BOUNDARY BETWEEN TURKEY AND ARMENIA

AS DETERMINED BY

WOODROW WILSON, PRESIDENT OF THE UNITED STATES OF AMERICA

ARMENIA

ARMENIA

THE CASE FOR A FORGOTTEN GENOCIDE

DICKRAN H. BOYAJIAN, LLM

EDUCATIONAL BOOK CRAFTERS, WESTWOOD, NEW JERSEY

This Work is
DEDICATED
To the Memory
of
Millions of Men, Women and Children
of the Armenian Nation
Who passed through death as
Heroes and Martyrs
to find
Resurrection

ISBN 0-912826-02-9

Library of Congress Catalog Card Number 73-188056

Educational Book Crafters, Inc., Westwood, N.J. 07675

PRINTED IN THE UNITED STATES OF AMERICA

Designed by Jan Kraner

Contents

Preface

Two purposes have guided me in writing this book. The first has been to assemble as much of the best testimony regarding the massacres of the Armenians as possible. Thereby I hope I shall awaken at least in part the dormant conscience of the civilized world with respect to what may well be its worst piece of unfinished business, the redress of a monumental grievance.

My second, and more important, purpose has been to press the case for the establishment of an Armenian homeland along the lines of the Israeli homeland. The reasons for such a settlement are clear: the territory I envision as the Armenians' future homeland has been theirs—barring the past few decades—for thousands of years, almost indeed since prehistory; the Armenians, a smaller group than the Jews, suffered under the Turks an even greater decimation of their total numbers on a proportional basis than the Jews did under the unspeakable persecutions of the Nazis; the plan for an Armenian homeland was not merely taken for granted in the years just after the terrible events of 1915–1916 and later but was embodied in state papers of the highest authority, emanating from the American presidency and the victorious councils of post-World War I Europe.

There are other reasons, practical as well as humanitarian, why an Armenian homeland inside Turkey should be established, not the least of them being that it would be good for the Turks themselves. I hope and believe that the material presented here will make all these reasons clear.

History is full of stories of persecution, massacres and murders. The strong have always forced their will upon the weak. Tyrants have invaded countries far and wide, tortured and killed their inhabitants, devastated their lands, outraged their women or carried them into captivity, and caused irreparable damage to life and property.

The stories told about Jenghiz Khan, Tamerlane and, in our own time, Hitler, are not fantasies of the imagination. They are facts amply recorded in history. For it is true that enemy invasions have created havoc in the lands they have invaded, and that horror, destruction, and desecration have inevitably followed each invasion.

But until the second decade of the twentieth century, one cannot find in any history the record of a plan comparable in savagery to the one set in motion by the Turks beginning with April 24, 1915.

A quarter of a century later, after the extermination of the Jews, the word *genocide*—the murder of a race—was coined. The word unquestionably applies to the Armenian massacres, for it was the murder of their race.

It was 1908 when a small group of men, ruthless in character and diabolical in the methods they applied, wrested power from an already corrupt and sick Turkish government, with the false promise that in the establishment of the new order all races and peoples of whatever religious beliefs would enjoy the same privileges, the same freedom and the same opportunities for progress and the same means for spiritual, cultural and material attainments.

Less than ten months after the young Turks came into power in July 1908, the falsity of the slogan of Liberty, Equality and Fraternity they had adopted for their government became evident. A dreadful story of massacres in Adana and its environs shocked the world and crumbled the hopes of the Armenians and other Christian minorities. Beginning on April 14, 1909 and within a matter of a week or two, about 30,000 Armenians of all ages were ruthlessly massacred. Heartless as it was, that event became a mere harbinger for even more horrible ones, soon to be unfolded, events which were meticulously planned to exterminate the Armenian people.

April 24, 1915 followed April 14, 1909.

April 24, 1915, one of the blackest of all days ever recorded in the history of mankind, was the day when "man's morality sank to the very depth in mire and blasphemy."

It was on that day when sinister men in the dark of night knocked on the doors of some three hundred unsuspecting victims, aroused them from their peaceful sleep and led them away from their homes and their families, never to be seen again. These men represented the cream of the Armenian intellectuals—writers, poets, journalists, clergymen, artists, professionals, businessmen, all men of culture, erudition and refinement.

Thus one of the most hideous crimes ever to be recorded began to unfold in Constantinople, and in the course of several months was repeated thousands of times in every nook and corner of Asia Minor. Hell broke loose upon an unfortunate people.

This publication, although it documents the events of that disaster, is not intended to rekindle old hatreds or arouse feelings of vengeance, but to remind the leaders of the civilized world of a crime which they may already have forgotten.

The world must be told of the events which in their magnitude and horror were far beyond the comprehension of man at the time of their occurrence. A people whose glories had penetrated the darkness of a barbarous age and imprinted on it their courage, their civility and their creative impulse, were brought near to total destruction.

In the pages that follow, the reader will see churches demolished, cultural and educational institutions torn asunder, whole cities, towns, villages and hamlets emptied of their inhabitants and laid waste. The reader will follow endless caravans of defenseless and terror-stricken men, women and children, gradually dwindling to the point of extinction.

Such was the fate of the Armenian people following April 24, 1915.

A group known as the American Committee on Armenian Atrocities was organized by a number of eminent humanitarians to render relief to the stricken thousands. In its first public report the Committee wrote: "A systematic attempt to uproot the peaceful Armenian population had been decided upon. [News of] torture, pillage, rape, murder, wholesale expulsion and deportation and massacres came from all parts of the Empire and was due not to fanatical or popular demand, but was purely arbitrary and directed from Constantinople."

An American physician holding an important position in one of the most important institutions of learning in the Turkish Empire wrote about only one episode: "I cannot describe the terrible sorrow of the past week, the utter despair of those people passing through here—refined, educated, wealthy, delicate people—women and girls, all treated worse than animals—beaten, robbed, outraged. It is too awful to think of."

The genocide of the Armenian people cannot be explained or justified either by logic or morality. For centuries the Armenians had suffered insults, endured hardships, tolerated indignities, and had been subjected to atrocities. There were, of course, many glorious instances when they courageously resisted attacks by their ruthless rulers in defense of their faith, their pride, their honor, their dignity, and their property rights.

The world does not know, or may have already forgotten, that more than one-and-a-half million defenseless and helpless Armenian men, women, and children suffered death in every form which "the most depraved nature, the most cruel instincts, the most bitter and fanatical hatred could devise," in the dreadful period covered in this book.

A sympathetic reader will find in this documentation a reminder of the crime of genocide, which the perpetrators and even their descendents, the new generation of Turks, have rarely acknowledged. Rather, the opposite is true. They have spared no effort to deny the truth of their crime. They have even gone so far as to distort history by blaming their victims as the cause of their own miseries.

The documented facts disprove their contention about the

guilt of the Armenians. Virtually all sources relied on are non-Armenian and no bias can be attributed to them. The authenticity of their statements is above reproach. One will even find among them a number of Turks who feel shame for their leaders and deplore their ruthless behavior.

It is the hope of this writer that the evidence herein presented will utterly convince men that Turkish authorities deliberately planned to exterminate the Armenians, and will thus set the historical record straight once and for all. This writer makes no apology for offering to the world the true story of the horrible crime committed by one race against another.

There are some who claim that the basic character of the Turk has changed for the better. There is evidence to refute that contention and to show that the Turk of today is no different from the Turk of 1915, that the so-called democratic state established by Mustafa Kemal Ataturk with its basic objective of Pan-Turanism remains the same.

The incident of September 6, 1955, in Istanbul, cannot be lightheartedly dismissed. It was on that day, some forty years after the Armenian massacres and deportations, that a Turkish mob, composed of men and women, young and old, numbering approximately 20,000, "armed with crowbars, pick axes and clubs," looted and destroyed the stores of many Greek and Armenian Christians. This was done under the condoning eyes of the police, and according to a predetermined scheme. One of the foreign correspondents of the New York *Times* reported that the "destruction was extensive and unrestrained."

Frederick Sondon, Jr. writes in the May, 1956 issue of the *Readers Digest:* "In six terrible hours, the frenzied Turkish crowds wrecked 2,000 houses, 4,000 shops, burned 29 churches to the ground and badly damaged 31 others. Before it was over, 100,000 people were made jobless." And all that was done when Turkey was a respectable member of the United Nations. What justification was offered by the Turks for this demonic act? Greek terrorists had defiled Ataturk's birthplace, was their answer. The Greeks and Armenians had to be taught a lesson.

As so often in the past, the civilized nations closed their eyes and ears and tacitly condoned the act as a disciplinary measure within the borders of a sovereign nation. No one, in short, had the right to interfere.

I will have succeeded in my mission if, by this documentation, I shall have been able to arouse a "more vigorous moral indignation" against an unspeakable crime and thereby to have assisted in the creation of a sympathetic and just attitude toward the case of the forgotten genocide.

ACKNOWLEDGMENTS

For the preparation of this volume I am greatly indebted to Mr. Antranig Antreasian, editor of *Nor Or,* an Armenian semiweekly published in Fresno, California, a distinguished author and speaker for co-authoring the Epilogue of this book; to Dr. A. O. Sarkisian, of the Library of Congress, Dr. Vahakn Dadrian, of the State University of New York, Miss Zabel D. Tahmizian, of Brookline, Massachusetts, Dr. Stephen G. Svajian, of Brooklyn, N. Y., and Mrs. Maritza M. Depoyan, widow of the late Rev. Hagop M. Depoyan, of Providence, R. I., for generously furnishing source material; to Prof. Marjorie Housepian, of Columbia University, author of *A Houseful of Love* and *Smyrna Affair*, Prof. William H. Thompson, of Harvard University, Mr. Manoog S. Young, Chairman of the Board of Directors of the National Association for Armenian Studies and Research, Cambridge, Massachusetts, and Mr. Jack Antreasian, of the Diocese of the Armenian Church of America, for their invaluable assistance in the choice and classification of the material for this volume; to Mr. X, a notable Armenian who wishes to remain anonymous, Mr. Edward Mardigian, of Detroit, Michigan, Mr. Hagop B. Barsamian, of Jamaica Plain, Massachusetts, Mr. Dadour Dadourian, of New York, and Mr. Charles Janjikian, of Detroit, whose generous support made possible the publication of this book, and many others, too numerous to mention, for their moral and material assistance and encouragement. A special debt of gratitude to my publisher, Mr. Harold Miller, President of the Educational Book Crafters, and to Mr. Frederick Highland, editor, for his collaboration and advice in the preparation of this book.

"Who, after all, speaks today of
the annihilation of the Armenians?
The world believes in success only."

Adolf Hitler, 1939, as quoted in
Louis Lochner, *What About Germany?*

Chapter 1

The Origins of Genocide

In February and March 1915 and for some months thereafter, the Turkish Minister of the Interior, Talaat Bey, issued a series of directives to officials of Turkey's eastern provinces that were to culminate, by early 1916, in the first real genocide of the modern age. By the time Talaat's orders had been carried out, a number of Armenians variously estimated between 800,000 and two million had been slaughtered in the cruelest manner conceivable, and Turkey had solved what Talaat ominously called the "Armenian Question."*

Talaat's directives to the government delegate in Adana, a city already infamous for previous atrocities against Armenians, express the intention "to exterminate all Armenians living in Turkey" with a minimum of delay and with no compassion whatsoever. They are thus the first modern record of an official policy of genocide, a genocide that has not yet had—and may never have—its Nuremberg. The orders for this crime could have had no higher authority, for Talaat, together with Enver Pasha, the War Minister, and Djemal Pasha, the Minister for Marine, shared absolute power in the Turkish dictatorship.

The consequences of Talaat's directives were incalculable. The deaths of as many as two million people—many of them children—the expropriation of their homeland, and countless acts of bestiality followed. The Armenians were indeed

* See Appendix, Chapter 1.

1

very nearly exterminated, for women, children, and men of sufficient youth to propagate the race were slaughtered with a systematic coldness not to be matched again until Hitler's concentration camps.

In some ways, the Turkish action against the Armenian minority was a prototype of the Nazi genocide. Talaat even bears some resemblance to Himmler, for he insists that compassion has no place in the necessary work to follow, as Himmler exhorted the SS to be strong enough for the disagreeable tasks of "the final solution." Like Himmler also, Talaat's private personality gave little indication of his murderous singlemindedness in the public sphere.

These then are the documents that brought about for the first time in modern history the systematic destruction on racial and religious grounds of an entire people by the highest officials of a legally constituted government.

February 28, 1915

To Delegate Jemal Bey of Adana:

The only force in Turkey able to frustrate the policies of Djihad[1] and Terakki[2] are the Armenians. Periodic news arriving from Cairo recently indicates that the Dashnagtzoutiun (the Armenian Revolutionary Federation) is preparing a decisive attack upon the Jemiyet (the Turkish Committee of Union and Progress, that is, the Turkish ruling party).

If we examine all the historical events in detail we shall see that all the agitations that have obstructed Jemiyet's patriotic efforts have been the result of seeds of turbulence sown by the Armenians. . . . Jemiyet has decided to free the fatherland from the covetousness of this accursed race and to bear upon its shoulders the stigma that might attach itself to Ottoman history.

Unable to forget the disgrace and bitterness of the past . . . Jemiyet, hopeful for the future, has decided to exterminate all Armenians living in Turkey, without allowing a single one to remain alive, and for this purpose has granted the Government extensive authority.

The Government shall give all necessary instructions to

the governors of provinces and the commanders of the Army for the arrangements concerning massacres. All delegates of the Ittihad and Terakki will be responsible for this matter in their respective localities.

All properties left behind will, for the time being, be seized and kept in the manner deemed best by the Government, with the understanding that they will be sold later for the expansion of the Jemiyet and for other patriotic purposes. . . . . Should you find any evidence of misappropriation of funds, you shall make appropriate reports to the governors and to us.

Minister of the Interior
Talaat[3]

Between the foregoing directive and the next occurred an event that truly altered the course of history, the attempt of British and French naval forces to break through the Straits of Gallipoli and to subjugate Constantinople itself. The failure of the campaign, which stemmed from an Allied failure of nerve as much as from the gallant Turkish defense, effectively crippled Russia's participation in the war and contributed to the Revolution of 1917. It may well have lengthened the war by two years, postponing the defeat of Turkey and the Central Powers until 1918 and thus insuring the slaughter of the Armenians.

At the time of Talaat's first directive, with the Allied fleet within sound of Constantinople, the entire Turkish government was preparing to flee to the interior. Indeed, Talaat himself had packed his papers and other belongings for this desperate removal. There seems little doubt that one more Allied naval thrust would have penetrated the Turkish defenses and brought about the speedy surrender of Turkey, perhaps with the sparing of countless Armenian lives.

As it was, the withdrawal of the Allied naval force and the disastrous landings on the Gallipoli peninsula, constituted Turkey's chief victory in the war. The fear that dictated Talaat's original directive was replaced by a feeling of triumph in the second, which was issued just a week after the withdrawal of the Allied warships.

March 25, 1915

To Delegate Jemal Bey of Adana:

It is the duty of all of us to realize . . . our intention to wipe out of existence the known elements who have obstructed the political progress of our State for centuries. . . . We must accept the full responsibility, and fully appreciating that the Government has entered the global war with great sacrifice, we must strive to carry to success all the activities that have been undertaken.
As was stated in our letter of February 28, 1915 the Jemiyet has decided to . . . annihilate various opposing forces that have obstructed our way for years, and for that purpose it is obliged, unfortunately, to resort to bloody means. Rest assured that we are also affected by the thought of these horrible means; but Jemiyet finds no other way to secure its eternal existence.
Ali Riza is criticizing us and appeals for compassion. This degree of naivete is stupidity. Go to Aleppo, try to convince him and work together if you can. Should that be impossible we will find a suitable place to play on his heartstrings. Until the successful completion of the activities undertaken for the Armenians, it would not be right to bother ourselves about the *others* (Greeks, Arabs, Syrians) . . . . I wish to remind you again about the abandoned properties. It is very essential. Their disposition should be under your very eyes. Examine the accounts and means of performance at all times. Let us also know the date of your departure.

Minister of the Interior
Talaat

On April 15, 1915, Talaat was joined by Enver Pasha and Nazim Bey in a more general order of the Committee of Union and Progress (the Jemiyet):

April 15, 1915

To the Excellent Governors, Honorable Mayors, and Esteemed Town Authorities:
You are familiar with the cruel political reasons which forced the mighty Ottoman Empire and the great Turkish

people to enter the war on the side of Germany and Austria against "The Triple Alliance." In order to emerge victorious from this fateful war, we repeat, every Mohammedan and Turk . . . should stand together as one man against our monstrous and infidel enemies and become a support to our valiant and wise leaders and to our army, which [is] waging a victorious war against treacherous foes.

. . . . In the event of victory [for Britain and Russia] they may agree upon a third competent inheritor, by finding a people that could serve their interests. . . .

And that third inheritor can only be the Armenian people. May God prevent it, but in case of our defeat, there will come to the fore during peace negotiations that "Armenian Question" that for more than half a century has been given an international character. . . .

Therefore, in order to protect our country, our nation, our government and our religion against the possibility of such a danger, the government which represents Islam and the Turkish people, and the Committee of Union and Progress, intending to forestall the presentation of the Armenian Question in any place and in any manner, taking advantage of the freedom which the war has granted us, has decided to end that question once and for all, by deporting the Armenians to the deserts of Arabia. . . .

The following serve as a justification for that plan:
  (a) The Armenian voluntary forces serving in the enemy armies;
  (b) The Armenian parties in the interior of the country, which have been organized to give a body blow to our Army;
  (c) The uncountable firearms and war materiel discovered and confiscated everywhere in the country.

With that justification we, the Government and the Central Committee of Ittihad appeal to you and to your patriotism and command you to assist with the means at your disposal the local organs of the Union and Progress Party, who at the sunrise of April 24th will undertake the implementation of this order, in conformity with secret instructions.

Any official . . . who opposes this sacred and patriotic work and fails to discharge the duties imposed on him or protects or hides this or that Armenian in any way, shall be branded an enemy of the country and religion and shall be punished accordingly.

The Minister of the Interior and Minister of War
Talaat   Enver
The Executive Secretary of the Union and Progress—Dr. Nazim

On the very day of this directive, at Van* in the eastern interior, the Turkish troops under Enver's brother-in-law, Djevdet Bey, were systematically slaughtering all young Armenian men of military age and killing at will Armenian women, children and old men. Their pretext for these outrages was that the Armenians had given aid to the enemy army of Russia.

Unfortunately, the Russians had retreated from the area of Van, leaving the Armenians almost defenseless. Nevertheless, the Armenians, numbering only 1,500 men, withstood a siege by 5,000 Turkish troops for almost five weeks, until help arrived with the return of the Russian forces. It was one of the most gallant defenses in modern history and is sacred to every Armenian. In and around Van during these dreadful days, 55,000 Armenians had been killed, according to the Russians, who performed the humane task of burying the Armenian dead.

Elsewhere in the interior the massacre of Armenians had already begun on a large if somewhat sporadic scale, but perhaps the most terrible day of all was in Constantinople itself during the night of April 24–25. On this night, the Turkish police rounded up more than 200 of the nation's most prominent Armenians for deportation to the interior, thus depriving the already beleaguered Armenians of their most effective leadership. For "deportation" in the Turkish lexicon was simply a euphemism for a horrible death. From this point on, the Armenian position became hopeless. Ap-

* See Appendix B, Chapter 4 for eyewitness accounts of the siege of Van.

peals to Talaat and Enver were pointless, for they served only to increase their vengefulness.

Talaat and Enver

Turkey's fortunes in this unhappy period had fallen largely into the hands of the Minister of the Interior, Talaat Bey, and the Minister of War, Enver Pasha. These two, whose frowns once inspired terror throughout the Western world, were the accidents of history, sorry examples of what can happen when there is a leadership vacuum in a nation that, whatever its weaknesses, has a pivotal role to play in world affairs. After half a century, the massive Talaat and the slight, dapper Enver appear as sinister clowns (Alan Moorehead calls them the Wallace Beery and Rudolph Valentino of their age) rather than as statesmen.[4]

Yet each was in his way a natural leader and in better times and places might have risen to a modest eminence, Talaat perhaps as mayor of a fair-sized city and Enver as a career officer in a well-regulated army.

Talaat was a huge man of obscure origins who had started as a postman and then had become a telegrapher. Active early in the Young Turk movement, which sought the overthrow of Sultan Abdul Hamid, he had risen to a place of considerable authority in that one-time conspiratorial organization, which was to become the new Turkish government. Instrumental in the revolutions of 1908 and 1909, which forced Abdul to restore the Constitution of 1876 and eventually ousted him, Talaat became Minister of the Interior in 1913. In that post he was, along with Enver, one of the two most powerful men in Turkey.

Ambassador Morgenthau has given an unforgettable portrait of the ex-telegrapher Talaat in *Ambassador Morgenthau's Story*.[5] Normally jocose, often seeming anxious to please, Talaat at times was open to advice and even criticism. On many points Morgenthau was able to appeal to

Talaat's keen wish to have Turkey appear more civilized to Western eyes than she usually did.

Mr. Morgenthau ends chapter XXV entitled "Talaat Tells Why He 'Annihilates' the Armenians," of his book, *Ambassador Morgenthau's Story*, with the following significant paragraph:

"Talaat's attitude toward the Armenians was summed up in the proud boast which he made to his friends: 'I have accomplished more toward solving the Armenian problem in three months than Abdul Hamid accomplished in thirty years.'" (p. 225)

Enver Pasha admits that the massacres were planned and carried out by the Central Government of Turkey:

Mr. Morgenthau, in chapter XXVI of his book, entitled "Enver Pasha Discusses Armenians," writes:

> In another talk with Enver I began by suggesting that the Central Government was probably not to blame for the massacres. I thought that this would not be displeasing to him.
>
> "Of course, I know that the Cabinet would never order such terrible things as have taken place," I said. "You and Talaat and the rest of the Committee can hardly be held responsible. Undoubtedly your subordinates have gone much further than you have ever intended. I realize that it is not always easy to control your underlings."
>
> Enver straightened up at once. I saw that my remarks, far from smoothing the way to a quiet and friendly discussion, had greatly offended him. I had intimated that things could happen in Turkey for which he and his associates were not responsible.
>
> "You are greatly mistaken," he said. "We have this country absolutely under control. I have no desire to shift the blame on our underlings and I am entirely willing to accept the responsibility myself for everything that has taken place. The Cabinet itself has ordered the deportations. I am convinced that we are completely justified in doing this owing to the hostile attitude of the Armenians toward the Ottoman Government, but we are the real rulers of Turkey and no underling would dare proceed in a matter of this kind without our orders." (p. 231)

There were even genuinely likeable traits about Talaat. He never forgot his origins and lived in a poor quarter of Constantinople in the old-fashioned Turkish style. He kept an old telegrapher's keyboard on his desk and loved to tap out messages as he had done in his obscurest days. When in good humor, he would bear Morgenthau's protests with a mixture of sheepishness and jocosity that made working with him an easy and fruitful task. But beneath the easygoing surface there existed a tough, backward-looking, and merciless Turk of the same stripe that has made Turkish history the dismal chronicle it has been for centuries.

On the Armenian question, Talaat was immovably vengeful. On May 12, 1915, when he was confronted by the two Armenian members of Parliament, Vartkes and Zohrab, over the mass arrests of April 25–26, he accused the Armenians of "forcing us to the brink" two years earlier by demanding Armenian reforms "in the days of our weakness." Now, he said, the tables were turned and Turkey will have its vengeance.

There was something gross and threatening in Talaat's presence. A huge man, he had wrists of an awe-inspiring thickness which he placed, flat and immovable, before him whenever he was indisposed to take advice. This physical peculiarity Morgenthau recalled long after his tenure as U.S. Ambassador to Turkey was over, for it seemed symbolic of the brutality and unreason of that extraordinary nation.

Enver stood in almost comic contrast to Talaat physically and temperamentally. Slight to the point of girlishness, delicate of feature and dapper, with mustaches waxed and upward-pointed in imitation of the Kaiser he so much admired, Enver seemed the born aristocrat, almost the matinee idol. His air of modest detachment, bordering on shyness, enhanced the image.

Yet Enver, the "would-be Napoleon," as Winston Churchill called him, compels a grudging admiration for his physical courage and decisiveness. From the meagerest of back-

grounds (his father a bridge-keeper and his mother a pre-
parer of corpses for burial), he had risen spectacularly,
graduating from the Military College at 25, leader of the revolt against Abdul at 26, ubiquitous and fearless in the disastrous Balkan and Italian campaigns, he had become
Minister of War—and co-dictator of Turkey—at 31.

If Enver had had Napoleon's ability, his courage might
have been more often capped with success. But his fool-
hardiness led him into one ruinous campaign after another.
Just before the massacres propagated by Talaat, Enver had
planned, if that is the word, an offensive against the Russian
army in the Caucasus. His troops were effectively trapped
by the winter at Sarikamish, with only a handful, including
Enver, of survivors.

It was typical of Enver that the Sarikamish disaster was
treated as if it had never occurred. News of it, whether in
print or in conversation, was strictly prohibited, and Enver
went on about his war-time activities quite unruffled. He
threw himself into the solution of the "Armenian Question"
with his customary elan.

Enver's desk was flanked by portraits of Napoleon and
Frederick the Great, but fate had a different end in view for
Enver than theirs. His country lost the war and he eventually died in a cavalry charge in an obscure corner of Asia
Minor. Even so, his end was less squalid than that of Talaat,
who was gunned down by a young Armenian in Berlin several years after the war.

Turkey in the War

As World War I approached in Europe, Turkey became an
increasingly desirable prize as an ally on either side. She
was wooed with promises and payments of all sorts, not so
much for her possible contribution to the war effort as for
her location, for without access to the Dardanelles through
the Bosphorus, there could be no movement between the
Black Sea and the Mediterranean.

Without free passage through the Bosphorus, Russia's participation in the war would become minimal, for she could then neither send nor receive food and supplies to maintain her war effort. It was the view of many British leaders that acquiring Turkey as an ally, or at least as a non-belligerent, would release as many as two million additional soldiers for the Western Front and shorten the war by as much as two years.

Conversely, the Germans knew that control of Turkey would pin down in the Near East vast numbers of Allied troops and would reduce Russia's part as an enemy to a small fraction of what it would otherwise have been. Thus was Turkey's importance magnified out of all proportion to its merits as a co-belligerent.

The Turkish armed forces were in such low regard that, long before hostilities began, Germany had sent scores of officers and technicians to reorganize the Turkish army. The French and British maintained military missions in Turkey as well.

Precisely how Turkey entered the war on the side of the Central Powers is still confused, although it has been written about at length. There were powerful pro-British and especially pro-French factions in the nation, although Enver, as Minister of War and Commander in Chief of the armed forces, was perhaps the deciding factor. He had been Turkish Military Attache in Berlin and had developed a pro-German attitude that verged on the slavish. Such incidents as the British refusal to deliver the two warships that had been built for Turkey and the Kaiser's prompt gift of the *Goeben* and the *Breslau* to replace them, certainly figured largely in Turkey's fateful decision to enter the war on Germany's side.

But one other factor probably counted for more than any other in the outcome, and that was Turkey's fear and hatred of Russia. And on that single element, more than any purely military considerations, hinged the fate of Turkey's Armenian population.

Russia herself contained a substantial number of Armenians who, like those within Turkey, had distinguished themselves for thrift, orderliness, and contributions to the commerce and culture of the nation. In general, the Russian Armenians had been fairly treated and had consequently become thoroughly loyal, even patriotic. Their service in the Russian army was ungrudging and even rather distinguished.

It is true that Russia, out of its historic enmity to Turkey, had attempted to exploit the disaffection of Turkish Armenians, but it is also true that the results had been minor. Nevertheless, Turkish politicians, especially the Turanian (Turkey for the Turks) magnified the threat of Russian influence among the Armenians of Turkey into a wholesale conspiracy.

How much of the Turkish paranoia over Armenian attachment to Russian interests was based on genuine belief (Who knows even now how sincerely Nazi leaders construed Jews as real enemies of the state?) is not easy to determine. That it was very deep and widespread is certain, for even the pledge on both sides of loyal military service by Armenians of fighting age ("brother against brother," as Churchill put it) counted for nothing with the Turks.

In this situation, the Armenians were truly helpless. With Turkey on the side of the Central Powers (she entered the war as Germany's ally in October, 1914) and the consequent crippling of Russia, there was no power that the Armenians could turn to for protection against the inimical state in which they dwelt.

Germany, the only western power in a position to cushion the severity of the Turks against their Armenian minority, dishonored itself by its hands-off policy. With the honorable exception of the heroic German pastor, Johannes Lepsius, and a few other German sympathizers, there was no one in that military state, least of all the Kaiser or the German ambassador, Wangenheim, to whom the Armenians might appeal. They were at the mercy of the Turks, hardly an enviable position at best.

Yet who could have envisaged the butchery that was to

follow? The very men who ran the nation, Talaat, Enver, Djemal, had overturned Abdul Hamid on a wave of liberalism and good feeling. A few short years before, Armenian and Turk had embraced in the streets in celebration of the new age of amity. Even the Turkish military disasters of 1911–1915 and the dismemberment of virtually all of European Turkey could not account, in any reasonable mind, for the wave of madness that ensued.

Even supposing there had been any considerable substance to Turkish suspicions of their Armenian minority—and there was not—how many comparatively humane ways might have been chosen to assuage Turkish fears? It is a measure of the Turkish government's fear, which Morgenthau judged the ruling passion of their policy, and the Turkish penchant for brutality, to which history has given sufficient testimony, that the government chose its policy of extermination. It was a policy that was to wipe out the most productive and progressive element in the nation and to earn the utmost loss of prestige in the world at large.

For all its irrationality, however, the Turkish policy of genocide had historical roots. The nation, once a threat to all of southeastern Europe and master of millions in the Balkans, had suffered a considerable diminution in the preceding centuries. In the years just before World War I, the process of reduction had been accelerated, and the Ottoman Empire had shrunk to a small portion of its former self. With centuries of misgovernment and gradual attrition of its hegemony behind it, Turkey was not, on the eve of the great war, in a position to judge its advantages and disadvantages dispassionately.

The elevation of Talaat and Enver, which had seemed so full of promise, had not proved to be the answer. The mirage of Westernization remained a mirage. The loss of territory continued. Turanianism* failed to unite the Turks and merely isolated the nation's minorities. By the early spring

* A sweeping policy of pan-Turkism aimed at making the nation "purely" Turkish in language, customs, etc.

of 1915, the war was going badly and showed signs of imminent disaster. From top to bottom, Turkey was a nation unnerved.

In this situation Turkey, already partially dismembered by the loss of its Balkan territories, and threatened with extinction if it lost the war, as seemed only a matter of days in February and March, 1915, sought an outlet for its fears and frustrations. Its Armenian population perfectly suited its need for a scapegoat.

Ironically, the comparative victory of Gallipoli, which was largely due to the inspired efforts of the then-obscure officer, Kemal Pasha, who would soon be known to history as Ataturk, served only to augment the fury with which the government turned on the Armenians. With the capital now secure and Russia effectively stalemated, the Turkish leaders could now prosecute their policy of genocide without threat of foreign interference or international justice, at least for the foreseeable future.

Talaat's charges that Turkey's Armenians were disloyal and actively working for a Russian victory were, as historian Howard J. Sachar has tersely commented, "a fabrication from beginning to end."[6] The Armenians' possession of firearms was, in fact, pitifully small in the light of the persecutions they had already undergone. The charge that the Armenians, who had been comparative models of responsibility and progress, had for centuries exploited their Turkish neighbors, was all the more effective with the Turks and Kurds of Eastern Anatolia for being a "big lie" par excellence.

The Turkish plan to seize Armenian land and property once the genocide was complete was as unrealistic as it was unprincipled. It was precisely the industry and ingenuity of the Armenians that had made the so-called Armenian vilayets among the most desirable provinces of the nation. Given the Turkish tradition of ineptitude and disorder, not even the motive of naked greed had any semblance of rationality in the unparalleled tragedy that was to follow.

For all the special circumstances creating the Armenian Gethsemane of 1915–16 (the Turkish military defeats, the peculiar barbarism of Talaat and the other leaders, the contraction of the Ottoman world, and the threat of invasion on several fronts), it was not, or should not have been, a matter of complete surprise except perhaps for its total savagery. The roots of genocide were deep, reaching back for centuries. The Young Turks' predecessor, Abdul Hamid, had truly earned his nickname of "The Assassin," more for his persecution of the Armenians than for any other single cause.

REFERENCES

1. Djihad—The historic "holy war" of Moslems against infidels, revived by Enver during World War I and aimed largely at the British.

2. Terakki—A shortened version of the name of the Young Turk party: "Ittihad ve Terakki."

3. Aram Andonian, *The Great Crime*, 1919.

4. Alan Moorehead, *Gallipoli*, p. 17.

5. Henry Morgenthau, Sr., *Ambassador Morgenthau's Story*, New York, 1919.

6. Howard J. Sachar, *The Emergence of the Middle East*, Knopf, 1969, p. 101.

Chapter 2

The Pre-World War I Era

The Imperial Edict, known as *Hatti Sherif* of Gulhané promulgated by Sultan Abd-ul-Mejid, November 3, 1839.

This was "a decree abolishing the arbitrary and unlimited power hitherto exercised by the state and its officials, laying down the doctrine of the perfect equality of all Ottoman subjects of whatever race or creed, and providing for the regular, orderly and legal government of the country and the security of life, property and honor for all its inhabitants. Yet the feeling of dismay, and even ridicule with which this proclamation was received by the Mussulmans in many parts of the country show how great a change it instituted, and how strong was the opposition which it encountered among the ruling race (Turks). The non-Mussulman subjects of the Sultan had indeed early been reduced to such a condition of servitude that the idea of their being placed on a footing of equality with their Mussulman rulers seemed unthinkable. Preserved merely as taxpayers necessary to supply the funds for the maintenance of the dominant and military class, according to a foreign observer in 1571, they had been so degraded and oppressed that they dared not look a Turk in the face. Their only value was from a fiscal point of view, and in times of fanaticism or when anti-foreign sentiment ran high even this was held of little account, so that more than once they very nearly became the victims of a general and state-ordered massacre." (*Encyclopedia Britannica,* 1922, Vol. 27, p. 458)

Imperial Edict, known as *Hatti Humayoun,* February 18, 1856.

The Sultan of Turkey, anticipating the demands of the European powers concerning the protection of Christian minorities in Turkey issued an Imperial Edict, which promised absolute equality of civil rights to all the subjects of the Empire without discrimination of race and creed. The following are the pertinent portions of that edict addressed to the Grand Vizier, Mohammed Emin Ali Pasha:

    1. All the assurances which we have granted by our Edict of Hatti Sherif of Gulhané the Tanzimat (program of reforms) to all the subjects of our Empire without discrimination as to religion and status, for the protection of their life, property and honor, are hereby ratified and strengthened. Stern measures will be taken to make these assurances effective.

    2. All the privileges and religious concessions which for a long time have been granted by our forefathers to all Christian and Mohammedan communities who live in the Empire and enjoy my protection, are hereby ratified and will be kept.

    3. Patriarchs, Metropolitans, Archbishops, bishops and rabbies upon assuming their respective offices will take an oath formulated between the sublime Porte and respective religious leaders; all ecclesiastical imposts, whatever their nature, shall be abolished and in their stead specific imposts will be established for the patriarchs and other religious leaders. The salaries of the clergy will also be determined according to the distinction, degree and importance of each individual.

    4. The personal and real estate of the various Christians shall be inviolate . . .

    5. No obstacles will be raised against the repairs and renovations of places of worship, schools, hospitals and cemeteries, according to existing plans, in all cities, small towns and villages where the entire population profess the same faith . . .

6. In cities, towns and villages where there is a mixed population, each group shall have the right to repair their church, school, hospital and cemetery within their own quarters . . .

7. In all these matters the intervention of executive authority shall be without charge. My sublime Porte shall take effective measures to see to it that the freedom of each sect, no matter how small their number, shall be safeguarded. Any intent to subordinate the subjects of my Empire one to the other because of their religion, language and race, shall be forever eradicated from civil records. Stern laws shall be enacted against the use of any dangerous and insulting remarks by officials of the government or individuals.—No one will be forced to change his religion.

8. The choice and the appointment of all functionaries and workers in my dominion depending only on my imperial will, all the subjects of my dominion, regardless of their nationality, shall be acceptable in any public service, in accordance with their qualifications and abilities . . .

9. All the subjects of my empire shall be accepted, without discrimination, in the military and civil schools of the State, if they satisfy the requirements as to age and entrance examinations, as determined by the authorities of these schools . . .

10. All controversies of business, emotional and criminal nature between Mohammedans and Christians or other non-Mohammedan subjects, or other sects, shall be tried before mixed tribunals. The trials shall be public. The opponents shall stand face to face and shall present their witnesses whose testimony shall be accepted without discrimination, after their taking an oath in accordance with their religious concepts . . .

11. No physical punishment shall be forced, even in jails, except in accordance with laws approved by the sublime Porte. Any means resembling torture shall be abolished.

12. The police force in the capital and in the cities and rural districts of all vilayets shall be organized in such a way that the strongest assurances shall be given to all the peaceful subjects in my dominion for the protection of their lives and properties.

13. Equality in taxes meaning equality in burden, and equality in obligations meaning equalities in rights. Chris-

tian subjects, as well as other non-Mohammedan communities, will be subject to military duties like Mohammedans, as has already been determined.

14. (Provides for free elections, the right to vote being accorded to all subjects without discrimination).

15. (Authorizes foreigners to acquire real estate).

16. (Provides for assessment and collection of taxes, effective measures to be taken to prevent misappropriations).

17., 19. and 20. (Provide further regulations and supervision of all collections and appropriations).

21. (Provides for stringent penalties for embezzlement, robbery, theft, extortion, etc. for everyone regardless of his position in the Empire).

22. (Regulates the establishment and administration of banks and other financial organizations).

23. (Provides means for unobstructed commerce and agriculture in order to benefit by European capital).

The Edict concludes in the following, significant words:

Such being my wishes and orders, you, who are my Grand Vizier, will publicize this, my Imperial Edict, as has been the custom, in my capital as well as in all other parts of my dominion, and you shall exercise utmost care and will take all necessary steps, so that all the orders contained in this edict are carried out most strictly and truly.

Rev. Frederick Davis Greene makes the following comment about that Edict: "Since the interpretation and enforcement of this edict has remained absolutely in the hands of the Turkish government, it is needless to add that it has been a dead letter." (*The Rule of the Turk, and the Armenian Crisis,* G. P. Putnam's Sons, New York and London, 1897).

The Treaty of Paris, March 30, 1856.

The Crimean War, in which all European powers—Great Britain, France, Austria, Prussia and Sardinia—fought against Russia on the side of Turkey, ended in a partial defeat of Russia and Turkey as well. With the fall of Sevastopol Napoleon's wishes had been satisfied and hostilities ceased.

After two months of negotiations between the warring nations the Treaty of Paris was signed. It will be noted that Armenia was never mentioned in the Treaty. The "Armenian Question" did not exist. But since the Treaty promises protection to the Christian minorities in Turkey, we deem it useful to quote clause 9 of the Treaty:

> 9. His Imperial Majesty the Sultan, having, in his constant solicitude for the welfare of his subject, issued a firman (edict) which, while ameliorating their condition, without distinction of religion or of race, records his generous intentions towards the Christian populations of his Empire, and wishing to give a further proof of his sentiments in this respect, has resolved to communicate to the contracting parties the said firman, emanating spontaneously from his soverign will. The contracting Powers recognize the high value of this communication. It is clearly understood that it cannot in any case give the right to the said Powers to interfere either collectively or separately, in the relations of His Majesty the Sultan with his subjects, nor in the internal administration of his Empire.

Note: The firman referred to in this clause is the Imperial Edict known as *Hatti Humayoun,* issued on February 18, 1856.

The Armenian National Constitution

On March 17, 1863, Sultan Abd-ul-Aziz of Turkey, by an Imperial decree, confirmed a document known as the Armenian National Constitution, which was intended to regulate the inter-relations within the Armenian communities in Turkey and the relations between the Imperial Government of Turkey and the religious and pseudo-political head of the Armenians, i. e. the Patriarch.

We find the English translation of that document at the end of volume II of H. F. B. Lynch's *Armenia, Travels and Studies,* devoted entirely to the Turkish provinces of Armenia. The author has traveled through the length and breadth of the country and has portrayed many intimate scenes of beauty, culture, progress, and the idiosyncrasies of the people, their likes and dislikes, their joys and sorrows, their successes and failures, their greatness and smallness, their pleasures and pains, their hopes and fears, their modesty and vanity, their love and hate, their benevolence and malevolence, their virtues and vices, and in short all of their characteristics.

Here is what he says about the so-called Constitution:

I have thought it worth while to include a translation of this lengthy document, and it will be found in my first appendix. It has the nature of a regulating statute, like the *Polojenye* in Russia, rather than of what we should understand by a constitution. But, unlike the *Polojenye*, it is mainly addressed to the development among the Armenians of systematic management of the affairs of their communities. These communities have always enjoyed the privilege of administering their own institutions, such as monasteries, churches, hospitals and schools. The statute of 1863 provides a complete and democratic machinery for the better organization and control of such institutions. It wisely avoids, except in the last resort, any interference by Government in these purely internal affairs. I cannot conceive any better training for the Armenian people than that which they would receive by the application of their great intelligence to such practical and concrete ideals. The pitfall which they should avoid, were the statute ever to revive, is the attempt to convert it into a political weapon. (pp. 436–437)

We do not think that the reproduction of the entire document will serve a useful purpose. We do not hesitate, however to make available to our readers documents leading to the preparation and adoption of the National Constitution of the Armenians in Turkey.

NATIONAL CONSTITUTION OF THE ARMENIANS IN THE TURKISH EMPIRE

Preliminaries

The Sublime Porte,

Ministry of Foreign Affairs,
        No. 191

To The Prudent Representative of The Patriarch
(Locum tenens)

Prudent and Dear Sir: The Imperial Firman concerning reforms requires that each community shall take into consideration within a given time the privileges and prerogatives which it enjoys, and, after due counsel, shall decide upon the reforms which are in accordance with the circumstances, the civilization and the learning of the present time. It shall present a list of such reforms to the Sublime Porte in order that the authority and rights granted to the spiritual heads of each community may be placed in harmony with the position and new conditions secured to each community. In accordance with these behests, the outlines of a Constitution for the Armenian nation have been prepared by a Committee composed of certain honourable persons. But at the same time it has been considered appropriate that the ecclesiastical members of the General Assembly and the delegates of the different Quarters should select by a majority of votes a Committee of seven, to whose consideration the above-mentioned project should be submitted. We therefore beg you to despatch within a few days the summons to hold the election of that Committee, and to direct that the Committee shall meet at the Sublime Porte the Committee and functionary specially appointed for this purpose. We beg you also to send us the names of the seven persons thus elected.

(Signature)
ALI

1862, Feb. 14 (Old style)

DOCUMENT PRESENTED TO THE SUBLIME PORTE
BY THE NATIONAL COMMITTEE AND THE
COMMITTEE OF THE GOVERNMENT

To the Sublime Porte,

Ministry of Foreign Affairs,

The Imperial Government has from ancient times granted
to the different nations under its righteous protection privileges and prerogatives for their religious liberty and the
special administration of their internal affairs.

These prerogatives are in their principles uniform for all
nations, but they are at the same time adapted to the particular religious regulations and customs of each nationality. And
each nationality has used and enjoyed them according to its
peculiar manners and customs.

The Armenian nation, like other nations, has had to this
day a Patriarch, who has been acknowledged by the Government as the President of the Patriarchal Administration, the
representative of the nation, and the medium of the execution of Imperial Orders, and who from ancient times has been
elected from the ecclesiastical body by a General Assembly,
composed of individuals representing the different classes of
the nation.

The Patriarch in his office, which is to preside over the
nation and to watch over its interests, has never been exempt
from the influence and supervision of the nation, exerted over
him through the General Assembly. The proof of this is that
the Patriarch has always invited and convoked the General
Assembly, and has applied to that Assembly for a decision
when a question has been raised by orders of the Sublime
Porte.

The Armenian nation about two years ago begged of the
Imperial Government to have two Assemblies established in
the Patriarchate under the presidency of the Patriarch, one
religious, the other political, that they might be participators

in and auxiliaries of the office of the Patriarch, and that any deviation on the part of the nation from its ancient regulations and customs, both religious and political, might be prevented.

When these assemblies were established it became necessary to organize other Councils for the administration of the minor affairs of the nation.

But as the authority and duties of each national officer were not definitely defined, it was evident that these efforts to improve the state of affairs in the nation would be the occasion of continual misunderstanding in the different branches of the National Administration, as well as between that administration and the nation. This naturally would be the cause of many irregularities in the execution of justice for all concerned, and of confusion and disputes in the National Administration.

With the object of doing away with the causes of such confusion and dissension, and with the nuisance of the undue claims of different parties, the Imperial Government, with its paternal solicitude for all its subjects, deems it necessary to organize a National Mixed Committee in order to prepare a Constitution in accordance with the peculiar religious and political customs and long-established manners.

Now that Mixed Committee considers it proper according to the outline of the Constitution presented for confirmation to the Sublime Porte,

I. That the office of the Patriarch as the medium between the nation and the Sublime Porte should remain as it was in the old system,

II. That the organisation of the General Assembly should be reformed. The national delegates, instead of being elected by the Esnafs (Artisans)—since the condition of the Esnafs is no longer what it used to be—should be elected by the Committee of Churches, that is, by different quarters, in a way that perhaps will be more regular and lawful than the one adopted by the Greeks.

And as Armenians living in the interior of the country

rightly complain that they are altogether deprived of participation in the deliberations and decisions of the Patriarchate, a number of delegates should be elected by the provinces to be added to the number of the delegates of the quarters or sections of Constantinople. The ecclesiastical members, twenty of them, should be elected by the clergy in Constantinople, so that the total number of the members of the General Assembly be 140; their term of office should last ten years, and once in every two years the tenth part should be changed, and new elections take place.

The General Assembly should nominate both the Patriarch and the members of the two Assemblies working under his presidency and should have the supervision of their acts,

III. The administration of religious affairs should belong to the Religious Assembly, the administration of political affairs to the Political Assembly, and that of mixed affairs to the Mixed Assembly, which shall consist of the other two Assemblies together,

IV. The Religious and Political Assemblies should manage through the Sectional and other Councils all national affairs of the church communities (that is to say, the people of different sections or quarters) under their jurisdiction, and the affairs of the churches, schools, hospitals, monasteries, and other similar national institutions,

V. The centre of the administration should be the National Patriarchate. The Patriarch, as the Official Head of the Patriarchate should preside both over the General Assembly and over the two National Assemblies, and he should under the inspection of the General Assembly manage all the affairs concerning the nation directly or indirectly,

VI. The administration of provincial communities should be connected with the Central Administration. The Metropolitans should preside over local assemblies which should be organized in the same way as these in Constantinople, and they should be the managers of these local assemblies,

VII. The Provincial Assemblies should be responsible to the Central Administration. Each of the Councils of this Central Administration should be responsible to the Assembly to which it belongs. The National Assemblies should be responsible to the General Assemblies, the Patriarch responsible on the one hand to the Imperial Government and on the other to the nation (through the General Assembly),

VIII. And, inasmuch as the Imperial Government considers the Patriarch as the natural medium of the execution of the orders given by it to the nation, and at the same time considers him as the head of the National Administration, and it is to him that it addresses its question, if the Government should command the Patriarch to give his opinion on the question asked, the Patriarch should act according to the decision of the Assemblies under his presidency; but, if he be ordered to communicate to the Government the opinion of the nation, then he should convoke the General Assembly and communicate to the Government the fiscal decision of that Assembly,

IX. The National Administration has three kinds of obligations. First towards the Imperial Government, that is to preserve the nation in perfectly loyal subjection and to secure to the nation in general and to individuals in particular the preservation of their rights and privileges on the part of the Government. The second obligation is to the nation, to treat it in true compassion and in a paternal way. The third is to the see of Edgmiatsin (Etchmiadzin), to act in accordance with the religious regulations and laws of the Armenian Church.

These are the features in the Constitution which the Mixed Committee considers desirable. These features are approved by the other Committee which was organised according to the orders to your Excellency, in order to present to the Sublime Porte on behalf of the nation their observations on the Constitution.

Constantinople, 1862.

Signatures of the members of the Committee of the Sublime Porte—Stephanos, Archbishop of Necomedia, Representative of the Patriarch Elect of Constantinople, three Armenian Ec-clesiastics, and eight notables.

Signatures of the members of the National Committee, seven notables.

ORDINANCE OF THE SUBLIME PORTE

To the Prudent Representative of the
    Patriarch Elect of Constantinople
    (Bishop Stephanos Maghakian)

The Constitution drawn up by the Committee formed at the Sublime Porte for the reforms of the condition and ad-ministration of the Armenian Patriarchate, after having un-dergone certain modifications concerning secular affairs only, was presented to His Imperial Majesty; the Imperial Decree, making a law of the features contained in it, was issued to be handed to your Beatitude.

In enclosing to you the above-mentioned Constitution, we commission you to superintend the perfect execution of those features according to the high will of the August Emperor.

1863. March 17.

INTRODUCTION

The privileges granted by the Ottoman Empire to its non-Mohammedan subjects are in their principles equal for all, but the mode of their execution varies according to the re-quirements of the particular customs of each nationality.

The Armenian Patriarch is the head of his nation, and in particular circumstances the medium of the execution of the orders of the Government. There is, however, in the Patri-archate a Religious Assembly for religious affairs and a Po-litical Assembly for political affairs. In case of necessity these two Assemblies unite and form the Mixed Assembly. Both the Patriarch and the members of these Assemblies are elected in a General Assembly composed of honourable men of the nation.

As the office and duties of the above Assemblies and the mode of their formation are not defined by sufficient rules, and for this reason different inconveniences and special difficulties in the formation of the General Assembly have been noticed,

As each community is bound according to the new Imperial Edict (Hatti Humayun, 6/18 Feb. 1856) to examine within a given time its rights and privileges, and after due deliberation to present to the Sublime Porte the reforms required by the present state of things and the progress of civilisation of our times,

As it is necessary to harmonise the authority and power granted to the religious chief of each nationality with the new condition and system secured to each community,

A committee of some honourable persons of the nation was organised, which Committee prepared for the nation the following Constitution.

Henry Finnis Blosse Lynch (1862–1913) made an extensive journey through Russia and Turkish Armenia and after his return published a book in two volumes entitled *Armenia—Travels and Studies* in 1901, Longmans, Green & Co., New York and London, from which we reproduce a number of passages:

> In the Armenians we have a people who are peculiarly adapted to be the intermediaries of the new dispensation. They profess our religion, are familiar with some of our best ideals, and assimilate each new product of European culture with an avidity and thoroughness which no other race between India and the Mediterranean has given any evidence of being able to rival. These capacities they have made manifest under the greatest of disadvantages—as a subject race ministering to the needs of Mussulman masters. They know well that with every advance of true civilisation they are sure to rise, as they certainly will fall at each relapse.

For nearly a thousand years they have been held in subjection; and it would be folly to expect that they should not
have suffered in character by the menial pursuits which
they have been constrained to follow. They have been *rayas*,
exploited by races most often their inferiors in intellect;
and I need not enlarge upon the results which have followed from such a condition. One should rather wonder
that their defects are not more pronounced.

On the other hand, they are possessed of virtues with
which they are seldom credited. The fact that in Turkey
they are rigorously precluded from bearing arms has disposed superficial observers to regard them as cowards. A
different judgment might be meted out were they placed on
an equality in this respect with their enemies the Kurds. At
all events, when given the chance, they have not been slow
to display martial qualities both in the domain of the highest strategy and in that of personal prowess. The victorious
commander-in-chief for Russia in her Asiatic campaign of
1877 was an Armenian from the district of Lori—Loris
Melikoff. In the same campaign the most brilliant general
of division in the Russian Army was an Armenian—Ter-
gukasoff (Der Ghugasoff). The gallant young staff-officer,
Tarnaieff, who planned and led the hare-brained attack on
the Azizi fort in front of Erzerum, was an Armenian, and
paid for his daring with his life. At the present day the
frontier police, engaged in controlling the Kurds of the
border, are recruited from among Armenians. These examples may be sufficient to nail to the counter an inveterate
lie, from which the Armenians have suffered, at least in
British estimation, more, perhaps, than from any other supposed defect.

If I were asked what characteristics distinguish the Armenians from other Orientals, I should be disposed to lay
most stress on a quality known in popular speech as *grit*.
It is this quality to which they owe their preservation as a
people, and they are not surpassed in this respect by any
European nation. Their intellectual capacities are supported by a solid foundation of character, and, unlike the
Greeks, but like the Germans, their nature is averse to superficial methods; they become absorbed in their tasks and
plumb them deep. There is no race in the Nearer East more
quick of learning than the Persians; yet should you be vis-

ited by a Persian gentleman accompanied by his Armenian man of business, take a book down from your shelves, better one with illustrations, and, the conversation turning upon some subject treated by its author, hand it to them after a passing reference. The Persian will look at the pictures, which he may praise. The Armenian will devour the book, and at each pause in the conversation you will see him poring over it with knitted brows. These tendencies are naturally accompanied by forethought and balance; and they have given the Armenian his pre-eminence in commercial affairs. (Vol. I, p. 466)

The Reign of Abdul Hamid

The Armenians, like all the non-Turkish peoples who suffered under the Ottoman hegemony, had been inured to misrule for centuries. Unlike most of the others, however, Armenians were condemned to developing their national destiny within what has been for almost a millennium the parent state of Turkey rather than on one or another of the Turkish Empire's foreign outposts. Turkish Armenia, roughly speaking, lies in that part of northeastern Turkish Anatolia which today borders on Syria and the Soviet Union. Where Serbs, Greeks, Bulgars, Egyptians, and other subjects of the Ottoman sultans endured their miseries at a distance from their Turkish masters, the Armenians were physically within range of the Turks of Asia Minor and such of their half-savage minions as the Kurdish and Circassian hordes. This physical fact is one of the keys—perhaps the most important one—to the intensity of their tragedy.

The Armenians, moreover, were condemned not merely to suffer from the caprices of a brutal, unpredictable government but from one that had already been in an advanced state of decay for more than two centuries when Abdul Hamid II, perhaps the worst of all Turkish sultans, assumed the Sultanate in 1876. Turkey had been denominated "the Sick Man of Europe" by Czar Nicholas more than three decades before Abdul came to power, and this too added to Armenian woes, for history has taught that there can be no greater source of suffering than the dissolution of an empire, such as the Turkish, when its subject peoples, whatever their irredentist or nationalist aspirations, are still within the physical control of the central—even if dying—power. The Armenians, like many other peoples under Turkish rule, had known this to their sorrow for some time when Abdul Hamid II became the supreme ruler at the beginning of the last quarter of the nineteenth century.

Not many months before Abdul's ascension to the imperial cushion, in fact, the Bulgarians, chafed beyond bearing by Turkish misrule, had attempted a rebellion. The Turks, in one of their last sucesses, had put down the revolt at Batak, but with such indescribable fury and bestiality as to arouse the entire civilized world. (One must allow for the fact that what the Turks did to the Bulgarians was insignificant in the light of what they did to the Armenians during and after the reign of Abdul in assessing the depth and intensity of Turkish cruelty.)

A British journalist, Edwin Pears, later Sir Edwin, was on the scene in 1876; his dispatches to his paper ignited an explosion of moral revulsion in Great Britain, led as it would be again and again by the great Gladstone:

> What seems now to be certain in this sense (besides the miserable daily misgovernment, which, however, dwindle by the side of the Bulgarian horrors) are the wholesale massacres
> 'Murder, most foul as in the best it is,
> 'But this most foul, strange and unnatural (Hamlet, i, 5)' the elaborate and refined cruelty—the only refinement of which Turkey boasts!—the utter disregard of sex and age—the abominable and bestial lust—and the utter and violent lawlessness which still stalks over the land. For my own part I have in the House of Commons and elsewhere, whatever my inward impressions might be, declined to speak strongly on these atrocities, until there was both clear and responsible evidence before me. . . . But this report of Mr. Schuyler, together with the report from Berlin, and the Prologue, so to call it, of Mr. Baring, in my opinion

turns the scale, and makes the responsibility of silence, at least for one who was among the authors of the Crimean War, too great to be borne.

An old servant of the Crown and State, I entreat my countrymen, upon whom far more than perhaps any other people of Europe it depends, to require, and to insist, that our Government, which has been working in one direction, shall work in the other, and shall apply all its vigour and concur with the other states of Europe in obtaining the extinction of the Turkish executive power in Bulgaria; let the Turks carry away their abuses in the only possible manner, namely by carrying themselves off. Their Zaptiehs and their Mudirs, their Binbashis and their Yuzbashis, their Kaimakams and Pashas, one and all, bag and baggage, shall, I hope, clear out from the province they have desolated and profaned.[1]

Rev. Frederick Davis Greene in his book *The Armenian Crisis in Turkey* further quotes from that paper as published in the *Christian Register,* Boston, as follows:

We may ransack the annals of the world; but I know not what research can furnish us with so portentous an example of the fiendish misuse of the powers established by God 'for the punishment of evildoers, and for the encouragement of them that do well.' No government ever has sinned; none has so proved itself incorrigible in sin, or, which is the same, so impotent for reformation. If it be allowable that the executive power of Turkey should renew, at this great crisis, by permission or authority of Europe, the charter of its existence in Bulgaria, then there is not one record, since the beginnings of political society, a protest that man has lodged against intolerable misgovernment, or a stroke he has dealt at loathsome tyranny, that ought not henceforth forward to be branded as a crime.[2]

Such enlightened views as Gladstone's, however, were not in the ascendant. Had they been, much of the terrible tragedy of the late nineteenth and early twentieth centuries might well have been averted. It was the advocates of *real-politik,* led in England by Gladstone's great adversary Disraeli, who conferred immunity from punishment on Turkey's worst

criminals, who were more often than not its legally constituted rulers.

It is hard at this date to recall Great Britain's fear and distrust of Czarist Russia. The anti-Russian policy makers
courted Turkey, no matter what bestial excesses it committed, as a buffer against Russian expansionism, real or fan-
cied. Thus Turkey became a pawn in the balance-of-power
struggle, with the consequence that its subject peoples, especially the Armenians, became as it were the pawns of a pawn.
Into this atmosphere in 1876 stepped Abdul Hamid II, the
last of a long line of bad or merely ineffectual sultans, and
undoubtedly the worst of them all.

It must be granted that Abdul was to prove clever to the
point of brilliance in exploiting the mutual distrust of Britain
and Russia in the first decades of his intolerable rule and to
do so again when Wilhelm's Germany became the British
bete noire. Initially, however, and with sad irony, Abdul's accession appeared to the Armenians almost to be an occasion
for rejoicing. Just as misleading, and even more tragically so,
were the signs when Abdul was finally overthrown by the
Young Turks thirty-three years later.

The sensation of Abdul's first year as Sultan was the announcement of a constitutional government, the first in Turkey's long, lamentable history. The constitution, in large part
authored by the great and enlightened Midhat Pasha, would
most certainly have been badly administered if it had survived—all Turkish laws were. But, as many commentators
have pointed out, the very existence of a constitution offers
some hope to the most helpless elements within a corrupt and
brutal nation. Even such residual tricklings of advantage to
oppressed citizens were soon to be denied, however, for in
1878 Abdul dissolved the parliament, declared the end of the
constitution, and hounded Midhat into exile. So ended the
dream that Turkey might at last be moving in the direction
of Western enlightenment and libertarianism.

Abdul's hatred of European ideals was all too evident in his dissolution of constitutional government. But to his anti-European policy he added features of his own, a pathological mixture of fear and suspicion on the one hand and savage cruelty on the other. It was by no means an untypical Hamidian act when a few years after his ouster of the noble Midhat, he had him murdered and his head brought to him in a box so that his fears of a coup might be allayed.

The Italian writer Luigi Olivero, after comparing Abdul Hamid with other tyrants, even including Ivan the Terrible, can find no shred of historical justification for the Red Sultan:

> Gille Roy . . . sought in vain to find a psychological explanation of his monstrous cruelty. Abdul Hamid was fully conscious of what he was doing; everything was premeditated, carefully calculated and then worked out with consummate intelligence and skill. While he was still a youth, the future Sultan had begun to compile his list of victims who, sooner or later, he had decided would have to pass over the threshold into eternity because it suited his purpose to get them out of the way.[3]

Under such a beast as Abdul even the most favored of his subjects might well feel cause for uneasiness. For the Armenians, Abdul's rule was an unmitigated disaster, for he hated them with a passion, even for a time forbidding the mention of Armenians in his presence.

It is a tribute to the courage and enlightenment of the Armenians that, even under Abdul, they prospered enough to be a permanent temptation to the marauding Kurdish and Circassian nomads, who were encouraged by the Turks to make Armenian life as miserable as possible. James Creagh, writing in 1880, put the position of the Armenians succinctly:

> Woe to the unhappy Armenian who was known to be the possessor of wealth! His only chance of preserving it was to simulate extreme poverty, for he was ever surrounded by spies ready to cite him for being too rich before a man in power. For the offence, or on the mere suspicion of it, he was sentenced to pay a fine, and flogged unmercifully or even killed if he could not do so.[4]

In all fairness, one must say that Abdul Hamid's position was so precarious that a certain amount of sympathy might have been engendered simply for his difficulties had he been any other kind of man than the unprincipled sadist he was. He ruled an empire that showed every sign of falling apart; his people were of an extreme backwardness and were dropping back further in relation to the progressive nations with every passing year; there was no money, hardly any schools; there was corruption and stagnation everywhere. It is hardly a wonder that "the Sick Man of Europe" seemed ripe for the acquisitive drives of every aggressive power. In 1877 the Russians could hold back no longer and launched a campaign that shortly proved entirely successful except for British resolves to risk war rather than see Turkey completely gobbled up.

Under the terms of the Treaty of San Stefano in 1878, Turkey lost large pieces of territory and the Armenians were guaranteed some protection. As Lord Eversley pointed out, however, the reforms and guarantees promised by Abdul meant less than nothing to him; indeed his animosity toward the Armenians increased. "It may be taken," says Lord Eversley, "that, if the Powers had conceived it possible that these promises would not be carried out, they would not have been so cruel as to restore these two provinces, (Erzeroum and Bayezid) inhabited so largely by Armenians, to Turkish rule."[5]

Virtually nothing in the reign of Abdul Hamid gives the humane, or even the detached, reader cause for cheer. The entire atmosphere of his thirty-three years is of a suffocating repressiveness, lighted by the glare of unspeakable official acts of cruelty and abnormal revenge, fear, and suspicion. In this supercharged air, the destiny of the Armenians was the most ominous of all, for if one can detect a pattern in Abdul's mercurial style of rule, it is simply that his hatred of the Armenians increased with the years and that power considerations alone prevented him from being the first promulgator of genocide. His unremitting hatred of this finest element in his domain is clear at all points, as was recognized by the British consul at Erzerum, Clifford Lloyd in a Minute on the Condition of Armenia which he submitted on October 2, 1890. Consul Lloyd was very well informed and dealt effectively with the canard encouraged by Abdul Hamid that the Armenians were disloyal. (One wonders in fact why the Armenians exhibited so few signs of disaffection in the light of the harassment they suffered and from which they were never free.)

Consul Lloyd's Minute is so apt and detailed as to deserve extensive quotation from the Reverend Malcolm MacColl's book of five years later, *England's Responsibility towards Armenia,* in which it is reproduced:

ARMENIAN SEDITION A MYTH

V. I am of the opinion that the question of protecting the Armenian peasantry from the attacks of the Kurds is of much greater importance than any other, and that, if the Christians were shielded from the ever-existing apprehension of being pillaged and killed, they would become a comparatively contented and prosperous people . . .

All the Christians asked for was protection, but this was the one thing the Government failed to provide . . . The result is that this summer the valley has been again overrun by the Kurds, *who here, as elsewhere, openly declare that their action meets with the approval of the Turkish Government.* I am fully justified in recording my opinion that, during the past year, had the Armenian peasantry been given security to life and property, their grievances in the provinces would not have been of that serious nature which now attracts to them the attention of Europe.

As to the second ground of complaint above mentioned, I need not go into any detail to show that the Turkish Government denies them any freedom of thought or action. In my despatch dated June 28, 1890, I fully explained the policy being locally adopted in this respect. *I believe that the idea of revolution is not entertained by any class of the Armenian people in these provinces,* whatever may be the aims of those outside them. *An armed revolution is, besides, impossible. Discontent or any description of protest is, however, regarded by the Turkish Local Gov-*

*ernment as seditious, and a policy such as I described in
my despatch alluded to is pursued, depriving the Armenian subject of every liberty to his person, and for which
no justification exists.* This materially aggravates the existing discontent, and produces a feeling of animosity between Mussulman and Christian which would otherwise
die out, or which would at least lie dormant.

The third cause is the inequality of justice and consideration shown to the Christian inhabitants of this country,
both by the Executive Government and by the Law Officers. This is well known to everyone conversant with the
condition of Kurdistan but, as an instance, I may mention
the fact that in all crimes of violence of which the Christians have been the victims during the past year in the
Province of Erzeroum, no one has been punished, nor,
with very few exceptions, has any effort been even made
to bring the offenders to justice.

On the other hand, Christians have been arrested and
detained in prison for long periods without any charge
being made against them. . . . The agricultural portion of
the Armenian people plead not as rebels, but as subjects of
His Majesty the Sultan, for protection; but, in the words of
the Note presented ten years ago to the Sublime Porte on
the same subject, the Local Government at Erzeroum
seems 'to refuse to recognise the degree of anarchy which
exists' in this province, or 'the gravity of a state of things
which, if permitted to continue, would, in all probability,
lead to the destruction of the Christian population of vast
districts.'

Colonel Chermside, who preceded Mr. Clifford Lloyd as
Consul at Erzeroum, writes in a similar strain, and admits
that the infamous treatment of the Christians by the Turkish Government is producing disaffection among the Armenians. He truly remarks that 'it would be strange were
it otherwise.'

ENGLAND'S RESPONSIBILITY TOWARDS ARMENIA

VIII. England's responsibility towards Armenia is at-
tested by a triple bond of obligation. Together with France,
she contracted through the Crimean War a special obligation towards all the Christian subjects of the Porte. Till
then Russia exercised, with the consent of Europe, a protectorate over the Christians of Turkey. The Treaty of

Paris in 1856 deprived Russia of that protectorate, and placed the rajahs under the collective protectorate of the Great Powers of Europe. That was precisely what the Porte wanted. Face to face with Russia alone, the Sultan was amenable to pressure, for experience had taught the Porte that war with Russia always ended in disaster to Islam. But the remonstrances of six Great Powers instead of one were another matter. What was everybody's business was nobody's business, and the Porte astutely trusted to the policy of *divide et impera*. Moreover, the Crimean War convinced the Porte that the integrity and independence of the Ottoman Empire were absolutely essential to the balance of power in Europe. We got no gratitude from the Turks for saving their Empire from ruin on that occasion. The Sultan and his pashas believed that France and England made war against Russia for their own selfish ends exclusively, and the ignorant Mussulman peasantry believed, and still believe, that the Powers of Christendom are the Sultan's vassals, and were bound to obey his mandate to help him to repel the invasion of rebellious Russia. The Porte, with that cunning which so often passes for statesmanship among Orientals, immediately fastened on the diplomatic advantage which the policy of the Crimean War had given it. (pp. 95–96)

The next landmark in our obligation to the Armenians is the Anglo-Turkish Convention of 1880, by which England undertook two things: a military obligation binding her to defend the Armenian frontier against Russia; a civil obligation giving her the right and imposing on her the duty of seeing that effectual reforms were carried out in the administration of that province. Article 1 stipulates that these reforms are 'to be agreed on between England and the Porte.'

From that day to this England has done nothing to fulfil her solemn obligation under that Convention. And the Armenians, meanwhile, have been enduring the life of agony which the Consular Reports reveal. (p. 99)

This third landmark in our obligation to Armenia is the Treaty of Berlin. In the 61st Clause of the Treaty of Berlin it is stipulated that the Porte shall carry out the reforms and general amelioration demanded by local requirements in the provinces inhabited by the Armenians. The Porte is a party to that agreement, and guarantees the security of the Armenians against Circassians and Kurds, and the

Sultan engages, in addition, that he 'will periodically make known the steps taken to this effect to the Powers, who will superintend their application.' That clause of the Treaty of Berlin has remained a dead letter ever since. The Porte has not once made known to the Powers the steps taken by it to fulfil its treaty engagements, and for the excellent reason that it has taken no steps whatever. And the Powers have calmly acquiesced in this cynical and contemptuous violation—I will not say of its honour, for a Government cannot violate what it does not possess, but—of its obligations under the sanctions of an international treaty. And for this most dishonouring fact England is principally and mainly responsible. (p. 101)[6]

. . . . At the same time every precaution was taken to prevent the news of these wholesale acts of rapine and massacre from being known to the outside world. . . . In the province of Bitlis twenty-four Armenian villages were destroyed by Zeki Pasha. Their inhabitants were butchered. Zeki was decorated by the Sultan for this infamy. In 1895 as again in 1896, wholesale massacres of Armenians took place, organized by Sultan Abdul Hamid, and effected through the agency of Shakir Pasha and other officials, civil and military. It was estimated that a hundred thousand Armenians were victims of these massacres, either directly or indirectly by starvation and disease which followed them. . . . In vain did Mr. Gladstone issue, for the last time, from his retirement and appeal to public opinion on behalf of these people, designating the Sultan as Abdul the Great Assassin.[7]

The years 1895–1896, midway in Abdul's reign, were sufficient evidence, if any had been needed, that Turkey was unfit to rule over any people, probably including its own. With his acts of these years Abdul reached the apotheosis of his reputation as perhaps the worst tyrant of his century.

What it was like to live through the Hamidian terror has been vividly recorded by an Armenian pastor of Diyarbekir, Abraham Hartunian, who survived both it and the more terrible massacre of 1915–1916. His account of his experiences in 1895 are recounted here (Hartunian, *Neither to Laugh Nor to Weep*. Copyright © 1968 by Vartan Hartunian. Reprinted by permission of Beacon Press):

The first attack was on our pastor. The blow of an ax decapitated him. His blood, spurting in all directions, spattered the walls and ceiling with red. Then I was in the midst of the butchers. One of them drew his dagger and stabbed my left arm, and I, convinced that they were about to torture me, instead of remaining standing, squatted on the floor with my head bent in front of me. Another second, and I lost consciousness. I felt as if I were in a dream and were flying down from a high place, and I remember clearly saying in my mind, "I shall see God. I shall see God."

What happened to me some women who had remained alive told me later. When I squatted on the floor, three blows fell on my head. My blood began to flow like a fountain, and I rolled over like a slaughtered lamb. The attackers, sure that I was dead and seeing no need to bother further, left me in that condition. Then they slaughtered the other men in the room, took the prettier women with them for rape, and left the other women and children there, conforming to the command that in this massacre only men were to be exterminated.

Blood-drenched and unconscious, I remained stretched out on the floor, surrounded by mutilated corpses, for seven hours. Sometime after midnight someone shook my body and consciousness returned. A blustering wind was blowing through the open windows and door of the room. It was bitter cold.

There is someone near me, handling me, trying to take off my clothes. Who is this person? A giant, savage, monstrous Kurd! Horror! If this murderer knows I am still alive, he will run his dagger through my heart and stop my breath. I try to control myself. I breathe as slowly as I can. I try to seem dead. He raises my head and lets it fall on the tiles. I bear the bitter pain silently. He moves my legs. He rolls my body, increasing the flow of blood. . . . In this way he succeeded in getting my coat, and now he was at my vest. He tried hard to take it off but not knowing how to unbutton it drew his dagger. O that moment! Would that dagger tear my heart?

The wife of the church sexton, Sister Mary, having escaped in some way from the hands of the enemy, was hiding in the next room, watching. As the Kurd drew his dagger to cut my vest, she, thinking he was about to stab me and unable to bear it, suddenly rushed upon him like a lioness and shouted, "Kurd, what are you doing!"

The Kurd, horrified, slunk back—who knows with what satanic superstition!—thinking perhaps that unseen evil spirits were persecuting him in the darkness. In a trembling voice he answered, "I'm not doing anything. I wanted this dead man's clothes. I couldn't untie his vest."

"Get back!" roared the voice. "I'll take it off and give it to you!"

The Kurd drew back like a cat. Sister Mary took off my vest and trousers and gave them to him. But coming closer he saw my underwear and asked for that too, and, taking it, disappeared. . . .

Suddenly there was a tumult. People were climbing the stairs, coming on the rooftops with torches and lamps in their hands. Some of these fiends approached us, and when they saw only a group of helpless women, they were about to leave to search for other victims. But the blood-drunk eye of one of them saw my prostrate form in the midst of the group. The women were driven away from my side and I was stripped of my quilt.

Were these Turks moved by my wounded, naked condition? No, the Turk does not know the meaning of compassion, love, pity. When they saw that I was not dead, one of them drew his sword to stab me with it. When I cried aloud and pleaded and begged for mercy, they turned more fierce and growled, "Gâvur gebermeli! The infidel must die like a dog!"

An old woman, unable to bear my woeful cries, threw herself on me. She covered me with her body and said, "Kill me first and then this man. Have pity. It is enough. He is already dead."

The sword was withdrawn. The devils turned away. But the Turkish conscience had a sting in it. To leave before the giavoor (infidel) died was to be irreligious. One of them picked up a large stone and hurled it at my head. And now, certain that I had received the fatal blow, the group left, satisfied in heart and calm in conscience, fully expecting twice ten virgins in heaven to crown this meritorious act. . . .

The women, feeling that my condition was hopeless, fled and left me alone. In the darkness, in the wind, in the cold, what was I to do? If I remained here I would be attacked again and killed. I had to escape. But was there enough strength in me? I turned my eyes toward heaven. Crying to God, I got on my feet and began to walk—no, I began to drive myself, to push and shove myself, sobbing, bending, stumbling, rolling, rising. Finally going down the stairs I passed through the yard and into the street. By chance I entered that same house to which the women had fled. This was an Armenian house adjacent to a Turkish agha's residence. On the floor was a little pile of wheat, and I stretched out on it to rest. This place too was attacked, but we managed to escape to the house of the agha, who received us and put us in a corner of his yard. We spent the last two hours of the night there, I prostrate on the ground, in a stupor.

On Sunday morning, November 3, 1895, the church bells were silent. The churches and schools, desecrated and plundered, lay in ruins. Pastors, priests, choristers, teachers, leaders, all were no more. The Armenian houses, robbed and empty, were as caves. Fifteen hundred men had been slaughtered, and those left alive were wounded and paralyzed. Girls were in the shame of their rape, mothers in the tears of their widowhood, orphaned children in wild bewilderment. The enslaved remnant was subject to nakedness and hunger, deprived of religion, honor, the very right to live.

But here and there some whose death had been decided upon beforehand, whose death warrant had been prepared, were still being hunted out. The Turks wanted to be sure that all these people had been destroyed. One of the names on this death list was mine. It had been discovered that the young Protestant teacher was not dead but missing.

This morning, a little after sunrise, a number of gendarmes and *basïbozuk* surrounded the agha's house and threatened him, saying, "There are giavoors hidden here. Give them up!" The agha showed me and another young man to them, and we were immediately arrested. With their bayonets at our backs, they forced us into the street. When they recognized me, one of them said, "Hoja, we're taking you to the *konak*. The Armenian leaders, aghas, and educators are having a meeting there. They are waiting for you." They drove us on, but we were not going in the direction of the *konak*. I asked one of them, "Why are we going by this road?" He answered mockingly, "The road that leads to your meeting place is this one." Now it was clear they were going to kill us.

Walking ahead, we soon reached our meeting place. The sight that met my eyes was a triple horror. All the Armenian leaders and religious heads, all those whose names were on the death list, were there. Slaughtered and soaked in kerosene, they were a burning hill of corpses. We two were pushed to the edge of this dreadful pile, and the Turk turned to me and said, "Here are your leaders! And here is your meeting place!" The guns were raised to shoot us.

In the very nick of time, when the command to shoot was about to be given, a Turkish ringleader turned the corner in front of us with his gang and, seeing us, shouted authoritatively, "Stop! Don't shoot!". . . .

On Thursday, November 7, the fifth day of our imprisonment, we were taken out and driven to the courtyard of a large inn. As we moved along in a file under guard, a crowd of Turkish women on the edge of the road, mocking and cursing us like frenzied maenads, screeched the unique convulsive shrill of the *zelgid,* the ancient battle cry of the women of Islam—the exultant *lu-lu-lu-lu* filled with the concentrated hate of the centuries. I said in my mind, as this scene impressed itself upon me, "Let Shimei's curse fall on David since the Lord hath bidden him. It may be that the Lord will look on mine affliction, and that the Lord will requite me good for his cursing this day" (II Samuel 16:11–12).

We reached the inn. Women and children engulfed us. They were weeping, wailing, choking, wild with despair. "In Rama was there a voice heard, lamentation, and weeping, and great mourning, Rachel weeping for her children, and would not be comforted, because they are not" (Matthew 2:18). One was saying, "Where is my father?" Another, "Where is my mother?" Still another, "Where is my child?" I think that even heaven does not know the heaviness of that day's suffering.

My stepbrothers' two young widows and four small orphans surrounded me, clung to me, wept and made me weep. They wanted their husbands and their fathers from me. I collected myself, struggling to preserve my moral strength. The hour to do my very best had come, to comfort not only my own but all the Armenian fragments, for I was the sole leader and shepherd of this unhappy flock.[8]

It would be interesting, if not especially profitable, to speculate on Turkish mistreatment of the Armenians. What, one wonders, could really have motivated it? Its source is most certainly not religious, for the Turks did not mistreat the Jews inside Turkey on anything like the scale of their merciless handling of the Armenians. Tales of Armenian disloyalty were transparently false; Russia's interests in the Armenians were as clearly prompted by political rather than humanitarian considerations.

It may well be that Turkish sadism regarding the Armenians will never have a satisfactory explanation. It was not merely insensate; it was positively self-defeating, for the Armenians were the most treasurable element within a nation rapidly sliding toward total ruin. One may have to seek the answer in Turkish feelings of inferiority to the one people who could manage their affairs, contribute to civilization, and make the inhospitable land flourish.

There are probable parallels between the Hamidian Turkish attitudes toward Armenians and Nazi attitudes toward the Jews. Superficially the resemblance may be merely the absurd myth that all Armenians were rich—as the Nazis persuaded themselves that the meagerest of Jewish paupers harbored diamonds in his rags. One of the more interesting likenesses, however, resides in the character of Turkish and Nazi German senses of personal failure, as opposed to comparative cohesiveness and purpose, as exhibited by Armenians and German Jews. This is merely the hint of an explanation—there is not much likeness between an illiterate, slovenly, lazy Turkish peasant on the one hand and a frustrated lower middle class German clerk on the other except the feeling of inadequacy and the convenient proximity of scapegoats in the form of a foreign body within the state.

The best analyses of Nazism have always emphasized the rejection of Western values (Greek, Judaic, and Christian) that was fundamental in its mythology, and this too may be an important clue. There can obviously be little connection between the rantings of a Hitler and the chilly murderousness of an Abdul Hamid except in their common rejection of those restraints, legal and moral, that have contributed to the advancement of civilization. Hitlerian Wotanism and Hamidian Ottomanism may have little in common, but they are one in their preference for quick solutions and their disregard of humane values.

All of Abdul Hamid's thirty-three years on the Turkish throne were troubled but none so much as the last ten or so. While he pursued his clever game of playing one Western power against another, he was at least coping with the situation so far as Britain, Russia, Germany, and France were concerned. One could at least say that he kept the world guessing. But internally Abdul had more to deal with.

The Hamidian regime had kept itself afloat with spying, assassination, midnight raids, xenophobia, corruption, and intrigue. All of these means had a way of doubling back in the form of internal insecurity, a process that rendered the Sultan's position increasingly shaky from 1890 on. Internal disaffection was extreme, especially among the comparatively few younger intellectuals and professionals within the empire, and there was little doubt, by the dawn of the twentieth century, that the sultanate had run its course.

Rise of the Young Turks

As might be expected, internal opposition to Abdul Hamid was widespread. It was also extremely difficult and dangerous to attempt any anti-Hamidian organization, for Abdul's spy system was ubiquitous and efficient. Punishment for even the mildest criticism was certain, swift, and savage. Nevertheless, groups against the Sultan began to form as early as the late 1880s.

The risk of infiltration of these groups by Abdul's spies was so great that the most elaborate precautions had to be taken to preserve the movement. It has been said that the great majority of the cell members knew the names of not more than one fellow conspirator, and that to know as many as six indicated a high position in the movement. Even with these elaborate precautions, the anti-Hamidian groups were often successfully infiltrated, and it is not surprising that organization tended to develop either outside Turkey, especially in Paris, or in such comparatively far-flung centers of the Empire as Salonika, rather than in Constantinople (now Istanbul). Egypt and Tunis were also centers of secret opposition.

In these difficult circumstances it is hardly surprising that success in opposing Abdul was long in coming. The brave conspirators against that unspeakable tyrant, some of them advanced pro-European constitutionalists, are now for the most part unknown, their names lost in the mists of late nineteenth-century political movements, of which there were so many.

Nevertheless, discontent was so widespread that the inchoate movement against the Sultan was eventually bound to succeed. When it finally assumed definite shape in the early twentieth century as the Party of Union and Progress it attracted large numbers of disaffected Turkish army members. When it secured the support of the army in 1908 its success was virtually assured.

In late July, 1908, the Committee of Union and Progress, under the leadership of Enver, threatened to march against Constantinople to force the Sultan to restore the Constitution, which for three decades had been in abeyance. The revolutionaries had no intention of deposing Abdul, at first, but simply to compel him to restore at least a comparative freedom to Turkey. They had prepared their revolution with great skill and thoroughness, so that even Abdul's bodyguard was with them. In great fear and trembling, Abdul capitulated, and constitutional government was restored.

There have probably not been many moments in recent history that have exhibited the unrestrained and touching joy that greeted the victory of the Young Turks under Enver, Talaat, Djavid, and other leaders. There was, literally, dancing in the streets. Jew embraced Moslem, Armenian embraced Turk, and an era of good will appeared to be dawning.

The revolution had gone off with such surprising ease and

with such an appearance of total victory that the Committee of Union and Progress was caught off guard by the counter-revolutionary conspiracy among such Hamidian elements as the Sultan's former spies. The matter came to a head in mid-April, 1909, when Abdul's lack of boldness resulted in a complete and almost bloodless victory for the Committee of Union and Progress. Abdul was deposed and succeeded by his brother Mahomet V, a virtual idiot and quite incapable of effective action.

In the short period of nine months between the Young Turks' first and final successes it had become all too evident that the initial outbreak of universal joy had been premature. There was a fierce internal struggle among the Young Turks for the establishment of an overall policy that would either be at least somewhat European and libertarian on the one hand or a species of mad-dog xenophobia known as pan-Turanism on the other. The latter, under the leadership of Enver, easily won, and proclaimed the complete Turkification of the nation, with consequent suppression of non-Turkish elements, their language, religion, even their property and lives being at risk. Foremost among these threatened groups, of course, were the Armenians, who received at Adana in 1909 a foretaste of things to come.

The tragedy at Adana had, as have so many Armenian disasters, capable and humane witnesses, as well as such outstanding commentators as the great Norwegian explorer, Dr. Fridtjof Nansen. A liberal selection from the testimony of the enlightened witnesses and scholars and journalists of the Adana massacres gives a vivid and heartbreaking account of the disaster which would soon pale in magnitude, if not horror, before the events of the 1915–1916 genocide.

Here, then, are some of the outstanding documents of the outrage at Adana:

First let us hear Dr. Herbert Adams Gibbons, author, scholar and historian (*The Blackest Page of Modern History*):

It was my fortune to go to Turkey during the first month of the new regime, and to live in Asia Minor and Constantinople until after the disastrous war with the Balkan States. From 1908 to 1913, I enjoyed exceptional opportunities of traveling in European and Asiatic Turkey, of becoming acquainted with the men who were guiding the destinies of the Ottoman Empire, and of witnessing the fatal events that changed in five years the hope of generations into despair and dissolution.

Above all, from the very beginning, I was in a position to become intimately acquainted with the Armenians of Turkey and to find out their real sentiments towards the Young Turks and the new regime. I was in Adana (Cilicia), in April, 1909, when their enthusiastic loyalty was rewarded by a massacre of thirty thousand of them in Cilicia and northern Syria. I was able to observe the attitude of the Armenians before the massacre. Their blood was spilled before my eyes in Adana. I was with them in different places after the fury of the massacre had passed.

. . . It is necessary, then, for me to state that the facts set forth here are given with intimate personal knowledge of their authenticity, and that the judgments passed upon these facts are the result of years of study and observation at close range. (pp. 13–16)

Next let us hear from David Brewer Eddy, in his book *What Next in Turkey?* of 1913:

April 14 will forever be the day of weeping in that city. Shops were broken open, looted and burned, the homes of Christians were entered and every man that could be found was shot, hacked to pieces, or thrown into the flames. No Christian woman's honor was spared. The bursting flames lit up the scene; homes, shops, even the church was utterly destroyed. Miner Rogers, a gallant young missionary who had been on the field but a few months, gave up his life with Maurer in their attempt to protect women and children in the buildings of a girls' school. Out from the city rushed bands of these devils in Turkish uniform to continue the destruction. Men were hunted in the mountains and murdered in the most horrible manner. Women were forced to watch the death of their husbands and little children while they themselves were reserved for an even worse fate. The murderers would make the most solemn promises of protection, tricking the villagers into giving their arms and then slaughter them in their defenseless condition. Sailors from British and American warships, who had passed through the Boxer riots, the siege of Port Arthur and the San Francisco earthquake said they had never seen anything to compare with the destruction of life and property in this district. From three to five thousand people fell in Adana alone, while something like 20,000 perished in the outside districts. Whole villages were wiped out.

Of the dreadful events Dr. Fridtjof Nansen says in his *Armenia and the Near East*:

> Not only did Young Turkish officers and soldiery join in the looting, but the subsequent legal inquiries were a scandal. The known leaders of the massacres went scot-free, while a few murderers chosen at random were hanged— with some Armenians who had resorted to armed resistance in defence of themselves and their families.

Another eloquent commentator, the French writer George Brezol, wrote in his *Les Turcs Ont Passe La . . . (The Turks Have Been There . . .)* of 1911:

> Here is how history is written in Turkey!
> In 1909, when M. Pichon in a speech made in the Chamber of Deputies in Paris, spoke of 20,000 Armenians massacred in Cilicia, the Turkish embassy of Paris, on the day following, published articles in the Parisian newspapers stating that only 4,000 persons had died.
> It is time to uncover the truth, to show the naked evil. We have undertaken this salutary work by rejecting all literary dissertations which could influence the mind. This volume is a collection of authentic documents—reports, letters, dispatches, speeches, interpellations, articles, etc., etc.,—the seal of originality of which has been loosened, respecting the limits of translation; they clear the responsibility overwhelmingly; the bloody charts, the scenes of carnage are one baffling horror and in reading them one too naturally evokes Victor Hugo's verse in *l'Enfant Grec:* '. . . all is in ruins and mournful/The Turks have passed by this place . . .'

The story of the massacre of the Armenians in Adana, Cilicia, in April, 1909, has been graphically described in the following dispatches from disinterested individuals, quoted by Mr. Brezol:

1. A dispatch sent by Dr. Chambers, director of the American Missionaries at Adana, dated May 1, 1909, from Mersini through Reuter agency of London.

A frightful massacre began on April 1/14; it subsided on the 16th, but it is continued in the suburbs. The following week an organized effort was made to bring help to 15,000 sufferers. The massacre began all over again furiously on the 12/25 of April, the *soldiers* and the *bashibozouk* (irregulars) began a terrible volley of firearms on the Armenian school where around 2,500 persons had taken refuge. Then the building caught fire and when the refugees tried to save themselves by running outside they were fired upon; many perished in the flames. The destructive fire continued until Tuesday morning. Four churches and the adjacent schools were burned as well as hundreds of homes in the most populated quarters of the city; following this incendiarism thousands of persons were left without lodging and in a worst kind of misery. Furniture and goods spared by the flames were pillaged.

On Monday the English consul, his arms bandaged, worked very hard to convince the local government to establish order and to organize a service for helping those who were located near the smoking ruins. The American missionary establishment and their school, the school of the Jesuit Sisters were equally in danger, they were now safe. Fire destroyed the Jesuit Church as well as the boys' school. More than 20,000 persons are hospitalized in two large factories. Wednesday morning provisions were distributed, that is to say 45 drams (145 grams) of rice and 35 drams (112 grams) of bread to this crowd that had not eaten for three days. The government help was absolutely insufficient and the measures taken to protect the goods and the persons are entirely ridiculous. *A group of soldiers are engaged in plundering.* More than 250 pounds sterling are needed to nourish the population of the city, that is dying of hunger.*

2. Dispatch from Adana on April 27, 1909 by missionary M. Gibbons, through Reuter agency.

* This dispatch entirely discredits the report of the Governor of Adana, Moustapha Zihni, who pretends that the soldiers did not budge from their place.

Woodrow Wilson, statesman, historian, and ardent champion of human rights. President of the United States before and during World War I, Wilson actively supported Armenian independence and claims for a homeland. *Underwood and Underwood News Photos*

Henry Morgenthau, Sr., U.S. Ambassador to Turkey during the Armenian massacres. Morgenthau exerted tremendous effort on behalf of Turkey's victims and left stirring records of Turkish brutality and German complicity in the genocide. *Underwood and Underwood News Photos*

Winston Churchill, statesman, warrior, author, and First Lord of the Admiralty until 1915. Churchill was largely responsible for the Gallipoli campaign, whose failure gave Turkish rulers a free hand in internal affairs. *The Bettman Archive*

David Lloyd George, British Prime Minister during World War I and a leading spirit in the Paris Peace Conference following the war. Lloyd George was a vigorous and outspoken proponent of the Armenian cause. *The Bettman Archive*

Viscount James Bryce, diplomat, historian, and author of *The Treatment of Armenians in the Ottoman Empire*. His championship of the Armenian cause extended from the late nineteenth century to the post-World War I peace settlement. *The Bettman Archive*

Johannes Lepsius, missionary, author, humanitarian. Dr. Lepsius was an eye-witness to much Armenian suffering and probably did more to awaken the world's conscience on behalf of the Armenians than any other person. *Underwood and Underwood News Photos*

Fridtjof Nansen, Norwegian explorer, author, humanitarian. Active in famine relief after World War I, for which he won the Nobel Peace Prize, Nansen bitterly attacked the postwar betrayal of the Armenian cause at Lausanne. *Underwood and Underwood News Photos*

Georges Clemenceau, French Prime Minister and Minister for War from 1917 until 1920. A great orator, Clemenceau pleaded eloquently for an Armenian homeland as part of the post-World War I peace settlement. *Underwood and Underwood News Photos*

After the commencement of the massacre of Adana on Friday evening, 250 Redif volunteers, without an officer to head them, settled in a convoy at the railroad station and forced the engineer to take them to Tarsous. There they helped to ruin and destroy the Armenian quarter which constituted the better part of the city. The grand Armenian historic cathedral was stripped. The marble statues were mutilated, the altars of historic value were cut to pieces and were all destroyed; however, the building withstood all efforts to demolish it by fire.

Fortunately, the number of the dead had not risen, thanks to the proximity of the American college which offered a safe refuge to more than 4,000 escapees, in a state of misery and without shelter.

Dispatch from M. Denys Cochin, deputy at Paris (Published in the *Journal Officiel*, May 18, 1909):

All our information is in accord with that of the European press establishing *the participation of the troops in the horrible butcheries of Adana and the province.* (Emphasis by D.C.) *The second massacre of April 25 was carried on by the troops themselves sent from Dediagatch to repress the disorders.* The scenes of indescribable atrocities appeared. All of Cilicia was ruined, a prey to hunger and misery.

The presence of European naval forces did not prevent the slaughter.

The concern of Europe is indispensable to punish the authors of the massacres.

Furthermore, at Erzeroum, Van and Moush the authorities and the troops are Armenophobes and Hamidian. In these conditions our strong warning given by the Chamber could alone avert these monstrous hecatombs.

We beseech you in the name of humanity to do everything necessary in this tragic moment. The most effective means shall be to assume the responsibility of governors and military chiefs in the Armenian provinces.

A Reuters dispatch to an English family, Adana, April 23, 1909:

The massacres have produced a terrible misery in this vilayet. As many as 15,000 persons are without shelter, without resources and are starving; there are thousands of widows and orphans to take care of. A relief commission is formed, composed of Christians and Moslems under the presidency of Mr. Chambers, the Canadian (?) missionary, who has much experience since the first massacre of Adana.

The missionary Kennedy wires as follows, Alexandretta, April 28, 1909:

Armenians have been massacred in Antioch—there are hundreds of widows and orphans—Dr. Martin and his family are safe and sound—The situation here is serious— The churches are filled with refugees. I am keeping more than 200 persons at my home. Foreign subjects find refuge at the governor's home.

The Official Report of the Commission of Inquest of Adana, categorically limiting the degree of responsibility and guilt of organizers of the massacres.

In our communication of May 30, 1325 (1909) we indicated that in consequence of the inquest made by our commission in Djebel-i-Bereket Assaf Bey, the former mayor (Mutessarif) of the said district had made known to the people the contents of the communication which he had received from the former governor of Adana, Djevad Bey. The latter had announced that he had freed the prisoners of Erzine and the convicts of Payas; that he had distributed arms and ammunition to these discharged prisoners and to the peasants. On the other hand, when the besieged inhabitants of Deur-vol asked him for protection, he sent against them the armed population; this former, Mutessarif of Djebel-i-Bereket is the only and chief culprit, by giving free rein to murderers, pillagers and arsonists of his district; he has destroyed the people by allowing the massacres to continue.

We are enclosing herewith a statement consisting of 15 pages, and containing our interrogatories together with the answers subscribed by Assaf Bey; as well as copies of telegrams which the above mentioned deputy governor has sent to the governor of Adana, the Minister of the Interior, the Caimakams of Hamidie, Baghdje and Iskenderoun (Alexandrette), to several Mudirs, to various commissariats, to commanders of Redifs, to the director of the fort of Payas, to the commander of the gendarmerie of that same fort, to other commanders of gendarmerie of various districts. Writings of the same import were equally addressed by him to the environs of the same province.

The reading of these copies will prove to you shockingly that Assaf Bey is the principal culprit and he must be declared responsible for the pillaging, arsons and massacres which have taken place in the sandjah of Djebel-i-Bereket.

The report of the commission describes in detail how Assaf Bey, many of his associates, the Governor-general, the Military Commander and others by their criminal acts or neglects incited the Mussulmans to attack and kill the Christians of Cilicia. They invented false rumors and circulated among the Islam population to the effect that Armenians were plotting a revolution. Even after the Ottoman soldiers arrived at Adana on April 12 to establish and safeguard peace and tranquility they deceived the Governor-general and the Military Commander by a false statement that the Armenians had fired upon a military encampment from the belfry of their church. The commission investigated this claim and found that the Armenian church was too far away from any military quarters and it was impossible to fire upon any such encampment. After refuting all accusations made against the Armenians, and proving beyond any doubt the guilt of various Turks the commission concludes its report as follows:

In view of all the above-mentioned considerations it is impossible not to recognize, as persons responsible for the grievous events of Adana and its surroundings, the Governor-general, the Military Commander, Ismail Sefa efendi and Ihsan Fikri efendi. The enclosed copies of the telegrams from the Governor-general and the military commander, are already a sparkling proof of their responsibility and guilt.

The Commission specifically names Salih effendi and Abdulkader effendi as the "ring-leaders of these terrible massacres." The report says:

The above-named Abdulkader and Bochnak Salih, on horseback, and accompanied by their accomplices, circulated through the city all the arms and they are regarded as the ringleaders of these terrible massacres, and this is also confirmed by all the religious heads and by persons of foreign nationality and absolutely impartial.

The solution to be given to the circumstances related in this Report depends upon the will of your Highness.
June 27, 1325 (1909).

The members of the Commission of Inquest of Adana
Haroutioun Mostidjian

Judicial Inspector of Saloniki
Faik

The President of the Court of the First Instance
of the Council of the State.

The author of *Les Turcs Ont Passé Là. . .* lists on page 254 of his book the persons convicted by a court-martial and given sentences which insult the intelligence of any fair-minded person. Here they are:

1. Djevad-Bey—The governor-general of Adana—six years of leisure, without any position in the employ of the government, and without pay.

2. Moustapha Remzi Pasha—Military Commander of Adana, three months in jail.

3. Assaf Bey—Governor of Djebel-i-Bereket, not guilty (later condemned to four years of rest).

4. Ihsan Fikri—publisher of "l'Ihidal" of Adana, author of articles inciting the Turkish population against Armenians—did not appear at the trial, no sentence.

5. Ismail Sefa—Ihsan Fikri's collaborator, one month in jail.

6. Osman Bey—Central military commander, three months in jail.

7. Abdullah Effendi—Vice-commander of Adana, three months in jail.

8. Bechir Agha, an officer at Adana, two months in jail.

9. Bagdatizade Abdulkader Effendi—Not guilty, but ordered to stay at Hidjaz for two years.

To refute the official statements of the Turkish authorities Mr. Brezol writes:

S. E. Ferid Pasha, the Minister of the Interior at the time of the 1909 happenings said to the newspaper correspondents of Constantinople: "How could 30,000 of the 40,000

Armenians in Cilicia be massacred, since there are still 25,000 living, according to our statistics? There is also a large group in Lattakia that is to be repatriated."

To counteract this false evaluation of Turkish statistics we are obliged to put the exact figures before the eyes of our readers, figures which came from Mr. Krikor Papazian, the secretary of the office of the Armenian bishop, a man much more competent in the matter. Certainly the office of the episcopate ought to know better than any other person about the exact number of its flock.

According to detailed statistics produced by the author, there were at the time 94,665 Armenians in Cilicia, not including the Vilayet of Aleppo, where there were numerous victims also.

"Now then," continues the author, "in a total figure of 95,000 Armenians, should one affirm that 25 to 30,000 were massacred that figure is not at all exaggerated, as the Turks wish to pretend.

"If we take into account the massacres in Antioch, Bei'lan, Alexandrette, Marash and other places in the vilayet of Aleppo we can establish without any doubt that the Armenian nation lost *thirty thousand persons* (italics by the author), without mentioning the sequels of massacres such as famine, cold, dysentery and other ailments which were brought about by suffering, which carried away thousands of women and orphans.

"Where are the 4,000 dead and the 40,000 Armenians at a maximum as indicated by Ferid Pasha? They are all far from reality; it is convenient for him to talk that way in order to mitigate as much as possible the guilt of the Turks; but why defend criminals and murderers instead of punishing them in his capacity as the Minister of the Interior? Mystery!"

The massacre of the Armenians at Adana coincided with the Young Turks' consolidation of their power. In the years between 1909 and Turkey's entry into World War I as an ally of Germany, the process of dismembering the Turkish Empire accelerated. In Tripoli and in the Balkans Turkish hegemony was reduced at a very rapid rate in this five-year period and the nation was shaken by almost unrelieved disaster on the battlefields of the Balkan areas which had for so long been under Turkish misrule. Shortsighted as always, the Turks, even when retreating from lost battlegrounds inflicted unnecessary and horrible suffering on the Christian populations in their path.

Out of all this defeat there came at least one Turkish victory of some substance, however, and that was the recovery of Adrianople (now Edirne) from the Greeks in European Turkey. The retaking of the city, which had a symbolic importance for the Turks, as effected by Enver Pasha, whose undoubted courage for once found a favorable theater of operations. This sorely needed success made him the man of the hour in Turkey and resulted in his elevation to Minister of War. Thus, on the eve of World War I, the nation was effectively delivered into the hands of three implacable enemies of the Armenians: Enver, Talaat, and Djemal Pasha.

REFERENCES

1. W. E. Gladstone, *Bulgarian Horrors and the Question of the East*, London: 1876, p. 38.

2. Greene, p. 130.

3. Olivero, *Turkey Without Harems*, London: Macdonald: 1952, p. 64.

4. Creagh.

5. Lord Eversley and Sir Valentine Chirol, *The Turkish Empire from 1288 to 1914*, New York: Howard Fertig, 1969, p. 339.

6. Clifford Lloyd, quoted by Malcolm MacColl, *England's Responsibility Towards Armenia*, London, 1895, pp. 95–96, 99, 101.

7. *Ibid.*, p. 106.

8. Abraham Hartunian, *Neither to Laugh Nor to Weep*. Boston: The Beacon Press, pp. 14–20.

Chapter 3

The Armenians: An Ancient Nation

1. *The Legend of Haig*

According to legend, which has acquired credibility by its transmission by word of mouth from generation to generation and was finally set to writing by the Armenian historian, Moses of Khoren (Khorenatzi) of the Fifth Century, the origin of the Armenian people may be traced back to 2350 B.C.

Even though historians have been unable to find a factual basis for the legend of Haig (or Haik), the persistent belief for fifteen hundred years that he was a direct descendant of Noah, the builder of the Ark of the Scriptures, gives an impressive air of authenticity to the legend.

According to Moses of Khoren, who is now the recognized father of Armenian history, Haig was a "handsome and sturdy" person with curly hair, sparkling eyes and strong arms. His forebears had travelled to the south and established themselves in the fertile lands of Mesopotamia. Moses of Khoren had as his source for this legend the "History of Mar Abas Katina" who was a native of Medsurch and wrote in Syriac about 380 A.D.

Vahan M. Kurkjian, an Armenian historian, writes in his *A History of Armenia*:

> The Armenians have their full share of legends regarding their origin, legends in which spirits, gods and superhuman heroes, the forces and phenomena of nature, play

dominant parts. In such myths may be traced occasional historical facts. The impossible thing is to disentangle the fact from fiction. The most pervasive figure in this national folklore, which has come down to us through songs and ballads, is that of Haik.

Haik, the wonderful archer, long ago became established in the national legend as the ancestor of the Armenians, bequeathing to them the patronymic *Hay*, the name which the Armenians apply to themselves. This legend takes us back to the prehistoric epoch when the first Armenians arrived in the land of Urartu, under the leadership of a great commander. Haik, according to the story, revolted against a tyrant, Bel of Babylon, and departed for the north with his family and followers. Bel, at the head of a large army, pursued and came upon him. Haik engaged Bel in battle, killed him with an arrow, dispersed his rabble of warriors and freed the land which is known as Hark—i.e., the country of the Hai people. . . . Haik, the *nahapet* (tribal chief), whose household included 300 men, waged his successful battle in the "land of Ararat." After his victory over Bel, the chieftain proceeded towards the northwest, whose inhabitants voluntarily submitted to his authority.[1]

2. *Pre-historic Armenia and Its People*

The land occupied by Haig and his descendants eventually became to be known as Armenia, or Hayasdan, as its natives called it.

Geographically, Armenia is a continuation westward of the great Iranian plateau. On the north it descends abruptly to the Black Sea; on the south it breaks down in rugged terraces to the lowlands of Mesopotamia; and on the east and west sinks more gradually to the lower plateaus of Persia and Asia Minor. Above the general level of the plateau, 6000 feet, rise bare ranges of mountains which run from north-east to south-west at an altitude of 8000-12000 ft., and culminate in Ararat, 17,000 feet. Between the ranges are broad elevated valleys, through which the rivers of the plateau flow before entering the rugged gorges that convey their waters to the lower levels. . . . Amongst the higher mountains are the two Ararats; Alageuz Dagh, North of the Aras; Bingeul Dagh, south of Erzeroum; and the peaks near lake Van. The rivers are the Euphrates, Tigris, Aras (Arax), Churuk Su (Chorokh) and Kelkit Ir- mak, all rising on the plateau. The more important lakes are Van, 5100 feet, about twice the size of the Lake of Geneva, and Urmia, 4000 feet, both salt; Gokcha or Sevan, 5870 feet, discharging into the Aras, and Chaldir, into the Kars Chai. The aspect of the plateau is dreary and monot- onous. The valleys are wide expanses of arable land, and the hills are for the most part grass-covered and treeless. But the gorges of the Euphrates and Tigris, and their trib- utaries, cannot be surpassed in wildness and grandeur. The climate is varied. In the higher districts the winter is long and the cold severe; whilst the summer is short, dry and hot. . . . Many of the early towns were on or near the Araxes, and amongst their ruins are the remains of churches which throw light on the history of Christian architecture in the East. Armenia is rich in mineral wealth, and there are many hot and cold mineral springs. *Encyc. Britannica*, Handy Volume, 1910, Vol. 2, p. 564.

Not until the 9th century B.C. can the origin of the Ar- menian people be traced. Some scholars find their origin in Khald; others claim that Armenians are descendants of the Hittites.

> In the 7th century B.C., between 640 and 600, the coun- try was conquered by an Aryan people, who imposed their language, and possibly their name, upon the vanquished, and formed a military aristocracy that was constantly re- cruited from Persia and Parthia. Politically, the two races soon amalgamated, but, except in the towns, there was apparently little intermarriage, for the peasants in certain districts closely resemble the proto-Armenians, as depicted on their monuments.[2]

But where did the Armenians come from? The consensus among historians is that they are of Indo-European stock and migrated from Thrace into Asia Minor with Macedonians and Phrygians. Jacques de Morgan quotes Herodotus as say- ing: "The Armenians were armed like the Phrygians, of which they were a colony."[3]

The migration took place sometime during the 12th or 13th century B.C. Later, the Phrygians and the Armenians were separated. The Phrygians remained in the western part of Anatolia and the land which they occupied became known as Phrygia. The Armenians on the other hand moved eastward, crossing the Euphrates, and established their homeland in the region of Ararat.

". . . about the time of their migration," writes Jacques de Morgan, "important moves were taking place in Asia Minor and seacoasts. The Hellenes were spreading all over the Black Sea shore, founding trading posts and colonies; Trebizond (756 B.C.) and Sinope (780 B.C.) both date from this period. The Kingdom of Urartu was disappearing, Nineveh even was falling (606 B.C.), whilst the Seythians were ravaging all western Asia. . . . And this frightful disorder was most auspicious for the realization of the Haikanians' (Armenians') ambitions."

As we have already seen the legend of Haig places the Hais in that biblical region much more than a thousand years before the dates established by later historians. A fiction though it may be, the Armenians of today claim the date of their origin, as legend has established, i.e., 2350 B.C.

Returning to history as accepted by contemporary and modern historians, we find in Xenophon's *Anabasis* the mention of the Armens. In that account, ten thousand Greek mercenary soldiers embarked upon a lengthy march, through unknown territories, in order to bring aid to Cyrus of Persia against his brother, Artaxerxes. The itinerary, which has not been definitely determined, took them through Armenia, which Xenophon describes as "a vast and rich country," with fertile lands wherein wheat, barley and cereals were raised in abundance. ". . . the Armen villages had in store raisins, perfumed wine, sesame, fragrant oil of almonds and turpentine. The people were both cattle-breeders and agriculturists. They exported many horses. Herodotus calls the Armens *polyprobatoi*, rich in sheep."[4]

For about 150 years after Alexander the Great occupied Armenia in 330 A.D., very little was written about the Armenians. In 190 B.C. the Artashesian Dynasty was established by Ardashes (or Artaxias), who was appointed by Antiochus the Great as his military governor. As soon as the circumstances became favorable he rebelled against his sovereign and declared the independence of Armenia. It was during his reign that the city of Ardashad was built on the River Araxes, "near the village of Khorvirab about 19 miles to the south of Erivan." It became the new capital of the Kingdom. King Ardashes ruled for about 30 years, and lost his life in battle with Antiochaiss Epiphanes.

From 159 or 160 B.C. to 95 B.C. several kings ruled Armenia, but the people would be denied dynamic leadership until a young prince, held hostage in the Parthian country, appeared to guide the nation to magnificent heights. Tigran or Tigranes II ascended the throne in the year 94.

He immediately began to organize the armed forces in order to bring all parts of Armenia into one united and greater Armenia. His first attempt was to conquer Sophene Armenia. His strategy was highly successful. His conquest of Sophene was completed in 93. After that "the immediate attention of the vigorous king was exercised in the unification of the country. . . . Tigranes was essentially a soldier, and by constant personal attendance in the activities of his army he both endeared himself to the men, and created among them that subtle quality, the morale, which is the secret of victory." (Hrant K. Armen, *Tigranes the Great*, p. 76)[5]

Tigranes the Great reigned for forty years, 94 to 54, and during his reign he conquered many countries and extended the influence of the empire as far south and southwest as Mesopotamia and Phoenicia, and was proclaimed "King of Kings."

"The expansion of his domain," writes Vahan Kurkjian, "to the south and west made necessary the creation of a new and more centrally located capital." So the walled city of Tigranocerta (Dikranaguerd) was built on the southernmost boundaries of the expanded empire on the shores of River Tigris. Its construction began in the year 77 B.C.

Political, social and economic reasons have been given for the building of this new capital. One of the most important, however, was the king's desire to invite and introduce Hellenic civilization into the country. As historian Hrant K. Armen writes: "The final thought of Tigranes was that his city will be a center of Greek civilization, Alexandria of the desert, and from this center the light and refinement of the preferred culture will spread throughout Armenia."[6]

The glory of the King of Kings was soon to fade, however, before the mighty power of Rome. Old age was creeping on Tigranes and for once the mighty ruler was forced to bow to a superior force. He felt that he had no quarrel with Rome, and that an amicable settlement of their differences might not be impossible.

Truly, it was not. The victorious Pompey received the vanquished Armenian king with royal courtesy. A pact was signed by the terms of which Tigranes junior, the arrogant son of the king, was to become his successor.

Tigranes the great died at the age of eighty-seven and with his passing the fate of Armenia became dependent upon two hostile countries: Rome and Parthia. The successors of Tigranes the Great were unable to sustain the independence of Armenia, and for a number of years the Armenians were forced to accept as their "ruler" any prince imposed upon them by the Parthians or the Romans.

3. The Pre-Christian Era

For about one hundred years after the death of Tigranes the Great the Parthians used every means to make Armenia a part of the Parthian empire, but all their efforts were frustrated by Rome. The country was divided into two spheres of influence: Parthia in the east and Rome in the west. The land of Armenia "became the field upon which East and West contended for mastery and the struggle ended for a time" with its partition in 387 A.D. between Rome and Persia.

Before that happened, however, the Parthians succeeded in placing upon the throne of Armenia kings of Parthian origin, and established what is known as the Arsacid or Arshakunian Kingdom.

It was just prior to the founding of the Arshakunian Kingdom that a new religion was secretly introduced in Armenia and was being clandestinely preached in underground meeting places, where many persons, including Princess Sandoukhd, the daughter of King Sanadruk, went to listen to St. Thaddeus, one of the apostles of Christ, who came to Armenia, according to a well-established tradition, in the year 43. King Sanadruk, who at the time ruled over a part of Armenia, upon being informed of the preaching of St. Thaddeus and his daughter's apostasy, condemned both to death. St. Thaddeus was soon followed by the apostle Bartholomew, who suffered a similar fate. Christianity, however, had gained a firm foothold in Armenia and its adherents were constantly gaining in numbers, in spite of ruthless persecutions and inhuman treatments at the hands of pagan kings and rulers.

4. *The Dawn of Christianity*

Nothing could stop the influx of Christian ideology which flooded the hearts of the common people of Armenia. By the end of the third century a great evangelist, endowed with divine power and an unshakeable faith, made his appearance on Armenian soil, changing the course of the history of the Armenian people and firmly establishing the Christian religion in that part of the world. The Christian world owes a debt of gratitude to St. Gregory the Illuminator, who in the year 301 (some scholars have placed the date as early as 287) converted King Tiridates (Drtad) of Armenia and his entire court to the Christian faith, thereby proclaiming Christianity as the national religion of the country and making Armenia the first state to embrace the new faith. "The conversion of this Tiridates by his cousin, St. Gregory, the Enlightener, whom he had confined for fourteen years in a dry well, is the turning-point in the history of the nation. From that day Armenia became the bulwark of Christianity in Asia." James Bryce, *Transcaucasia and Ararat*, 1877.

". . . it was some time before the emperor Constantine the Great allegedly saw the flaming cross in the sky with the words *In Hoc Signo Vinces*—'In this Sign shalt thou conquer'—on the morning of a battle, and thereupon decreed that the Roman Empire should be Christian. Armenia, therefore, claims to have been the first among the nations to adopt Christianity."[7]

"The conversion of Armenia was accomplished in a miraculous manner. It was not Gregory's intention to destroy the old in order to make room for the new. He introduced reforms whereby the old modes of worship retained their form and continued under new names, wrought into and enriched by the new religion and its mode of worship. The pagan priests, who had secured their livelihood from public offerings to their gods, were assured that 'not only should the sacrifices continue, but they should have larger prerequisites than ever.'" (*The Pillars of the Armenian Church* by Dickran H. Boyajian, 1962, p. 11.)[8]

The building of the Cathedral of *Etchmiadzin* ("his only begotten son descended") on the very foundation of a pagan temple, was the beginning of an intensive work for the construction of places of worship over the length and breadth of the country.

5. *The Discovery of the Armenian Alphabet and the Translation of the Holy Bible*

Teachers and preachers of Christian faith soon realized that conducting services in languages foreign to the general public was gradually losing its effectiveness and that the services could have greater relevance if they were recorded in the native language of the people.

The task was enormous, but the saving of Christianity in Armenia was at stake and the need to find effective means of communication was urgent. Hence the assignment of that sacred task to one of the greatest leaders of the Church and nation, St. Mesrob Mashdotz, who, assisted by several of his pupils, after many months of arduous work in study and research, returned to Armenia with 36 Armenian characters capable of expressing each sound in the Armenian language. The people, led by Catholicos Sahag Bartev and King Vramshabuh, received him with adulation.

Joachim Marquart (1812–1882), the German historian and writer, in his *History of the Armenian Alphabet,* makes the following remarks: "If we consider the extremely difficult circumstances in which Mashdotz succeeded in awakening the national consciousness of the Armenian people and compare his work with that of Pippin [III., who died in 768] and his collaborator, Wynfrith [St. Boniface, 680–754], these last two seem like poor dwarfs, compared to the great mental giant." (*The Pillars of the Armenian Church,* by Dickran H. Boyajian, *op. cit.*, 62)[9]

6. *The Golden Age*

Having lost its political independence in 428 and being governed by alien rulers, "the Armenians would have been completely inundated in the whirlpools of foreign influence had they not possessed the means of self-expression. The alphabet became an indestructible foundation upon which were built their hopes and aspirations. It became a source of inspiration, a fountain of spiritual wealth from which the life blood of the Armenian people flowed into the future and endowed the Armenian Church and nation with inexhaustible vitality.

It is difficult to believe that our erudite fathers could have visualized such far-reaching consequences. It can, however, be safely assumed that their greatest incentive for exploring the need and discovering the Armenian alphabet originated primarily in their unquenchable desire to translate the Holy Bible, so that God might converse with Armenians in their own tongue. . . .

The translation of the Bible and the preparation of the *Mashdotz* by no means constituted the culmination of the Armenian literature of the Golden Age. Well-known books and treatises on philosophy, mathematics, history, astronomy, art, architecture and other subjects were translated from the Greek. The works of Aristotle, Plato and others became an indispensable part of classical Armenian literature.[10]

Vahan M. Kurkjian has summed up the impact of Mashdotz' achievement: "So swiftly did the Armenian language grow, blossom and flourish that the intellectual success achieved in so short a space of time is one of the most inspiring chapters in the history of civilization. The Armenian mind longingly turned towards the light of knowledge. No longer did it need the services of self-seeking alien tutors. The various clans, separated from each other by physical and social barriers—mountains, rivers, dialects and traditions—were now being linked together by the spiritual tie of the written and spoken word. The Church, therefore, enriched by its own letters, became a moral light, as well as a stronghold for national consolidation. It was the champion of the new spirit amidst brute selfishness and under the oppressive Asiatic atmosphere, spreading the gospel of love and charity, brotherhood and equality."[11]

Church and nation had been wrought together indissolubly and formed an indestructible union that was destined to live forever, enduring all manner of persecution, threat, physical destruction and even scorning death. That was amply proven by the courageous stand of the Armenian clergy and nobility against the demands of the Persian ruler to renounce Christianity and accept Mazdeism as their religion. In the Council of Ardashad in 449, numerous bishops, suffragans, priests and nakharars had gathered to discuss and formulate a reply to the letter of the Grand Vizier of Persia. A few sentences from their carefully composed answer sufficiently express the depth of their devotion and the resoluteness of their attitude:

"From this [Christian] faith no one can shake us, neither

angels nor men; neither sword nor fire, nor water, nor any, nor all other tortures. All our goods and possessions are in your hands; our bodies are before you; dispose of them as you will. If you leave us to our belief, we will, here on earth, choose no other master in your place, and in heaven choose no other God in place of Jesus Christ, for there is no other God. But should you require anything beyond this great testimony, here we are; our bodies are in your hands; do with them as you please. Tortures from you, submission from us; the sword is yours, the neck ours. We are no better than our forefathers, who, for the sake of their faith, surrendered their goods, their possessions, and their bodies." (*Yeghisheh*, 451 A.D., English Translation by Dickran H. Boyajian, 1952, p. 45)[12]

Hence the Armenian war against the Persians about May 26, 451, commonly known as the Battle of Avarair, wherein 66,000 stalwart Armenians fought against a Persian army of 300,000 men and a "herd of trained elephants." The battle ended in the defeat of the Armenians who suffered 1036 losses including their valiant commander, Vartan Mamigonian, as against 3544 Persians who lost their lives on the battlefield.

The Armenians continued the fight in guerrilla warfare, under the leadership of Vahan Mamigonian, Vartan Mamigonian's nephew, and the constant harassment of the Persians by the Armenian guerrillas forced the Persian king to make peace. A treaty was signed at Nuvarsak in 484, containing the following terms:

"I. Religious worship in accordance with Christian doctrines and rites to be declared free. No Armenian to be appointed as a Magian officer; no public position to be given as a reward for conversion to Mazdeism. Fire altars to be removed from Armenia.

"II. The rights and privileges of the *nakharars* [satrapal houses] to be restored.

"III. The King himself to direct the investigation and render judgment whenever an Armenian *nakharar* shall have been charged with some offense."[13]

7. *The Pakradunian Dynasty (Bagratids)*

For over four hundred and fifty-seven (428–885) years the Armenian people lived an insecure, precarious, and despairing life under Persian, Byzantine and Arab rule. Internally they were exploited by Marzbans, or Governors-general, externally by the ruling power, whichever it might be.

During the first half of the seventh century the Arabs invaded Armenia and resorted to any means to convert the Armenians to Mohammedanism, while on the other hand the Greeks were trying to force them to accept the Orthodox creed. "Thus the Armenians were persecuted by the Moslems because of their Christianity and the Byzantine Greeks because of mere differences in creed."[14]

The fall of the Persian empire in the year 652 gave Arabs a splendid opportunity to take over almost all of Armenia. In place of Marzbans, Ostikans were appointed to govern the country. This lasted for two centuries. There were occasional revolts, which however failed to bring any reform until open hostilities between the Arabs and the Byzantine Empire created the opportunity for the Armenians to take advantage of the situation and take up arms against the Arabs. An autonomous state was created with a prince at its head, followed by a king in 885, when Prince Ashod Pakraduni was crowned King of Armenia.

Ani became the city of a thousand and one churches, built on a high plateau on the shores of the Akhurian River (Arpa-tchai) because the capital of Armenia was turned by massive walls into a fortress which, in the course of its short duration, withstood many onslaughts, and repelled many attacks.

The Bagratid Dynasty did not enjoy a peaceful existence. For a time the population of Ani became prosperous. Magnificent palaces, beautiful churches, and colorful homes were built. But its glory was soon to be engulfed in sorrow and disaster. The Seljuk Turks had begun to spread death and destruction.

During many engagements, the Armenians put the Turkish hordes to flight. But these military successes did not prevent the collapse of the Bagratid Dynasty. The loss of the
independence of Armenia was due more to the treachery of
the Greeks than to the prowess of the enemy. The king was
invited to Constantinople and was asked to relinquish his
throne and surrender Ani to the Greek emperor. When he
refused he was shown "a letter in which the Armenian nobles
affirmed their allegiance to the Empire and offered to deliver
to the Emperor the keys of Ani. Betrayed by his own nobles,
forsaken by all, and alone in a foreign city, Gaghik (the
king) gave up his kingdom (1045). . . ."[15]

Less than twenty years later, on June 6, 1064, the Turks
entered the city. "A frightful butchery followed, blood flowed
in torrents in the streets, and in public places thousands fell
by the sword. Those who had taken refuge in the churches
perished and were buried in the ruins of the burnt edifices.
Such survivors as were believed to be wealthy were tortured
in an effort to force them to reveal the hiding places of their
treasures."[16]

Ani was left in ruins never to rise again. But even in its
ruins she was majestic. Here is what Jacques de Morgan
wrote about an episode that happened in the year 1064:

Ani, the city of a thousand churches . . . is nothing
more today (1918) than a ruin-covered wilderness, the
abode of wild animals. This very abandonment of the Bagratid capital gives, however, an ineffable charm to the remains of its one-time glory. On this promontory fringed
with the deep gorges where its two rivers flow, the dead
city stretches out into the mystery-laden air, where the
great churches and the ramparts above survive. Shapeless
heaps of rubbish hidden by the brushwood mark the spots
where once stood princely dwellings; the streets and
squares have vanished, the palaces have crumbled, and
yet, amid this tangled mass of bits of walls, are still to be
seen imposing sanctuaries, stately in their ordered lines
and entrancing in their ornate lace-like carvings and their
quaint frescoes. The majestic remains of these sacred edifices, the names of which are mostly forgotten today, bear

witness to the refined taste both of the kings of Ani and their architects. The double wall defending the city on the north, with its towers, castle, and keep, call forth count-less memories linking Armenia with the West. One cannot help but feel intense pity as one walks through these desert places today, pity for the victims of the terrible deeds here committed, of the massacres and sackings so poignantly related by Aristanes. *Turkish mis-government during the ensuing centuries is indeed seen to be Satan's handiwork.* [Emphasis ours—D.H.B.][17]

De Morgan makes another remark about Ani worth repro-ducing: "We have in Europe a good number of towns still surrounded by their medieval fortifications . . . while ruins of this kind are also numerous in the East. . . . No site, how-ever, is comparable to that of Ani in the deep impression this dead city makes on the Traveler. Lost in the middle of a vast solitude, it bears yet the deep wounds it received at its hour of destruction."[18]

8.   *Princedoms or the Barony of Cilician Armenia*

The fall of Ani and the end of the Pakradunian Dynasty did not destroy the ideal of independence cherished by the Armenian people. Of course there were those, the so-called defeatists, who preferred Greek domination to a struggle for independence, the success of which was by no means certain. Any revolt against the Turkish rule in the Araratian plateau might be disastrous. The Armenians had neither the capacity in men and equipment nor the hope of securing outside help to form an army strong enough to overpower the Turks. They had to look elsewhere.

Many of the nobles had moved westward and had estab-lished homes beyond the Taurus mountains, on the northern shores of the Mediterranean. It would not be impossible, the Armenians thought, to establish a homeland on Cilician soil. All they needed was a leader. And such a leader emerged in the person of Roupen, who was "according to some chron-iclers, of direct royal issue." Many Armenians gathered around him and expressed their devotion to the cause of freedom.

Roupen with his warriors moved westward, crossed the mountain ranges forming the boundary of Cilician plains and occupied "the fortress of Partzerpert [high castle] . . . about a day's march above Sis. That location became the cradle of the Cilician Armenian Kingdom."[19]

The Barony of Cilician Armenia was established in 1080. Several barons followed in succession after the death of Roupen in 1095, some of whom distinguished themselves in defense of their independence. Their struggles continued until an Armenian kingdom was established there.

The Greek pressure never ceased during this period. They were bent upon forcing the Armenian Church to accept the superiority of the Greek Orthodox church. The acceptance of Greek demands would have meant the loss of independence and identity of the Armenian Church. These demands were categorically rejected. History was repeating itself. The Armenians of the fifth century in the same manner had rejected the Persian demands to renounce Christianity and accept Mazdeism.

9. *The Roupenian Dynasty, the Crusaders and the Loss of Independence*

For several years prior to his coronation as King, Baron Leon II oscillated between the Romans and the Greeks, seeking and receiving favors and promises from one, then the other. He was determined to wear the King's crown. The third crusade was moving eastward from Macedonia and "made a halt in Cilician Armenia" on its way to Antioch and Jerusalem.

There was Leon's opportunity to achieve his goal. "He, therefore, eagerly supplied the Third Crusaders with provisions, guides, pack animals and all manner of aid, besides pledging the co-operation of his army."

The fateful hour arrived. On January 6th, 1199, Baron

Leon was crowned and took the name and title of "Leon I, by the grace of the Roman Emperor [Henry VI], King of Armenia." Later, Leon discarded the designation "by the grace of the Roman Emperor, etc." and called himself "King by the Grace of God."

Of course the granting of the crown by the Pope entailed the change of some of the traditional rites of the Armenian Church, such as (a) celebrating Christmas on December 25; (b) reciting in church the prayers of the hours of the day and night, long discarded by the Armenians; (c) permitting the use of fish and oil on Christmas Eve and Easter Eve.

During King Leon's reign Cilician Armenia prospered. Commerce with East and West benefited the Armenians immensely and the royal treasury was enriched. He earned the title "the Great," or "the Magnificent."

He named his minor daughter Zabel (Isabelle) as his successor under a regency. After an unfortunate marriage which lasted only a short time, the youthful queen was married again at the age of twelve, this time to a handsome Armenian prince named Hetoum, who ascended the throne in the year 1226.

The Armenian kingdom in Cilicia was destined to be in constant turmoil. No sooner had the threats of Jenghiz Khan and his son subsided than a new "scourge came upon the scene to harass western Asia." The Memlouks invaded Cilicia, captured many cities and slaughtered their inhabitants.

Peace was finally obtained at a tremendous sacrifice. The king, weary and disillusioned, abdicated his throne in favor of his son Leon and retired to a monastery, where he died in 1270.

King Leon II was an intelligent and vigorous young man endowed with many good qualities. But he had hardly begun to improve the conditions of his realm, when he was attacked by a formidable army led by the emirs of the Sultan. The King's uncle, General Sempad, "lured his foes into a mountain pass and dealt them such a mortal blow that the bodies of the dead impeded the flight of the survivors."[20]

King after king tried to defend the country against foreign threats of destruction. The Greeks, the Romans, the Memlouks, the Bibars, the Arabs, Egyptians, Tartars, and the Turks, one after the other, sometimes two or three together, including even the Greek and the Roman churches, continued to menace the independence and existence of Armenia.

King Leon VI, died without a male heir to succeed him. However, prior to his assassination at the age of thirty-two he had named as his successor his nephew, Guy de Lusignan, of French descent.

Jean Dardel is quoted by Jacques de Morgan as saying: "When the good King Guy de Lusignan (Constantine II) reigned in Armenia (1342–1344) he governed the country with puissance, valiancy and sovereignty. He loved and served God with all his heart, and upheld and defended the common cause with all his power, and the country's freedom did he most diligently protect, without paying any truce-money whatever to the infidels."[21]

Guy de Lusignan's successor, Constantine III, who was chosen by the nobles, had no relationship to the royal house, of the Cilician Armenia. He was a tyrant and his reign was turbulent and insecure at all times. "Things were becoming more critical every day, but no power in Europe intervened in behalf of the Armenians, notwithstanding the repeated entreaties of Pope Clement VI."[22]

Upon the death of Constantine III on April 19, 1364, the so-called Armenian Nationalist Party, opposing the selection of an heir of Guy de Lusignan as King of Armenia, succeeded in their efforts by placing on the throne a descendant of the Roupenians and named him Constantine IV, who ruled for eight years with tyranny and selfishness "indifferent to the welfare of his country and to any possibility of its deliverance from its Moslem oppression." He was assassinated in 1373 in a palace revolution.

Constantine IV was succeeded by Leon de Lusignan as the proper choice of the Armenian clergy and nobles. He was then in Cyprus, where he was detained by the Genoese and

Cypriots. However, he bought his way out of the island and when he approached Sis, the capital of Cilician Armenia, on July 26, 1374, he was greeted with unprecedented enthusiasm. Catholicos Boghos I, bishops, vartabeds, the nobles and a multitude of men and women, with music and fanfare hailed their new king as their deliverer in a time of tragic events. The new king took his oath on the following day. The coronation was to take place at a later date. Leon wanted to be crowned by a Roman bishop. The Armenians were displeased with the decision, and it was agreed to have a double ceremony, first by Roman ritual, to be followed by the Armenian. On September 14, 1374 Leon was crowned in the Cathedral of St. Sophia at Sis with the title of Leon V.

The new king inherited an empty treasury, internal discord and external threats. The Catholic ceremony had caused so much discontent that many within and without that small kingdom did not hesitate to resort to betrayal, which eventually brought on war. In February of 1375 the Turcomans, encouraged and assisted by the Sultan of Egypt and the governor of Aleppo besieged Sis, the capital city. All the surrounding territory was seized by the enemy. The city was finally taken by the Moslems after it was set afire by its inhabitants. The king was wounded in an attempted assassination. "He made his confession, heard mass, and took communion; then, hardly able to walk, with his head completely bandaged, he came down from the keep followed by his family. This was April 13, 1375, less than ten months after King Leon V of Lusignan had left the island of Cyprus and set foot on Armenian soil. The Sultan offered to restore him to his kingdom provided he embraced Islam. Leon refused with dignity. He was offered one of the castles in Cilicia to live in, but he declined, realizing that within a few years the Moslems would get rid of him."[23]

The downfall of the Kingdom of Cilician Armenia was partly due to the treachery of ambitious barons, a number of whom claimed the right to the throne. King Leon finally found refuge in Paris, where he was received with honors due to royalty and was given an opportunity to use his talents in diplomatic service. The relations between the French and the British were not cordial, and King Leon felt confident that he could bring about an accord, which in his mind "was indispensable for the political rebirth of Armenia." He pleaded with the French Parliament to entrust him with that delicate mission. "No friendly connection whatsoever binds me to the English," he said in his fervent plea, "and yet an appeal by me, may, perhaps, be more fruitful than one by a delegate from your own nation against which they [the English] cherish inexorable hatred."[24]

King Charles VI of France and the members of the Parliament were so impressed by King Leon's emotional utterances that the dethroned king of Armenia was sent to the Court of King Richard II of England, where he was received with affection and was offered "a reverential hospitality."

We consider it highly important to pay tribute to the last King of Armenia by reproducing the speech delivered by him before King Richard and the Lords in Westminster Palace at the beginning of the year 1386.

" 'I wish to tell you, not by way of flattery, but prompted by brotherly love, that the people of the Orient have until now admired your accomplishments, and they would not forbear to praise you, had you and France consented to achieve friendliness between you. But fate compels me, helas! to make a sorrowful and bitter confession. It was only because of your discord that the unbelievers were able to oppose me victoriously with their arms. I declare to you that I, once a king and now an exile, ruled in tears and mourning. The fickleness of fortune cast me into an abyss. Henceforth, the Crown is to me only a mournful adornment, and the royal turban, once the decoration of my brow, will be as a veil of sacrifice, destined to immolation. O mighty princes! had you been willing to dedicate the support of your arms to Christ, the Christians of the East, who were saved by the blood of Christ, would not have been condemned to languish in grief, misery and slavery. The places long identified with the Christian faith, especially the Holy Cradle of Jesus in Bethlehem, and Zion, glorified through His miracles, would not have been subjected to the intolerable yoke of the Turks, Saracens, and Persians. You, however, straying from the true course, have been supplying deadly weapons against the Christian world.

" 'Through a stretch of full sixty years, neither side can boast of anything but invasion and destruction of cities, the plundering or burning of villages and the imprisonment of the inhabitants of the countryside. The war was marked by alternate successes, the net result being only bloodshed. Tell me, I adjure you, which side is the winner? Let men of experience and erudition answer. If you boast of your victories, you must at least confess that their cost is too high. Should you count the French fortresses subjugated by you—all but one, by the way, lost already—your opponents might retort that it is better to preserve a country than to expand its frontiers. Illustrious princes, if I am to speak the truth rather than utter honeyed words, I shall not hesitate to declare that the motive which has so far kept the flame of war alive, is your ambition to invade France. The kings of that country had, by long possession, assured themselves of the crown which they had so valiantly earned; and if the strength of a throne is based upon the obedience of its subjects, I must consider the throne of France unshakable. The hostility between the two nations has dragged on too long. In my opinion, both rivals should be implored to be satisfied with their vast territories, to cease the struggle between their peoples, so that they might be able to smite the enemies of Christ and to throw off the yoke of the Christians scattered through the Orient—those Christians who are day by day waiting for your help and humbly solicit it, O exalted princes!' "[25]

There was a note of sincerity and hope in the words of King Leon, which moved his audience, and he returned to France believing that he had served the cause of peace between two hostile countries. But history tells us otherwise. Other conferences were held "but the desired objective, alas!

was not realized. War was again declared and carried on with the usual fury and obstinacy."[26]

For almost eight years after Leon made that eloquent plea for peace and his return to France, he visited many European courts, conversed with many rulers and received many honors, but his main objective of redeeming the independence of Armenia was never realized. Promises for aid in that direction never materialized. Death came to him on November 29, 1393, exactly 59 years and six months before the Turks occupied Constantinople. His remains were interred in the monastery of the Celestins*. Later his tomb was "placed in the basilica of St. Denis."

Certain reflections of historian Jacques de Morgan about the Kingdom of Cilician Armenia are worth reproducing:

"Nevertheless," he writes, "this small kingdom founded by men from far off in the East and Europeanized by contact with the Crusaders wrote a handsome page in the great epic of the Middle Ages. Despite disturbances and wars, amid the greatest perils, the Armenians of Cilicia devoted themselves to literature and art, built churches, monasteries, castles and fortresses, and engaged in commerce. In short, even throughout the horror of war, this principality showed surprising vitality. The downfall was caused by the disaster that befell the Crusaders, but whereas the Latins withdrew to their western lands the Armenians had to endure for centuries the yoke of their conquerors. From the time that the Westerners' domains were reduced to the island of Cyprus, discouragement seized the Christians in Asia, and the drama that ended the death-throes of the city of Sis, now that we can view it at a distance of five centuries, deserves censure less severe than that passed by its contemporary, Dardel. Mistakes were made, but if we compare the heroic resistance of the Armenians for two centuries with the supineness with which most Eastern Christians bowed to Islam's yataghan

---

* But during the French Revolution his ashes, together with those of other sovereigns, were scattered to the winds.

(dagger), we cannot but admire this small number of brave people, and find their faults effaced by the courage they manifested up to the last hour, until every hope had faded."[27]

Armenian independence was lost in 1375, not to be retrieved until 543 years later, on a small segment within its historical boundaries, far removed from Cilicia.

10. *Armenia Under Foreign Domination*

Hostile elements surrounding that small Armenian kingdom on the northern shores of the Mediterranean Sea finally caused its downfall. Now the territory known as Armenia Major and Armenia Minor, which once extended from the Caspian Sea to the Mediterranean and from the Black Sea to Mesopotamia and Palestine, was occupied and exploited one after another by the Mongols, Seljuks, Memlouks, Turcomans and Turks. The hordes of Timur-Lang, (Tamerlane) Jenghiz Khan and others swamped the country like locusts devastating the land and destroying its inhabitants. At times, however, under certain humanitarian rulers the Armenians enjoyed certain privileges, from which the ruling people benefited more than their subjects.

Soon after their capture of Constantinople in 1453 the Turks ruled over all the territories formerly belonging to the Armenians. Mohammed II, the conquering sultan, recognized and appreciated the progressive and industrious qualities of his Armenian subjects and treated them with compassion. It was during his reign that the patriarchate of Constantinople was established, having as its head Bishop Hovakim of Brusa, enjoying the same rights and privileges as the Ecumenical patriarch of the Greek Orthodox Church. In the course of time the patriarch became the only spiritual and communal representative of the Armenian people before the Sublime Porte.

In spite of the distinguished title and apparent authority granted to the Armenian patriarchs, the conditions in the interior of Turkey grew worse. Hostilities between Turkey and Persia had disastrous effect upon the Armenian population.

Localities changed hands, now in favor of Turkey, then in favor of Russia or Persia, the losers being the Armenians, because of their geographical location. They were forced to migrate in great numbers and established colonies in Persia or joined their kinsmen in Crimea, the Ukraine, Moldavia, Bukovina, Poland and other Baltic and Balkan countries. The Ottoman yoke was very heavy and destructive. A contemporary writer, Thomas of Sepasdia, gives the following testimony: "They [the Turks] left no village or town, all burnt in fire; they uprooted the vineyards, set fire to all the fields, and put to sword the inhabitants."

It was in the 16th century when all Armenian children from two to five years of age were collected and placed in military establishments, later to form the famous Janisaries.

There were many Armenians, however, who refused to surrender their ancestral homes. Many took up arms to defend their honor and the sanctity of their home. The Meliks (feudal Lords) of Karabagh distinguished themselves as fearless chieftains and warriors. The story of heroic exploits of David Beg, the son of a nobleman, may be compared favorably with famous patriots of other lands, such as Garibaldi, who effected the unity of Italy.

However, the heroism of David Beg and others could only give temporary relief to the suffering thousands. Outside help was sorely needed. An appeal to the Western Powers for the liberation of the Armenian provinces was considered the only avenue of escape, no matter how hopeless.

Unfortunately, no one was interested in espousing the Armenian cause, and all attempts to find a friend in the Christian West met with dismal failure. Even the Pope turned a deaf ear to plaintive supplications of his brothers in Christ.

Among all the so-called Great Powers, Russia displayed the most interest in the Armenians. When Catherine the Great became Empress of Russia she manifested a strong desire to restore to the Armenian people their lost independence. She even proposed to place the crown of the new kingdom on the head of her general, Grigori Alexandrovitch Potemkin, whose sympathies for the Armenians were well known. Unfortunately, however, the creation of an autonomous Armenian state under Russian sovereignty was objected to by the Viceroy of the Caucasus, General Paskevitch and never materialized, to the bitter disappointment of the Armenians.

By the Treaty of Adrianople in 1829, which was influenced by the Western Powers, all Turkish territories occupied by Russia during the war, with a few minor exceptions, were restored to Turkey, forcing the migration of more than 90,000 Armenians westward.

The situation of minorities under Turkish domination continued to cause concern to the European statesmen, in spite of the Imperial Edicts, such as Hatti Sheriff of Gulhane's (Tanzimat) of November 3, 1839 and Hatti Humayoun's of February 18, 1856, giving assurances "to all the subjects of our Empire without discrimination as to religion and status, for the protection of their life, property and honor" as well as "all the privileges and religious concessions which for a long time have been granted by our forefathers to all Christian and Mohammedan communities who live in the Empire and enjoy my protection."

Truly for a decade or so there seemed to be a sincere effort on the part of the Turkish government to give full and equal protection to all its subjects without discrimination. The Armenians, the largest minority in Turkey, were given the right to regulate the affairs of their own communities, under the so-called "Armenian National Constitution," which was confirmed on March 17, 1863 by the Imperial decree of Sultan Abdul-Aziz. This document was also intended to regulate the relations between the Imperial Government and the religious and pseudo-political head of the Armenians, namely the patriarch.

This document, petitioning for the ratification of the Constitution and presented to the Ministry of Foreign Affairs, sets forth the following:

IX. The (Armenian) National Administration has three kinds of obligations. First towards the Imperial Government, that is to preserve the (Armenian) nation in perfectly legal subjection and to secure to the nation in general and to individuals in particular the preservation of their rights and privileges on the part of the government. The second obligation is to the (Armenian) nation, to treat it in true compassion and in a paternal way. The third is to the See of Etchmiadzin, to act in accordance with the religious regulations and laws of the Armenian Church.

Unfortunately, the solemn promises made by the Imperial Edicts and set forth in the Constitution above referred to were to be discarded as scraps of paper.

When Abdul Hamid ascended the throne of the Sultans on August 31, 1876, he was forced to proclaim a constitutional form of government, under a plan conceived by Mihtad Pasha, the Grand Vizier, and approved by the Sultan. A parliament was created and its first session was opened by Abdul Hamid in person on March 19, 1877. That constitution, had it remained in force, might have been a blessing for Turkey and the salvation to all the Christian minorities for years to come. But it was abrogated in less than a year and tyranny once again took hold of the country with devastating consequences.

The Turkish atrocities committed in Bulgaria in 1876 evoked the anger and condemnation of men like Lord Gladstone and others. However, it was the Russo-Turkish war of 1877 that gave the Armenian Question an international significance. In the Treaty of San Stefano (March 3, 1878), resulting from Russia's defeat of Turkey, direct reference was made to the Armenian situation.

Inasmuch as the evacuation by the Russian troops of the territories they occupy in Armenia, and which are to be restored to Turkey, might give rise to conflicts and complications detrimental to the good relations of the two countries, the Sublime Porte engages to realize, without further delay, the ameliorations and the reforms demanded by local requirements in those provinces inhabited by the Armenians, and to guarantee their security against the Kurds and the Circassians.

Russia had the upper hand over Turkey and that could not be tolerated by the European states, especially Great Britain. The ink on the San Stefano Treaty had hardly dried when the so-called Cyprus Convention was negotiated between Turkey and Great Britain, by the terms of which the island of Cyprus was given to Great Britain which enabled her "to check Russian influence in Western Asia."

Russian victory over Turkey not only "settled the Eastern question to the Czar's advantage" but gave her a decided advantage in Balkan affairs. The European powers countered with the convocation of the Berlin Conference which resulted in a treaty (July 13, 1878) wherein "Russia lost the fruits of her victory."

A memorandum containing numerous proposals for the formulation of certain rules pertaining to Turkish Armenia, was presented to the Conference by the Armenian delegation and copies were circulated among all the delegates, but no one seemed to have paid any attention to it.

Thus article 16 of the Treaty of San Stefano was replaced by article 61 of the Berlin Treaty, which reads:

> The Sublime Porte undertakes to carry out, without further delay, the ameliorations and the reforms demanded by local requirements in the provinces inhabited by the Armenians, and to guarantee their security against the Kurds and the Circassians. The Sublime Porte will periodically render account of the measures taken with this intent to the Powers who will supervise them.

The Eastern question remained unsolved, and the world once more accepted from Turkey promises of reforms for the Armenians and other Christian minorities, promises which were never meant to be kept. Atrocities continued unabated in spite of numerous complaints by European powers individually and collectively.

The reader will find in this volume many eye-witness reports by reliable men of various nationalities and races giving details of the inhuman torments the Armenian people were subjected to during and after Abdul's reign.

In 1894–1896, over 300,000 Armenians were massacred in the interior of Turkey. The red sultan of Turkey was determined to do away with the Armenians. His solution to the Armenian problem was to destroy the people. "The way to get rid of the Armenian question is to get rid of the Armenians," he had said.

11. *The Turn of the Century*

A revolution against the despotic rule of Sultan Hamid was seething among the Young Turks and in 1908 it erupted and forced the establishment of a parliamentary government. The Sultan was rendered impotent and served as a tool for the Committee of Union and Progress, whose basic policy was the complete Turkification of the Empire. The ideals of liberty and equality professed by the revolution, were soon discarded completely.

In a matter of nine months, the honeymoon was over and once again the policy of extermination became the driving force in the Young Turks' determination to create a homogeneous Empire. The first sign came from Adana where 30,000 Armenians were slaughtered in cold blood, after being disarmed by snare and treachery.

The Young Turks appeased the Western Powers with promises and at the same time secretly worked on a plan to exterminate the Armenians.

They did not have to wait long. The assassination of Archduke Ferdinand of Austria-Hungary set a spark to the torch which grew into a horrible conflagration enveloping the entire world. Turkey sided with Germany in the global war which caused universal death and destruction.

The time had come to deal with the Armenians with a vengeance. Total extermination became the order of the day to be understood literally and to be carried out ruthlessly. No one was to be spared. Old and young, men, women and children, even babes in arms or yet to be born, were to be eliminated, to "get rid" of the Armenian nation once and for all.

The Armenian Church

Any history of Armenia, no matter how comprehensive, will fail to depict the true life of the Armenians, without a comparable presentation on the Armenian Church. The Armenian Church and the Armenian nation have been so intertwined that one could hardly be conceived without the other.

Since the formal reorganization of the Armenian Church about the year 287, its lofty position in the life of the Armenian people has been universally recognized. Christianity is universal in character and scope, but its practice among the Armenians through their church is unique. No people in Christendom can claim a church as exclusively their own. The Catholic Church envelops within its folds all peoples who profess it, regardless of their national or ethnic origin. The Orthodox Church, which was originally propagated by the Greeks, spread its wings over many other peoples. The Protestant denominations, with the exception of the Anglican Church and to some extent the Episcopal Church, are independent organisms, and no nation can claim any one denomination to the exclusion of others.

Because of that singular and distinctive position, the Armenian Church has exerted tremendous influence upon the Armenian people and in the molding of the character of their creative arts, such as music, sculpture, architecture, poetry, philologic studies, etc. The Church, in a word, became and remained the storehouse of the greatest treasures of the people and their inspiration.

The Armenian Church is of Apostolic origin, which means that it has a direct relation with the Founder of the Church. This relation is proved in two ways: first, that a church is established by the preachings of one of the apostles of Christ; second, that it is established by the intermediacy of a church founded by one of the apostles.

The accepted theory is that St. Thaddeus preached the gospel in Armenia for eight years—35 to 43. He suffered martyrdom and was followed by St. Bartholomew who served Christ for 16 years, 44–60. He suffered a similar fate. These two are recognized as the First Illuminators of the Armenians. The places where their remains were interred, have been consecrated shrines visited by many millions during the course of centuries.

Christianity was persecuted not only in Armenia but wherever it was preached during the first few centuries. The first official acceptance of that creed was affected in Armenia in the year 301 (some historians are inclined to believe the date to be 287 or thereabouts), when King Tiridates (Dertad) of Armenia, his royal family, retinue and the entire people of his kingdom were converted to Christianity. Thus the Armenians were the first to adopt Christianity as their national religion. It was twelve years later that Emperor Constantine of Rome claimed and perhaps believed that he saw a flaming cross in the sky, with the words *in hoc signo vinces* (in this sign thou shalt conquer) and officially recognized the new faith and proclaimed it as the national religion of Rome.

King Tiridates soon realized that the propagation of the principles of his new faith required an authoritative spiritual head duly chosen by the people. Of course he had the undisputed authority to choose whomever he wished for that exalted office, but he thought that a popular vote would invest the leader so chosen with importance, prestige, dignity and power to determine all spiritual matters and give proper guidance. He, therefore, summoned the nobles of the entire kingdom to a conference where Gregory was unanimously elected as the supreme head of the Armenian Church.

That act established a precedent to be followed at all times in the selection of their spiritual leaders—supreme patriarchs as well as diocesan bishops and parish priests.

After his election Gregory, attired in royal garments and accompanied by sixteen nobles went to Caesarea, Cappadocia, where numerous bishops headed by the Archbishop of Cesarea, took part in the sublime ceremony of ordination and anointment.

During his return journey to Armenia St. Gregory passed

through many cities and towns in all of which he caused the destruction of pagan temples and the erection of churches and chapels. He baptized thousands of persons and ordained many priests and placed them at the head of newly organized parishes; historical records indicate that within several months after his return to Armenia about four million persons were baptized.

It took very little time for the holy man to establish himself in the hearts of the people whom he wanted to serve and guide by teaching them the ways of worshipping their new God and instructing them about their new faith.

The conversion of Armenia was accomplished in a miraculous manner. The Patriarch introduced reforms, whereby the old modes of worship retained their form and continued under new names, wrought into and enriched by the new religion and its mode of worship.

Christianity enjoyed universal favor throughout Europe, parts of northern Africa and the Middle East where the Armenian Church had become the most influential. In spite of the general acceptance of the doctrine, however, controversies rose among diverse nationality groups as to the nature of Christ and His dual personality, creating a situation which threatened to destroy the unity of the Church of Christ. It was believed by the most prominent leaders of Christendom that an ecumenical conference, where all Christian churches were represented, would reconcile the differences by adopting a formula which would best express the ideals of Christianity.

Invitations were sent out in the name of Emperor Constantine to all Christian churches and 318 bishops from all parts of the world answered the call and congregated in Nicaea, a town near the imperial summer residence of Nicomedia (Ismid). The Synod met in the imperial palace from May 20 to July 25, in the year 325. The Armenian Church was duly represented at the Council, where a creed of faith was adopted which became known as the Nicene Creed. This was later confirmed and was more fully established at the Council of Constantinople in the year 381.

"The Armenian Church confesses the doctrine which was approved and formulated by the first three ecumenical Councils, and which is summed up in the Creed of Nicea and Constantinople." (*The Armenian Church* by Papken Catholicos Gulesserian, translated by Terenig Vartabed Poladian, New York, 1939, p. 22)*

Hereditary succession to the Patriarchate continued for a century or more, with an interruption of about fifty years after the death of Nerses the Great, and in the year 387 or 388 the line of St. Gregory was restored by the ascension of Sahag to the patriarchal throne. His ordination on Armenian soil put an end to the custom of going to Caesarea for ordination as Catholicos. The autonomy of the Armenian Church was thoroughly established.

St. Nerses had introduced numerous reforms in order to achieve organizational solidarity in the Church, to secure its stability and strength. He recognized the dangers and evaluated the need. Before his very eyes stood a Christian church surrounded by a sea of pagan tradition. Ancient customs and modes of worship had become so immutable in the course of centuries that they would not easily yield to the new religion. A return to these customs was a natural inclination and offered great temptation to nobility as well as to the peasantry. He recognized the enormity of his task and fully realized that his powers, capabilities, experience and devotion would fall short of adequacy without the cooperation and dedication of his associates and the public in general.

All the bishops and many of the lay leaders of the country were called to a conference or a general assembly where positive or mandatory and negative or preventive rules were

* Due to his advanced age St. Gregory transferred his authority and all his responsibilities as Supreme Patriarch to his son Aristakes who was one of the delegates representing the Armenian Church at the Council of Nicaea St. Gregory's mission had been accomplished; his dream to build a cathedral, as the spiritual center of Christianity in Armenia for all generations to come, had been realized. He could retire in peace and contentment, confident that the life of his people and their new faith would be well guarded by his successors in office.

adopted. The former or the positive rules were based on Christian compassion or evangelical love, as means to obliterate the forces of waste and exploitation for the guidance of the king, princes, nobles, heads of families and schoolmasters; the latter, or the preventive rules, were intended to deal with social evils such as lewdness, intoxication, avarice, lust, deceit, intrigue, gossip, falsehood, perjury, and many other offences which plagued society.

His only son Sahag followed his father's footsteps and has been credited with greater achievements. He enjoyed the unreserved and scholarly cooperation of Mesrob. With the invention of the Armenian alphabet the Armenian people were blessed with the means of self-expression. The alphabet became an indestructible foundation upon which were built their hopes and aspirations. It became a source of inspiration, a fountain of spiritual wealth, from which the life blood of the Armenian people flowed into the future and endowed the Armenian church and nation with eternal life.

The fruits of the joint endeavors of the two holy fathers, Sahag and Mesrob, surpassed all imagination. Aside from the translation of the Holy Bible, which has been hailed as the "Queen of all translations" numerous noteworthy books and treatises on philosophy, history, astronomy, art, architecture, etc., were translated from Greek, thus enriching the classical Armenian literature.

Church services assumed new splendor and meaning; men and women attended the services in huge numbers; psalms were read and hymns were sung in the squares, on the streets and in homes. The exultation of the people was boundless. Courses of instruction in Armenian were instituted in various parts of the country. Schools were opened everywhere and illiteracy was lessened.

The fall of the Arshagunian (Arsacid) Dynasty in the year 428 brought with it the loss of the independence of Armenia and the Armenian people. The Persians were not satisfied with the replacement of the Armenian King by a Marzban (Governor-General) appointed by their king. They made a serious attempt to place at the head of the Armenian Church a pontiff of foreign origin to determine the destiny of the Christian faith in Armenia. The threat to obliterate that faith was real. Hence the War of the Armenians against the Persians in the spring of 451, where Vartan Mamigonian, the supreme commander of the Armenian forces, reached immortality in martyrdom.

In spite of the defeat of the Armenian forces in the Battle of Avarayr, the struggle continued for 33 years. A new leader had emerged in the person of Vahan Mamigonian, Vartan's nephew, who forced the Persians to accept the inviolability and immutability of the Christian faith among the Armenians. The hostilities ended by the signing of a peace treaty in the year 484, wherein the Armenians were guaranteed freedom of worship and unmolested enjoyment of life in honor, peace and security.

The year 451 established another landmark for the Armenian Church and people. That was the year when the ecumenical Council of Chalcedon was called by Emperor Marcia and held in October. Close to six hundred bishops took part in the deliberations. Due to political upheavals in Armenia the Armenian Church was not represented. Pope Leo, by his famous tome, or the *Epistola Dogmatica* (dogmatic letter) to Florianus, "dictated a decision by authority," rather than by discussion. The Armenian Church rejected the decisions of the Council of Chalcedon and reaffirmed the Cyrilian formula which had been adopted and confirmed at the Council of Ephesus in 431, expounding the doctrine that the divinity and humanity of Jesus Christ were united, forming one single nature: One Nature United of the Incarnate Word. This faith was again affirmed and proclaimed in Douin, where in the year 506 Armenian bishops as well as those from Georgia and Azerbaijan congregated and firmly rejected the doctrine adopted in Chalcedon.

Papken Catholicos Guleserian in his concise history of the origin and development of the Armenian Church, writes:

"From the moment when the Armenian Church obtained

her administrative independence, she elaborated her theology, her rites, her traditions. She has known how to defend herself against all attacks with a firmness and perseverance worthy of admiration. Byzantium caused her many injuries. Its emperors often attacked her and persecuted her with an incomprehensible fanaticism. Later, from the time of the Crusades, it was Rome which took up the Byzantine policy and which has continued her efforts until our own days to restore 'the lost sheep' of the Armenian Church into the fold of Catholicism." (*The Armenian Church,* translation by Terenig Vartabed Poladian, 1939.)

The Holy See

Social and political upheavals brought about by foreign powers who ruled over Armenia at one time or another, necessitated the removal and establishment of the seat of the Catholicate now here and now there. Locus of the seat was determined by the existence of an independent government, or where the political center of the Armenian nation was found.

It was, of course, first established in Etchmiadzin at the beginning of the fourth century, and it remained there until 484 A.D. That is about 56 years after the fall of the Arshagunian Dynasty. That was when Vahan Mamigonian had forced the Persians to sign the Treaty of Nuarsag granting a complete freedom of worship to the Armenians.

Vahan Mamigonian was the Governor-General (Marzban) of Douin, where he had established a peaceful government. It was considered safe and advisable to remove the seat of the Catholicate to Douin, in the year 485. Thereafter it was forced to migrate from place to place until finally it came to rest at Etchmiadzin, its place of birth, in the year 1441.

The periodical migration of the Holy See was due to social and political upheavals. The seat of the Supreme Patriarch was then located wherever political and social circumstances required, with the hope always of returning to its place of origin.

In the year 485, after Vahan Mamigonian had forced the Persians to acknowledge the right of Armenians to worship their God in a manner of their choice, under the provision of the Treaty of Nuarsag, the seat of the Catholicate was removed to Douin, where a magnificent cathedral was constructed. There it remained for more than four centuries. Doctrinal disputes, however, between the Armenians and the Greeks, continued to plague the peace and security of the Armenian Church.

During the first half of the seventh century the Arabs invaded the land of the Armenians. These disputes were somewhat minimized, but the pressure often brought on by the Greeks, to place the Armenian Church in a subservient position, was never totally eliminated. However, all threats of intimidation, cajolery and bribery, were of no avail. The Armenian Church was determined to maintain its independence.

Armenians had given a logical meaning to the union between the Churches of Christ—a spiritual communion without the supremacy of one and the subservience of the other. Each church was to be free within itself, free from interference from without.

In the year 885 the Pakradunian (Bagratid) Kingdom was founded with Ani, the city of one thousand churches, as capital. A little more than a century later the Holy See was removed to the new capital.

Internal disorders and external pressures threatened the stability and the security of the Holy See and forced its removal from place to place until it found what appeared to be a permanent home in Western Armenia, commonly known as Cilicia, where a new Armenian Kingdom was established after the fall of the Pakradunian Dynasty.

Even in Cilicia the Armenian Church was prevented from enjoying peace and tranquility. It had to resist pressures both from Roman Catholic and Greek Orthodox churches.

Fortunately, all efforts to destroy or nullify the identity and independent existence of the Armenian Church failed, because of the unshakable faith of the Armenian people who had vowed as far back as the fifth century to remain steadfast in their belief: "From this faith no one can shake us, neither angels nor men; neither sword, nor fire, nor water, nor all other horrid tortures."

There were times, however, when the desire for political independence became a strong factor in leaning towards catholicism. The promise of the western powers to grant a royal crown to one of the Armenian princes in 1197 encouraged the Armenians to renew negotiations with the Latins seeking union with the Catholic Church. These negotiations continued for two years but failed to gain their objectives. There were vigorous and powerful resistances on the part of the great majority of the Armenian bishops who were convinced that submission to the demands of Rome would mean total loss of identity for the Armenian Church.

Completely disregarding the possibility of these dire consequences, twelve bishops joined the Catholicos and Prince Leon in signing an agreement to accept the supremacy of the Pope, so that Leon might be crowned King of Armenia, and in fact on January 6, 1199, the Papal Nuncio performed that ceremony.

After gaining the royal crown King Leon, recognizing the strong opposition of the dissident bishops, refrained from carrying out the terms of the agreement, and the Armenian Church continued to give spiritual comfort to her faithful without effective hindrance. The influence of the Roman Church, however, continued to harass the leaders in the hierarchy of the Armenian Church, but failed to subdue the Armenian bishops. The Armenian Kingdom in Cilicia was destroyed in the year 1375, and the Armenian people, left without political independence, turned to the Church for direction, supervision, advice, guidance and spiritual comfort. The seat at Cilicia was no longer in a position to withstand assaults from Rome. A so-called Latino-Armenian brotherhood was formed under the deceptive title "Unitors," who were determined to dissolve the Armenian Church within the Roman Church.

The threat was real and strong, not only from without but from within the confines of the Church itself. The moral standard of the clergy had fallen deplorably. The lust for power and the yearning to capture the highest office in the Church hierarchy caused irreparable damage to the prestige and honor of the Catholicate. The situation had become intolerable.

There existed, therefore, the basic reasons guiding the thoughts of the clergy and lay leaders in the East to cause the removal of the seat of the Catholicate from Sis to Etchmiadzin.

(a) The overpowering influence of the Catholic Church on the Holy See of the Armenian Church in Cilicia,

(b) The scandalous acts of the clergy in legal and administrative affairs.

The Armenian clergy in the East, recognizing the visible danger of later infiltration within the folds of high-ranking clergymen who professed allegiance to the Holy See at Sis, which had fallen under the domination of the Egyptians, decided to call a National Church Assembly in Etchmiadzin and to invite the incumbent Catholicos to reinstate the Holy See at its place of birth. The Assembly convened in May, 1441, and was attended by more than 700 representatives consisting of bishops, heads of monasteries, vartabeds, priests, princes and civic leaders of great repute.

The Catholicos at Sis had rejected the invitation, but did not object to the reinstatement of the Holy See at Etchmiadzin and the election of a new Patriarch of All Armenians, and the clerical order under his immediate jurisdiction tacitly acquiesced to the plan. The assembly at Etchmiadzin unanimously decided and formally proclaimed the removal of the Holy See to its place of origin and elected a Supreme Patriarch of All Armenians. It was clearly understood between all parties concerned that upon the passing of the incumbent

Catholicos at Sis a successor would not be elected and the patriarchal See would cease to exist.

In spite of that, however, some five years after the death of the occupant of the patriarchal seat at Sis the Cilician See was restored by the election of a Catholicos, mainly due to political exigencies. Under the harsh rule of the Egyptian *Meliks* (rulers) the Armenians of Cilicia would have had difficulty in communicating with the spiritual head of the Armenian Church located in a far corner of Eastern Armenia suffering under the repressions of another tyranny.

The relations between the two Sees were not always cordial. Misunderstanding, dissensions, recriminations, disharmony and disunity often disrupted peaceful attempts of cooperation in the service of the Church. At all times, however, the people considered the Holy See of Etchmiadzin as the guiding light of Armenian Christendom, the supremacy of which was beyond question.

In the course of its history the Armenian Church has had many illustrious supreme Patriarchs conducting its affairs and dispersing spiritual benefits to the faithful. From the time of St. Gregory (c. 239–c. 326), who had earned the epithet Illuminator of Souls to Vasken I, the incumbent Catholicos of All Armenians, the Armenian people were blessed with many eminent religious leaders of whom the following are probably the most distinguished:

St. Nerses Bartev the Great—329–373, A.D.
St. Sahag Bartev—348–439
St. Mesrob Mashdotz—361–440
St. Gregory of Nareg—950–1010
St. Nerses the Gracious—1100–1173
Gregory of Datev—1346–1409
Nerses of Ashdarag—1770–1857
Mugrditch Khrimian—1820–1907
Maghakia Ormanian—1841–1918
Karekin Hovsepian—1867–1952

The ending of hostilities upon the termination of World War II had a decidedly favorable effect upon the existence of the Armenian Church. Relations between the Mother See and its spiritually subordinate hierarchies became gratifyingly harmonious. It appeared as if a complete unity in the Church had been achieved, with the Catholicos of All Armenians in Etchmiadzin as its titular head.

After his consecration and anointment in 1955, Catholicos Vasken I made great progress at the Holy See with the active encouragement and tacit cooperation of all the prominent leaders of Armenia—political, civic, social, educational and scientific. He restored several of the ancient monasteries of historical renown; he renovated and beautified the palatial residence (Veharan) of the Supreme Patriarch with marble floors, marble stairs and walls which were adorned by relief carvings representing historic churches and monasteries; he endowed the Holy See with a modern printing establishment and has enormously improved its finances. He has organized dioceses in various parts of the Soviet Union and has maintained close relationship with the dioceses in many countries outside of the Soviet Union.

In a locality where religious worship is not encouraged, thousands of persons, young and old, literally invade the Holy See from near and far corners of the country to make offerings and to commune with the God of their forefathers. Thousands upon thousands take their children of various ages to the monastery of Keghart to be baptized. There a sacrificial lamb is slaughtered as an offering to God. Only a few years ago the approach to the monastery was made on foot to a distance of more than a mile. Keghart is a veritable shrine, where several chapels have been hewn out of solid rock, where the floors, the walls and the ceilings form one continuous piece of carving of solid rock. The church has been renovated and a clergymen is in constant attendance to perform religious services and to administer sacraments. Keghart is now a thriving symbol of Christian devotion.

The Armenians in their homeland and in the dispersion have been blessed with a spiritual father who has devoted himself to the perpetuation of the Armenian Church and its Christian ideology and worship with a liberal interpretation of the principles laid down by his predecessors in the past many centuries.

From the time of the adoption of Christianity as a national religion and a way of life in 287, to the founding of the Armenian Republic in 1918, the Armenians have had a limited independence; and always in fear of being invaded by one or the other of their hostile neighbors. The Church has served as a bulwark against all intrusions. It has been the strongest factor in all efforts to perpetuate the national spirit of the Armenians.

Hierarchal Sees

Aside from the Mother See of Etchmiadzin there are three hierarchal Sees: (a) The Great House of Cilicia; (b) The Patriarchate of Jerusalem; and (c) The Patriarchate of Constantinople.

The Great House of Cilicia

As we have noted above, after the transfer of the Catholicate of All Armenians from Sis to Etchmiadzin, the House of Cilicia continued in its existence due to political exigencies. Its jurisdiction spread over a large territory in Turkish Armenia and as many as fourteen dioceses. However, with the annihilation of the Armenians in Turkey through massacres and deportation in 1915 the Cilician See literally ceased to exist. The seat of the Catholicos, Sis, was destroyed; the inhabitants in all dioceses were driven away or slaughtered, and the entire country was laid waste. The incumbent Catholicos finally sought refuge in Lebanon, where a new Seat was established with a jurisdiction over the dioceses of Damascus, Beirut, Aleppo, and Cyprus. This territory was transferred to the aged Catholicos of Cilicia by the Armenian

Patriarch of Jerusalem "in a fine gesture of brotherly solicitude." "A new catholicate was built at Antelias, near Beirut, which soon became a flourishing religious center." The occupants of the Seat of Cilicia have not always manifested spiritual loyalty to the Holy See of Etchmiadzin, but the Great House of Cilicia, "under patriotic, high-minded catholicoi, has been a loyal collaborator of the Mother See . . . for the greater glory of the Armenian Church."

The Patriarchate of Jerusalem

The Patriarchate of Jerusalem was established soon after the Council of Chalcedon in 451, when the controversy concerning the nature of Christ divided the Church of Christ and plagued it with doctrinal conflicts.

Papken Catholicos Gulesserian in his book entitled *The Armenian Church* as translated by Terenig Vartabed Poladian (Gotchnag Press, New York, 1939) writes:

"The Patriarch of Jerusalem for centuries has had the task of guarding in Palestine and chiefly in the Holy City, the special rights of the Armenian Church and also the rights which she shares with Greek and Roman Churches.

"The common rights of the three churches extend over the Church of the Nativity in Bethlehem, the Church of the Resurrection (Holy Sepulchre) in Jerusalem, and the Church of the Blessed Virgin in Gethsemane. In addition, the patriarch superintends, conjointly with the Greek patriarch, the ruins of the Church of the Ascension on Mount Olives, where divine service is held two times each year." (page 54)

The patriarch is the head of the monastic Order and supervises over the seminary, where students of theology are trained and prepared for service in the church in various dioceses in the Armenian diaspora as priests and vartabeds (celibates), as well as over elementary schools conducted under the jurisdiction of the patriarchate.

Independent in its internal administrative affairs the Patriarchate of Jerusalem is, however, an integral part of the

Armenian Church and recognizes the supremacy of the Catholicos of All Armenians in all doctrinal and spiritual matters.

The Patriarchate of Constantinople

Soon after the occupation of Constantinople by the Turks, Sultan Mohammed Fatih, recognizing the need of a responsible body to represent the Armenians in Turkey, established a patriarchate similar to the Greek Patriarchate, with jurisdiction over religious, ecclesiastical, and educational matters as well as over marriages, baptisms, divorces, descent and distribution, wills, and all philanthropic and benevolent institutions.

In the year 1461 Bishop Hovakim, the religious head of the Armenians in Asia Minor, with headquarters in Brussa, was brought to Constantinople, where he was invested with the titles, honors and privileges similar to those accorded to the Greek Patriarch.

For over 450 years the Patriarch of Constantinople was the recognized leader of the Armenians before the Sublime Porte. At times he fought valiantly in defense of his people in the interior of Turkey. Protests, petitions, supplications and demonstrations short of threats flooded the palace of the Sultan, searching for a gleam of hope to protect and defend helpless and unarmed Armenians against fanatic and savage Kurds, Turks and Circassians, who marauded the country, robbed the people, seduced young women and girls, killed mercilessly and laid waste the lands they invaded.

At times the Sultan appeared to be receptive to these pleas, at other times he turned a deaf ear to the pleading patriarch, who on one side tried to placate the despotic rulers of the country and on the other side did everything in his power to hold in check any outbursts among his own people that might resemble anything like rebellion.

The role of the patriarch in Constantinople was unique. Over three million of his flock, some concentrated in large centers, others scattered all over the Anatolian plateau, sought guidance, encouragement and protection.

The Armenians living in Constantinople and other metropolitan cities on the shores of the eastern Mediterranean, enjoyed comparative freedom in their religious worship, educational endeavors and commercial activities. They were not subject to constant harassment from Kurdish and Circassian hordes.

Then came 1915 when the entire Armenian nation was subjected to violence beyond belief, violence which was planned to exterminate a whole people to the last man, woman and child. True, the deportation of Armenians from Constantinople was limited to the elite class—doctors, lawyers, men of letters, artists, merchants of international repute and the most outstanding leaders of the clergy.

The patriarchate was reduced to a hollow shell, divested of all the power, dignity, pride, authority, prestige, honor and usefulness of the office, and the patriarch became a helpless pawn in the hands of the wicked and immoral, unable to render a helping hand to his dying flock.

The office of the patriarch was maintained in Constantinople, where he was able to dispense spiritual comfort, consolation and guidance to the approximate number of 60,000 Armenians who were spared deportation. The incumbent patriarch occasionally dispatched a priest to a very small number of Armenians scattered in the interior of Turkey, who are now gradually losing their identity or whose memory about the tragic past is shrouded with mist and uncertainty. Some have already forgotten their origin and believe themselves to be Mohammedans.

The past glory of the patriarchate is only a dim memory with no hope for revival or rejuvenation. The undying faith of the patriarch and his people in the indestructibility of the Armenian Church and people is the only force that maintains and strengthens the ideal of a free and independent existence to enjoy the blessings of God so abundantly distributed among all men of good will and charity.

In the succeeding pages the reader will find the unbiased opinions of world leaders, from all walks of life, contemporaneous to that tragic event, and it is our ardent hope that all civilized men and women will fully comprehend and evaluate the magnitude of the crime of genocide committed against the Armenians.

More than half a century has elapsed since the Armenian tragedy. The world has seen a number of wars, devastation, terror and attempted genocide in other lands and upon other people, but the memory of the 1915 episode can never be erased by subsequent events. It is impossible for the surviving victims of such a crime and their descendants to forget the terror suffered by them or their forefathers.

REFERENCES

1. pp. 49–50.
2. *Ibid.*, p. 51.
3. *History of the Armenian People*, Boston, 1918.
4. Kurkjian, *op. cit.*, p. 58.
5. p. 76.
6. Armen, p. 102.
7. Kurkjian, *op. cit.*, p. 118.
8. p. 11.
9. *Ibid.*, p. 62.
10. *Ibid*, pp. 43–44.
11. Kurkjian, *op. cit.*, p. 134.
12. p. 45.
13. Kurkjian, *op. cit.*, p. 161.
14. *Ibid.*, p. 178.
15. Jacques de Morgan, *op. cit.*, p. 177.
16. Kurkjian, *op. cit.*, p. 208.
17. de Morgan, *op. cit.*, p. 183.

18. *Ibid.*, p. 145.

19. Kurkjian, *op. cit.*, p. 216.

20. *Ibid.*, p. 229.

21. de Morgan, *op. cit.*, p. 252.

22. *Ibid.*, p. 254.

23. *Ibid.*, pp. 269–270.

24. Kurkjian, *op. cit.*, p. 273.

25. *Ibid.*, pp. 274–275.

26. *Ibid.*, p. 275.

27. de Morgan, *op. cit.*, p. 273.

Chapter 4

The Unthinkable Crime

It is no doubt fruitless to speculate on "what might have been" if certain events which were not of the first magnitude themselves but which precipitated others of world-wide import had turned out differently. Many commentators have pointed out that a strong French opposition to Hitler's re-occupation of the Rhineland in 1936 would undoubtedly have succeeded and would thus almost certainly have destroyed Hitler as a political figure and quite possibly have spared the world the disaster of World War II.

Similarly, the failure of nerve by the British leadership of the Gallipoli Campaign in early 1915, when victory was possibly a matter of hours away, had incalculable consequences for the civilized world generally, for Czarist Russia in particular, and for the Armenians within Turkey above all. The Allies' loss of the Straits to the Turkish and German forces crippled Russia, which was the only effective partisan of the Armenian community's rights in the Western world, and it enabled the Turkish leadership to proceed with impunity on a campaign of extermination that it had considered as far back as 1911 and explicitly formulated in the early months of 1915. Even the presence of large numbers of Germans was no deterrent to Enver and Talaat, for the German Ambassador von Wangenheim himself was anti-Armenian in outlook, and showed no inclination to interfere in any Turkish affairs other than the conduct of the war, which was largely in the hands of German military missions, in any case.

Ironically, the Turkish government, whose name was a byword for inefficiency, approached its terrible "solution" of the so-called Armenian problem, with a kind of Germanic efficiency that Heinrich Himmler might have admired twenty-five years later. There was no Turkish equivalent of Zyklon-B or elaborately constructed death camps but simply a plan of deportation to the Mesopotamian desert.

The plan was simplicity itself. All Armenians of whatever age or condition of health were to be driven on foot to the totally barren Der-El-Zor region of what is now Syria, there to expire if they did not do so on the way. They were to be driven there by units of the Turkish armies or by released convicts, neither of whom were to be discouraged from acts of vandalism, physical cruelty, or even murder. Vast though the plan was, it was virtually cost-free, and, better still, would result in the Armenian lands becoming the property of the Turkish marauders.

The plan of genocide was conveyed to the internal authorities, as we have seen, by a series of telegrams from Interior Minister Talaat beginning in February 1915 and continuing for about a half year thereafter. On the night of April 24–25 the leaders of the Armenian community were rounded up with such completeness that now there was not even internal leadership to plead for the defenseless Armenians scattered throughout Turkey and concentrated in the east.

As it happened, there were many men of good will inside Turkey at the time. To their credit, many of these men bore witness against the Turks, and many of them worked heroically on behalf of the Armenians. Of these splendid men and women, undoubtedly the greatest was the German pastor Dr. Johannes Lepsius, who viewed with the deepest horror his own countrymen's indifference to the bestial acts he himself witnessed. Dr. Lepsius, whose name ought forever to be remembered for his services to the highest ideals of humanity, has left us a record of what took place in Turkey in

1915 and 1916 in his book entitled simply *La Rapport Secret*,[1] published in 1919. The following pages are drawn largely from his account.

The deportation of the Armenians took place in three different areas at three consecutive periods. The three regions where the Armenians were established somewhat closely and formed a considerable portion of the population (from ten to forty percent) are:

> I. Cilicia and Northern Syria
> II. Eastern Anatolia
> III. Western Anatolia.

According to Dr. Lepsius in the various regions the deportations began as follows:

1. The deportation of the Armenian population began at the end of March and was systematically continued during the months of April and May.

2. The deportation in the Eastern Vilayets (with the exception of the Vilayet of Van) began at the end of May and was systematically pursued to the 1st of July.

3. The deportation in the Western district of Anatolia began at the beginning of August and continued during the month of September.

4. In northern Syria and in Mesopotamia, at first the massacres were limited to the imprisonment of the notables. The deportations began at the end of May and continued until October. (p. 10)

The following is a schedule of deportations and massacres as reported by Dr. Lepsius on pages 8–10 of his book:

May 15, 1915—	The rural parts of Erzeroum
June 15–July 15 and	
July 26, 1915—	The city of Erzeroum
June 24, 1915—	Shabin Karahisar
June 25, 1915—	Sivas
June 26, 1915—	Harpout and Trebizond

June 27, 1915—	Samson
July 1, 1915—	Medzpin (Nisibis), Armenians & Assyrians
	Tel-Ermen
	Bitlis
	Mardin and surroundings
July 10, 1915—	Moush
	Malatia

Deportations from Cilicia

July 27, 1915—	The seashore areas in Cilicia
	Antioch
July 28, 1915—	Aintah
	Kilis
	Adiyaman
July 30, 1915—	Suedia

Deportations from Western Asia Minor

August 10–19, 1915—	Izmit (Nicomedia)
	Bardizag
	Brusa
	Adahazar and surroundings
August 16, 1915—	Marash
	Konia
August 19, 1915—	Ourfa

George Horton refers to *La Rapport Secret* in his book entitled *The Blight of Asia:*[2]

We have lists before us of 550 villages whose surviving inhabitants were converted to Islam with fire and sword; of 568 churches thoroughly pillaged, destroyed and razed to the ground; of 282 Christian churches transformed to mosques; of 21 Protestant preachers and 170 Gregorian (Armenian) clergymen who were, after enduring unspeakable tortures, murdered after their refusal to accept Islam. We repeat, however, that these figures reach only to the extent of our information, and do not by a long way reach to the extent of the reality. Is this a religious persecution or is it not?

Dr. Lepsius' *Deutschland und Armenien, 1914–1918,*[3] is a remarkable book that may well be compared with Lord Bryce's *The Treatment of Armenians in the Ottoman Empire,* edited by the well-known historian Arnold J. Toynbee. It is well worth quoting at some length:

Upon his return from the Caucasian front during February of the year 1915, Enver Pasha, in his dual capacity as Minister of Defense and Commander-in-chief of the Turkish Army, replied to a greeting by the Bishop of Konia as follows: 'I wish to express my gratitude and use this opportunity to tell you how conscientiously the Armenian soldiers in the Ottoman Army fulfill their duties on the battlefield as I have personally witnessed. I wish to convey to the Armenian nation, which is known for her absolute devotion to the Imperial Ottoman government, the expression of my satisfaction and gratitude.' (*Osmanischer Lloyd,* January 26, 1915). To the Armenian Patriarch, too, Enver Pasha expressed his 'special satisfaction about the conduct and bravery of the Armenian soldiers, who gave an excellent account of themselves,' but already then had significantly added that 'in the event of the smallest occurrence he would intervene with most drastic measures.' How did it come to pass, then, that on April 20 the judgment of the Armenian people's devotion was suddenly reversed? The 'uprising' of Van had constituted the tragic moment in the fate of the Armenians. The signal for Enver Pasha's 'drastic measures' had been given.

With the fixing of this moment it is not meant to say that the will for destruction within the driving powers that stood behind the Minister of Defense, had not existed previous to the events of Van. Already at the Congress of the Young-Turk 'Committee for Union and Progress' in Saloniki, October 1911, the nationalistic-panislamic thought —the sole reign of the Turkish race and the construction of the Empire on a purely islamic basis—had been wrought into the governmental program:

"Sooner or later the total Islamization of all Turkish subjects must be accomplished, but it is clear that this can never be achieved by verbal persuasion, therefore the power of arms must be resorted to. The character of the Empire will have to be Mohammedan, and respect for

Mohammedan institutions and traditions is to be enforced. Other nations must be denied the right to organize because de-centralization and self-government would constitute treason against the Turkish Empire. The nationalities will become a negligible quantity. They could keep their religion, but not their language. The proliferation of the Turkish language would be a principal means to secure Mohammedan predominance and to assimilate the remaining elements."

Since the outbreak of the war this program stood behind all the proceedings which treated the "Raya" of the Christian nations as a "herd" of subjects: the general disarmament of the Christian population, the degradation of the Armenian soldiers, who had been inducted to bear arms but were reduced to the status of porters and road laborers, the dismissal of Armenian officers and physicians from administrative posts and military hospitals, etc. The pan-Turkish program loomed behind the deportations and mass arrests in Cilicia and in the Vilayet of Erzeroum already, prior to the days of Van and dictated the campaign of destruction Turkish and Kurdish troops undertook in the winter of 1914–1915 in Northern Persia against the peaceful Assyrian and Armenian population of Urmia and Salmas. This program provoked the general persecution of Christians in the Vilayets of Diarbekir and Mossul, where Jacobites, Chaldeans, Nestorians and Armenians were indiscriminately victimized.

This program would have been executed even without the "uprising of Van," since this uprising was only an act of self-defense against the threatening massacre, which began in several localities simultaneously, when Djevdet Bey gave the signal by assassinating the Armenian leaders during the same days that the deportation measures in Cilicia were expanded to large districts outside of the battle zones.

The "uprising" of Van only served as a widely visible pretext to shroud the execution of the plan intended to insure Turkish predominance and Islamization by making it appear to the outside world as a military necessity, and also to destroy within the Committee itself any resistance against its execution by the most radical means, with the view of annihilating the Armenian people.

From which side came the decisive turning point in the policy of the government in Constantinople concerning

the Armenians, whether through Enver Pasha or Talaat
Bey, or through a decision by the Young-Turk Committee,
will only become evident when the internal affairs of the
Young-Turkish government become known.*

It appears that within the Committee itself conflicts existed between the radical and the more moderate factions,
which, during the period between April 24 and May 27
escalated into a confrontation that resulted in the victory
for the radical group.

From these struggles ensued the decision which sealed
the fate of the Armenian people: the general deportation.

Turkish Acceptance of Responsibility

After the publication of the German documents the
question of responsibility for the universal deportation and
its consequences warrants no further discussion. The
Turkish government and their executive ministers themselves acknowledge having been the originators of the proceedings they embarked upon. Any outside stimulus or
co-responsibility—especially coming from Germany—was
not only vehemently disputed by them, but categorically
denied. In a pamphlet distributed to the representatives of
foreign powers in Constantinople on March 1, 1916 the
Porte said:

"The statements to the effect that the measures of the
Sublime Porte were suggested by certain powers, are totally untenable. The Imperial Government, having firmly
decided to maintain its absolute independence, naturally
would not permit any participation even by their friends
and allies in their internal affairs."

When vilifying statements were issued inside Turkey,
and through the press of other nations, claiming that Germany had inspired the deportation measures and had
organized their execution, the [German] Embassy demanded the complete retraction of those statements by
the Porte, whereupon the Porte issued orders to the provinces, officially forbidding such publications which were
spread by Turkish officers, officials and the clergy and

* In a conversation I [Lepsius] had with Enver Pasha on August 10 in
Stambul [Istanbul, then Constantinople], he explained that he would take
responsibility for whatever happened in the interior.

found wide-spread belief among Christians and Mohammedans alike. The more sensitive elements among the
Mohammedans, who were ashamed of the atrocities committed against the Armenian people, of course found it
preferable to place the odium of guilt for these deeds on
their German ally. They refused to believe that their government was the originator of such horrors. And yet, no
matter how frequently the German government and embassy protested to the Porte about these lies, which frequently found all too willing belief abroad, no matter how
often the Grand Vizir and the Minister of the Interior declared their sole responsibility for the acts committed most
recklessly against the Armenians, the Turkish mollahs and
functionaries did not cease to spread the belief in such
slander.

The consequences of this government policy against
the Armenians, which might affect the economic future of
the country as well as her peace negotiations, have been
pointed out to the Porte both by the German government
and embassy, but these warnings have made no impression on the leaders. Whose fault was it?

The soul of the policy for Armenia was the Young-Turk
'Committee for Union and Progress;' the Minister of the
Interior, Talaat Bey, and vice-generalissimo Enver Pasha
were formally responsible for the execution of these
politics. 'Nobody any longer has the power,' Count Wolff-
Metternich writes on June 30, 1916, 'to restrain the many-
headed hydra of the Committee, the chauvinism and the
fanaticism. The Committee demands the elimination of
the last remainders of the Armenian people and the government has to give in. The Committee means not only
the organization of the government party in the capital;
it is spread over all the vilayets. At the side of each Vali,
and on down to the Kaimakam, a Committee member
stands with instructions to either support or restrain.'

Abstract from Section 4, "Steps of the Ambassadors at the
Porte."

Through the announcement of the deportation decision
of 'not quite impeccable families' from the 'centers of
insurrection,' the German embassy had been deceived
about the character and extent of the Committee's decision. It was not a matter of 'families' but rather of the

entire Armenian people; it was not 'centers of insurrection,' but all of Anatolia and Mesopotamia. Every town and village deep into the innermost provinces where Armenians lived, were declared 'rebellious,' even though the whole area of deportation had been in Russian hands since the incident of Van, and no insurrection existed. But, after the ordinance of May 27, 'suspicion' was sufficient grounds for deportation.

Duke Hohenlohe-Langenburg, who was sent to Constantinople to represent the Ambassador, handed a memorandum to the Porte on August 9, and reports about it to the Reichs-Chancellor on August 12:

'The systematic slaughter of the Armenians driven from their homes has reached such dimensions during the past few weeks, that a renewed, urgent protestation from us seems appropriate against this wanton conduct, which the government not only permits, but obviously encourages, especially since in various areas the Christians of other races are no longer left unmolested."

The tireless efforts of the Ambassador did not seem to make an impression upon Talaat Bey until September 2. It was only then when he issued a series of telegraphic orders to administrations of the provinces to deliver proof of the central government's serious endeavors to bring an end to these excesses, and to procure some care for the evacuated people. The Embassy informed the consuls of these orders from the government.

It took no more than one week for the reports to come in from the consuls in the deportation areas of Mossul (September 9), Aleppo (September 9 and 12), and Adana (September 10 and 13). The orders of the Porte to the Vilayets remained ineffectual; the deportations continued; the number of starving people grew, and the measures against widows, orphans, the sick and the blind and even the families of soldiers were becoming more stringent. The Inspector, Ali Mumif Bey, who was sent to Cilicia to organize support for the deportees upon the orders of the Porte, even rescinded the few remaining mitigations. 'The officials,' the Consul, Dr. Buege, writes from Adana, 'act naturally only after the second directive and continue with the deportation regardless of religious conversion. The message from the Porte to the Imperial Embassy is merely an impudent trickery.'

The sport of promises begins anew. Assurances are given, restricted, renewed, withdrawn again, renewed again, and once more withdrawn, and the promises were never kept. A series of continuing diplomatic steps are being undertaken because of the threatened deportation of the Armenians in Constantinople, who already have been secretly moved away by the thousands, and whose total deportation is being prepared by registering 70,000 more.

Excerpts from the text, in Dr. Lepsius' words:

To visit the concentration camps and to bring clothes, bread or money to the starving prisoners was nearly impossible, as the government tried to prevent this with all means at its disposal. Only very few Germans succeeded in completing the daring mission. The German nurses were forbidden to leave the towns even though they would have gladly exposed themselves to the dangers. The Germans were treated no better than neutrals. Among the deportees and the starving were many German-speaking children educated in German schools and orphanages. The Armenian teaching and assisting staff in German institutions and schools, Armenian physicians, pharmacists, nurses in German hospitals, were indiscriminately deported, imprisoned, shot, hanged, or, at best, forced to convert to Islam. Four buildings of the German orphanage in Mamuret-ul-Asis, filled with orphan children, were requisitioned for military purposes, but never used.

The German Embassy did what it could to lend weight to the wishes of the Pope, Protestant and Catholic Mission, and Relief Organizations, that were presented to the Porte. But all was in vain.

In his report to the German Military Mission in Constantinople,[4] a Lieutenant-Colonel Stange dealt convincingly with the expulsion of the Armenians.

The expulsion of the Armenians began approximately during middle of May, 1915. Until then everything had remained relatively calm; the Armenians were permitted to pursue their businesses and professions and to practice their religion undisturbed and they seemed generally content with their situation. However, on February 10, the second director of the local Ottoman Bank, an Armenian, was shot to death in the open street around six o'clock. Despite the so-called efforts of the government the culprit was never apprehended; today there is no longer any doubt that the motive for this murder was a political one. The Armenian bishop of Ersindjian was also murdered during that time.

Toward May 20 Kiamil Pasha, the Commander-in-Chief, had ordered the evacuation of the Armenian villages north of Erzeroum, an order which was executed in the most brutal manner by the Turkish authorities. Regarding this a copy of a letter written to the bishop by Armenian villagers exists: within the briefest of notice these people were chased from their homes and land, rounded up and the majority were not even allowed the time to pack the meanest necessities before being taken along by the gendarmes. Property that was left behind, as well as that which they carried with them, was subsequently simply taken from them, or pilfered from their homes by the gendarmes.

Despite the bad weather the refugees had to sleep under open skies; in most cases the gendarmes gave permission to go to the villages to procure food or water only against special payment. Rapings did occur and desperate mothers actually cast their infants into the Euphrates river when they saw no further possibility to nourish them. The German Consul had his German consular employees distribute bread among the refugees upon several occasions, and these employees are in a good position to testify as to the misery of these refugees.

It is an undisputable fact that these Armenians were murdered in the vicinity of Mamachatun (Terdjan) almost without exceptions by the so-called Tchettas (volunteers), Ashirets, and similar rabble with the sanction of the military accompaniment, and often even with their assistance. The Vali reported these facts—of course only in a limited scope—to the German Consul, who interviewed an old Armenian who had managed to escape the slaughter. A large number of corpses was seen in that area by Schlimme, the porter of the consulate.

The expulsion of the Armenians from the town of Erzeroum began in the first part of June. The manner in which this was conducted by the government, police authorities and other menials lacks any sign of order and organization. On the contrary, it is a prime example of reckless, inhuman and lawless abandon and of the animal brutality of all the participating Turks against a group of people which they deeply hated and considered fair game. A multitude of certain examples is available to confirm this. The government did nothing whatsoever to assist the refugees, and since the police were aware of the sentiments of their leaders, they did everything they could to increase the misery of the Armenians. Deportation orders were issued and rescinded; then the granted residence permits withdrawn again by the police a few days later. In many cases this happened between evening and morning of one night. Complaints and appeals were ignored and often answered by maltreatment.

The government never informed the deportees of their destination. This permitted the rising of prices for transportation to almost inaccessible heights; accompanying military personnel was authorized only in unsatisfactory numbers; they were poorly trained, and, as it later became apparent, did not at all take seriously their duty to protect the refugees. It had become known that the insecurity of the streets in the country had reached a high degree, which did not deter the official agencies to expose the Armenians to these dangers. They were supposed to perish. After they had received their deportation orders it was prohibited for the Armenians in Trapezund to either sell their property or take it along. The porter of the local German consulate, Schlimme (who had undertaken an official trip via Baiburt, Erzindjian to Trapezund on orders from the consulate) saw himself how police crews removed all the bundles from refugees filing by the police station. The above may be sufficient to render an impression—albeit a weak one—of the cruel treatment the Armenians were subjected to. Many further details are available.

As far as it can be judged with the government's efforts at minimizing and obfuscating events, the situation is as follows:

Of the first group, which departed on June 16 directly for Kharpout and which primarily consisted of Armenian notables, carrying large amounts of luggage, the men have been murdered with few exceptions, and this has been admitted by the Vali for thirteen Armenians. The women seemed to have arrived in Kharpout with their smallest children, but nothing certain is known about the adult girls. The rest of the troops were led via Baiburt and Erzindjian and on in the direction of Kemach (Euphrates valley). In general, they are 'supposed' to have crossed the Euphrates valley safely, but still have to cross a dangerous area on their march to Kharpout and to the vicinity of Urfa.

Of the Armenians from Trapezunt [Trebizond] the men were led aside into the mountains, and, with the help of the military, slaughtered, while the women were driven to Erzindjian in miserable condition. It is not known what happened further to them. In Trapezunt men were taken out to sea and thrown overboard. The Bishop of Trapezunt was summoned to the court martial in Erzeroum and was strangled on the way, together with his Kawass. An Armenian military physician was murdered between Trapezunt and Baiburt.

The Armenians from Erzindjian were all chased into the Kemach (Euphrates) valley and were slaughtered there. It is credibly reported that the corpses were carted away on carriages that had been standing ready from before, and thrown into the river. The Bishop of Erzindjian accompanied his fellow believers and must have shared their fate. There are now only very few Armenians left in Erzeroum after the originally established regulation permitting women and children without men to remain in the city, had been rescinded, and their deportation was now pursued stringently and unscrupulously. Even those who were needed for the operation of military and administration, skilled workers, blacksmiths, drivers, hospital personnel, bank and government officials and military physicians were planlessly evicted.

The removing of the Armenians from the war-zone in Erzeroum was authorized by law, and is being justified as a military necessity. In fact, Armenians in certain areas did prove themselves unreliable. Rebellions flared up in the vicinity of Van-lake and in Bitlis and Moush. Occasionally, telephone wires were cut and not a few espionage cases occurred. On the other hand, the Armenian population in Erzeroum had remained absolutely calm. Whether they would have continued to remain calm in the event of a possible Russian approach to Erzeroum is not too accu-

Armenian refugees fleeing from the Turks. The massacre of Armenians remaining within Turkey was called the "most colossal crime of all ages" by the examining American Military Mission's report to the U.S. Congress. *UPI*

Armenian victims of one of the widespread forced marches. *Brown Brothers*

Survivors of forced marches were herded into central camps, which were called concentration camps even in World War I. Pictures like this recall the Nazi death camps in the world war that followed. *Wide World Photos*

Many atrocities during the Armenian genocide were reported and described by foreign eyewitnesses in Turkey. *Wide World Photos*

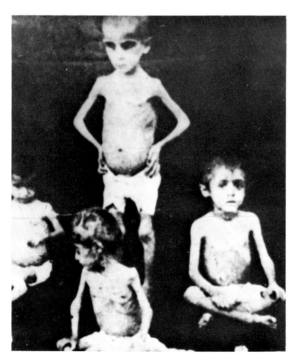

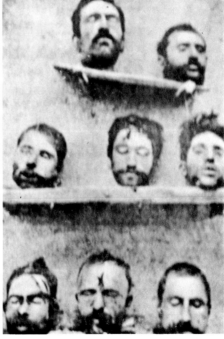

Children of Armenian refugees at Marasch fed by Near East Relief workers. *UPI*

Armenian orphans silently cross the snow to their barracks, mute testimony to the slaughter of a large segment of the Armenian adult population. *UPI*

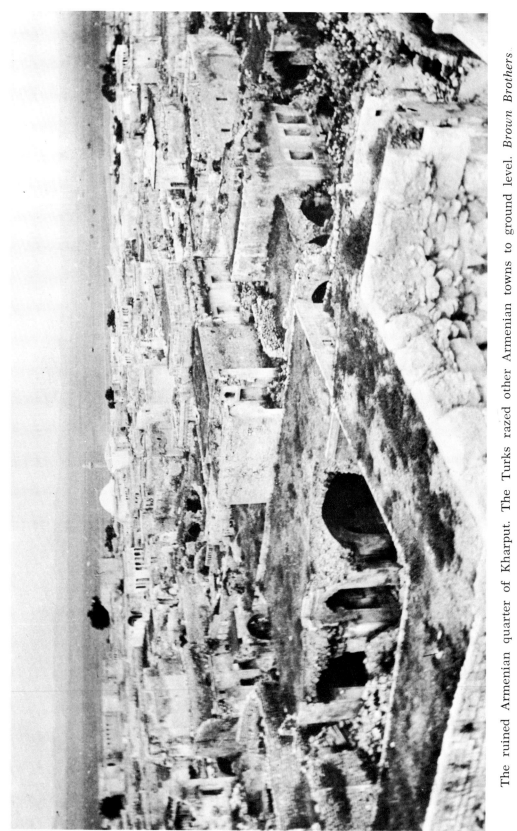

The ruined Armenian quarter of Kharput. The Turks razed other Armenian towns to ground level. *Brown Brothers.*

A loaf of bread meant life. Without bread, many hundreds of thousands of Armenians slowly died of starvation. *UPI*

Enver Pasha, leader of the Young Turk movement which came to power in 1909. Minister of War, and co-dictator of Turkey with Talaat and Djemal, Enver was a principal author of the plan to exterminate the Armenians. *Ewing Galloway*

Djemal Pasha, Minister of Marine, shared with Enver Pasha and Talaat Bey absolute power over Turkey and the fate of the Armenians during World War I. *Radio Times Hulton Picture Library*

Talaat Bey, Turkish Minister of the Interior and one of the ruling triumvirate. The ex-telegrapher was merciless in directing the slaughter of the Armenians and was unmoved by any human appeals. *Radio Times Hulton Picture Library*

Mustafa Kemal, the Young Turks' chief of staff under Enver Pasha, whom he later opposed. Kemal organized the Turkish Nationalist party and was elected the Turkish republic's first president after the Conference of Lausanne in 1923. When the conference had ended, Turkish nationalism had won, and Armenian independence had been forgotten. *Underwood and Underwood News Photos*

rately determined at this time. All Armenians fit for military service had been conscripted, with only a relatively small fraction exempted. Therefore, there was no special reason to fear a rebellion. Despite this, the government seemed to have had such a fear of such an action by the Armenians, which was in no relation to the relatively powerless situation the Armenians were in at the time. Even if the decision for the eviction of not altogether reliable elements remains that of the High Command, it ought to be expected that these measures are carried out without damage to life and property of the deportees, especially since not the smallest proof exists as to their personal guilt. This does not touch upon the right and duty to afford a trial for the individual guilty. But that hundreds and thousands are being literally murdered, that the authorities wilfully manipulate property left behind (houses, shops, goods and household wares)—there were stores valued at approximately 150,000 Ltq in the Armenian church—that the eviction was conducted in the most inhuman form and that families and women were expelled without the protection of their men, and that those Armenians that had converted to Islam were no longer considered to be under suspicion and thence left in peace, gives reason to the assumption that military reasons were considered as secondary in the deportation of the Armenians, and that it primarily was a good opportunity to execute a long before established plan to weaken, if not destroy, the Armenian population without outside interference. Military considerations and rebellious efforts in various parts of the country offered a welcome smoke screen.

The authorities seemed to consider justified the principle to practice revenge on the innocent for the deeds of the guilty ones, who could not be apprehended.

During the execution of the deportation measures the Vali referred to orders from the High Command at one time, and orders from Constantinople at another. On the other hand, the High Command constantly urged reckless acceleration of the eviction and not a few times issued orders for the execution of which the Vali was made responsible, without having been given the means for the execution. The High Command must have been aware of the murder of the first Armenians as well as of the conduct of the accompanying gendarmes; they knew the insecurity of the streets and did nothing to rectify that situation, and ordered Armenians to be deported over these same roads. This behavior corresponds of course to a remark made to the consul, stating that 'after the war there no longer will exist an Armenian Question.'

After all this has happened, the following can be concluded safely: The deportation and destruction of the Armenians was decided by the Young-Turk Committee in Constantinople, probably organized by them, and executed by them with the assistance of the armed forces and bands of volunteers. For this purpose members of the Committee were present here.

Hilmi Bey, Shakir Bey, the deputy for Erzeroum, Seyfulla Bey; also in office here: The director of police, Chulussi Bey, and the High Commander, Mahmud Kiamil Pasha.

> Signed
> Lieutenant-Colonel Stange
> Erzeroum, August 23, 1915

In June, 1916, Count Wolff-Metternich, whose memory should be revered by all civilized men, sent a message to Reichs-Chancellor von Bethmann-Hollweg. Dr. Lepsius gives it in full:

I have discussed with Talaat Bey and Halil Bey the deportation of the Armenian workers from the Amanus stretch, which deportation hampers the conduct of the war. These measures, I told the ministers among other things, gave the impression as if the Turkish government were itself bent on losing the war.

These developments are instructive in several directions. People like Talaat and Enver know well that the war effort is being stunted by endangering railroad service and construction at Amanus. But no one any longer has the power to control the many-headed hydra of the Committee, to control the chauvinism and the fanaticism. The Committee demands annihilation of the last remainders of Armenians, and the government must bow to their demands. The committee means not only the organization of the government party in the capital; it is spread all over the Vilayets. At the side of each Vali, and on down to the Kaimakam, a Committee member stands with instructions to either support or restrain. The expulsion of the Armenians has begun anew everywhere. But the hungry wolves of the Committee can no longer expect more from these unhappy people except the satisfaction of their fanatic rage for persecution. Their goods have long since been confiscated, and their capital has been liquidated by a so-called commission, which means that if an Armenian owned a house valued at 100 Ltq, for instance, a Turk, friend or member of the Committee, could have it for around 2 Ltq. Thus, there is not much to gain any longer from the Armenians. The mob is therefore preparing itself for the moment when Greece, forced by the Entente, must turn against Turkey and her allies. Massacres of far greater scope will occur then. The victims are more numerous and the booty more enticing. Greekdom constitutes the cultural element of Turkey and it will be destroyed like the Armenian segment if outside influence will not put a stop to it. 'Turkification' means to expel or kill everything non-Turkish, to destroy, and to forcefully acquire others' properties. In this, and in the parroting of French freedom phrases, lies at present the famous rebirth of Turkey. People like Talaat, who have an honest will to advance Turkey, although he as well is only familiar with power politics, must bow to the many-headed hydra.

> Signed
> Count Wolff-Metternich
> Imperial German Embassy
> Therapia, June 30, 1916

Dr. Lepsius' book contains a moving report by a neutral American eye-witness, also published by the American Relief Commission for Armenia and Syria:

> I had obtained permission to visit the camps of the Armenians along the Euphrates from Meskene to Deir-el-Zor, and to give an account of the conditions under which they live, and, if possible, the approximate numbers of these deportees.
> The purpose of this report is to outline the results of this mission. I take the liberty of sending you this report with the request to take the conclusions arrived therein into consideration. If you should accept these conclusions they will only serve in a very minor degree to alleviate some-

what the daily sufferings of an unhappy people which is in the process of disappearing from the face of the earth.

It is impossible to render an image of the horrible impressions I received on my journey through the dispersed camps along the Euphrates river. I travelled on the right-hand bank of the stream. To speak of 'camps' is actually not possible.

The major portion of these miserable people brutally driven from home and land, separated from their families, robbed of everything they owned and stripped of all they carried underway, have been herded like cattle under the open skies without the least protection against heat and cold, almost without clothing, and were fed very irregularly, and always insufficiently. Exposed to every change in weather, the glowing sun in the desert, the wind and rain in spring and fall, and the bitter cold in winter, weakened through extreme want and their strength sapped by endless marches, deplorable treatment, cruel torture and the constant fear for their lives, those that had some shreds of their strength left dug holes at the banks of the river to crawl into them.

The extreme few who managed to salvage some clothes and some money and who are in a position to purchase some flour are considered fortunate and rich people. Fortunate are those, too, who could obtain a few watermelons or a sick and skinny goat from the nomads in exchange for the same weight in gold. Everywhere one only sees pale faces and emaciated bodies, wandering skeletons conquered by disease and surely soon victims of starvation.

When the measures to transport the entire population into the desert were adopted, no appropriations were made for any kind of nourishment. On the contrary, it is obvious that the government pursued a plan to let the people die of starvation. Even an organized mass-killing such as during the times when liberty, equality and fraternity had not yet been proclaimed in Constantinople, would have been a much more humane measure, since it would have saved these miserable people from the horrors of hunger and the slow death and the excruciating pains of tortures so fiendish that the most cruel of the Mongols could not have imagined them. But a massacre is less constitutional than death by starvation. Civilization is saved!

What remains of the Armenian nation, scattered along the banks of the Euphrates, consists of old men, women and children. Men of middle age and younger people, as far as they have not been slain, are scattered over the roads of the country where they smash stones or do other labors for the Army in the name of the state.

The young girls, many still children, have become the booty of the Mohammedans. During the long marches to the destination of their deportation they were abducted, raped if the opportunity arose, or sold if they hadn't been killed by the gendarmes who accompanied these gloomy caravans. Many have been carried by their robbers into the slavery of a harem.

The entrances to these concentration camps could well bear the legend imprinted on the gates of Dante's hell 'Ye who enter here, abandon all hope.'

Gendarmes on horseback made the rounds to punish all those that tried to escape, to seize and punish them with their whips. The roads are well guarded. And what roads they are! They lead into the desert where death awaits the refugee as surely as under the whips of their Ottoman guards.

In various locations in the desert I came upon six such refugees lying in the throes of death. They had managed to escape their guards. And now they were surrounded by half-starved dogs; the crazed animals waiting for their last convulsions so that they could leap upon them and feed on them.

Everywhere along the way one can find remainders of such unhappy Armenians, who had simply dropped to the ground. There are hundreds of these mounds of earth under which they rest, the victims of unqualified barbarism, sleeping without a name.

On the one hand they are prevented from leaving the concentration camps in search of food, and on the other it is made impossible for them to utilize those capabilities characteristic to their race, namely to adapt themselves to their terrible fate and to improve their sad lot in their ingenious ways.

One could build some sort of shelter such as stone or earth huts. If, at least, they would have such shelters they could perhaps apply themselves agriculturally. But this hope has been taken from them as well; under threat of death they are continually dragged from one place to another, to bring variety to their suffering. They are scared into endless forced marches, without bread, without water, exposed to fresh sufferings and new maltreatment under the whips of their overseers, miseries that would not even occur to a slave dealer from the Sudan; the entire stretch of the way is a fearsome row of suffering, marked by the victims of these transports.

Those who still carry some money are constantly robbed by their wardens, who threaten them with even further deportations, and when their small means are exhausted, they execute these threats. To speak here of 'one thousand and one nights of horror' means to say nothing. I literally believed to cross hell. The few impressions I would like to report are occasional and hastily assembled. You can only form a weak impression of the terrible and gruesome picture that was before my eyes. Everywhere I travelled I saw the same images; everywhere the terror-regime of barbarism, which has as its goal the systematic annihilation of the Armenian race, rampages. Everywhere one finds the inhuman bestiality of these henchmen, and the self-same tortures with which these unhappy victims are tormented. From Meskene to Der-es-Zol—everywhere the banks of the Euphrates are witness to the same atrocities.

2.

As a result of its geographical location at the border of Syria and Mesopotamia, Meskene ideally offers itself as the point of concentration for the deported Armenians from the Vilayets from where they had been dispersed along the Euphrates river. They arrived at this point by the tens of thousands, but a large portion lost their lives. The impression the great Plain of Meskene leaves is deeply melancholy and depressing. Information I gathered at that place gives me the right to state that nearly 60,000 Armenians are buried here who fell victim to the hunger, deprivations, dysentery and typhus. As far as the eye reaches there are earth mounds, each containing about two-hundred dead. Women, old men, children are all thrown together regardless of social position or family relationship.

At present, there are still 4,400 Armenians herded between the town of Meskene and the Euphrates river. They are no more than living ghosts. Their overseers distribute a slice of bread to them very irregularly and very sparingly. It happens often that for three or four days they receive nothing.

A frightful dysentery rages, demanding terrible sacrifices especially among the children. In their hunger these unhappy youngsters pounce upon everything they can find, and they devour grass, soil, and even excrements.

Inside a tent measuring perhaps five or six meters square, I saw roughly four-hundred orphan-children—they were starving. These miserable children are supposed to receive 150 grams of bread per day. It happens often that they receive nothing for two or three days. Of course the mortality rate is fearfully high. As I was able to ascertain myself, the dysentery claimed seventy victims within eight days.

Abu Herere is a small town north of Meskene, located at the banks of the Euphrates. It is the most unhealthy spot in the desert. Two hundred yards away from the river banks, on a hill, I found 240 Armenians guarded by two gendarmes who let them die mercilessly under the horrible pains of starvation. The scenes I have witnessed surpass any conceivable imagination of horror. Near the place where my cart stopped I noticed women, who, hardly after they saw me come, prepared to pick out of the horses' excrements the few undigested oat kernels, to eat them. I gave them bread. They threw themselves at it, shredding it in night-marish avarice with their teeth, like starving dogs, among jerks and convulsions of epileptic proportions, and as soon as any of these 240 people—or rather 240 hungry wolves—who had eaten nothing for seven days, received wind of my arrival, the entire horde swarmed upon me, racing down the side of the hill, reaching out toward me with their skeleton arms, and among sobs and hoarse screams, begged me for a piece of bread. Among them were only women and children, and maybe a dozen of old men.

Upon my return I brought with me bread for them and for more than an hour I was the compassionate, albeit powerless, spectator to a veritable battle over a piece of bread, a battle as vicious as even starving animals could have performed.

3.

Hama is a small village where 1,600 Armenians are imprisoned. Here as well, the same scenes of hunger and horror take place every day. The men have been inducted into penal companies to do road work. As a reward for their labor they receive daily one piece of inedible and indigestible bread, which is utterly insufficient to provide them with strength for their hard labor.

In this village I met several families who still had some money left, and therefore tried to live under slightly less lamentable conditions. But the majority had no other living quarters but the naked earth without the smallest shelter, and nourished themselves from water melons. The poorest among them tried to cheat their hunger by eating melon peels which the others threw away. Mortality is enormous, especially among the children.

4.

Rakka is a more significant town on the left bank of the Euphrates. Here, around 5-6000 Armenians—chiefly women and children—are divided into groups of between fifty and sixty, and dispersed in various parts of the town where they have been quartered in decrepit and collapsed buildings, which the goodness of the governor provided for them. One should give credit where credit is due. Something that should be nothing but the most elementary duty of a Turkish official toward his Ottoman subjects must, under the present circumstances, be considered an act of special, yes, almost heroic humane-ness. Although the Armenians in Rakka are treated better than elsewhere, their misery is bad enough. Bread is distributed by the authorities only very irregularly and in absolutely insufficient quantities. Every day there are cues of women and children before the bakery shops begging for a morsel of flour. One comes across hundreds of beggars in the streets. Always the cruel torture of starvation! One must also consider that among the starving population there are not a few who have held high positions in the social life, and who must conceivably suffer doubly under these deprivations. Yesterday they were rich and envied. Today they do not hesitate to beg the poorest for a piece of bread.

On the right bank of the Euphrates, opposite Rakka, I found also thousands of Armenians, crammed into tents and guarded by soldiers. They were similarly starved. They were waiting to be transported further on to fill the rows of their dead predecessors. But how many of them will ever reach their destination?

5.

Sierrat is situated north of Rakka. 1,800 Armenians camp there and they suffer more under the hunger than anywhere else. In Sierrat there is nothing but desert. Groups of women and children roam along the river in search of a few strands of herbs to still their hunger. Others collapse under the eyes of their indifferent, merciless guards. A barbaric order, barbaric in every sense, prohibits anyone to leave the confines of the camp without special permission, under punishment of bastonnade.

Semga is a small village where 250 to 300 Armenians are kept under the same conditions, the same sad situation as everywhere else.

6.

Der-el-Zor is the seat of the governor of the province by the same name. A few months ago, 30,000 Armenians in various camps outside of town were encamped under the protection of the governor, Mutessarif Ali Suad Bey. Although I would like to abstain from any personal remarks, I would like to remember this man's name, who has a heart, and to whom the deportees are grateful, for he tried to lighten their miseries. He is to be thanked for the fact that some of the Armenians were permitted to earn something for themselves by dealing in the streets, and they did fairly well at that.—This proves that even if one is prepared for a moment to admit a reason of state for the mass-deportation of the Armenians to preclude a solution to the Armenian Question, it was surely not necessary for the Turkish authorities to betray basic humanity in the interests of the state, had they only sent the Armenians into areas where they could have found work, or could have engaged in trade. They could have been sent to more cultivated regions, where agriculture is so neglected, that plenty of work would have been available to them. But no, it was a premeditated plan to annihilate the Armenian race, and thus to settle the Armenian Question once and for all. This would not have been achieved under more humane conditions.—The mitigating circumstances, under which the Armenians of Der-el-Zor existed, became the cause for a denunciation at the Central Authorities in Constantinople. The 'guilty' Ali Suad Bey was sent to Baghdad and replaced by Zekki Bey who is well known for his cruelty and barbarism. I was told horrible things that happened under the rule of the new governor. Imprisonments, fiendish tortures, bastonnades, and hangings were the order of the day. They were the daily bread of the deportees in this town. Young girls were raped and left to the Arabic nomads in the vicinity. Children were thrown into the river. Ali Suad Bey, this rare example of a Turkish official, had lodged about 1,000 children in a large house, where they were fed at the cost of the municipality. His successor, Zekki Bey, drove them into the streets, where they died like dogs from starvation and deprivation. There is more. The 30,000 Armenians, who were located in Der-el-Zor, were sent into the region along the Chabur river, a tributary of the Euphrates; this is the worst region of the desert, where it is impossible to find any kind of food. From the information I have received, a major portion of these deportees are already dead. Those that still remain alive, will inevitably share the same fate.*

It is not our purpose here to quote all or even most of the many hearbreaking accounts of suffering and death that are available to us. The tragedy was too immense to be grasped through repetition or an endless recital of horrors. For a unique view of the genocide by one of the survivors, the reader might well go to the recently published work by Abraham H. Hartunian, an Armenian clergyman, whom we have already liberally quoted in Chapter 2 in connection with the Hamidian massacres of 1895–1896.

It was the Reverend Hartunian's lot to live through both of the massacres and to set down the experiences he shared with millions of the less fortunate. His memoirs of the terrible events were for many years confined to his family (he died in 1938), but his son Vartan Hartunian has ably translated them from the Armenian so that this eloquent document is available to all who would know what it was like to endure the agony of the forgotten genocide.

Despite the unimpeachable evidence of witnesses, the accu-

* The preceding quotations from Dr. Johannes Lepsius' book *Deutschland und Armenien, 1914–1918* were translated from the German by Wolfgang K. Herrmann.

rate documentation, and the almost universal outcry against the Turkish actions, amazingly enough Turkey has had its apologists, most notoriously perhaps Pierre Loti, the French poet. One of the abler Turkish writers on the subject is Ahmed Emin, whose book, *Turkey in the World War,* discusses the Armenians in Chapter XVIII.

The book in general seems to be a scholarly presentation of the conditions in Turkey prior to, during, and subsequent to the Great War. We are primarily, I should say, solely, concerned with the chapter pertaining to the Armenians.

The author begins with some statistics and credits the *Encyclopedia Britannica* with the following, as quoted from his book:

> The population of the nine Turkish villayets, Erzerum, Van, Bitlis, Kharput, Diarbekir, Sivas, Aleppo, Adana, and Trebizond, was 6,000,000 (Armenians, 913,875 or 15 per cent; other Christians 632,875 or 11 per cent; Moslems, 4,453,250, or 74 percent). In the first five villayets which contain most of the Armenians, the population was 2,642,-000 (Armenians 633,250 or 24 per cent; other Christians, 179,875, or 7 per cent; Moslems, 1,828,875 or 69 per cent); and in the seven Armenian kazas or districts, the population was 282,375 (Armenians 184,875 or 65 per cent; other Christians 1,000 or 3 per cent; Moslems 96,500 or 34.7 per cent). (p. 212)[5]

Now let us see the statistics published in the *Encyclopedia Britannica,* The Twelfth Edition, Volume 30, 1922, p. 197.

Since Mr. Emin accepts *Encyclopedia Britannica* as expressing the truth, let us pursue the matter a little further. We quote the following from the said Volume 30:

> Armenian estimates of the losses suffered by their people as the result of the Young Turk measures are liable to be excessive. It is in the nature of things that they should be. But if we place the loss of life directly and indirectly caused by massacre and deportation since the year 1914 as being in the neighbourhood of three-quarters of a million we cannot be far from the truth. In addition are what may be called the legitimate losses of war, and those, in proportion to the manhood of the Armenian race, were enormous. . .

The Six Armenian Vilayets of Asia Minor in 1914

	Bitlis	Diarbekir	Erzerum	Mamuret el Aziz	Sivas	Van	Total
Armenians	185,000	82,000	205,000	130,000	200,000	190,000	992,000
Moslems	261,000	400,000	540,000	480,000	977,000	260,000	2,918,000
Other elements	19,000	78,000	15,000	2,000	108,000	133,000	355,000
Totals	465,000	500,000	760,000	612,000	1,285,000	583,000	4,265,000

Note: According to the above chart the Armenians constitute 23.5% of the total population. Further, the *Britannica* does not mention Aleppo, Adana and Trebizond and the figures given therein as to the Vilayets of Erzerum, Van, Bitlis, Kharput (Mamuret el Aziz) and Diarbekir do not correspond with the figures presumably quoted by Mr. Emin. Let us repeat:

	Erzerum	Van	Bitlis	Kharput	Diarbekir	Total
Total population	760,000	583,000	465,000	612,000	500,000	2,920,000
Armenians	205,000	190,000	185,000	130,000	82,000	792,000

The percentage of the Armenians according to the above chart is 27% plus.

Probably not less than one sixth of the males of the whole race perished in warfare in addition to loss by massacre and deportation. (p. 198)

Taking those figures as accepted by Mr. Emin, i.e., 913,875 Armenians of whom 750,000 lost their lives, we can truthfully state that 82% of the Armenians were killed in one way or another, and all by the order of the leaders of Turkey.

It may not be entirely out of place if we quote a little more of the *Encyclopedia Britannica:*

It is unnecessary to follow in detail the execution of the infamous policy for the destruction of the Armenian population of Asia Minor. Suffice to say it was begun soon after the outbreak of war by *concocting* [Emphasis ours—D.H.B.] reports of Armenian revolutionary plots in support of the Allied Powers; and then, as far as possible, by a general disarmament of Ottoman Armenians. Though British operations in Gallipoli and Mesopotamia and Russian operations against the eastern vilayets, kept the Turks occupied in a military sense, they did not prevent Turkish activity against Armenians. During the spring and summer of 1915, indeed, when the fate of Constantinople and Turkey hung in the balance and inhabitants of the Imperial City daily scanned the Sea of Marmora for signs of an approaching British fleet, the Young Turk government prosecuted their Armenian policy with the utmost vigour. But when the Gallipoli operations had plainly failed, and the outcome of the war was thought to be no longer in doubt, a Turkish defeat in Russian Armenia, attributed by Enver Pasha to the Armenians, was revenged upon the race by massacres of even greater ferocity. From first to last they were organized and carried out systematically. Massacres on the largest scale took place at Bitlis, Mush, Sivas, Kharput, Trebizond—wherever, in fact, a considerable and more or less defenseless Armenian population existed. The people were butchered in masses, butchered in groups, drowned in the Black Sea and in rivers, burnt in buildings —killed by whatever processes were found most ready and convenient. Girls were placed in Turkish harems. It should not be supposed, however, that no resistance was offered, that the Armenian people sold their lives cheaply. Although supposed to have been disarmed, weapons remained, and on numberless occasions, in untold villages and towns, a hopeless resistance inflicted severe losses on the attackers.

Deportation, too, became an easy indirect means of destroying Armenian life. On the long routes of eastern Asia Minor by which movement took place; on the subsidiary roads leading to these routes; at the great concentration centers on which the columns of suffering humanity were directed, the Armenian people died of hunger, exhaustion, exposure, disease, in tens of thousands, perhaps in hundreds of thousands. Only a comparatively small proportion of those who set out reached the destination assigned to them. The policy of transferring an Armenian population to Mesopotamia and Syria became in execution a wholesale means of destroying those who were dispatched. (p. 198)

In defense of their actions, Mr. Emin writes, the Party of Union and Progress, in a report presented to their party conference in 1916 offered the following justification of the deportation:

"As soon as the order of mobilization was issued, Turkish Armenians crossed the frontiers on their way to Egypt, Bulgaria, Rumania, and Russia, and joined the Russian army or bands of Armenian irregulars. The various revolutionary organizations temporarily dropped their differences and held a general meeting. They decided to start disorders, massacres, and acts of incendiarism behind the front in case Turkey entered the War, and to induce Armenian soldiers to desert with their weapons. Bands composed of such deserters were to menace the lines of communication of the Turkish army."[6]

There are numerous sources, other than M. Mandelstam whom the author of the book quotes, who emphatically refute these charges and brand them as false. But since Mr. Emin likes to quote the *Encyclopedia Britannica* we would refer him to the passage quoted above: "Massacres on the largest scale took place at Bitlis, Mush, Sivas, Kharput, Trebizond— wherever, in fact, a considerable and more or less *defenseless* [Emphasis ours—D.H.B.] Armenian population existed."

The truth is that a definite scheme to exterminate the

Armenian people was adopted years before "the order of mobilization was issued." Many people have testified to the existence of such a scheme. Among these many we refer to an authoritative source, the letter of Mehmed Cherif Pasha to the Editor of *Journal de Geneve* and reproduced in *The New York Times,* September 21, 1915. (See pp. 345–346)

Speaking about the Turkish policy of massacre and deportation *Encyclopedia Britannica* says:

How the policy for dealing with the Armenian part of the question took form we do not know. Probably Tal'at Pasha and Enver Pasha had as much to do with it as any —Tal'at at least is credited with its application—but they only sought to follow, on a greater scale, the example set in past years by Abdul Hamid. A preposterous and cynical scheme of compulsory colonization as part of the policy has been attributed to German theorists; but it was not even a mask except as affording greater opportunities for destroying the Armenia population. Described in a few words the policy was that of deportation coupled with extermination. The Armenian race was to be uprooted from the wide territories of Asia Minor beyond the hope of continuance or return . . . Armenians from provinces too distant for deportation to be practicable were to be exterminated or driven to a fugitive existence." (*Encyclopedia Britannica,* Vol. 30, p. 197)

Mr. Emin writes on page 218 of his book:

"On the eve of the World War, the Armenian Dachnakzoutioun party applied for permission to hold a party congress in Erzeroum. Permission being withheld, the congress was held secretly. It came to the conclusion that a Russo-Turkish war might mean calamity for the Armenians, that they should therefore abstain from hasty action until the outcome of such a war should become clear, and that they should cooperate with the Russians in case of a Russian invasion."

According to a report published in the *Gazette de Lausanne,* February 13, 1916 (reprinted from the Russian press) Mr. Emin's assertions are not correct. The following are extracts from that report published in *The Treatment of Armenians in the Ottoman Empire, 1915–1916,* pages 80–82:

> At the beginning of the European War, the 'Dashnak-tzoutioun' party met in congress at Erzeroum in order to decide on the attitude to be observed by the Party. As soon as they heard of this congress, the Young Turks sent their representatives to Erzeroum to propose that the Party should declare its intention of aiding and defending Turkey, *by organizing an insurrection in the Caucasus* [Emphasis ours—D.H.B.] in the event of a declaration of war between Turkey and Russia. According to the project of the Young Turks, the Armenians were to pledge themselves to form legions of volunteers and to send them to the Caucasus with Turkish propagandists, to prepare the way there for insurrection . . . The Erzeroum Congress refused these proposals, and advised the Young Turks not to hurl themselves into the European conflagration—a dangerous adventure which would lead Turkey to ruin.

"A short time after the proclamation of war by Russia (in the first days of December 1914)," writes Mr. Emin, "the whole plain was invaded by the Armenian volunteer division wearing Russian uniforms. One of the regiments was commanded by M. Pastirmadjian, the deputy from Erzeroum in the Turkish parliament. The local Armenian population amounted to 10 or 12 per cent of the total. The Turco-Kurdish population was entirely defenseless, because government forces did not exist, and the tribal warriors, who formed a light cavalry division, had been sent to the front. Within eighteen days the whole local Mohammedan population had been massacred by Armenian soldiers helped by local Armenians. Only one-tenth managed to escape, and only a small part of them managed to reach the other side of the mountains.

"These events created an unofficial state of war between the Armenians and the Turks. By April, 1915, hostilities were general. On April 20, the town of Van, in which the Armenians were in the majority, was seized by local Armenians

with the aid of leaders coming from Russia, and a temporary Armenian government was instituted."[7]

The facts have been exaggerated by Mr. Emin if not wholly
distorted. Let us see what the *Encyclopedia Britannica* says
about the Armenian troops in the Russian army:

"Here it may be remarked that when Russia mobilized in
August, 1914, for the World War, her Armenian troops, numbering, it is said, more than 120,000 men, were dispatched,
to the European fronts. When war with Turkey demanded
great armies in Trans-Caucasia these troops were not available. But as a matter of policy Russia raised an auxiliary volunteer army of Armenians including *many thousands* of
refugees [Emphasis ours—D.H.B.] from Asia Minor, for
service against the mortal enemy of their race." (Vol. 30,
p. 198)

Mr. Emin quotes a paragraph from the "War Memoirs" of
Lieutenant Colonel Tucerdo Khlebof, "commander of the second Russian fortress artillery regiment stationed at Erzeroum until the recapture of the town by the Turks on
February 27, 1918." That paragraph merits reproduction:

> At the time of the Russian occupation of Erzeroum, in
> 1916, not a single Armenian was allowed to approach, and
> so long as General Kalivine, head of the First Army Corps,
> was in command of this district, divisions in which there
> were Armenians were not sent there. After the Revolution
> all earlier measures were annulled. The Armenians forced
> their way into Erzeroum, immediately began to pillage the
> town and villages, to measure the inhabitants, and to com-
> mit all sorts of excesses.[8]

It is a known fact that the Russian Revolution took place
in the fall of 1917, when the entire Armenian population of
Turkey, with the exception of Constantinople and the extreme western part of the country, had been deported, massacred, or died on route by exhaustion, slaughter, disease or
criminal assault. How can one blame the Armenian volunteers for reprisals, at the sight of their devastated homes,

desecrated churches, and slaughter of their loved ones?

Mr. Emin categorically rejects the assertion of Djemal Pasha that 1,500,000 Turks were "massacred by Armenians after the Russian Revolution." Here is what he says:

". . . with the Russian military authorities acting vigilantly to save the lives of the Turks, those actually massacred by Armenians in the period between the Russian Revolution and the Turkish reoccupation can hardly have exceeded 40,000."[9]

The statement about the institution of "a temporary Armenian government in Van" is intended to give a false impression by the deliberate omission of pertinent facts that would be decisive if expressed truthfully. We refer the reader (see Index) to the lengthy report of Miss Grace Higley Knapp, an eye-witness to the happenings in Van, and to the statements made by Dr. Clarence D. Ussher in his book entitled *An American Physician in Turkey*.

Under the sub-heading "Russian Armenians and Local Revolts," the author of *Turkey in the World War*, after mentioning the alleged desertions in the army, writes:

After Russia's proclamation of war Armenian volunteer formations crossed the border in Bayizid, devastated villages, massacred Mohammedans, cut the railroad between Van and Bitlis, destroyed bridges and telegraph lines, attacked Turkish detachments, and engaged in out and out war with the forces of Turkey. They seized Zeitoun in February, massacring all Mohammedan families. Twenty-five hundred armed Armenians seized the town of Van on April 20, and set up a temporary Armenian government. On April 12, several thousand armed deserters created disorders around Diar-Bekr. In Sivas, an Armenian force of 30,000 deserters was organized, with a view of making rear attacks upon the army on the Russian front. On June 12, the Armenians of Kara-Hissar revolted and massacred the Mohammedans in the town. In Marash, armed bands of five hundred or more Armenians disturbed the public peace. Revolutionary documents and arms were seized almost everywhere. The Turkish army, being thus between two fires, it became necessary to deport Armenians from the neighborhood of the front and from the vicinity of railroad and other lines of communications.[10]

We have already mentioned the volunteer units in the Russian army, for whom the Armenians in Turkey were not responsible. We have also exploded the myth of the "revolt" in Van. Speaking about these "volunteers" or "deserters" as having been "engaged in out and out war with the forces of Turkey" Mr. Emin states that they seized Zeitoun in February, massacring all Mohammedan families. Here is what the editor of *The Treatment of Armenians in the Ottoman Empire* writes:

> The case of Van, which the apologists have made so much of, simply falls to the ground, and they cannot rehabilitate themselves by adducing any previous revolt at Zeitoun. It is true that twenty-five fugitive conscripts defended themselves for a day in a Monastery near Zeitoun against Turkish troops and decamped into the mountains during the night. *But this happened only one day before the deportation* [Emphasis ours—D.H.B.] and the deportation must have been decided upon far in advance, for it was preceded by a protracted inquisition for arms, and there were Moslem refugees from the Balkans concentrated on the spot, ready to occupy the Zeitounlis' houses the moment the rightful owners were carried off. During all these preliminary proceedings—most of which were violations of the charter of liberties held by Zeitoun from the Ottoman Government—the population as a whole (15,000 individuals as against the 25 who rebelled) very scrupulously kept the peace. This was the policy of the leaders, and they were obeyed by the people. Nothing happened at Zeitoun that can account for the Government's scheme of deportation.[11]

The diary of "a foreign resident" in a town in Cilicia communicated to a Swiss gentleman of Geneva, printed on pp. 482–486 of the same volume is worth reading.

> A foreign resident in a letter dated July 13, 1915 writes in part: To begin with the all-important fact which may have reached you by now, the Armenians of the interior are being deported in the direction of Mosul. At the time

we left Sivas, two-thirds of them had gone from the city
. . . This general movement against Armenians began
months ago in arrests for alleged revolutionary activity
and in searches for guns and bombs. In Sivas, the winter
passed rather quietly, and it was late spring before much
was done. About two months ago a general endeavor was
made to imprison all the leading Armenians, and within
a week more than 1,000 were arrested. I estimate the whole
number of Sivas men in prison to be between 1,500 and
2,000 (*The Treatment of Armenians in Turkey.*)[12]

Mr. Emin further alleges that "In Sivas, an Armenian force
of 30,000 deserters were organized, with a view of making
rear attacks upon the army on the Russian front." The writer
fails to state just when and where these forces were concentrated. The city of Sivas is about 250 miles from Erzeroum
and 400 miles from the Russian border, as the crow flies.

The myth of "30,000 deserters" is no more than this: "a
few villages took up arms in the vilayet of Sivas, after the
rest of Sivas Armenians had been deported." If Mr. Emin
had been sincere in his efforts he would have been able to
ascertain and report the true facts; that every act of "desertion" and "rebellion" took place *after* the major act of genocide had been put into operation, and that they "were simply
attempts at self-defence by people who had seen their neighbours massacred or deported, and they themselves were
threatened with the same fate." He writes: "The Armenians
in Kara-Hissar revolted and massacred the Mohammedans
in the town." But here is how the editor of *The Treatment
of Armenians in Turkey* puts it: ". . . at Shabin Kara-Hissar
the Armenians *drove out* [Emphasis ours—D.H.B.] their
Turkish fellow townsmen and stood for several weeks at bay,
when they heard how the exiles from Trebizond and Kera-
sond had been murdered on the road." (pp. 628–629). Mohammedans of Kara-Hissar were *driven out*, not *massacred.*

Mr. Emin further alleges: "Revolutionary documents and
arms were seized almost everywhere."

On page 296 of *The Treatment of Armenians in the Ottoman Empire* there is a footnote wherein the editor says that

"the Armenians of Kara-Hissar had been overwhelmed by force and massacred to the last woman and child, with their bishop at their head."

Mr. Emin as well as the Turks generally "make sweeping allegations about secret stores of bombs and arms, which prove to be false in every case when they can be checked." The Armenians certainly possessed a moderate number of rifles and revolvers because, for the past six years, under the Young-Turkish regime, they had been permitted to carry arms for their personal security, a privilege that had always been enjoyed, as a matter of course, by every Moslem in the Ottoman Empire. But evidently there were not enough arms in their possession to go around, even among the comparatively few men left behind after mobilization; for when, in the winter of 1914–15, the Ottoman authorities made a house-to-house search for arms, and conducted their inquisition by atrocious physical tortures, the Armenians bought arms from each other and from their Moslem neighbours, in order to be able to deliver them up and suffer no worse punishment than mere imprisonment. This practice is recorded independently by several trustworthy witnesses from various localities.

We respectfully refer our readers to the following documents in *The Treatment of Armenians in Turkey*: Document 68, p. 271; Document 82, p. 320; Document 94, p. 328; and Document 122, p. 479.

> The stories of bombs are still more extravagant. In the town of X., for instance, a bomb was unearthed in the Armenian cemetery, which was made the pretext for the most atrocious procedure against the Armenian inhabitants. Yet the bomb was rusty with age, and was believed to date from the days of Abd-ul-Hamid, when the Young Turks, as well as the Armenian political parties, were a secret revolutionary organization and not averse to using bombs themselves. In the same town, a blacksmith in the employment of the American College, was cruelly tortured for "constructing a bomb"; but the "bomb" turned out to be a solid iron shot which he had been commissioned to

make for the competition of "putting the weight" in the College athletic sports.[13]

After asserting that "the deportations taken as a whole were meant to be only a temporary military measure," Mr. Emin admits that "for certain influential Turkish politicians they meant the extermination of the Armenian minority in Turkey with the idea of bringing about racial homogeneity in Asia Minor."[14]

REFERENCES

1. Johannes Lepsius, *Deutschland und Armenien,* Tempelverlag, Potsdam, 1919.

2. George Horton, *The Blight of Asia* (Indianapolis: Bobbs-Merrill), 1926, p. 263.

3. Lepsius, *op. cit.,* pp. 220ff.

4. Lt.-Col. Stange, quoted by Lepsius, *op. cit.,* pp. 138ff.

5. Ahmed Emin, *Turkey in the World War* (New Haven: Yale University Press), 1930, p. 212.

6. *Ibid.,* p. 215.

7. *Ibid.,* p. 218–219.

8. *Ibid.,* p. 222.

9. *Ibid.,* p. 222.

10. *Ibid.,* p. 216.

11. Viscount Bryce, ed., pp. 267–268.

12. *Ibid.,* p. 302.

13. Bryce, ed., *op. cit.,* p. 630.

14. Emin, *op. cit.,* p. 220.

Chapter 5

After the Holocaust

Almost from the very beginning of the genocide of 1915–16, as reports reached America and Western Europe of the unbelievable atrocities being inflicted on a helpless, abandoned people, reaction was swift and strong. Before the genocide had even run its course, there was widespread demand for compensation of the Armenians to the degree possible; and the assumption that the survivors would be granted a homeland, either independently or under an Allied mandate, was soon incorporated into official agreements and treaties.

The agony of the Armenians came to no merciful end with 1916, however. It was destined to continue indefinitely, even though the defeat of Turkey in October, 1918; the formation of a short-lived independent Armenian Republic in that same year; the prevailing opinion at the Paris Peace Conference; and the Treaty of Sevres all indicated at least minimal justice in the settling of their case.

Events in the postwar years were to provide the ultimate disillusionment in the Armenian community. Divisions among the victorious Allies, the French abandonment of Cilicia, the Greek disaster at Smyrna in 1922, with its attendant massacre yet again of thousands of Armenians, and the final betrayal at Lausanne in 1923, all of these were crucial in depriving the Armenian remnant of even the semblance of justice. Never has so worthy a supplicant for justice been so callously abandoned as in this critical period.

The period 1916–1924 saw many efforts by the most enlightened men of the age to secure justice to the Armenians, and their validity remains to this day. Of all the testimonials left us from this period, perhaps none carries the weight of the Harbord Mission report to the U.S. Congress in 1920. A document of the utmost importance, the Harbord report is reproduced in full in this chapter—read today, after more than half a century, it is still a model of fairness, balance, and unvengeful eloquence.

This chapter, then, attempts to recreate the conditions of the years just after the genocide. They were eventful years in the world at large, for they coincided with tremendous convulsions within a war-exhausted Europe and a newly isolationist America. In Turkey, the rise at this time of Kemal Ataturk had incalculable effects on the Armenian cause, for it was just the appearance of strength that he was able to project that made Allied pressure on Turkey ultimately ineffectual, especially where Armenia was concerned.

1.   *The Sykes-Picot Agreement, May 16, 1916*

Sir Mark Sykes, representing Great Britain and M. George Picot, representing France entered into an agreement, by the terms of which Turkey was divided into arbitrarily defined spheres of influence. The French sphere was to include Cilicia, Southern Armenia and Syria. The British sphere was to include Haifa and Mesopotamia. Russia was to obtain the Armenian provinces of Erzeroum, Trebizond, Van and Bitlis, and the land in the southern part of Kurdistan.

In a later agreement, known as the St. Jean de Maurienne Agreement, signed on April 17, 1917 between Great Britain, France and Italy, after Italy declared war on Germany and her allies, she was allowed to keep the Dodecanese islands and a sphere of influence on the adjacent mainland (Adalia).

2.   *The Treaty of Mudros, October 30, 1918*

This Treaty "ended the hostilities between the Allied Powers and Turkey. Better days seemed now to be in sight for the Armenian race. Turkey was crushed, the Young Turk Government had fallen into disrepute, the chief leaders were in flight, and it was the avowed purpose of the Allies to force the subject races of the Ottoman Empire from Turkish rule. The armistice contained conditions that speedily relieved the position for the Armenians." (*Encyclopedia Britannica*, Vol. 30, page 200)

According to the terms of the Treaty the Allies reserved the right to occupy any part of Turkey which may have had strategic importance. The Treaty further provided that the six Armenian vilayets—Van, Bitlis, Harpoot, Erzeroum, Diarbekir and Trebizond—and the Cilician territory be given to the Armenians.

On May 28, 1918 the Armenians declared their independence after 543 years of subjugation and servitude. The nation, weak though it was, raised its head through misery, devastation and want, and was determined to assert itself and defend its rights, whatever the cost. Born to misfortune and bloodshed, surrounded by enemies, and inaccessible to its friends, the Armenian state had to survive. There was one thing in its favor—its people were *united*. There was no dissension, no division, no parting of ways; the Armenian people had to become "one nation indivisible under God," for survival. The needs were enormous: food, clothing, munitions and medical supplies, as well as experienced administrative and executive officers.

In September 1918, Turkish armies on the Palestine front crumbled before the British Expeditionary forces which contained an American contingent commanded by a French colonel and French and Armenian officers. The Armenian soldiers distinguished themselves in the battle of Arara on that front, and their bravery was well recognized by the Supreme Commander of the Army, Marshall Edmund Allenby.

With its armies completed defeated and dispersed, Turkey sued for peace. Most of its leaders who had plunged Turkey into war and had caused the near extermination of the Armenian people, fled the country. On October 30, 1918 the Armistice of Mudros was signed, giving new hope to Armenians. By the opening of the Straits, it became possible to supply the people of an almost destitute country with food and clothing.

The signing of the armistice with the Central Powers on November 11, 1918, and subsequent peace negotiations, led the Armenians to believe that an independent Armenia containing within its boundaries all of the Armenian provinces in Turkey, including Cilicia, would be created.

Anxious months rolled on without a definite plan. All the Allied Powers had been lavish in their praise of the Armenians and had made excessive promises.

3.   *The Situation in the East*

The government of the Armenian Republic had not fared well. In January of 1919 a dispute over boundaries resulted in war between Armenia and Georgia, countries which had existed side by side for centuries and had often joined forces in their mutual defense against common enemies. It was not a major war but was bad enough to weaken the Armenians further.

Then came the Bolshevik invasion of Caucasia. Batum was occupied in April, 1920. Azerbaijan succumbed to Communist threats and established a Soviet government. Pressure was brought upon Armenia by the Russians in the North and by the Turks in the south. An attack on Erivan by the Bolshevik forces in Azerbaijan in May, 1920, met with determined resistance by the Armenians and failed. An abortive revolt within the country was also subdued.

But that did not insure a safe existence for the tottering government of Armenia. A larger and much more serious threat was in the offing. By the end of September, when Bolshevik forces of Azerbaijan were deployed on the northern frontier, a Turkish Nationalist army attacked Armenia without warning. The enemy advance was checked temporarily, but not decisively. Soon the fortress of Kars fell. The city of Alexandropol (now Leninakan) was occupied, "the resistance of the Republic collapsed," and the Armenians sued for peace.

A humiliating treaty was forced on the Armenians by triumphant Turks at Alexandropol, on December 2, 1920, less than four months after the victorious Allied Powers had solemnly created an independent Armenia.

S. Vratzian, the Premier of the provisional government, following the overthrow of the Communist regime, in his *Armenia Between the Bolshevik Hammer and Turkish Anvil*, Beirut, 1953, quotes the Treaty of Alexandropol as summarized by A. Khadisian, President of the Armenian Delegation. The following excerpts will suffice for our purpose:

1. The Great National Assembly of Turkey is bound to recognize the independence of Armenia in the following boundaries: (Sets forth the boundaries).
2. The province of Kars and Sourmalou shall remain unsettled for three years, during which the Armenian government shall submit the question to referendum to determine the final fate of these provinces. A mixed Armenian-Turkish gendarmerie shall supervise the voting.
3. The Armenians shall renounce the Treaty of Sevres and shall recall all the committees and representatives that exist in Europe, and shall maintain in Armenia no Allied representatives until Turkey signs a treaty of peace with them.
4. Armenia shall have the right to maintain an army with not more than 1500 firearms and a comparable number of officers and a necessary number of gendarmes. There may be forts for the defense of the country, armed with only defensive guns. Compulsory military conscription shall be abolished.
5. In the event of an attack on Armenia, Turkey, at the request of the Armenian government will actively defend Armenia.

– – – – –

9. All agreements of Armenia against Turkey are declared invalid. (pp. 134–135)

Within hours after the signing of the Treaty of Alexandropol the Government of the Armenian Republic capitulated by surrendering their powers to a provisional government organized by the Communists consistent with the Manifesto which was made public on November 29th. Armenia became a part of the Soviet Union as one of its republics.

Atrocities continued in localities which remained in Turkish hands. It has been reliably reported that in Kars alone more than 10,000 Armenians were killed. In the region of Alexandropol, where the notorious treaty was signed, 30,000 men and 30,000 women and children were mercilessly slaughtered. Besides these, about 32,000 perished by starvation.

The Soviet government of Armenia inherited nothing but a disillusioned and discouraged citizenry and a bankrupt country deprived of the most essential needs for existence. The new administration, led by men of limited experience but with an exaggerated opinion of their abilities to govern, was unable to allay the fears of the people that the Bolsheviks had come to dominate as autocrats, not to rule as liberators.

Then came the "revolution." In February 1921 a segment of the people revolted against the Communist regime and overthrew the government, causing bloodshed, misery and destruction at a time when the Armenian people were in desperate need of peace and quiet, more than anything else, to make total use of their skill and energy to rebuild their homes and stabilize their economy.

The "revolutionary" government was not able to rule peacefully. The fighting continued with a vengeance in all parts of the country and in a matter of weeks, the Communist forces were in complete control of the situation and the Communist government came into power again, this time for good. A new set of leaders was entrusted with guiding the destiny of the Armenian people.

For twenty years (1921–1941) the Armenian S.S.R. as one of the 15 Soviet Socialist Republics, with a population of about 1,500,000 and an area of 11,500 square miles, devoted itself to the development of all the resources of the country and to the improvement of the living conditions of its people. With a large portion of the country arid and unproductive, it required superhuman efforts to build canals for irrigation purposes. The waters of Lake Sevan, locked in a mountain valley 6,000 feet above sea level, were tapped by an enormous hydro-electric plant designed and constructed by Armenian engineers and architects. Powerful turbines were installed by the lake about 250 feet deep in the ground, in which the waters rushed with a terrific speed and down the side of the mountain to enrich the barren soil of the country. Vast areas were thus reclaimed and once treeless mountainsides were converted into vineyards, orchards and tillable land to produce wheat, rye and other grains and to raise vegetables and fruits.

The plans for public education from kindergarten to university level received tremendous impetus. Attendance in public schools is compulsory and is rigidly enforced by the state. In August 1930, a project for the reconstruction of the State University of Erevan, was formally adopted and set to work. Programs for adult education gradually reduced illiteracy in Armenia to a minimum. Public education, however, received a severe blow by the tragic persecutions, or purges, as they were generally called, during the years between 1936 and 1938. Men of great literary and intellectual attainments were victimized ruthlessly without any justifiable cause.

There was a period in the thirties when the situation in Armenia reached a tragic stage. In the entire Soviet Union mistrust, suspicion, purges, executions and mass exiles were the order of the day. Men and women of notable achievements and great responsibilities in the life of the people became victims of these purges. The Armenian people suffered a similar fate. Many of its leaders were executed; tens of thousands of its people were exiled to Siberia. Only a small percentage survived and was allowed to return home.

World War II further reduced many of the activities of

the people to a minimum. All able-bodied men and women became engaged in the defense of the Soviet Union, of which Armenia was an integral part. The role played by Armenia in that war can be measured by the tremendous losses in manpower it suffered. It carried more than its proportionate share in the global conflict.

With the ending of hostilities, the government and people of Armenia tightened their belts and embarked upon new programs to industrialize the country, to expand its building construction, to tap its natural resources, to increase the acreage of its tillable land, to improve their production methods, to enlarge the scope of their educational institutions and scientific establishments, to provide more adequate hospitals, better medical and nursing care, to increase medical facilities and in general improve their conditions in every way possible.

Blessed with continued peace since the ending of the second global war and completely free from external threats and internal disturbances, the Armenians in Soviet Armenia have made tremendous strides in every line of endeavor. They have enriched the country physically, intellectually, morally and industrially, by building roads, bridges, parks, factories, public buildings, educational, scientific and cultural institutions, hospitals, infirmaries, health resorts, etc. The Government Printing Press prints and distributes annually over 1,000 books in several million copies. Complete works of men of letters of the recent and distant past are being reproduced in accordance with a meticulously prepared plan.

Cultural endeavors enjoy top priority in Armenia. Poet, writer, musician, playwright, actor, teacher, scientist, etc., command unusual respect. Culture is considered the greatest single factor in the life, progress and accomplishments of the people.

The population in Armenia has almost tripled since 1920, from about 800,000 to well over 2,500,000. The population of Erivan, the capital of the country, was 37,000 in 1926; it now has over 750,000. That is an increase of almost 2000%.

It is estimated that by 1980, the population of Armenia will pass the 3,000,000 mark.

Let us now return to the period just after World War 1. Speaking in Paris, Paul Painleve, former president of the Council of France, is quoted in *France et Armenie:*[1]

> We have gathered to-day to pay homage to Armenia, not only to martyred Armenia, but heroic Armenia. You are aware of the sinister, diabolic plan of deportations, the plan by which 1,500,000 Armenians were driven to fara-away deserts, without food, and were massacred on long routes, without mercy! You know that thousands of women and children were thrown into the Euphrates, the sight of which defies all imagination. We know this from the re-ports of German missionaries and Germans who witnessed its horror. One should read the descriptions by such mis-sionaries from Munich who declare that their eyes were unable to keep from their sight the spectacle of long lines of children so sweet, with long blond hair, with innocent looks, who were going towards the river into which they were to be thrown! All these little angels who are around God's throne to-day raise their protests.
>
> But let us talk no more about these horrors; we know them, they are very well known. I dare say, because a sim-ple description of the facts appears as a martyrdom of a whole people to such an extent that in the imagination of many Armenia seems only a memory of a people that ex-ists no more. I am convinced also that this idea runs through the minds of certain people that Armenia was a country doomed to destruction, that the Armenians from a long time of slaves led to slaughter, because they were too gentle, incapable of defending themselves, and per-haps for that reason certain opinions adapt themselves to the old saying, I do not know by which Machiavelli, that after the executioner what is most odious in a persecution are the victims who should have been able to defend them-selves!
>
> This legend must be dispelled: the Armenian people have not been without strength, without courage, without resistance, who would allow themselves to be massacred, to extend their neck to the butcher's knife! On the con-

trary, there is nothing in history more admirable than the resistance against all forces of destruction and, in particular, I would like to make this statement as the basic theme of this brief speech, because it is Armenia that has been placed in the cross-beam of the pan-Germanic plan, because it did not want to let the Touranian hordes proceed towards India, that it has suffered abominable massacres for the likes of which history has given no example to this day.

We must not forget that more than a million women were subjected to cruel tortures because they refused to be converted by force. Oh! certainly, Armenians are artists profoundly; they are gentle, they hate violence; but that does not mean that they are only musical people, a people whose admirable liturgy utters a cry of anguish and thought . . . Armenians are a valiant people, and from the moment they obtained arms, they fought heroically with all their means, and I wish to give you examples, true examples, examples which history will record as lofty deeds of a people with the right to live.

At the start of the war there were in France several thousand Armenians: the young volunteered. A column of 800 men was formed. Do you know how many of those remained alive? One-hundred, of whom fifty were unscathed and fifty wounded.

There were 150,000 men in the Russian Army, they were called the Armenian legions who followed the footsteps of Loris Melikoff, and upon notice by the Russian leaders, they fought in a manner to pay back to their enemies all the cruelties to which their ancestors were subjected. At Van, when the Russians were not yet in a position to attack, massacres began and were turned loose around the city. There were no arms; they were forged, they improvised, and with these home-made arms, the city drove away the Turks and Kurds and for many weeks stood against forces ten times greater, until the time when Russians arrived to free it.

At Lebanon, on an isolated hill* near the sea, 3,000 women and children left their homes to escape Turkish massacre. There were 500 young men with the group, with a few firearms, several projectiles, insufficient arms; courageously, with heroic strength, they held their position for

* M. Painleve refers to Musa-Dagh.

a month (40 days), in spite of the famine, against the repeated attacks of Turkish hordes, until they were liberated
by a French flotilla.

There is a beautiful page, very great, in the Armenian
defense. There lives in Armenia a legendary hero, Andra-
nik, called by the people "the hero of Armenian freedom."
At the beginning of the war he was the chief organizer of
the corps of volunteers; to the last day he fought against
the cruelty and tyranny of the persecutors . . .

You know that at all times a great effort has been exerted by the western civilization to maintain the peace
among the peoples of the old Orient. The humanitarian
work of France, among all the nations, has been persistent
and at the same time very generous. France in the East
—and that is where its prestige comes from—has always
searched for the welfare of humanity, to have peace and
harmony reign, same as Christian France, France of the
Crusades and France of the Revolution, and that is why in
these last years, since so much misfortune fell upon Armenia, men of all factions in France did their best to help
the persecuted nation and you have been able to listen to
eloquent words of a Jaures, a du Mun, a de Pressense, a
Marcelin Barthelot, and so many others, and all about this
sacred name: Armenia, as a sort of sacred union. Ah, well!
France should, in line with its past, be the first to raise
its voice so that the peril which I have just mentioned be
set aside once and for all. The tricolor flag and the flags
of other allies should finally shelter within their folds the
orphans and women of Armenia! On this venerable land,
where the sun rises, the sun of justice and liberty should
rise finally.

4. *Major General James G. Harbord,* a report of the American Military Commission, 1919.

A personal statement from Major General James G. Harbord, head of the American Military Mission which had in
1919 travelled by automobile, carriage, horseback and on
foot through practically all sections of Armenia, making a
full detailed investigation and report of conditions to the
United States Government:

Thousands must inevitably perish in the Near East this
winter unless American relief is continued. I speak of this

with conviction because of my recent investigation of conditions in Turkey in Asia and the Trans-Caucasus. Practical American philanthropy has kept alive a large portion of the Armenians, Syrians and Greeks and other destitute peoples of the Near East who certainly would have died of starvation and disease but for contributions from America. I was everywhere impressed with the pathetic trust with which these people depend upon America for the simplest necessities of life. Several hundred thousands of these people are still refugees in the Caucasus, unable to return to their homes until conditions are more settled.

Colonel Haskell, Allied High Commissioner for Armenia, reports that more than 800,000 are destitute in the Caucasus alone. Unless supplies are continued, at least 7,000 tons of wheat flour each month, there will inevitably be death from starvation there this winter on an unprecedented scale. In addition to food supplies, the hospitals, orphanages, soup kitchens and other institutions of the Near East Relief must be supported.

Most of the refugees are huddled in concentration camps. These people are normally industrious and thrifty. Now they are helpless. There are many thousands of children, many of whom have lost both parents and do not even know their own names. The Near East Relief is working with splendid courage and in spite of inadequate funds to save these little children. Their work is worthy of and demands the support of all Americans.

5. *Committee of the District of Alexandropol,* a report in 1920; translated from the *Distortion of the Modern Armenian History,* by E. Sarkisian and R. Sahagian.

In a report made by the Committee of the District of Alexandropol on December 20, 1920, the following appears:

Hitherto unseen and unheard-of crimes are being committed in the rural districts . . . All the villages have been pillaged, there is no live-stock, no provisions, no clothes, no fuel. The village streets are filled with corpses, to complete the picture hunger and cold arrive one after the other to take away more and more victims. This is nothing yet; all this became more intolerable, when soldiers ridicule their captives and are trying to punish the people in more horrible ways, and still not satisfied they seek more pleasure by subjecting them to various tortures; they force the parents to surrender to their executioners their own eight-year-old daughters and 20–25 year old sons. They rape the girls and murder the boys, and all this takes place before the very eyes of the parents. This is the way they treat all the villages; they cause the girls and women up to forty years of age to disappear, and they kill men up to 45 years of age. These villages are depopulated. This is a situation beyond description, without precedent.[2]

6. *J. Ellis Barker*, a review of *Deutschland und Armenien*, by Dr. Johannes Lepsius, published in the *Quarterly Review*, April 1920.[3]

The review comments in detail on the contents of the book wherein are described "authentic documents relating to Armenia, comprising more than 400 dispatches and telegrams exchanged between the Berlin authorities and the German Embassy in Constantinople . . . and between that Embassy and the German Consulates throughout the Turkish Empire . . . ."

A few quotations and the reproductions of several important documents from that highly illuminating review will be of great interest to our readers, especially since Dr. Lepsius' book has not been translated into English in its entirety, or at least we have not been able to find such translation in the public libraries in our region.

"The massacre of the Armenians is probably the greatest crime in modern history," writes Mr. Barker:

> The Armenians are an old and highly civilized Christian race. They are a peaceful people engaged in agriculture and especially in commerce and industry. The business of Turkey was chiefly carried on by the industrious Armenians . . . The murder of the Armenians was due not to Moslem fanaticism but to cold calculation on the part of the governing Turks. In their policy of extermination the Committee of Union and Progress followed in the footsteps of Sultan Abdul Hamid, Gladstone's "great assassin," whom they had deposed. At the Young-Turkish Congress held in Salonica in October 1911 the Committee of Union and Progress had formulated a Pan-Islamic programme

according to which the Mohammedans were to secure for themselves the paramountcy in Turkey by extirpating those non-Turkish and non-Islamic nationalities dwelling in Turkey which were not willing to amalgamate voluntarily with the Turks.

Turkey entered the war on November 1, 1914. On April 20, 1915 the Turkish Government reported that a grave Armenian rising had occurred in Van. This "rising," which furnished a welcome pretext to the Turkish Government, was according to Dr. Lepsius, not an act of aggression on the part of the Armenians but merely an act of legitimate self-defense. The Turks had arrested and murdered some of the leading Armenians and had then attacked the Armenian quarter at Van. Not unnaturally the Armenians resisted. In the fighting the Turks lost 18 men killed. This justifiable resistance of the inhabitants was henceforward described by the men in power as a treasonable act against Turkey. In its desire to put the Armenians in wrong, the Turkish Government asserted, through its accredited representatives in Berlin and elsewhere, that the Armenians had killed not 18 Turks but 180,000.

The ruling Turks resolved to destroy the Armenians by what they euphemistically called deportation. In the night between April 24 and 25, 1915, the Turkish authorities arrested in Constantinople 600 leading Armenians—politicians, priests, scientists, merchants, doctors, authors, journalists, etc.,—and on May 27, the Turkish Government published a Provisional Law for the Deportation of Suspected Persons. Article II of the Law ran as follows:

"The commanders of the armies, army corps and divisions may, if military requirements demand it, deport and settle in other localities, either individually or jointly, the inhabitants of the towns and villages whom they suspect of being guilty of treason or espionage."

It will be noticed that no proof of guilt was required. Mere suspicion was considered sufficient for deporting the population of entire districts. In fact all Armenians were considered to be suspect.

7. *Carlton J. H. Hays, A Brief History of the World, 1920.*

Christian Armenia, throughout the first 8 months of 1915 had been the scene of the most wholesale and cold-blooded massacres in the long history of the distracted country. At Angora, Bitlis, Mush, Diarbek(i)r, at Trebizond and Van, even at distant Mosul many thousands were butchered like sheep, partly by the gendarmerie, partly by the mob. Women were violated, and they and their children were shamelessly sold to Turkish harems and houses of ill fame. Hundreds of thousands of wretched creatures were driven into the deserts and mountains to perish miserably of starvation. The protesting voices were few and ineffective; the Sheikh-ul-Islam resigned; the pope remonstrated; the American ambassador at Constantinople did his best. The Turkish Government was obdurate; 'I am taking the necessary steps,' its premier told the American Ambassador, 'to make it impossible for the Armenians ever to utter the word autonomy during the next fifty years,' and the Germans, quite used themselves to committing outrages in Belgium, shuddered not at the newest and gravest atrocities inflicted by their friends, the Mohammedan Turks, upon the hapless and helpless Christian Armenians.

8. *Daily Telegraph*, an article by the Diplomatic Correspondent, June 6, 1921.[5]

On April 28, 1921, Mr. Charles P. Grant, the representative of the American Committee at Karakilissa, having been informed that in the Akboulagh regions, where the Turks had recently returned, *a large number of bodies, most of them children, had been found*, went to the locality accompanied by Rev. T. Acton and Mr. George Bey Mamikonian, who were also members of the American Committee. Their guide conducted them from Akboulagh to the Djardour mountains. Before reaching the gorge of Djardour the guide stopped the group in the cars and asked them to follow him on foot. All along the river which flowed in the deep and straight valley, they found a large number of bodies, mostly children. They also saw bodies on the banks of the river partially covered with sand. A number of bodies were found over the rocks. They were undoubtedly thrown ashore by an overflow of the river.

After examining the nature of the wounds the travelers were convinced that they were the bodies of the inhabitants of surrounding Armenian villages, who had been massacred some four months before. That theory seemed plausible since the surviving villagers were able to identify several bodies. The approximate number of the victims was surely 12,000, two-thirds of whom were refugees, from Kars and Alexandropol. The Americans picked up some cartridges, but most of the victims had been killed with a bayonet or sword. The absence of male bodies was striking, the oldest of the male was one young boy about fourteen years of age.

9. *Rev. Joseph Naayem, Shall this Nation Die?* New York, 1921. In Chapter X of his book, under the heading "Rape, Loot, and Murder,"[6] Rev. Naayem writes as follows:

It was during the afternoon of Saturday, July 18th, 1918, that we were informed that all Christians were to be deported from Trebizond. . . . The whole town was stricken. The Christians were in tears. Trebizond was a city of mourning. A crowd of breathless women were running about the streets, pursued by soldiers deaf to their prayers. The men had been torn from their homes and taken to a monastery called Astuazatzin. On the 13th of July, five days before the order for deportation, all men who were Russian subjects and all the members of the Tashnaktzagan Committee were collected and placed on board a motor boat; treated with great harshness and told that they were to be taken to Sinope or Constantinople to be tried by court martial. All were men of position. Once well out to sea they were thrown overboard and drowned. We learned of their sad end and some days later we found about four hundred of their bodies on the seashore.

After describing the march of the caravan of 5,000 to an unknown destination, the author writes:

One hundred and fifty girls and ten teachers belonging to a group of young women confided to the care of the American Mission, had been deported from Trebizond with a number of boys from fifteen to nineteen years of age. For days afterwards some of the more handsome girls were chosen and carried off. The remainder, together with the boys, were shot down there and then, or otherwise done to death.

10. *Daily Telegraph,* an article by the Diplomatic Correspondent, May 15, 1922.[7]

The diplomatic correspondent of the publication reports eye-witness stories in the May 15, 1922, issue of the paper, quoting "neutral and independent" witnesses. The reporter writes in part:

> The actual deportations and massacres in Asia Minor are without precedent in Turkish history. They exceed in importance those of the Gladstone era, and even those that took place in 1915. *They are not isolated incidents, but systematic, with the complete extermination of Christian races as the only motive* [Emphasis ours—D.H.B.]. They were intensified and augmented during the course of the following months, since the question of the armistice and the protection of the minorities was made a part of the terms of the peace treaty. An important Kemalist official recently declared that *with one minute's peace there would no longer be a need to protect the minorities* [Emphasis ours—D.H.B.], and that a mistake made in 1915 in not doing away, once for all, with Christianity and the Christians in Turkey, might very well be rectified to-day. The deportations which are being carried out now are all in the territory occupied by the Kemalists, from the shores of Pontus, near the Caucasus and north to Odalia in the southwest.
>
> The methods of extermination are keen and double. Here are concrete examples: The entire Greek male population of Trebizond and the land beyond were at last brought together, incorporated into battalions called 'labor battalions,' and were sent to far distant localities, such as Kars and Sarikamish. The older men, the women and children of the same area and the same race, after having been gathered in the neighborhood of Amasia, were led to Cesarea, on foot, via Sivas, then were brought back always on foot and were finally sent to Kharput and Diarbekir, where the civilized observers lost their trace. The worst months, when the Anatolian mountains were covered with snow, were chosen for these marches. The majority of the deportees froze to death, exhausted on route, thus escaping outright massacre at the hand of their executioners. Over a small portion of the route a reliable witness of the faith has counted 1,500 bodies, in another part, 2,000.
>
> The persecutions began [writes the *Daily Telegraph*], from the month of May, 1919. At that time the witnesses were from the British marines, who reported that 80% of

the country's gendarmerie was recruited from among bandits. At the end of the same year the British authorities in Turkey declared that the persecutions were still continuing in certain areas and that Mustapha Kemal and his associates were the authors of the system which was very much like the system used by Talaat in 1915. At the beginning of 1920 massacres took place in Cilicia, at Marash (15,000 to 20,000 victims, according to British estimates) and at Hadjin (9,000 victims).[8]

11. *Mrs. D. C. (Blanche) Eby*, in *At the Mercy of Turkish Brigands*, 1922.[9]

Mrs. Eby commences Chapter V of her book with the following words:

> Words fail to convey to our imagination the actuality of what happened to the Armenian nation. It is altogether beyond our experience in this land of Christian freedom. The Turkish Administration, calling themselves The Committee of Union and Progress, instigated the tortures inflicted on the Armenians. This Committee, led by the Turkish statesmen, Talaat and Enver, spent nights planning the deportations, discussing new methods of inflicting pain and devising new tortures—even delving into the old records of the Spanish Inquisition. Everything possible was done to rid themselves of the Armenian nation. Talaat Bey had said: "After this there will be no Armenian Question for fifty years." To blot out a nation was their aim.[10]

After describing the heroic defense of Hadjin against overwhelming Kemalist hordes in detail, in spite of the miserable failure of the French to send help, Mrs. Eby writes:

> Though it seems incredible, the brave defenders of Hadjin held out until October, over seven long months of siege. They managed to make raids on the surrounding villages and captured enough livestock to eke out a miserable existence during that time.
> The Turks then brought more cannon, and reinforcements enough to overwhelm the Armenians and turn the tide in their favor. Entering the city, they closed with the brave defenders in a terrible death struggle, and a most revolting massacre ensued. The entire city was mercilessly swept with fire and sword, only a small section near the government buildings was spared. (p. 284)

(Editor's Note: Hadjin had been repopulated by Armenian repatriates after the defeat of Turkey. Its population numbered more than 8,000, all of whom—men, women and children,—perished, except about 400, who escaped.)

12. *Edward Hale Bierstadt*, in *The Great Betrayal*, 1924.[11]

Smyrna. Mrs. Anna H. Birge, the wife of an American missionary stationed at Smyrna, when the cavalry regiment of the Turkish army entered the city, reports the following:

> The first that entered were dressed in black, with black fezzes with their red crescent and red star, riding magnificent horses, carrying long curved swords, proudly they rode into the city. With one hand raised they called out to the terrified inhabitants, "Fear not! Fear not!" but the inhabitants of Smyrna, knowing the reputation of the Turks, were filled with horror. All morning long the Turkish army marched into the city, and about three o'clock that Saturday afternoon they started the most terrible looting, raping and killing that it is impossible to describe in words. Whole companies of soldiers broke into the stores on the business streets and swept them clean of their goods. . . The city was systematically looted, and things were carried in carts down to the Turkish quarters. The American teachers in our American Girls' School watched the soldiers kill civilians in the street in front of the school, enter homes and kill families and throw them out into the street, and then take loads of goods along with them. When the sun set that evening dead bodies were lying all over the streets of that doomed city.

Commenting on Mrs. Birge's eyewitness story, Mr. Bierstadt says: "It is probable that the worst of what Mrs. Birge described happened in the Armenian quarters, where a fire had been set Saturday night."

> During the first three days of the occupation looting, murder and outrage continued. It was a massacre, with all its attendant atrocities, but Turkish guards were stationed at all approaches to the Armenian quarter in order to prevent Europeans, so far as possible, from knowing what was going on.

Full details of what happened during the first four days of the occupation, September 9th, 10th, 11th and 12th, can never be given. There are many instances, however, that serve to indicate the trend of events: eight hundred Christians who had taken refuge in the Catholic Cathedral were dragged out and massacred; twenty women who had fled to the house of a British citizen for safety were outraged and killed; the grave of an American soldier was violated, the body exhumed and subjected to every indignity by Turkish troops; a naturalized American citizen was shot himself when the Turks seized his wife and sister; hundreds of Greek and Armenian girls were placed in brothels for the delectation of the Turkish soldiery. . . massacre, raping and pillage without stint and on a scale unequalled.

Before and after the occupation the people of the city had been crowding on to the long quais begging that they might be taken away by any ship that could and would carry them. But now, with this city in flames, the quais were soon packed close with those whose only hope lay in flight. It is impossible to achieve complete accuracy as to the figures involved in the Smyrna debacle, but by checking one authority against another it is computed that approximately 100,000 persons were massacred, 280,000 were crushed together on the quais praying for safety, and still another 160,000 were deported by the Turks into the interior, never to be seen again. It is a picture too large and too fearful to be painted. The girl students of the American Collegiate Institute, along with those of the Armenian Girls' School across the street, fell into Turkish hands. With them were 1,300 refugees who had been sheltered in the college grounds. It is very dreadful to contemplate the fate of these girls, trained in an American institution to American ideals and ways of thought, at the complete mercy of men who knew no mercy, and who combined the savagery of the Mongol with the cunning cruelty of the low caste Oriental. But in spite of the fact that Smyrna harbour was full of Allied war ships there was no one to save them, and they were lost.

Yes. Great Britain, France, Italy and the United States all had war vessels in Smyrna Harbour. The United States had four destroyers there.

But why did they not lift one finger to save the struggling and dying human beings, Christian human beings, who were trying to escape total destruction by murder, rape and fire? Here is the answer given by the author of *The Great Betrayal:*

"It was a matter of common knowledge that the sympathy of the French and the Italians was strongly Turkish, for these nations had supported Turkey in her war with Greece, whose rather passive ally was Great Britain. *The United States was neutral, very neutral.*"

"Smyrna today is in ruins," relates the author ruefully. "It will probably be years before it is rebuilt, for those who made it what it was are dead or in exile. While those ruins stand there will be no need to raise any other monument to commemorate the great crime that marked the end of the Christian civilization in Turkey."

13. *Edward C. Little,* speech before the U.S. House of Representatives, on February 17, 1918, discussing the House Bill H. R. 9214 concerning an appropriation for Diplomatic and Consular Service. We quote the pertinent portions of the speech dealing with Armenia and Turkey:

When Noah stood on Ararat, the great plateau of Armenia lay all about him. To the northeast he could see the fertile and beautiful valley of Arazes running 150 miles to the salt waters of the Caspian Sea. To the southwest were the fountainheads of the Tigris and the Euphrates and the hills and valleys and the plateaus extending to the waters of the Mediterranean in the vicinity of Tyre and Sidon. To the northwest was the Black Sea, and later the famous city of Trebizond, while Persia lay to the southeast. When our Aryan ancestors left the roof of the world and entered Europe north of the Caspian, our Armenian cousins, for such they are, marched to the south of that sea and after a bit established themselves around Mount Ararat, where they have lived more than 3,000 years, and it is not quite 311 since John Smith landed in Jamestown.

The 2,000,000 Russian Armenians are an efficient and contented factor in the life of Tiflis and the Caucasus, with fine farms, towns, schools and cities, taking part in all its activities. Within the territory of Turkish Armenia, three years ago, over a million and a half Armenians lived. There is some little difference of opinion as to how many of them have been slain since then. I think it is a fair statement to make that at least 500,000 Armenians have been killed since 1915 in this country, to which I now point, by the Turks and Kurds. Their effort is to exterminate the Armenian race that they may possess their lands and stock and destroy the Christian Church there. We talk much about the tribulations to which Belgium has been subjected. I think I can safely state to the House that Armenia has suffered a thousand times as much as Belgium has endured. The sultan has been killing off small nations much longer than the Kaiser. For hundreds of years this has gone on to a greater or less extent. To deflower the maids, to rape the matrons, to slay the young men, to butcher the old, to assemble them together in the Armenian churches and steal everything they have, to burn their furniture, to drive away such as are left from their homes is a most everyday occurrence in Armenia. Hundreds of thousands have so suffered since 1914. I would hesitate about making such a statement on the floor of this House if I were not absolutely satisfied of the correctness of my statement.

The Turks themselves, as you know, of course, came from up in Mongolia. They have learned nothing since they have been there that makes them capable of conducting a government. They came in as soldiers and conquerors and never have been anything else. With them the collection of taxes is an adventure and they can not govern anybody except by cutting them in two. That is the Turkish idea of administration. (Laughter)

Fifty-four villages in Bulgaria forty-odd years ago were ruined and everybody in them was destroyed; the massacres in Chios and the other Grecian islands some 90 years ago were awful, but hardly a circumstance to what has been done in Armenia. In 1915 thousands upon thousands of men were slain and thousands upon thousands of women were dishonored. Slaughter often began by the sound of a bugle, and ended each day by the same signal. Hundreds of thousands of Armenian men, women, and children, driven from their good homes, were hurried on foot, without provisions, for unknown destinations, in the hope of extermination. Many women sprang into the Euphrates to escape dishonor. Three thousand died in the burned church at Orfa in the massacre of a few years ago. Circumstances have been such in the last few years that hell would not have been a right good vestibule for Armenia. In hell they do not dishonor women. I do not think it is to the benefit of civilization to exterminate Armenia. I do not believe it is to the safety of that empire that the only race which has any capacity for administration and business should be completely wiped out or driven out. They can not build up business communications in that fashion. They cannot develop a country by such methods. The rape of Belgium, the murder of Serbia, the collapse of Russia have appalled a world that would stand aghast if it knew the horrors of Christian life in Armenia. Vengeance is mine, saith the Lord.

In answer to a question posed by representative Fairfield as to whether the Armenians were "wholly disarmed," Mr. Little said:

Yes; and whenever they accumulate property it is the signal for assault by Kurds and Turks. For 400 years the Kurd and Turk have had the Armenian down, and they keep somebody sitting on his stomach to assure permanence in his position. Surrounded for centuries by his enemies, cut off from all the modern world, the wonder is the Armenian has lived at all. The Jews abandoned their native land generations ago, and many a nation has disappeared from history since the last Armenian king died 500 years gone by.

The Armenians have long had a hope that they could be given a representative government in Turkish Armenia under a protectorate established by the great Christian powers that would extend from the Mediterranean at Mersina and Alexandretta to the Russian border. The possible disintegration of Russia may have Russian Armenia in a position where the great powers would determine that it should be placed under the same protectorate. They would then hope to build railroads from the Mediterranean to Erzeroum and connect with those to Tiflis and the Black and Caspian Seas. In such an event in a few months Armenia would be a part of the modern world, life would be safe, property secure, education assured, and religious freedom attained. Farms, villages, towns, and cities would thrive; schools, newspapers, and colleges would spring up, following the results already achieved by the work of the American missions. The world could make no better financial and moral investment than to promote the best development of Armenia. Boghos Pasha Nubar, son of the great Nubar of Egypt, is now the chief spokesman of the Armenian race. He formulated their plans for a protectorate and presented them to the great powers. Recent events have been a menace to the Armenians, so great that self-defence is their most immediate necessity. As I have said, with the Georgians they could put 200,000 men in the field to fight the Turks. They ask the allies now the means to arm, equip, and maintain the 200,000 soldiers. Their best protection would be the total defeat of the Turk, and they could not afford to pause till that was accomplished. Every touch of sympathy, every dictate of reason, every requirement of our own interest, every rule of common sense, demands that the allies comply with their wish for financial assistance and aid them to attain the realization of their highest hopes. (Appendix, Congressional Record, February, 1918)

14. *Major General Harbord*, in a report October 16, 1919, Senate Document 266, Congressional Record May 29, 1920.

Major General James G. Harbord reports to the 66th Congress of the United States about his mission to Armenia:

Conditions in the Near East.

American Military Mission to Armenia,

From: Major General James G. Harbord, United States Army

To: The Secretary of State

Subject: Report of the American Military Mission to Armenia.

The undersigned submits herewith the report of the American Military Mission to Armenia. The mission, organized under authority of the President, consisted of Maj. Gen. James G. Harbord, United States Army; Brig. Gen. George Van Horn Moseley, United States Army; Brig. Gen. Frank R. McCoy, United States Army; Col. Henry Beeuwkes, Medical Corps, United States Army; Lieut. Col. John Price Jackson, United States Engineers; Lieut. Col. Jasper Y. Brinton, judge advocate, United States Army; Lieut. Col. Edward Bowditch, jr., Infantry, United States Army; Commander W. W. Bertholf,

United States Navy; Major Lawrence Martin, General Staff, United States Army; Major Harold Clark, Infantry, United States Army; Capt. Stanley K Hornbeck, Ordnance Department, United States Army (Chief of Far Eastern Division, American Commission to Negotiate Peace); Mr. William B. Poland, Chief of the American Relief Commission for Belgium and Northern France; Prof. W. W. Cumberland, economic advisor to the American Commission to Negotiate Peace; Mr. Eliot Grinnell Mears, trade commissioner, Department of Commerce, with other officers, clerks, interpreters, etc.

The instructions to the mission were to—

Proceed without delay on a Government vessel to Constantinople, Batum, and such other places in Armenia, Russian Transcaucasia, and Syria, as will enable you to carry out instructions already discussed with you. It is desired that you investigate and report on political, military, geographical, administrative, economic, and other considerations involved in possible American interests and responsibilities in that region.

The mission proceeded by ship to Constantinople. From there it traveled by the Bagdad railway to Adana, near the northeastern coast of the Mediterranean Sea, the scene of the massacres of 1909, and the principal city of the rich Province of Cilicia, where two days were spent visiting Tarsus and the ports of Ayas and Mersina; thence continued by rail via Aleppo to Mardin; from there by motor car to Diarbekir, Kharput, Malatia, Sivas, Erzinjan, Kars, Erivan, and Tiflis; thence by rail to Baku and Batum. Erivan, Tiflis, and Baku are the capitals, respectively, of the Republics of Armenia, Georgia, and Azarbaijan, and Batum is the seat of the British military government of the Georgian district of that name. Members of the mission also traveled by carriage from Ula Kishla to Sivas; from Sivas to Samsun; visiting Marsovan, where there is much apprehension among the Armenian population at this time; from Trebizond to Erzerum; by horseback from Khorasan to Bayazid; from Erivan to Nakhichevan, near the Persian border. The Armenian Catholicos, His Holiness Kevork V, was visited at Etchmiadzin, the historic seat of the Armenian church, with its ancient cathedral, dated from 301 A. D. The mission traversed Asia Minor for its entire length and the Transcaucasus from north to south and east to west. All of the vilayets of Turkish Armenia were visited except Van and Bitlis, which were inaccessible in the time available, but which have been well covered by Capt. Niles, an Army officer, who inspected them on horseback in August, and whose report corroborates our own observations in the neighboring regions; as well as both Provinces of the Armenian Republic as well as the Republic of Azarbaijan and Georgia. The Turkish frontier was paralleled from the Black Sea to Persia. On the return voyage from Batum the mission visited Samsun, the port of one of the world's great tobacco regions, and Trebizond, the latter a principal port on the south shore of the Black Sea, terminus of the ancient caravan route to Persia, of historic interest as the point of where the Greek 10,000 reached the sea under Xenophon over 2,300 years ago.

The mission spent 30 days in Asia Minor and Transcaucasia, and interviewed at length representatives of every Government exercising sovereignty in that region, as well as individual Turks, Armenians, Greeks, Kurds, Tartars, Georgians, Russians, Persians, Jews, Arabs, British, and French, including Americans for some time domiciled in the country. It also gave consideration to the views of the various educational, religious, and charitable organizations supported by America. In addition to this personal contact the mission before leaving Paris was in frequent conference with the various delegations to the peace conference from the regions visited. It has had before it numerous reports of the American Committee for Relief in the Near East, and Food Administration, and that of the mission of Mr. Benjamin B. Moore, sent by the peace conference to Transcaucasia, as well as the very complete library on the region, its geography, history, and governments, loaned by the Librarian of Congress, the American Mission to Negotiate Peace, and others. It has listened to the personal experiences of many witnesses to the atrocities of 1915, and benefited by the views of many persons whose knowledge of the various peoples in the regions visited is that obtained by years spent among them.

The interest, the horror, and sympathy of the civilized world are so centered on Armenia, and the purpose and work of this mission so focus on the blood-soaked region and its tragic remnant of a Christian population that this report should seem to fall naturally under the following heads: (a) history and present situation of the Armenian people; (b) the political situation and suggestions for readjustment; (c) the conditions and problems involved in a mandatory; (d) the considerations for and against the undertaking of a mandate.

The report is accordingly so presented.

THE HISTORY AND PRESENT SITUATION OF ARMENIAN PEOPLE

The Armenians were known to history under that name in the fifth century B.C., and since that period have lived in the region where their misfortunes find them to-day. Their country is the great rough table land, from 3,000 to 8,000 feet above the level of the sea, of which Mount Ararat is the dominant peak. In ancient times it touched the Mediterranean, Caspian, and Black Seas. In later days it has dwindled to about 140,000 square miles, an area about as large as Montana, with political identity, but existing in 1914 in two parts, the eastern belonging to Russia, which consisted of Kars and Erivan, and some portions of the present territory of Azarbaijan; the remainder being Turkish Armenia, comprised in the villayets of Van, Bitlis, Erzerum, Diarbekir, Kharput, and Cilicia, though Armenians were scattered more or less throughout the whole of Transcaucasia and Asia Minor. Armenia was an organized nation 1,000 years before there was one in Europe, except Greece and Rome. For over 12 of the 25 centuries of its history Armenia enjoyed independence within borders that shifted with the events of the times. Its last king, Leon VI, an exile from his own land, spent his last years in the effort to bring about an understanding between France and England, then in the struggle of the Hundred Years War, and actually presided at a peace conference near Boulogne in 1386, which brought about the understanding which led to the end of the war. Armenia was evangelized by Apostles fresh from the memory of our Lord, as early as 33 A.D., and as a nation adopted Christianity and founded a national church in 301 A.D., which has outridden the storms of the centuries and is vital today. Armenia was the first nation to officially adopt Christianity, with all that act involved in a pagan world.

The first two centuries following the foundation of the church were a golden age of Armenian literature, witnessing the invention of an Armenian alphabet; the translation of the Bible into the vernacular; the thronging of Armenians to the great centers of learning at Athens, Rome, and Alexandria; and the development of a flexible literary language, one of the great assets of national life.

By its geographical location on the great highway of invasion from east and west the ambitious kings of Persia, the Saracens and the rising tide of Islam, and the Crusades found Armenia the extreme frontier of Christianity in the East. Persians, Parthians, Saracens, Tartars, and Turks have exacted more martyrs from the Armenian church in proportion to its numbers than have been sacrificed by any other race. The last Armenian dynasty was overthrown by the Sultan of Egypt 78 years before the fall of Constantinople to Mahomet II in 1453. From that time until to-day the story of their martyrdom is unbroken. In the Persian, the Roman, the Byzantine, the Armenian found Aryan kinsmen and tyranny was tempered with partial autonomy. Even the Saracen was a high racial type, and reciprocal adjustments had been possible. The Turk to whom they now fall prey was a raiding nomad from Central Asia. His mainsprings of action were plunder, murder, and enslavement; his methods the scimitar and the bowstring. The Crusades were long ended. Europe

busy with her own renaissance contented herself with standing on the defensive against the Moslem, and the eastern
Christian was forgotten. For more than three centuries the
Armenian people figure little in the history of the times,
though at an earlier period 16 Byzantine emperors were of
that race, and ruled the Eastern empire with distinction.
Many individuals, and even colonies, however, played a part
in distant lands. Europe, India, and Persia welcomed them.
They were translators, bankers, scholars, artisans, artists,
and traders, and even under their tyrannical masters filled
posts which called for administrative ability, became ambassadors and ministers, and more than once saved a tottering
throne. They carried on trades, conducted commerce, and
designed and constructed palaces. Nevertheless as a race they
were forbidden military service, taxed to poverty, their property confiscated at pleasure, and their women forced into the
harems of the conqueror. Such slavery leaves some inevitable
and unlovable traces upon the character, but in the main the
Armenian preserved his religion, his language, and his racial
purity, persecution bringing cohesion.

Time, temperament, and talent eventually brought most
of the industry, finance, commerce, and much of the intellectual and administrative work of the Ottoman Empire into
Armenian hands.

The progress of events in Europe brought about in the
early nineteenth century a revival of interest in the forgotten
Near East. As early as 1744 the treaty of Kainardje had placed
Imperial Russia in the role of a protector of the Christians of
the Near East, an attitude many times under suspicion by
contemporary statesmen, but whatever its motives, the only
genuine attempt by any European nation to afford such protection to helpless Armenia. A plebiscite in Russian Armenia,
if fairly held, would probably vote a reconstituted Russia into
a mandatory for that region.

With Armenian consciousness of their own capacity to
trade, to administer, and to govern in the name of others,
there came in the last quarter of the nineteenth century the

opportunity to throw their weight into the scale for reform of Turkey from within, at a time when the dismemberment of Turkey was balanced in European politics against the possibility of her self-redemption. In 1876 a constitution for Turkey was drawn up by the Armenian Krikor Odian, secretary to Midhat Pasha, the reformer, and was proclaimed and almost immediately revoked by Sultan Abdul Hamid.

The foregoing inadequately sketches the story of the wrongs of Armenia down to our own times. From 1876 it is a story of massacre and of broken and violated guarantees.

The Russo-Turkish War ended in 1877 by the treaty of San Stefano, under which Russia was to occupy certain regions until actual reforms had taken place in Turkey. This treaty, through British jealousy of Russia, was torn up the following year and the futile treaty of Berlin substituted, asking protection but without guaranties. Meantime there had been the convention of Cyprus, by which that island passed to Great Britain, and the protection of Turkey was promised for the Armenians in return for Great Britain's agreement to come to the aid of Turkey against Russia. A collective note of the powers in 1880 was ignored by Turkey. Then followed the agreement of 1895, which was never carried out, and the restoration of the constitution of 1876 in 1908. A further agreement in 1914 was abrogated at the entrance of Turkey in the war—and the last of the series is a secret treaty of 1916 between Great Britain, France, and Russia, the existence and publication of which rests on Bolshevik authority, by which Armenia was to be divided between Russia and France. Meanwhile there have been organized official massacres of the Armenians ordered every few years ever since Abdul Hamid ascended the throne. In 1895 100,000 perished. At Van, in 1908, and at Adana and elsewhere in Cilicia in 1909, over 30,000 were murdered. The last and greatest of these tragedies was in 1915. Conservative estimates place the number of Armenians in Asiatic Turkey in 1914 at over 1,500,000, though some make it higher. Massacres and deportations were organized in the spring of 1915 under definite system, the soldiers going from town to town. The official reports of the Turkish government show 1,100,000 as having been deported. Young men were first summoned to the government building in each village and then marched out and killed. The women, the old men, and children were, after a few days, deported to what Talaat Pasha called 'agricultural colonies,' from the high, cool, breeze-swept plateau of Armenia to the malarial flats of the Euphrates and the burning sands of Syria and Arabia. The dead from this wholesale attempt on the race are variously estimated from 500,000 to more than one million, the usual figure being about 800,000.

Driven on foot under a fierce summer sun, robbed of their clothing and such petty articles as they carried, prodded by bayonet if they lagged, starvation, typhus, and dysentery left thousands dead by the trail side. The ration was a pound of bread every alternate day, which many did not receive, and later a small daily sprinkling of meal on the palm of the outstretched hand was the only food. Many perished from thirst or were killed as they attempted to slake thirst after crossing of running streams. Numbers were murdered by savage Kurds, against whom the Turkish soldiery afforded no protection. Little girls of 9 or 10 were sold to Kurdish brigands for a few piasters, and women were promiscuously violated. At Sivas an instance was related of a teacher in the Sivas Teachers' College, a gentle, refined Armenian girl, speaking English, knowing music, attractive by the standards of any land, who was given in enforced marriage to the beg of a neighboring Kurdish village, a filthy, ragged ruffian three times her age, with whom she still has to live, and by whom she has borne a child. In the orphanage there maintained under American relief auspices there were 150 'brides,' being girls, many of them of tender age, who had been living as wives in Moslem homes and had been rescued. Of the female refugees among some 75,000 repatriated from Syria and Mesopotamia we were informed at Aleppo that 40 per cent are infected with venereal diseases from the lives to which they have been forced. The women of this race were free from such diseases before the deportation. Mutilation, violation, torture, and death have left their haunting memories in a hundred beautiful Armenian valleys, and the traveler in that region is seldom free from the evidence of this most colossal crime of all ages. Yet immunity from it all might have been purchased for any Armenian girl or comely woman by abjuring her religion and turning Moslem. Surely no faith has ever been put to a harder test or has been cherished at greater cost.

Even before the war the Armenians were far from being in the majority in the region claimed as Turkish Armenia, excepting in a few places. To-day we doubt if they would be in the majority in a single community, even when the last survivors of the massacres and deportations have returned to the soil, though the great losses of Turkish population to some extent offset the difference brought about by slaughter. We estimate that there are probably 270,000 Armenians today in Turkish Armenia; some 75,000 have been repatriated from the Syrian and Mesopotamian side, others are slowly returning from other regions, and some from one cause or another remained in the country. There are in the Transcaucasus probably 300,000 refugees from Turkish Armenia and some thousands more in other lands, for they have drifted to all parts of the Near East. The orphanages seen throughout Turkey and Russian Armenia testify to the loss of life among adults. They are Turkish as well as Armenian, and the mission has seen thousands of these pathetic little survivors of the unhappy years of the war. Reports from 20 stations in Turkey show 15,000 orphans receiving American aid, and undoubtedly the number demanding care is double this, for many were seen cared for under the auspices of the Red Crescent, the organization which in Moslem countries corresponds to our Red Cross. Twenty thousand are being cared for at the expense of the various relief agencies in the Transcaucasus. On the route traveled by the mission fully 50,000 orphans are today receiving Government or other organized care. We estimate a total of perhaps half a million refugee Armenians as available to eventually begin life anew in a region about the size of New York, Pennsylvania, and Ohio, to which would be added those not refugees who might return from other lands. The condition of the refugees seen in the Transcaucasus is pitiable to the last degree. They subsist on the charity of the American relief organizations, with some help, not great, however, from their more prosperous kinsmen domiciled in that region. Generally they wear the rags they have worn for four years. Eighty percent of them suffer from malaria, 10 per cent from venereal troubles, and practically all from diseases that flourish on the frontiers of starvation. There are also the diseases that accompany filth, loathsome skin troubles, and great numbers of sore eyes, the latter especially among the children. The hospitals are crowded with such cases.

The refugees in Russian Armenia have hitherto drifted from place to place, but an effort is now being made by the administration of Col. Haskell to concentrate them in several refugee camps. The winter season will see many deaths, for the winters there are extremely severe, fuel is scarce, and shelter inadequate. Medicines are scarce and very dear. Quinine costs approximately $30 a pound. On the Turkish side of the border where Armenians have returned they are gradually recovering their property, and in some cases have received rent for it, but generally they find things in ruins, and face winter out of touch with the American relief, and with only such desultory assistance as the Turkish Government can afford. Things are little if any better with the peasant Turks in the same region. They are practically serfs, equally destitute and equally defenseless against the winter. No doctors or medicines are to be had. Villages are in ruins, some having been destroyed when the Armenians fled or were deported; some during the Russian advance; some on the retreat of the Armenian irregulars and Russians after the fall of the empire. Not over 20 per cent of the Turkish peasants who went to war have returned. The absence of men between the ages of 20 and 35 is very noticeable. Six hundred thousand Turkish soldiers died of typhus alone, it is stated, and insufficient hospital service and absolute poverty of supply greatly swelled the death lists.

In the region which witnessed the ebb and flow of the Russian and Turkish Armies the physical condition of the country is very deplorable. No crops have been raised for several years and the land ordinarily cultivated has gone to weeds. Scarcely a village or city exists which is not largely in ruins. The country is practically treeless.

Where the desperate character of the warfare, with its reprisals of burning and destroying as one side and then the other advanced, has not destroyed the buildings, which are generally of adobe, the wooden beams have been taken for fuel and the houses are ruined. In the territory untouched by war from which Armenians were deported the ruined villages are undoubtedly due to Turkish deviltry, but where Armenians advanced and retired with the Russians their retaliatory cruelties unquestionably rivaled the Turks in their inhumanity. The reconstruction of this country will be little short in difficulty of its original reclamation from virgin wilderness in days when the world was young.

Where the Russian went he built fine macadam highways, and even the main Turkish roads generally built during the war, over which our mission traveled, were passable, and some quite good. All highways are rapidly going to ruin for lack of maintenance. A country once fairly equipped for motor traffic is sliding back to dependence on the camel caravan, the diminutive pack donkey, and the rattly, ramshackly araba wagon. The ox is the principal draft animal. A good highway existed from Erzerum to Trebizond, on the line of the most ancient trade route in the world, that from Persia to the Black Sea, through which, in all ages, the carpets and jewels of Persia have reached the western world. The distance is about 150 miles. The freight rate is now between $145 and $150 per ton.

In the portion of Turkey traversed we heard of brigandage,

but experienced no inconvenience. Apparently the Turkish Government, inefficient and wicked as it sometimes is, can control its people and does govern. In the region once policed by Russia the relaxation from its iron hand has been great, and life and property are unsafe in many regions. Our mission was fired upon by Kurds in Russian Armenia and several motor cars struck by bullets, and over half the party were kept prisoners one night by Moslems who claimed to have been driven from their villages by Armenians.

In Azarbaijan we were also fired upon. Train wrecks for robbery are frequent on the Transcaucasian railroad, and the Georgian Government took the precaution to run pilot engines ahead of our train for safety. The highways are unsafe even to the suburbs of the large towns. Practically every man in Georgia and Azarbaijan, outside the cities, carries a rifle. If he desires to stop a traveler on the highway, he motions or calls to him, and if unheeded fires at him.

The relief work consists of the allotment made to the Transcaucasus from the unexpended balance of the hundred millions appropriated by Congress for relief in allied countries, and of the funds contributed through the American Committee for Relief in the Near East. All circumstances considered, the relief administration in the Transcaucasus seems to have been conducted with more than average energy. It has rescued the refugees there from starvation and brought the name of America to a height of sympathy and esteem it has never before enjoyed in this region. It extends now throughout the Near East, and is felt by the wild, ragged Kurd, the plausible Georgian, the suspicious Azarbaijan, the able Armenian, and the grave Turk with equal seriousness. With it, or probably because of it, there has come widespread knowledge of the fourteen points submitted by the President, and 'self-determination' has been quoted to the mission by wild Arabs from Shamar and Basra, by every Government in Transcaucasia, by the mountaineers of Daghestan, the dignified and able chiefs of the Turkish nationalist movement at Sivas and Erzerum, and the nomad Kurds who 10

minutes before had fired at our party, thinking us to be
Armenians. Undoubtedly some charges of corruption on the
part of native officials connected with the relief could be
substantiated. Charges of partially favoring Christian against
Moslem in equal distress are not infrequent. Due to inex-
perience, to difficulties of communication, and other causes,
there has been inefficiency on the part of American officials
and employees. Enthusiastic young Americans out of touch
with the sources of their funds, confronted with the horrors
of famine in a refugee population, drew drafts on the good
faith and generosity of their countrymen, procedure not
usual in the business world, but drafts that were honored
nevertheless. Any criticism of unbusinesslike methods must
be accompanied with the statement of work accomplished,
which has been very great and very creditable to America
and her splendid citizens who have so generously contributed to this cause. Col. Haskell has reorganized the work in
the Transcaucasus and is getting better results. In some way
funds must be found and this work must be continued and
the people be sustained until they can harvest a crop. If seed
is available for planting, a crop should be due in August,
1920. Even this prospective amelioration only applies to
those repossessed of their lands.

There is much to show that, left to themselves, the Turk
and the Armenian when left without official instigation have
hitherto been able to live together in peace. Their existence
side by side on the same soil for five centuries unmistake-
ably indicates their interdependence and mutual interest.
The aged Vali of Erzerum, a man old in years and in official
experience, informed us that in his youth, before massacres
began under Abdul Hamid, the Turk and the Armenian lived
in peace and confidence. The Turk making the pilgrimage
to the holy cities of Mecca and Medina left his family and
property with his Armenian neighbor; similarly the Armenian on the eve of a journey intrusted his treasures to his
Turkish friend. Testimony is universal that the massacres
have always been ordered from Constantinople. Some Turk-

ish officials were pointed out to us by American missionaries as having refused to carry out the 1915 order for deportation. That order is universally attributed to the Committee of Union and Progress, of which Enver Bey, Talaat Bey, and Djemal Pasha were the leaders. A court has been sitting in the capital practically since the armistice, and one man, an unimportant subordinate, has been hung. Talaat, Enver, and Djemal are at large, and a group of men charged with various crimes against the laws of war are at Malta in custody of the British, unpunished, except as restrained from personal liberty. Various rumors place Enver Bey as scheming in the Transcaucasus, and a French officer is authority for the statement that he has been in Tiflis within two months conferring with Government officials. This man is in Turkish eyes a heroic figure; risen from obscurity by his own efforts, allied by marriage to the Imperial House of Osman, credited with military ability, the possibilities of disturbance are very great should he appear in command of Moslem irregulars on the Azarbaijan-Armenian frontier.

Such are conditions to-day in the regions where the remnant of the Armenian people exist; roads and lands almost back to the wild; starvation only kept off by American relief; villages and towns in ruins; brigandage rampant in the Transcaucasus; lack of medicines and warm clothing; winter coming on in a treeless land without coal. We saw nothing to prove that the Armenians who have returned to their homes in Turkey are in danger of their lives, but their natural apprehension has been greatly increased by unbalanced advice given by officers on the withdrawal of foreign troops from certain regions. The events at Smyrna have undoubtedly cheapened every Christian life in Turkey, the landing of the Greeks there being looked upon by the Turks as deliberate violation by the Allies of the terms of their armistice and the probable forerunner of further unwarranted aggression. The moral responsibility for present unrest throughout Turkey is very heavy on foreign powers. Meantime, the Armenian, unarmed at the time of the deportations and massacres, a brave soldier by thousands in the armies of Russia, France, and America during the war, is still unarmed in a land where every man but himself carries a rifle.

THE POLITICAL SITUATION AND SUGGESTIONS FOR READJUSTMENT

In seeking a remedy for political conditions which shriek of misery, ruin, starvation, and all the melancholy aftermath, not only of honorable warfare but of bestial brutality, unrestrained by God or man, but which nevertheless prevail under an existing government with which the powers of Europe have long been willing to treat on terms of equality, one's first impulse is to inquire as to the possibility of reform from within. The machinery of government existing, can it be repaired and made a going concern, affording to its people the garanties of life, liberty, and the pursuit of happiness which the modern world expects of its governments? The case of the Turkish Empire was duly presented to the peace conference in Paris on June 17 last by the Turkish grand vizier, Damad Ferid Pasha, in which he admitted for the Turkish Government of the unhappy region under consideration the commission of 'miseries which are such as to make the conscience of mankind shudder with horror forever,' and that 'Asia Minor is to-day nothing but a vast heap of ruins.' In the reply made by the council of 10 of the peace conference to the plea of the grand vizier for the life of his empire, the probability of that Government being able to accomplish reforms from within which will satisfy modern requirements and perhaps make amends for past crimes is well weighed in the following words:

'Yet in all these changes there has been no case found, either in Europe or in Asia or in Africa, in which the establishment of Turkish rule in any country has not been followed by a diminution of prosperity in that country (a diminution of material prosperity and a fall in the level of culture). Neither is there any case to be found in which the withdrawal of Turkish rule has not been followed by material prosperity and a rise in culture. Never among the Christians in Europe, nor among the Moslems in Syria, Arabia, or Africa, has the Turk done other than destroy wherever he has conquered. Never has he shown that he is able to develop in peace what he has gained in war. Not in this direction to his talents lie.'

It seems likely, therefore, that, as far as the Armenians are concerned, the Turk has had his day, and that further uncontrolled opportunity will be denied him.

With the break-up of Russia, the Transcaucasus found itself adrift. This Transcaucasian region is ethnographically one of the most complicated in the world. In all ages it has been one of the great highways of mankind. Here stragglers and racial remnants have lodged during all the centuries that the tides of migration have swept the base of the great Caucasus Range until to-day its small area contains five great racial groups, divided into some 40 distinct races. Nine of these have arrived in comparatively recent times, but the remaining 31 are more or less indigenous. There are here 25 purely Caucasian races. This racial diversity is complicated by the fact that with the exception of the fairly compact group of Georgians, and one of Tartars, these peoples are inextricably commingled throughout the region. Their civilization varies from the mountain savage to individuals of the highest type. Of the 40 distinct races, the most important groups are the Georgians, the Azarbaijanese Tartars, and the Armenians.

A Transcaucasian confederation formed by all the peoples in that region was followed by an alignment in these small Republics—Georgia, Azarbaijan, and Armenia. Georgia is Christian, and its Iberian population are in the majority; Azarbaijan is Tartar and Moslem; Armenia is made up of the former Provinces that composed Russian Armenia, less the part that went to Azarbaijan in the split, and the majority of its people are the blood brothers of the Armenians of Turkey in Asia. These republics have been recognized by none of the powers except Turkey. The Armenian Republic seeks at the peace conference a union with the Turkish Armenians, and the creation of an Armenian State to include Russian Armenia and the six Turkish Vilayets—Van, Bitlis, Diarbekir, Kharput, Sivas, Erzerum—and Cilicia, to be governed by a mandatory of the great powers during a transition state of a term of years in which Armenians of the dispersion may return to their homes, and a constituent assembly be held to determine the form of the eventual permanent government. Georgia and Azarbaijan ask independence at the peace conference with certain adjustments of disputed boundaries in which all Transcaucasia is interested.

Both Georgia and Azarbaijan, living on the salvage from the wreck of Russia, have persuaded themselves that the civilization and governmental and business machinery they have taken over have been theirs from the beginning. The Georgians, with a church of their own antedating that of Russia, and traditions of a Georgian dynasty of Armenian origin which reigned in Tiflis for a thousand years before Russia took over the country in 1802, are a very proud and plausible race. They have been much influenced by the proximity of Bolshevism, fly the red flag of revolution over their own, and have nationalized land, taking it from the original owners without compensation, to sell to peasants. This measure has been unsatisfactory to both peasant and proprietor. The Azarbaijanese are Tartars by blood and Moslem by religion and sympathy. The varied topography of their little country and the diversity of its products make them more independent of outside help than either of the other Transcaucasian Republics. Both Georgian and Azarbaijan Governments live in terror of the forces of Deniken coming south of the Caucasus Mountains. Georgia has her little army on her northern frontier; and Azarbaijan has a tacit agreement with Gen. Deniken to refrain from hostilities against him in return for immunity from attack by his gunboats on the Caspian Sea.

The Russian Armenians are the blood brothers of those in Turkey, and came under Russian domination in 1878. They

absorbed many Russian manners and customs, and the
wealth and ability of the race gave them a predominant role
in the Transcaucasus under Russia. Tiflis, which was the
Russian capital, has probably the largest Armenian population of any city in the world except New York and Constantinople. They are friendly to Deniken and a reconstituted
Russia, and their refusal to join Georgia and Azarbaijan
against Deniken caused the break-up of the Transcaucasian
Federation.

The dominant civilization in Transcaucasia is Russian.
Everything worth while in the country is due to Russian
money and Russian enterprise. Besides this common bond,
these countries are interdependent in the matter of transportation. From Tiflis, the capital of Georgia, a railroad runs
west to the Black Sea at Batum and east to the Caspian Sea
at Baku, the capital of Azarbaijan, and south to Erivan, the
capital of the Republic of Armenia. The road is one of system, of the Russian gauge, with the three radii from Tiflis,
each ending in a different country something like the following:

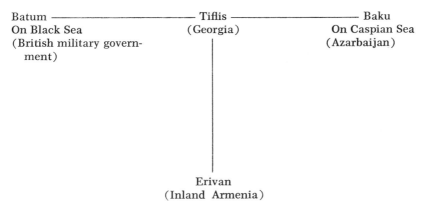

Batum ————————————— Tiflis ————————————— Baku
On Black Sea   (Georgia)   On Caspian Sea
(British military govern-   (Azarbaijan)
  ment)

Erivan
(Inland Armenia)

Under Russia the road was, of course, under one management, with shops, rolling stock, and policy in common. Georgia now controls the shops, Azarbaijan the oil fuel, and each
of the three such rolling stock as it can get. No one of the
three trusts the others; no through or continuous traffic is

possible without an outside power guaranteeing the return of the rolling stock when it passes from one jurisdiction to another. Georgia does not hesitate to embargo freight against Armenia, and from her position of vantage simply censors the railroad traffic to that unfortunate country. Azarbaijan controls the fuel supply and combines with Georgia against Armenia, which alone of the three has nothing by which to exert leverage. The railroad can neither be consolidated nor properly operated under native control. Roadbed and rolling stock are rapidly deteriorating. An example of the power of Georgia over Armenia is that the latter is not permitted to import either arms nor ammunition, though under almost constant menace from its neighbors.

The three Governments from an occidental standpoint are now thoroughly inefficient, without credit, and undoubtedly corrupt. Alone each faces inextricable financial difficulties. Religious differences, added to racial, threaten to embroil them unless brought under a common control. Two of them have no outlet to the Black Sea except through Georgia over the railroad. They have no present intermonetary, postal, or customs union, and, as stated, no definite agreement for common control and use of the railroad, and are in continual squabbles over boundaries. Azarbaijan has no educated class capable of well administering a government; Georgia is threatened by Bolshevism; Armenia is in ruins and partial starvation. All our investigation brings conviction that the people in each would welcome a mandatory by a trustworthy outside power. Russian Armenia would to-day probably vote a mandate to Russia if that power were reconstituted. Georgia recalls its ancient independence and was never thoroughly reconciled to Russian rule. Azarbaijan, Tartar and Moslem, feels a double tie to Turkey and distrusts the Christian, but the more intelligent people realize that outside control is inevitable and even necessary to their relations with Christian countries, and that Turkey is beyond consideration. So closely are the countries related geographically, commercially, and by the habit of generations that this mission not only believes that a mandatory is necessary for them but that it is imperative from the standpoints of peace, order, efficiency, and economy that the same power shall exercise a mandate over them all, leaving for the present their interior boundaries unsettled. The ultimate disposition or form of government of these States, other than that they may look forward to autonomy, but not necessarily independence, should, in our opinion, not now be announced. Their capacity for self-government and their ability to sustain amicable and workable relations among themselves remain to be tested under control by such power as may be induced to undertake its supervision, facing a long period of tutelage for possibly unappreciative and ungrateful pupils, much expense, probably diplomatic embarassment from a reconstitution of Russia, and little reward except the consciousness of having contributed to the peace of the world and the rehabilitation of oppressed humanity.

The covenant of the League of Nations contemplates that certain communities *formerly* belonging to the Turkish Empire' shall be subject to a mandatory power for an unstated period, thus appearing to recognize in advance the dismemberment to some degree of that Empire. [Emphasis ours—D.H.B.] This, in connection with the arraignment of the Turkish Government in the reply of the peace conference, . . . may not unreasonably be construed to apply to any or all parts of the Turkish Empire as fast as they reach a certain stage of development. As between actual dismemberment and a receivership for his entire country, the Turk would beyond doubt prefer a mandatory for the whole Empire as it may stand after adjudication by the peace conference. Bad as he is, without the pale of consideration from many standpoints, there would seem to be no objection to action taken in his interest and in line with his preference if the interest and inclination of the world lie in the same direction.

A power which should undertake a mandatory for Armenia and Transcaucasia without control of the contiguous territory of Asia Minor—Anatolia—and of Constantinople, with its hinterland of Roumelia, would undertake it under most unfavorable and trying conditions, so difficult as to make the cost almost prohibitive, the maintenance of law and order and the security of life and property uncertain, and ultimate success extremely doubtful. With the Turkish Empire still freely controlling Constantinople, such a power would be practically emasculated as far as real power is concerned. For generations these people have looked to Constantinople as the seat of authority. The most intelligent and ambitious Armenians have sought the capital as a career. The patriarch of the Armenian Church in Constantinople, although subordinate in matters of doctrine to the Catholicos at Etchmiadzin, is in reality the political head of the Armenian people by his location in Constantinople. Every people in the Empire is numerously represented at the capital, the Armenians reaching before the war the number of 150,000, with business connections ramifying to distant corners of the entire country. To no small degree the future business and industrial development of their native land will depend upon these men. Transportation lines and commerce center at Constantinople. Before the war Constantinople was the most important part in continental Europe, reckoned upon the basis of shipping clearances. There are well-informed business men who believe it is destined to become the third most important commercial city in the world. But, through generations of habit, unless put under a mandatory, Constantinople will continue to be a whirlpool of financial and political currents. Concession hunting, financial intrigue, political exploitation, and international rivalries will center there in the future as in the past. Concerted international action for administration of Constantinople is impracticable. All concerts for governmental action are cumbersome; all concerts must have a leader to secure effectiveness, and were it possible to agree upon one power which should really lead, the reality of a mandate would exist with the handicap of a camouflage concert. In any concert for

the future government of Constantinople there would still
exist the temptation for single powers to play politics and
befriend Turkey for value received. There must be actual
control, for responsibility without authority is worse than
useless in a land of oriental viewpoints.

As Americans, supposed to be disinterested, this mission
was the recipient of confidences from the various sources.
Turks when not deriding foreign efforts were deploring their
effect on their unfortunate Empire. Without dependable cen-
tralized control of Constantinople, a power exercising mandate in Armenia would be crippled in administration,
restricted in trade development, ridden by concessionaries,
dependent on Turkish discredited diplomacy for redress of
local and boundary grievances, and in extreme case practically cut off from communication with the western world.
It is believed that allied sentiment is so crystallized in the
opinion that Constantinople must be placed under a mandatory that it may safely be assumed for the purposes of this
report that this will be done.

Conceded that there shall be a mandate for Armenia and
Transcaucasia and one for Constantinople and Anatolia,
there are many considerations that indicate the desirability
of having such mandates exercised by the same power. If
separate powers exercised such mandate the inevitable jealousies, hatreds, exaggerated separatist tendencies, and economic difficulties would compel failure. With all its faults
the Turkish Empire is an existing institution and it has some
rusty, blood-stained political machinery which under control
of a strong mandatory can be made to function. The peoples
in question live in adjacent territory and whether they wish
it or not are neighbors. A single mandatory for the Turkish
Empire and the Transcaucasus would be the most economical solution. No intelligent scheme for development of railroads for Transcaucasia and Armenia can be worked out
without extension into Anatolia. Natural highways through
the high mountains of Armenia are few, and transportation
development will, with proper feeders, at best be costly and

difficult; without access into Anatolia it will be impossible. For many years the expenses of exploitation will not be met by equivalent receipts. This situation would be alleviated by control of both regions. With Constantinople, Anatolia, and Armenia in different hands, the manufacturers and exporters of Armenia could not hope for an equal share in the commerce and trade of the Near East.

The Armenian Patriarch, the head of the Armenian Protestants, and others at Constantinople, on our return from Armenia, called and volunteered the belief that the Armenian question could not be settled within the boundaries of that country, and that they were prepared to pass under a single mandate which should include the other parts of the Turkish Empire. In a later written statement, however, they modified this, stating that while 'Different nations of this Empire may enjoy the help of the same mandatory power' they felt that to bring Armenia under the same system of administration as that of the Turks would defeat the object of the development of Armenian ideals, 'because by assuring the individual rights of a people the national rights and ideals of the same people can not necessarily be assured'; that 'Giving a good government to the whole Turkish Empire will not induce the Armenians to gather to their native land. They will still be scattered people, etc.'

A party of distinguished Turks, including a former cabinet minister of high standing and a diplomat who for eight years represented his country at one of the European courts, stated that as between the independence of Turkey as it existed in 1914 and a mandate for the Empire given to the United States, they greatly preferred the latter, and believed that they spoke for the educated classes of all Turkey.

It has been very evident to this mission that Turkey would not object to a single disinterested power taking a mandate for her territory as outlined in the armistice with the Allies, and that it could be accomplished with a minimum of foreign soldiery, where an attempt to carve out territory for any particular region would mean a strong foreign force in constant occupation for many years. The aim of the Nationalist, or National Defense Party, as its adherents style it, as stated by Mustapha Kemal Pasha, its head, is the preservation of the territorial integrity of the Empire under a mandatory of a single disinterested power, preferably America.

The mission, while at Sivas, had a conference with the chiefs of this party, which held a congress at Erzerum in July and one at Sivas in September. This movement has been the cause of much apprehension on the part of those interested in the fate of the Armenians, to whose safety it has been supposed to portend danger. The leader, Mustapha Kemal Pasha, is a former general officer in the Turkish Army, who commanded with distinction an army corps at the Dardanelles, and appears to be a young man of force and keen intelligence. He is supposed to have resigned from the army to lead this movement. It sought, as a means to its end, the overthrow of the Ferid Pasha cabinet, which has since fallen, claiming that it was entirely under the influence of one of the great powers which itself desires a mandate for the Empire. While professing entire loyalty to the Sultan, the Nationalist leader had gone to the extremity of cutting all official telegraph communications between the capital and the interior, pending the removal of the cabinet. The fall of the Ferid Pasha ministry in October would seem to put the Empire behind the movement, for the Turkish officials in the interior were already identified with it. In a statement given out October 15, Mustapha Kemal said:

'The Nationalist Party recognized the necessity of the aid of an impartial foreign country. It is our aim to secure the development of Turkey as she stood at the armistice. We have no expansionist plans, but it is our conviction that Turkey can be made a rich and prosperous country if she can get a good government. Our government has become weakened through foreign interference and intrigues. After all our experience we are sure that America is the only country able to help us. We guarantee no new Turkish violences against the Armenians will take place.'

The events of the Greek occupation of Smyrna and the uneasiness produced by the activities and propaganda of certain European powers have so stirred the Turkish people in the long interval since the armistice that the mission fears that an announcement from Paris at this time of an intention to carve from Turkey a State of Armenia, unless preceded by a strong military occupation of the whole Empire, might be the signal for massacres of Christians in every part of the country. There is no wisdom in now incorporating Turkish territory in a separate Armenia, no matter what the aspirations of the Armenians. Certainly it is unwise to invite trouble which may be avoided by the consolidation of the mandate region under a single power. Under one mandatory they will be neighbors. Under two or more they will be rivals, their small differences subjected to the interminable processes of diplomatic representation, with the maintenance of duplicate and parallel establishments in many lines of governmental activity. Only under a single mandatory can the matter of ultimate boundaries be deferred, which is believed by this mission to be important.

In the proposition to carve an independent Armenia from the Ottoman Empire there is something to be said on the part of the Turk; namely, that his people, even when all the refugees shall have returned to their homes, will be in the majority in the region contemplated for a reconstituted Armenia—and they were in the majority before the deportations took place—even though due, as it may be, to the gerrymandering of provincial boundaries and the partial extermination of a people. Notwithstanding his many estimable qualities, his culture, and his tenacity of race and religion, the Armenian generally does not endear himself to those of other races with whom he comes in contact. The Armenian stands among his neighbors very much as the Jew stands in Russia and Poland, having, as he does, the strong and preeminent ability of that race. He incurs the penalty which attaches among backward races to the banker, the middleman, and the creditor. Unjust as it may be, the sentiment regarding him is expressed by this saying current in the Near East: 'The Armenian is never legally in the wrong; never morally in the right.' Even the American missionary, who in so many instances has risked his life for his Armenian charges, does not, as a rule, personally like the Armenian as well as he does the more genial but indolent and pleasure-loving Turk. The Armenian is not guiltless of blood himself: his memory is long, and reprisals are due and will doubtless be made if opportunity offers. Racially allied to the wild Aryan Kurd, he is cordially hated by the latter. Kurds appealed to this mission, with tears in their eyes, to protect them from Armenians who had driven them from their villages, appealing to be allowed to go back to their homes for protection against the rigorous winter now rapidly approaching on the high interior plateau. The Kurds claim that many of their people were massacred under the most cruel circumstances by Armenian irregulars accompanying the Russian Bolshevists when the Russian Army went to pieces after the collapse of the Empire.

Similar claim is made by the people of Erzerum, who point to burned buildings in which hundreds of Turks perished, and by the authorities of Hassan-Kala, who give the numbers of villages destroyed by the Armenians in their great plain as 43. According to British Consul Stevens, at Batum, these statements were verified by a commission which examined into the allegations and on which Armenians had a representation. In Baku the massacre of 2,000 Azarbaijanese by Armenians in March, 1918, was followed by the killing 4,000 Armenians by Azarbaijanese in November of the same year. From the standpoint of this mission the capacity of the Armenian to govern himself is something to be tested under supervision. With that still in doubt, the possibility of an Armenian minority being given authority over a Moslem majority, against whom its hearts are filled with rancor for centuries of tyranny, may well justify apprehension. There are very many who believe that the best elements of the Armenian race have perished. It is believed that with the reestablishment of order in their native country many of those who have emigrated to other countries will return. That, however, can only come with time, and even then it is doubted if many of the wealthy and influential Armenians long domiciled in happier lands will return to their somewhat primitive ancient home, even though such absentees have raised their voices most loudly for an autonomous Armenia. Certainly with arbitrary boundaries on the Anatolia side determined only by Armenian wishes, expediency, tradition, or even verified historical claims of former occupation, without regard to the present population, the mandatory powers for both Anatolia and Armenia should inaugurate government by placing a cordon of trustworthy foreign soldiers from the Black Sea to the Mediterranean. With a single power in control of both peoples and boundaries unannounced except as they have hitherto existed, such difficulties would not arise. Against such combination of authority and postponement of delimitation of boundaries is to be weighed the unchangeable belief of many that the Turk at the end of his tutelage will still be the Turk, bloodthirsty, unregenerate, and revengeful, and that it is unthinkable that Armenia shall ever again form part of a country which may be governed by him; that the sufferings of centuries should now be terminated by definite and permanent separation of Armenia from Turkey, and that this plan seems to contemplate a tutelage of indefinite length. To this the reply is that the Armenian should have no fear to submit his case to the League of Nations—the court of the world—and that he must in the meantime prove his capacity not only to govern himself but others, and that at the behest of the great powers a plebiscite could be had and the mandatory at any time be terminated by detachment of his territory from Anatolia as well as now and with much greater safety to him and convenience to his benefactors.

The conclusion of the American military mission to Armenia is that the remedy for the existing conditions in Armenia and the Transcaucasus is a mandatory control to be exercised by a single great power. The Armenian question can not be settled in Armenia. It can not be finally settled without answering two questions:

What is to be done with Turkey?
What is Russia going to do?

Pending the ultimate settlement of these questions the mission believes that, for reasons set forth, the power which takes a mandate for Armenia should also exercise a mandate for Anatolia, Roumelia, Constantinople, and Transcaucasia; the boundaries of the Turkish vilayets of Armenia and Anatolia and the interior boundaries of Russian Armenia, Georgia, and Azarbaijan to remain substantially as they are for the present. The divisions of such mandate are an administrative detail to be worked out by the mandatory power. Good administration indicates that there should be some intermediate authority between the provinces and the capital. A natural subdivision of such a mandate as has been indicated would probably be: Roumelia, city of Constantinople (federal district), Anatolia, Armenia, district of Transcaucasia (less Russian Armenia).

The inclusion of the whole Turkish Empire under the government of a single mandatory would be simpler and proportionately more economical than to divide it. A plebiscite fairly taken would in all probability ask for an American mandate throughout the Empire. Syria and Mesopotamia, however, not being considered essential to the settlement of the Armenian question or as being the field for possible American responsibilities and interests in the Near East as contemplated in the instructions to the mission, because actually occupied by France and Great Britain at this time, have been considered by us as excluded from our considerations, as is for a similar reason Arabia. In its belief that the Armenian problem is only to be solved by a mandatory which should include also Constantinople, Anatolia, Turkish Armenia, and the Transcaucasus, the mission has the concurrence of many Americans whose views by reason of long residence in the Near East are entitled to great weight. Such Americans are practically a unit in believing that the problems of Armenia, Anatolia, Constantinople, and Transcaucasia must be considered as an inseparable whole.

The mission has a strong conviction that the nation which may be induced by its colleagues to undertake this mandate should be one prepared to steadfastly carry out a continuity of policy for at least a generation, and to send only its most gifted sons to leadership in the work without regard to political affiliations. Only on the certainty of continuity of a nonpartisan policy would the best men forsake their careers in their own country to take up the burdens in these eastern lands. No disinterested nation would undertake such a mandatory except from a strong sense of altruism and international duty to the peace of the world in this breeding place of wars and at the unanimous wish of other parties to the covenant of the League of Nations.

No duty of modern times would be undertaken under so fierce a glare of publicity. Such nation would hold the center of the international stage, with the spotlight from every foreign office and from every church steeple in the world focussed upon it. No nation could afford to fail, or to withdraw when once committed to this most serious and difficult problem growing out of the Great War. No nation incapable of united and nonpartisan action for a long period should undertake it.

THE CONDITIONS AND PROBLEMS INVOLVED IN A MANDATE FOR TURKEY, AND TRANSCAUCASIA

This report has heretofore endeavored to consider the conditions and questions of which it treats in the abstract sense applicable to any nation which might be induced to assume the task of a practical regeneration of this region. Its interest for our country, however, lies in the possibility that the United States may be called upon by the world to undertake the task, and the necessity, therefore, of knowing what it would mean for America. The problems for the United States would not be identical with those of any other nation which might undertake it. A not too sympathetic Old World, without pretensions to altruism or too much devotion to ideals, will expect of America in the Near East the same lofty standards shown in Cuba and the Philippines—the development of peoples rather than of material resources and commerce. Distance, our time-honored detachment from the affairs of the Old World, our innocence from participation in the intrigues which have hitherto characterized intercourse with the Turk, our freedom from bias through the necessity of considering Moslem public opinion in other parts of the world, and the fact that we have no financial interest in the great foreign debt of the Ottoman Empire, give America a viewpoint and an advantage in approaching the situation that are enjoyed by no other great power.

A great part of the work of the mission has been devoted to a consideration of the situation as it would affect our own country should it be invited to assume a mandate in the Near East. The problem as a whole has been kept in mind while individual members of the mission have made special inquiry into different matters of which knowledge is necessary to reach an intellectual appreciation of the difficulties to be solved in this region. Each of these studies constitutes a unit on the subject with which it deals, too important to justify the risk of an attempt at epitomizing for this report. They are therefore submitted as appendices, as follows:

A. Political Factors and Problems, by Capt. Stanley K. Hornbeck, Ordnance Department, United States Army.

B. Government in Turkey and Transcaucasia, by Lieut. Col. Jasper Y. Brinton, Judge Advocate, United States Army.

C. Public and Private Finance of Turkey and Transcaucasia, by Prof. W. W. Cumberland.

D. Commerce and Industry in Turkey and Transcaucasia, by Trade Commissioner Eliot Grinnell Mears.

E. Public Health and Sanitation, by Col. Henry Beeuwkes, Medical Corps, United States Army.

F. Population; Industrial and Other Qualities; Maintenance, by Lieut. Col. John Price Jackson, Engineers, United States Army.

G. Climate, Natural Resources, Animal Industry, and Agriculture, by Lieut. Col. E. Bowditch, Infantry, United States Army.

H. Geography, Mining, and Boundaries, by Major Lawrence Martin, General Staff, United States Army.

I. The Press of Turkey and Transcaucasia, by Maj. Harold W. Clark, Infantry, United States Army.

J. The Military Problem of a Mandatory, by Brig. General George Van Horn Moseley, General Staff, United States Army.

K. Transport and Communications in Asia Minor and the Transcaucasus, by William B. Poland, engineer member of the mission.

L. Bibliography.

THE MILITARY PROBLEM

Our country has so recently sent its young manhood to war overseas and the heart of the Nation is so sensitive to any enterprise which calls for its sons to serve as soldiers in distant lands that the greatest interest attaches to the military problem involved in any mandate to which our people may ever give consideration.

The immediate problems which would lie before the Army and Navy of a mandatory power in Turkey and Transcaucasia are:

(a) The suppression of any disorder attendant upon withdrawal of occupying troops and the initiation of the government.

(b) The maintenance of order until a constabulary could be organized for the rural police of the mandatory region.

(c) To help organize and train a native constabulary.

(d) To constitute a reserve for moral effect, for possible actual use in supplementing the local constabulary in case of emergency, and for the prestige of the mandatory government in a region which has been governed by force since the beginning of history.

The inauguration of a mandatory government would be followed at a very early date by the withdrawal of the foreign troops now occupying the region and by the dissolution as soon as practicable of the permanent military establishments now maintained by Turkey and Transcaucasia. The United States accepting the mandate at the request of the other great powers and of the peoples interested, no resistance to her troops would be anticipated; on the contrary, they would doubtless be welcomed. No problem of external defense of the country occupied would exist.

(a) The present occupying force of the regions now under consideration, Roumelia, Constantinople, Anatolia, and Transcaucasia, excluding five Greek divisions occupying Smyrna, is the Army of the Black Sea and the troops in Cilicia, comprising about 50,000 of the British, French, Italian, and Greek Governments. The regular troops of Turkey and Transcaucasia to be disbanded in the same region at the convenience of the mandatory government aggregate about 92,000 men. The gendarmerie of Turkey amounts to about 30,000 men. The loss of man power in Turkey has been appalling, and too many men are still absent from work and carrying rifles.

It is not thought that any serious disorder would attend this substitution of the troops of the mandatory power for the army of occupation and for the native regular forces.

(b) During the formation of an efficient native constabulary, a period of six months to a year, small garrisons would have to be furnished along the railroads and in isolated towns, especially on the old frontiers, where feeling runs high between races. This would give security while the various nationals are being repatriated, reconstructing their homes, and adjusting themselves to new conditions. The suppression of outlaw bands, which already exist in some localities, and the formation of which in eastern countries invariably follows the disbandment of armies after a long war, would call for constant use of a certain number of United States troops pending the completion of the constabulary organization for service. During this period the disarmament of the civilian population would be accomplished.

(c) The first duty of a mandatory would be to guarantee the safety of life and property through the country, and to this end its earliest efforts should be directed to the establishment of a native rural police or constabulary for the suppression of brigandage, outlawry, and other crimes outside the towns. This force, with a military organization, should be a force of peace officers as that term is used in our own country, empowered to make arrests of criminals of all kinds, serve warrants, execute orders of arrest, etc. While decentralized in its administration, and destined eventually to operate in small bodies, it should be a Federal force, operating with but not serving under provincial officials. Its personnel should absorb the best elements of the present gendarmerie, and also provide suitable employment for deserving officers of the disbanded armies. For a considerable period its highest officers would necessarily be Americans, but as fast as the quality of the native officers justifies, the force should become native. The strength of the constabulary should be such as to enable it to take over the whole task of maintaining orders outside of towns and release American troops at the earliest practicable date. Coincident with the organization of the constabulary would be the creation of efficient municipal police.

(d) Considering the uncertain character of the neighboring populations, the traditional lawlessness of migratory Kurds and Arabs, and the isolation of certain regions where the temptation to reprisals for past wrongs will be strong for at least a generation, a certain force must be kept in hand to supplement the native constabulary when needed. Such a force will also be necessary for general moral effect. Its mere existence will prevent organized disorder on a scale too large for a peace force to handle. Such a force would be stationed near a capital, trained for quick expeditionary work, and sent where needed.

The character of the troops should be suited to the purpose for which used. For expeditionary purposes, marines or infantry with artillery would be best. For moral effect in the interior and during the period of constabulary organization, cavalry would be preferable. A small, efficient air service should be maintained. The aeroplane is not only a means of very rapid communication, but its value for dealing with a distant small problem among half-wild tribes can not be overestimated. The country much resembles Mexico, and the conditions would be not unlike our border cavalry service. A regiment of railway engineers would be a necessity. During the initial period of the mandatory, troops would be needed in connection with the general problem of sanitation and cleaning up, and an extra proportion of sanitary troops would be necessary.

Estimates of the necessary number of mandatory troops vary greatly—from 25,000 to 200,000. Conditions change so rapidly that plans made to-day for the use of troops might be obsolete in six months. Uncertainty as to the time the mandate will be tendered and accepted make estimates merely approximate. Under conditions as they exist to-day the undersigned believes that a force of two American divisions, with several hundred extra officers, or a total force of 59,000, would be ample. Such force would be specially organized; one aeroplane squadron; a minimum of artillery; not to exceed one regiment of 75's motorized; a minimum of the special services; four times the number of the usual sanitary troops; four regiments of cavalry, with minor changes in organization at the discretion of the senior general officer on duty with the mandatory government. This force should be substantially reduced at the end of two years, and by 50 percent at the end of the third year. After that some further reduction could be slowly effected, but the irreducible minimum would be reached at about the strength of one division.

The annual cost for the force of the Army above stated would be at the maximum:

For the first year $88,500,000
At the end of two years perhaps $59,000,000
At the end of three years $44,250,000

with thereafter a continuing appropriation of that sum less such amount as the local revenues could afford, probably a very substantial fraction of the cost.

To offset our expenditures there would be available at least a part of the naval and military budget hitherto used for the support of the disbanded armies in the region. In Turkey before the war this totaled about $61,000,000 annually for the Army, including $5,000,000 for the Navy.

The Naval Establishment should consist of a station ship for the capital, and probably one each for Smyrna, Mersina, Batum, and Baku, to meet local needs in quick transportation of troops. A transport of light draft capable of carrying a complete regiment should be permanently on station at the capital. Four to six destroyers would be needed for communication and moral effect. Collier, repair, and hospital service afloat should be in proportion. Old ships of obsolete type would probably answer for all except the station ship at the capitals and the destroyers. Some ships of the Turkish Navy, of which there are over 30, could doubtless be used with American crews soon to be replaced by natives.

The Naval Establishment might not entail any additional Federal appropriations. Ships and personnel could probably be drawn from existing establishment; the only additional expense would probably be the difference in cost of maintenance in near eastern and home waters.

It is very important that a proper military and naval setting be given the mandatory government at the beginning. In no part of the world is prestige so important, and in no region have people been so continuously governed by force. The mandatory could at the outset afford to take no unnecessary risks among such a population in densest ignorance as to our resources and our national traits.

CONCLUSION

This mission has had constantly in mind the moral effect to be exercised by its inquiry in the region visited. Very alarmingly reports had been received from Transcaucasia for several months before its departure from France, particularly as to organized attacks by the Turkish Army impending along the old international border between Turkey and Russia. The itinerary of the mission through Turkey was planned with those reports before it and with the intention of observing as to their truth and, if possible, to exert a restraining influence. We practically covered the frontier of Turkey from the Black Sea to Persia, and found nothing to justify the reports. The Turkish Army is not massed along the border; their organizations are reduced to skeletons; and the country shows an appalling lack of people, either military or civilian. At every principal town through which we passed the chief of the mission held a conference with the Turkish officials. Inquiry was made as to the Christian community, some were always interviewed; the interest of America in its own missionaries and in the native Christians was always emphasized; the Armenian deportations, the massacres, and the return of the survivors were discussed on each occasion, as well as other matters intended to convince Turkish officials that their country is on trial before the world. The visit of the mission has had a considerable moral effect in securing the safety of Christian lives and property pending action by the peace conference.

We would again point out that if America accepts a mandate for the region visited by this mission it will undoubtedly do so from a strong sense of international duty, and at the unanimous desire—so expressed at least—of its colleagues in the League of Nations. Accepting this difficult task without previously securing the assurance of conditions would be fatal to success. The United States should make its own conditions as a preliminary to consideration of the subject—

certainly before and not after acceptance, for there are a multitude of interests that will conflict with what any American would consider a proper administration of the country. Every possible precaution against international complications should be taken in advance. In our opinion, there should be specific pledges in terms of formal agreements with France and England and definite approval from Germany and Russia of the dispositions made of Turkey and Transcaucasia, and a pledge to respect them.

Of particular importance are the following:

Absolute control of the foreign relations of the Turkish Empire, no ambassador, envoy, minister, or diplomatic agent to be accredited to Turkey, and the latter to send none such abroad.

Concessions involving exclusive privileges to be subject to review if shown to be contrary to the best interests of the State.

Concessions undesirable from the standpoint of the mandatory upon which work has not been started to be canceled. Compensation to be allowed to holders when necessary.

The system by which specified revenues are assigned for particular purposes to be discarded. All revenues to be controlled by the treasury, and all creditors to look only to the treasury as the source of payment.

Foreign control over Turkey's financial machinery to cease, meaning the dissolution of the council of administration of the Ottoman public debt, reserving the right to retain some individual members of the council as advisers because of their familiarity with Ottoman finances.

All foreign obligations of the Empire to be unified and refunded.

Those countries receiving territory of the Turkish Empire, e.g., Syria and Mesopotamia, to assume their reasonable share of the paper currency, of the foreign obligations, and of obligation for possible reparation payments.

Abrogation, on due notice, of existing commercial treaties with Turkey.

All foreign Governments and troops to vacate territorial limits of mandate at dates to be fixed by the mandatory power.

Consent to many of these measures would not easily be obtained. Many nations now have some sort of financial control within the Ottoman Empire, and they would not see this control taken away without protest.

It needs no argument, however, to show that the United States could not submit to having her financial policies controlled from foreign capitals. The refunding of the debt, possibly with a reduction of the capital amount, would raise a storm of protest, but it should be insisted upon. Otherwise an American administration would be embarrassed and run the risk of being discredited.

The mission has not felt that it is expected to submit a recommendation as to the United States accepting a mandate in the Near East. It, therefore, simply submits the following summary of reasons for and against such action, based on all information obtainable during six weeks' constant contact with the peoples of the region:

Reasons for

1. As one of the chief contributors to the formation of the League of Nations, the United States is morally bound to accept the obligations and responsibilities of a mandatory power.

2. The insurance of world peace at the world's crossways, the focus of war infection since the beginning of history.

Reasons against

1. The United States has prior and nearer foreign obligations, and ample responsibilities with domestic problems growing out of the war.

2. This region has been a battle ground of militarism and imperialism for centuries. There is every likelihood that ambitious nations will still maneuver for its control. It would weaken our position

Reasons for	*Reasons against*
	relative to Monroe doctrine and probably eventually involve us with a reconstituted Russia. The taking of a mandate in this region would bring the United States into the politics of the Old World, contrary to our traditional policy of keeping free of affairs in the Eastern Hemisphere.
3. The Near East presents the greatest humanitarian opportunity of the age—a duty for which the United States is better fitted than any other— as witness Cuba, Porto Rico, Philippines, Hawaii, Panama, and our altruistic policy of developing peoples rather than material resources alone.	3. Humanitarianism should begin at home. There is a sufficient number of difficult situations which call for our action within the well-recognized spheres of American influence.
4. America is practically the unanimous choice and fervent hope of all the peoples involved.	4. The United States has in no way contributed to and is not responsible for the conditions, political, social, or economic, that prevail in this region. It will be entirely consistent to decline the invitation.
5. America is already spending millions to save starving peoples in Turkey and Transcaucasia and could do this	5. American philanthropy and charity are world wide. Such policy would commit us to a policy of meddling or

Reasons for

with much more efficiency if in control. Whoever becomes mandatory for these regions we shall be still expected to finance their relief, and will probably eventually furnish the capital for material development.

6. America is the only hope of the Armenians. They consider but one other nation, Great Britain, which they fear would sacrifice their interests to Moslem public opinion as long as she controls hundreds of millions of that faith. Others fear Britain's imperialistic policy and her habit of staying where she hoists her flag.

For a mandatory America is not only the first choice of all the peoples of the Near East but of each of the great powers, after itself.

American power is adequate; its record clean; its motives above suspicion.

7. The mandatory would be self-supporting after an initial period of not to exceed five years. The building of

Reasons against

draw upon our philanthropy to the point of exhaustion.

6. Other powers, particularly Great Britain, and Russia, have shown continued interest in the welfare of Armenia. Great Britain is fitted by experience and government, has great resources in money and trained personnel, and though she might not be as sympathetic to Armenian aspirations, her rule would guarantee security and justice.

The United States is not capable of sustaining a continuity of foreign policy. One Congress can not bind another. Even treaties can be nullified by cutting off appropriations. Nonpartisanship is difficult to attain in our Government.

7. Our country would be put to great expense, involving probably an increase of the Army and Navy. Large num-

Reasons for	*Reasons against*

railroads would offer opportunities to our capital. There would be great trade advantages not only in the mandatory region but in the proximity to Russia, Roumania, etc.

America would clean this hotbed of disease and filth as she has in Cuba and Panama.

bers of Americans would serve in a country of loathsome and dangerous diseases. It is questionable if railroads could for many years pay interest on investments in their very difficult construction. Capital for railways would not go there except on Government guaranty.

The effort and money spent would get us more trade in nearer lands than we could hope for in Russia and Roumania.

Proximity and competition would increase the possibility of our becoming involved in conflict with the policies and ambitions of States which now our friends would be made our rivals.

8. Intervention would be a liberal education for our people in world politics; give outlet to a vast amount of spirit and energy and would furnish a shining example.

8. Our spirit and energy can find scope in domestic enterprises, or in lands south and west of ours. Intervention in the Near East would rob us of the strategic advantage enjoyed through the Atlantic, which rolls between us and probable foes. Our reputation for fair dealing might be impaired. Efficient supervision of a mandate at such distance

Reasons for	*Reasons against*
	would be difficult or impossible. We do not need or wish further education in world politics.
9. It would definitely stop further massacres of Armenians and other Christians, give justice to the Turks, Kurds, Greeks, and other peoples.	9. Peace and justice would be equally assured under any other of the great powers.
10. It would increase the strength and prestige of the United States abroad and inspire interest at home in the regeneration of the Near East.	10. It would weaken and dissipate our strength, which should be reserved for future responsibilities on the American continents and in the Far East. Our line of communication to Constantinople would be at the mercy of other naval powers, and especially of Great Britain, with Gibraltar and Malta, etc., on the route.
11. America has strong sentimental interests in the region —our missions and colleges.	11. These institutions have been respected even by the Turks throughout the war and the massacres: and sympathy and respect would be shown by any other mandatory.
12. If the United States does not take responsibility in this region, it is likely that international jealousies will result	12. The peace conference has definitely informed the Turkish Government that it may expect to go under a man-

Reasons for	*Reasons against*

in a continuance of the unspeakable misrule of the Turk.

date. It is not conceivable that the League of Nations would permit further uncontrolled rule by that thoroughly discredited Government.

13. "And the Lord said unto Cain, 'Where is Abel, thy brother?' And he said, 'I know not; am I my brother's keeper?'"

Better millions for a mandate than billions for future wars.

13. The first duty of America is to its own people and its nearer neighbors.

Our country would be involved in this adventure for at least a generation, and in counting the cost Congress must be prepared to advance some such sums less such amount as the Turkish and Transcaucasian revenues could afford, for the first five years as follows:

FIRST YEAR

General government	$100,000,000
Communications, Railroads, etc.	20,000,000
Relief, repatriation, education, etc.	50,000,000
Army and Navy	88,500,000
Sanitation	17,000,000
Total	275,500,000

SECOND YEAR

General government	75,000,000
Communications, railroads, etc.	20,000,000
Relief, education, etc.	13,000,000
Army and Navy	59,000,000
Sanitation, etc.	7,264,000
Total	174,264,000

Reasons for   *Reasons against*

THIRD YEAR

General government	50,000,000
Communications, rail-roads, etc.	20,000,000
Relief, education, etc.	4,500,000
Army and Navy	44,250,000
Sanitation, etc.	5,000,000
Total	123,750,000

FOURTH YEAR

General government	25,000,000
Communications, rail-roads, etc.	20,000,000
Relief, education, etc.	4,500,000
Army and Navy	44,250,000
Sanitation, etc.	3,000,000
Total	96,750,000

FIFTH YEAR

General government	15,000,000
Communications, rail-roads, etc.	20,000,000
Relief, education, etc.	4,500,000
Army and Navy	44,250,000
Sanitation, etc.	2,000,000
Total	85,750,000

SUMMARY

Total first year	275,500,000
Total second year	174,264,000
Total third year	123,750,000
Total fourth year	96,750,000
Total fifth year	85,750,000
Grand total	756,014,000

14. Here is a man's job that the world says can be better done by America than by any

Reasons for   *Reasons against*

other. America can afford the
money; she has the men; no
duty to her own people would
suffer; her traditional policy
of isolation did not keep her
from successful participation
in the Great War. Shall it be
said that our country lacks
the courage to take up new
and difficult duties?

Without visiting the Near East it is not possible for an
American to realize even faintly the respect, faith, and affection with which our country is regarded throughout that region. Whether it is the world-wide reputation which we enjoy
for fair dealing, a tribute perhaps to the crusading spirit
which carried us into the Great War, not untinged with hope
that the same spirit may urge us into the solution of great
problems growing out of that conflict, or whether due to unselfish and impartial missionary and educational influence
exerted for a century, it is the one faith which is held alike
by Christian and Moslem, by Jew and Gentile, by prince and
peasant in the Near East. It is very gratifying to the pride of
Americans far from home. But it brings with it the heavy
responsibility of deciding great questions with a seriousness
worthy of such faith. Burdens that might be assumed on the
appeal of such sentiment would have to be carried for not
less than a generation under circumstances so trying that we
might easily forfeit the faith of the world. If we refuse to
assume it, for no matter what reasons satisfactory to ourselves, we shall be considered by many millions of people as
having left unfinished the task for which we entered the war,
and as having betrayed their hopes.

Respectfully submitted,

JAMES G. HARBORD
Major General, United States Army, Chief of Mission.

REFERENCES

1. pp. 8–13.

2. p. 606.

3. pp. 385–387.

4. p. 139.

5. p. 80.

6. pp. 230–233.

7. pp. 32–33.

8. p. 50.

9. p. 49.

10. *Ibid.*, p. 284.

11. Bierstadt, *op. cit.*, pp. 26–45.

Chapter 6

Proposals for a Mandate:
An Armenian Homeland

The Armenian survivors of the Turkish plan of extermination had the sympathy of the civilized world with them from the end of World War I. More substantive than sympathy, however, was their right to a homeland, which was theirs by virtue of several millennia of occupation, outstanding contributions to the fruitfulness and culture of the region, ownership and cultivation of the land and its resources, and the demonstrated unfitness of the Turkish government either morally or administratively to remain in control. Turkey was, moreover, an abjectly defeated power without a defender of any consequence anywhere.

In 1919, then, and for several years thereafter, the case for Armenia seemed strong and clear. The victorious powers were all in favor of granting an Armenian homeland: the logic of it and the moral imperative seemed to guarantee it. President Wilson, acting upon expert advice from Henry Morgenthau and other qualified persons, and answering to the clear wishes of the Allied Powers, urged the creation of such an Armenian homeland and went so far as to formulate its boundaries in considerable detail, with a scrupulous regard to Turkish interests so far as they could conceivably be considered legitimate.

The following pages show clearly not only the justice of

the Armenian case for a homeland but its tragic betrayal in the years that followed upon the Allied victory.

President Woodrow Wilson, message to Congress, May 24, 1920, *Congressional Record,* May 24, 1920:

MANDATE OVER ARMENIA (H. DOC. NO. 791).

The VICE PRESIDENT laid before the Senate the following message from the President of the United States, which was read and referred to the Committee on Foreign Relations, and ordered to be printed:

GENTLEMEN OF THE CONGRESS:

On the fourteenth of May an official communication was received at the Executive Office from the Secretary of the Senate of the United States conveying the following preambles and resolutions:

Whereas the testimony adduced at the hearings conducted by the subcommittee of the Senate Committee on Foreign Relations has clearly established the truth of the reported massacres and other atrocities from which the Armenian people have suffered; and

Whereas the people of the United States are deeply impressed by the deplorable conditions of insecurity, starvation, and misery now prevailing in Armenia; and

Whereas the independence of the Republic of Armenia has been duly recognized by the Supreme Council of the Peace Conference and by the Government of the United States of America: Therefore be it

Resolved, That the sincere congratulations of the Senate of the United States are hereby extended to the people of Armenia on the recognition of the independence of the Republic of Armenia without prejudice respecting the territorial boundaries involved; and be it further

Resolved, that the Senate of the United States hereby expresses the hope that stable government, proper protection of individual liberties and rights, and the full realization of nationalistic aspirations may soon be attained by the Armenian people; and be it further

Resolved, That in order to afford necessary protection for the lives and property of citizens of the United States at the port of Batum and along the line of the railroad leading to Baku, the President is hereby requested, if not incompatible with the public interest, to cause a United States warship and a force of marines to be dispatched to such port with instructions to such marines to disembark and to protect American lives and property."

I received and read this document with great interest and with genuine gratification, not only because it embodied my own convictions and feeling with regard to Armenia and its people, but also, and more particularly, because it seemed to me the voice of the American people expressing their genuine convictions and deep Christian sympathies, and intimating the line of duty which seemed to them to lie clearly before us.

I cannot but regard it as providential, and not as a mere casual coincidence, that almost at the same time I received information that the conference of statesmen now sitting at San Remo for the purpose of working out the details of peace with the Central Powers which it was not feasible to work out in the conference at Paris, had formally resolved to address a definite appeal to this Government to accept a mandate for Armenia. They were at pains to add that they did this, 'not from the smallest desire to evade any obligations which they might be expected to undertake, but because the responsibilities which they are already obliged to bear in connection with the disposition of the former Ottoman Empire will strain their capacities to the uttermost, and because they believe that the appearance on the scene of a power emancipated from the prepossessions of the Old World will inspire a wider confidence and afford a firmer guaranty for stability in the future than would the selection of any European power.'

Early in the conferences at Paris it was agreed that to those colonies and territories which as a consequence of the late war have ceased to be under the sovereignty of the States which formerly governed them and which are inhabited by peoples not yet able to stand by themselves under the strenuous conditions of the modern world there should be applied the principle that the well being and development of such peoples form a sacred trust of civilization, and that securities for the performance of this trust should be afforded.

It was recognized that certain communities formerly belonging to the Turkish Empire have reached a stage of development where their existence as independent nations can be provisionally recognized, subject to the rendering of administrative advice and assistance by a mandatory until such time as they are able to stand alone.

It is in pursuance of this principle and with a desire of affording Armenia such advice and assistance that the statesmen conferring at San Remo have formally requested this Government to assume the duties of mandatory in Armenia. I may add, for the information of the Congress, that at the same sitting it was resolved to request the President of the United States to undertake to arbitrate the difficult question of the boundary between Turkey and Armenia in the Vilayets of Erzeroum, Trebizond, Van and Bitlis, and it was agreed to accept his decision thereupon, as well as any stipulation he may prescribe as to access to the sea for the independent state of Armenia. In pursuance of this action, it was resolved to embody in the treaty with Turkey, now under final consideration, a provision that 'Turkey and Armenia and the other high contracting parties agree to refer to the arbitration of the President of the United States of America the question of the boundary between Turkey and Armenia in the Vilayets of Erzerum, Trebizond, Van and Bitlis, and to accept his decision thereupon as well as any stipulations he may prescribe as to access to the sea for the independent State of Armenia': pending that decision the boundaries of Turkey and Armenia to remain as at present. I have thought it my duty to accept this difficult and delicate task.

In response to the invitation of the council at San Remo, I urgently advise and request that the Congress grant the Executive power to accept for the United States a mandate for Armenia. I make this suggestion in the earnest belief that it will be the wish of the people of the United States that this should be done. The sympathy with Armenia has proceeded from no single portion of our people, but has come with extraordinary spontaneity and sincerity from the whole of the great body of Christian men and women in this country by whose free-will offerings Armenia has practically been saved at the most critical juncture of its existence. At their hearts this great and generous people have made the cause of Armenia their own. It is to this people and to their Government that the hopes and earnest expectations of the struggling people of Armenia turn as they now emerge from a period of indescribable suffering and peril, and I hope that the Congress will think it wise to meet this hope and expectation with the utmost liberality. I know from unmistakable evidences given by responsible representatives of many peoples struggling towards independence and peaceful life again that the Government of the United States is looked to with extraordinary trust and confidence, and I believe that it would do nothing less than arrest the hopeful processes of civilization if we were to refuse the request to become the helpful friends and advisers of such of these people as we may be authoritatively and formally requested to guide and assist.

I am conscious that I am urging upon the Congress a very critical choice, but I make the suggestion in the confidence that I am speaking in the spirit and in accordance with the wishes of the greatest of the Christian peoples. The sympathy for Armenia among our people has sprung from untainted consciences, pure Christian faith, and an earnest desire to see Christian people everywhere succored in their time of suffering, and lifted from their abject subjection and distress and enabled to stand upon their feet and take their place among the free nations of the world. Our recognition of the independence of Armenia will mean genuine liberty and assured happiness for her people, if we fearlessly undertake the duties of guidance and assistance involved in the functions of a mandatory. It is, therefore, with the most earnest hopefulness and with the feeling that I am giving advice from which the Congress will not willingly turn away that I urge the acceptance of the invitation now formally and solemnly extended to us by the council at San Remo, into whose hands has passed the difficult task of composing the many complexities and difficulties of government in the one-time Ottoman Empire and the maintenance of order and tolerable conditions of life in those portions of that Empire which it is no longer possible in the interest of civilization to leave under the government of the Turkish authorities themselves.

WOODROW WILSON.

THE WHITE HOUSE,
24 May, 1920.

Speeches in the Cathedral of St. John the Divine, November 11, 1920:

(1) Henry Morgenthau
(2) Josephus Daniels
(3) General J. G. Harbord
(4) Dr. Henry Van Dyke
(5) Resolution adopted

Quoted in *The New Armenia*, December, 1920.[1]

On November 11, 1920 a mass-meeting was held at the Cathedral of St. John the Divine in New York, with participants of Messrs. Henry Morgenthau, Hamilton Holt, Rev. George R. Montgomery, Rev. Herbert Shipman, Mr. Oscar Straus and other prominent Americans.

Mr. Morgenthau said in part: "Although the Armistice was signed two years ago, the war between right and might, between justice and spoilation is still in progress. They expected the United States to take a mandate for Armenia. We were simply tired. We again fell back to our state of complacency and indifference and refused to take up our share of the white man's burden. Isn't it about time for us to see the gross neglect we are perpetrating? The American people shirked nothing during the war. They are not going to shirk now in the last act of the war."

Hon. Josephus Daniels, Secretary of the Navy, in a telegram said: "The heart of America is in Armenia and the sympathy it has for these Christian comrades will continue to express itself in such benefactions as will contribute to their comfort."

General J. G. Harbord's message was: "True to their religion, language and race through a thousand years of persecutions, the Armenians must not be permitted to perish. Americans should aid them with moral, financial and political support."

Dr. Henry Van Dyke had sent a message which read in part: "Everybody who has memory, a mind, and a heart, must be concerned for the future of the Armenian people, and not only wish them well in their present distress and danger, but also desire to help them out of their trouble, and into a peaceful and secure life. I think that all civilized nations should concur in this wish, and co-operate, so far as may lie within their power, in this work."

The meeting adopted a resolution which concluded: "The time has come when expressions of sympathy should crystalize into action and the Armenians, who were our allies in the great war, should not be deserted in the time of their need. America, because of her long interest in the Armenians, her generous contributions for the perishing and dying and for the care of orphaned children, has not only gained the right to offer her services for their further protection, but also is brought face to face with a responsibility which she cannot escape."

President Woodrow Wilson, Letter to the President of the Supreme Council of the Allied Powers, November 22, 1920:

MR. PRESIDENT:

By action of the Supreme Council taken on April 26th of this year an invitation was tendered to me to arbitrate the question of the boundaries between Turkey and the new state of Armenia. Representatives of the powers signatory on August 10th of this year to the Treaty of Sevres have acquiesced in conferring this honor upon me and have signified their intention of accepting the frontiers which are to be determined by my decision, as well as any stipulation which I may prescribe as to access for Armenia to the sea and any arrangement for the demilitarization of Turkish territory lying along the frontier thus established. According to the terms of the arbitral reference set forth in part III, Section 6, Article 89, of the Treaty of Sevres, the scope of the arbitral competence assigned to me is clearly limited to the determination of the frontiers of Turkey and Armenia in the Vilayets of Erzerum, Trebizond, Van and Bitlis. With full consciousness of the responsibility placed upon me by your request, I have approached this difficult task with eagerness to serve the best interests of the Armenian people as well as the remaining inhabitants, of whatever race or religious belief they may be, in this stricken country, attempting to exercise also the strictest possible justice toward the populations, whether Turkish, Kurdish, Greek or Armenian, living in the adjacent areas.

In approaching this problem it was obvious that the existing ethnic and religious distribution of the population in the four vilayets could not, as in other parts of the world, be regarded as the guiding element of the decision. The ethnic consideration, in the case of a population originally so complexly intermingled, is further beclouded by the terrible results of the massacres and deportations of the Armenians and Greeks, and by the dreadful losses also suffered by the moslem inhabitants through refugee movements and the scourge of typhus and other diseases. The limitation of the arbitral assignment to the four vilayets named in Article 89 of the Treaty made it seem a duty and an obligation that as large an area within these vilayets be granted to the Armenian state as could be done, while meeting the basic requirements of an adequate natural frontier and of geographic and economic unity for the new state. It was essential to keep in mind the new state of Armenia, including as it will a large section of the former Armenian provinces of Transcaucasian Russia, will at the outset have a population about equally divided between Moslem and Christian elements and of diverse racial and tribal relationship. The citizenship of the Armenian Republic will, by the tests of language and religion, be composed of Turks, Kurds, Greeks, Kizilbashis, Lazes and others, as well as Armenians. The conflicting territorial desires of Armenians, Turks, Kurds and Greeks along the boundaries assigned to my arbitral decision could not always be harmonized. In such cases it was my belief that consideration of healthy economic life for the future state of Armenia should be decisive. Where, however, the requirements of correct geographic boundary permitted, all mountain and valley districts along the border which were predominantly Kurdish or Turkish have been left to Turkey rather than assigned to Armenia, unless trade relations with definite market towns threw them necessarily into the Armenian state. Wherever information upon tribal relations and seasonal migrations was obtainable, the attempt was made to respect the integrity of tribal groupings and nomad pastoral movements.

From the Persian border southwest to the town of Kotur the boundary line of Armenia is determined by a rugged natural barrier of great height, extending south of Lake

Van and lying southwest of the Armenian cities of Bitlis and Mush. This boundary line leaves as a part of the Turkish state the entire Sandjak of Hakkiari, or about one-half of the Vilayet of Van, and almost the entire Sandjak of Sairt. The sound physiographic reason which seemed to justify this decision was further strengthened by the ethnographic consideration that Hakkiari and Sairt are predominantly Kurdish in population and economic relations. It did not seem to the best interest of the Armenian state to include in it the upper valley of the Great Zab River, largely Kurdish and Nestorian Christian in population and an essential element of the great Tigris river irrigation system of Turkish Kurdistan and Mesopotamia. The control of these headwaters should be kept, wherever possible, within the domain of the two interested states, Turkey and Mesopotamia. For these reasons the Armenian claim upon the upper valley of the Great Zab could not be satisfied.

The boundary upon the west from Bitlis and Mush northward to the vicinity of Erzingan lies well within Bitlis and Erzerum vilayets. It follows a natural geographic barrier, which furnishes Armenia with perfect security and leaves to the Turkish state an area which is strongly Kurdish. Armenian villages and village nuclei in this section, such as Kighi and Temran, necessarily remain Turkish because of the strong commercial and church ties which connect them with Kharput rather (than) with any Armenian market and religious centers which lie within Bitlis or Erzerum vilayets. This decision seemed an unavoidable consequence of the inclusion of the city and district of Kharput in the Turkish state as determined by Article 27 II (4) and Article 89 of the Treaty of Sevres.

From the northern border of the Dersim the nature and the direction of the frontier decision was primarily dependent upon the vital question of supplying an adequate access to the sea for the state of Armenia. Upon the correct solution of this problem depends, in my judgment, the future economic well-being of the entire population, Turkish, Kurdish, Greek, Armenian, or Yezidi, in those portions of the vilayets of Erzerum, Bitlis and Van which lie within the state of Armenia. I was not unmindful of the desire of the Pontic Greeks, submitted to me in a memorandum similar, no doubt, in argument and content to that presented to the Supreme Council last March at its London Conference, that the unity of the coastal area of the Black sea inhabited by them be preserved and that arrangements be made for an autonomous administration for the region stretching from Riza to a point west of Sinope. The arbitral jurisdiction assigned to me by Article 89 of the Treaty of Sevres does not include the possibility of decision or recommendation by me upon the question of their desire for independence, or failing that, for autonomy. Nor does it include the right to deal with the littoral of the independent Sandjak of Djanik or of the Vilayet of Kastamuni into which extends the region of the unity and autonomy desired by the Pontic Greeks.

Three possible courses lay open to me: to so delimit the boundary that the whole of Trebizond Vilayet would lie within Turkey, to grant it in its entirety to Armenia, or to grant a part of it to Armenia and leave the remainder to Turkey. The majority of the population of Trebizond Vilayet is incontestably Moslem and the Armenian element, according to all pre-war estimates, was undeniably inferior numerically to the Greek portion of the Christian minority. Against a decision so clearly indicated on ethnographic grounds weighed heavily the future of Armenia. I could only regard the question in the light of the needs of a new political entity, Armenia, with mingled Moslem and Christian populations, rather than as a question of the future of the Armenians alone. It has been and is now increasingly my conviction that the arrangements providing for Armenia's access to the sea must be such as to offer every possibility for the development of this state as one capable of reassuming and maintaining that useful role in the commerce of the world which its geographic position, athwart a great historic trade route, assigned to it in the past. The civilization and the happiness of its mingled population will largely depend upon the building of railways and the increased accessibility of the hinterland of the three vilayets to European trade and cultural influences.

Eastward from the port of Trebizond along the coast of Lazistan, no adequate harbor facilities are to be found and the rugged character of the Pontic range separating Lazistan Sandjak from the Vilayet of Erzerum is such as to isolate the hinterland from the coast so far as practicable railway construction is concerned. The existing caravan route from Persia aross the plains of Bayazid and Erzerum, which passes through the towns of Baiburt and Gumushkhana and debouches upon the Black Sea at Trebizond, has behind it a long record of persistent usefulness.

These were the considerations which have forced me to revert to my original conviction that the town and harbor of Trebizond must become an integral part of Armenia. Because of the still greater adaptability of the route of the Karshut valley, ending at the town of Tireboli, for successful railway construction and operation I have deemed also essential to include this valley in Armenia, with enough territory lying west of it to insure its adequate protection. I am not unaware that the leaders of the Armenian delegation have expressed their willingness to renounce claim upon that portion of Trebizond Vilayet lying west of Surmena. Commendable as is their desire to avoid the assumption of authority over a territory so predominantly Moslem, I am confident that, in acquiescing in their eagerness to do justice to the Turks and Greeks in Trebizond I should be doing an irreparable injury to the future of the land of Armenia and its entire population, of which they will be a part.

It was upon such a basis, Mr. President, that the boundaries were so drawn as to follow mountain ridges west of the city of Erzingan to the Pontic range and thence to the Black Sea, in such a way as to include in Armenia the indentation called Zephyr Bey. The decision to leave to Turkey the harbor towns and hinterland of Kerasun and Ordu in Trebizond Sandjak was dictated by the fact that the population of this region is strongly Moslem and Turkish and that these towns are the outlets for the easternmost sections of the Turkish vilayet of Sivas. The parts of Erzerum and Trebizond Vilayets which, by reason of this delimitation, remain Turkish rather than become Armenian comprise approximately 12,120 square kilometers.

In the matter of demilitarization of Turkish territory adjacent to the Armenian border as it has been broadly described above, it seemed both impracticable and unnecessary to establish a demilitarized zone which would require elaborate prescriptions and complex agencies for their execution. Fortunately, Article 177 of the Treaty of Sevres prescribes the disarming of all existing forts throughout Turkey. Articles 159 and 196–200 provide in addition agencies clearly adequate to meet all the dangers of disorder which may arise along the borders, the former by the requirement that a proportion of the officers of the gendarmerie shall be supplied by the various Allied or neutral Powers, the latter by the establishment of a Military Inter-Allied Commission of Control and Organization. In these circumstances the only additional prescriptions which seemed necessary and advisable were that the Military Inter-Allied Commission of Control and Organization should, in conformity with the powers bestowed upon it by Article 200 of the Treaty, select the superior officers of the gendarmerie to be stationed in the vilayets of Turkey lying contiguous to the frontiers of Armenia solely from those officers who will be detailed by the Allied or neutral Powers in accordance with Article 159 of the Treaty; and that these officers, under the supervision of the Military Inter-Allied Commission of Organization and Control, should be especially charged with the duty of preventing military preparations directed against the Armenian frontier.

It is my confident expectation that the Armenian refugees and their leaders, in the period of their return into the territory thus assigned to them, will by refraining from any and all forms of reprisals give to the world an example of that high moral courage which must always be the foundation of national strength. The world expects of them that they give every encouragement and help within their power to those Turkish refugees who may desire to return to their former homes in the districts of Trebizond, Erzerum, Van and Bitlis remembering that these peoples, too, have suffered greatly. It is my further expectation that they will offer such considerate treatment to the Laz and the Greek inhabitants of the coastal region of the Black Sea, surpassing in the liberality of their administrative arrangements, if necessary, even the ample provisions for non-Armenian racial and religious groups embodied in the Minorities Treaty signed by them upon August 10th of this year, that these peoples will gladly and willingly work in completest harmony with the Armenians in laying firmly the foundation of the new Republic of Armenia.

I have the honor to submit herewith the text of my decision.

Accept (etc.)

WOODROW WILSON

Washington, November 22, 1920.

Post War Treaties and Declarations:

The Allied Powers, Jointly

(a) *Anglo-French Declaration,* November 2, 1918, quoted *in La Société des Nations et les Puissances devant le Probleme Armenien.*[2]

> To pursue these intentions France and Great Britain agree to encourage and help the establishment of native governments and administrations in Syria and Mesopotamia, actually liberated by the Allies, or in territories the liberation of which they pursue, and to recognize those that have already been effectively established.
>
> Far from wishing to impose upon the peoples of these regions such and such institutions, they have no concern other than to insure by their support and by efficient help the normal functioning of governments and administrations which shall be freely given.
>
> To insure an impartial and equal justice for all, to facilitate the economic development of the country by reviving and encouraging local initiative, to favor diffusion of instruction, to put an end to the divisions exploited by Turkish politics for a long time, such is the role which the two allied governments demand in the liberated territories.

(b) *United States, Great Britain, France, Italy and Japan,* a joint declaration, January 30, 1919, quoted in *The Great Betrayal,* by E. H. Bierstadt.

On January 30, 1919, at the Quai d'Orsay, representatives of the above countries, meeting in conference, adopted a resolution from which the following is abstracted:

"(1) That in settling the issues of the Turkish Empire, account may rightfully be taken of any 'menace' to 'the function and security of all nations';

"(2) That the 'historical misgovernment by the Turks of subject peoples and the terrible massacres of Armenians and others in recent years' constitute a special reason for separation of territory but 'without prejudice to the settlement of other parts of the Turkish Empire';

"(3) That this separation of territory should be taken as a

special opportunity to apply 'the principle that the well-being and development of subject peoples are a sacred trust of civilization and that securities for the performance of this trust should be embodied in the constitution of the League of Nations';

"(4) That this principle should be carried out through the mandatory system, which the remaining resolutions carefully define."[3]

(c) *Reply to President Wilson by the Chief Ministers of Great Britain, France and Italy,* December 25, 1916, quoted in *Memoirs of the Peace Conference,*[4] by David Lloyd George.

On Christmas Day 1916 the Chief Ministers of Great Britain, France and Italy met in London and prepared a joint reply to President Wilson's quest for the Allied conditions of peace. This reply cabled to the President contained the following declaration:

"The liberation of non-Turkish peoples who then lay beneath the murderous tyranny of the Ottoman Empire, and the expulsion from Europe of that Empire, which had proved itself so radically alien to Western civilization."

(d) *Proposal by the Council of Four,* May 14, 1919, quoted in *Memoirs of the Peace Conference,*[5] by David Lloyd George.

In a meeting of the Council of Four David Lloyd George, after consultation with President Wilson and M. Clemenceau, proposed the following:

(1) A mandate over the province of Armenia as constituted within frontiers to be agreed upon between the U.S.A., British, French and Italian delegations with recommendations, if unanimous, shall be accepted without further reference to the Council.

The proposal was accepted by all the European delegations. President Wilson accepted the proposal "on behalf of the U.S.A. and subject to consent of the Senate thereof," but, says Lloyd George, "made it quite clear to M. Clemenceau and myself that he was not in a position to state definitely that the U.S. would assent to the proposal."

(e) *James B. Gidney, A Mandate for Armenia.* Kent,

Ohio: The Kent State University Press, 1967.

As to documents submitted to the Peace Conference Professor Gidney writes:

The conference was swamped by a flood of documents of all kinds; it is impossible to estimate how many of the delegates, or even the experts, read any of them. Any who took the trouble to read the Armenian case found the following demands:

1) Recognition of an independent Armenian state formed by a union of the seven vilayets (the six—Erzeroum, Van, Bitlis, Harput, Sivas, Diarbekir, Kharput—plus Trebizond), Cilicia and the Armenian Republic of the Caucasus, its precise boundaries to be settled by a commission of the great powers;

2) The state thus created to be guaranteed by the powers and the League of Nations in which it claimed membership;

3) A mandate not to exceed twenty years' duration, with the Armenian National Conference, which had been sitting in Paris since before the war, to be consulted on the choice of a mandatory;

4) An indemnity for massacres, spoliations and devastation to be fixed by the peace conference and paid by Turkey, in return for which Armenia would assume a share of the Ottoman debt;

5) The mandatory to be responsible for the following:

a) expulsion of all Turkish and Tartar authorities,

b) disarmament of the population,

c) expulsion and punishment of those guilty of massacre, violence and pillage or profiting therefrom,

d) expulsion of disruptive elements and nomad tribes which could not be brought under the control of the government,

e) repatriation of *muhajjirs*, i.e., Moslem colonists settled during the Hamidean and Young Turk periods,

f) restoration of Christian women forcibly placed in harems, with the Turks paying damages in such cases, as well as indemnities for the destruction of schools, churches, and monasteries.

It was further demanded that Armenian religious authorities should be allowed to dispose of any Armenian community property remaining in Turkey after the boundaries had been fixed, with the proceeds of such sales to their (respective) congregations.

Any person of Armenian origin in any other country was to be given five years in which to choose the new nationality for himself and his minor children. The document concluded by rejecting all Syrian and French claims to Cilicia.[6]

Referring to the U.S. mandate for Armenia Professor Gidney quotes from Vol. V, p. 583 of *The Paris Peace Conference*, 1919 (U.S. State Department, Washington, D.C., Government Printing Office) the following suggestions made by Lloyd George on May 13, 1919:

"The United States should take a mandate for Armenia, France should take a mandate for northern Anatolia, Italy for southern Anatolia; and Greece should be dealt with as proposed by President Wilson (i.e.,—sovereignty for Smyrna and the adjacent district and a mandate for the rest of the territory claimed by Venizelos). The United States, he earnestly hoped, would also take a mandate for Constantinople."[7]

In spite of President Wilson's hesitations, the Big Three (Great Britain, France and the United States) accepted Lloyd George's suggestion and adopted the following resolution, "subject to the consent of the Senate:"

"(It gave to the United States) a mandate over the Province of Armenia as constituted within frontiers to be agreed upon between the United States, British, French and Italian delegations, whose recommendations, if unanimous, shall be accepted without further reference to the Council."[8]

The King-Crane Commission*

Henry Churchill King, President of Oberlin College "a man of sound judgment and high ideals, author of several theological works and serving as chairman of the Committee on the War and the Religious Outlook."

* In order to have complete and authentic knowledge of the conditions in Asia Minor, President Wilson proposed the appointment of a commission to study the situation and report thereon with a desirable recommendation, which might do away with unnecessary arguments and controversies. His suggestion, however, met with lukewarm reception on the part of

Charles R. Crane, a former president of the Crane Company, . . . "member of a special commission of inquiry in Russia, headed by Elihu Root."

The King-Crane Commission included among its personnel George R. Montgomery, a Congregationalist minister, who served as special assistant to the (American) Ambassador in Constantinople in 1917, Professor Albert H. Lybyer, a teacher of mathematics at Robert College in Turkey, of History at Harvard, Oberlin, and the University of Illinois; Captain William Yale, a member of the American Commission to Negotiate Peace, Armenian military advisor assigned to General Allenby's headquarters.

After several months of unnecessary delay caused by constant squabble, the membership of the Commission was completed and it embarked upon its journey to review the conditions in areas presenting special problems. They were to visit Turkey, Syria and near-eastern localities. They met various groups in various countries; received testimonies from opposing groups.

In his discussion of the Armenian situation as regarded by the King-Crane Commission, Professor Gidney writes:

> Although it had been pretty clear from the first days of the peace conference that a separate Armenia would be created, the Commission felt obliged to justify it. It found its reason for an Armenian state in the unfitness of the Turks to rule even themselves, the bad treatment accorded by Turkish governments to the Turkish people and their much worse treatment of subject peoples. However, the 'great and primary' reason for breaking up Turkey was the massacre of the Armenians. The only way in which Armenians could be protected in a Turkish state would be to establish a permanent mandate, while the League of Na-

---

the British and vehement objection by the French and Italians. The French insisted upon the enforcement of the Sykes-Picot Agreement by the terms of which Turkey was to be divided into spheres of influence and control among the British, French and Italians and the Russians. In spite of violent disagreements between the Allied Powers, President Wilson named the two outstanding members of the Commission—Henry Churchill King and Charles R. Crane—by whose names the Commission came to be known— King-Crane Commission.

tions mandates were to be temporary. Since nothing less would guarantee the Armenian's safety or satisfy the world's conscience, a separate mandate for Armenia was imperative.[9]

Admiral Mark Bristol, commander of the American Naval Forces at Constantinople, Caleb F. Gates, President of Robert College at Constantinople and Mary Mills Patrick, former President of Constantinople Women's College, opposed the "creation of an Armenian state," while Dr. James L. Barton, former president of Euphrates College in Khraput, William W. Peet, Treasurer of the American Board of Foreign Missions, George E. White, President of Anatolia College at Marsovan, and Mary Graffam, an American Missionary from Sivas argued that "it was no longer possible for Turks and Armenians to live under the same government . . ." White went further than the others in believing the Turks could not be trusted with even a "shred of independence."

The reader would please note that those who defended the political and territorial integrity of Turkey were stationed in Constantinople and could not be credited with knowledge of the conditions in the interior of Turkey, or whatever knowledge they possessed was based on biased information and distorted facts. Whereas those who defended the right of the Armenians to be free had lived among the people in the interior of Turkey and had first-hand knowledge of the misrule and barbaric character of the Turk.

Gates had made his position clear as early as April 1919, by a statement sent to the State Department from Constantinople. In that statement he deplored the fact that "armed Armenian soldiers" were employed in Cilicia. "It is feared," he wrote, "that the creation of an Armenian kingdom will be a signal for serious trouble all over the country." He advised (advocated) the policy of "an undivided Turkey under the control of some power that will administer it, giving equal justice to all races and nationalities." (*National Archives*, State Department, 860j, 01/5, 93–94)

James W. Gerard vehemently condemned Gates' statement

by accusing him of far greater interest in Robert College than in the welfare of Armenia.

As to Admiral Bristol it seems that his support of the Turks was only surpassed by his opposition to the Armenians, as may well be seen by the sentiments he displays in his statements and letters of which we reproduce only part of one written to Frank L. Polk, Undersecretary of State and the head of the American delegation in Paris. This letter was dated January 15, 1920 which we quote from Professor Gidney's book: *"I certainly hope that under no circumstances will our government recognize Armenia, even as a de facto government."*[10] [Emphasis ours—D.H.B.]

The King-Crane Commission did not propose to ". . . establish the rule of a minority of Armenians over a majority of other peoples . . . But such a separated state should furnish a definite area into which Armenians could go with the complete assurance that they would never be put under the rule of the Turks. It should also be a region to which Armenians could gradually concentrate, and from which the Turkish population might increasingly tend to withdraw, though no compulsion should be put on any people." (Quoted from *Paris Peace Conference*, XII, 819–820)

Professor Gidney comments:

> However, if the state were restricted to an area more nearly equivalent to ancient Armenia, if as many Armenians as possible were repatriated to that area, and if the movement of Armenians from other parts of Turkey were facilitated while those Turks who wanted to move out were helped to do so, there existed a strong possibility that by 1925 a small Armenian majority would have been created. That purpose would be advanced by incorporating the Republic of Armenia into the new state.
>
> Because an Armenian majority would not exist at the outset* and because even when a majority was created, it would be a small one, a short term mandate would not serve the purpose. A mandate of longer term was therefore

---

* Because the Armenians were driven away from their homes, were slaughtered or died on route during their deportation.

recommended with the United States as mandatory power. An American mandate was desired by the Armenians, approved by the Allies, and even preferred by the Turks, if there had to be a mandate. (Professor Gidney refers to PPC XII, 819–820)

The Commission would not recommend the American acceptance of the mandate as proposed by it unless it was definitely established.

> . . . that she (the United States) is really wanted by the Turks; that Turkey should give evidence that she is ready to do justice to the Armenians, not only by the allotment of the territory within her borders, recommended for the Armenian state, but also by encouraging the repatriation of Armenians, and by seeing that all possible just reparation is made to them as they return to their homes; that Turkey should also give evidence that she is ready to become a modern constitutional state, and to abolish military conscription; that Russia should be ready to renounce all claims upon Russian Armenia; that the Allies should cordially welcome America's help in the difficult situation in Turkey; and especially that all plans for cutting up Turkey for the benefit of outside peoples into spheres of influence and exploitation areas should be abandoned. These conditions are necessary to a successful solution of the Turkish problem. Unless they are fulfilled, America ought not to take the mandate for Asia Minor. And the commissioners do not recommend that the mandate be given to America if these conditions cannot be substantially met." (Quoted by Professor Gidney from PPC XII, 847–848)

"The report of the King-Crane Commission was completed late in August, 1919," he continues, and "On the 28th the full text was delivered to the peace conference in Paris. President Wilson was advised of its recommendations on the 31st but the full report did not reach the White House until September 27. It was, therefore, not available to the President until after the physical collapse which caused the cancellation of his nation-wide speaking tour in support of the Covenant of the League of Nations."[11]

Unfortunately the report of the King-Crane Commission

never saw the light officially. It was "suppressed" both by Washington and the Peace Conference to whom it had been submitted. Professor Gidney makes the following comment:

"However we describe it, the disappearance of the King-Crane Report* can only be accounted a misfortune for the Armenians. It could have done them no harm; it might have done them some good. The similarity of its findings to those of the Harbord Mission would surely have lent some weight to the argument for the mandate."[12]

REPORT
of the
KING-CRANE COMMISSION

Pursuant to the Resolution adopted by the Representatives of the United States, Great Britain, France, Italy and Japan at Quai d'Orsay, on January 30, 1919, President Wilson, Mr. Lloyd George, Mr. Clemenceau and Mr. Orlando agreed to send Commissioners from the Peace Conference "to make inquiries in certain portions of the Turkish Empire which are to be permanently separated from Turkey and put under the guidance of governments acting as Mandatories for the League of Nations."

Upon the suggestion of the then Secretary of State, Robert Lansing, President Wilson, on April 15, 1919, appointed Henry Churchill King, President of Oberlin College, Ohio, and Charles R. Crane, Treasurer of the American Committee for Armenian and Syrian Relief as the two American Commissioners.

The American Section of the International Commission on Mandates in Turkey submitted reports upon Syria, Mesopotamia and non-Arabic-speaking portions of the former Ottoman Empire.

The itinerary of the American Commissioners began at Jaffa, Palestine, and ended in Adana, Turkey. The Commissioners visited many cities and towns and interviewed a

* The text of the missing report is herewith presented.

great many persons, including government officials, civic leaders, educators, business men, leaders in many walks of life, as well as representatives of the common people. The trip lasted 41 days, from June 10 to July 21, 1919.

Our immediate concern is that part of the Report dealing with the Armenian situation and the Commissioners' recommendation for the solution of the Armenian problem. The pertinent portions of the Report shall be set forth in the following pages.

The Commissioners consider the situation "unique" in Turkey as to mandates, compared to the situations existing in Syria and Mesopotamia. "For in the case of the proposed State of Armenia, for example," they report, the territory was not yet set off, nor its boundaries even approximately known; the Armenians were not largely present in any of the territory to be assigned; the wishes of the Armenians themselves as to mandate were already known; and the wishes of the rest of the population could not be taken primarily into account, since the establishment of the Armenian State would be in a sense penal for the Turkish people, and naturally to be accepted only as a necessity."

The Peace Conference had already taken pertinent action concerning the fate of certain areas in Turkey. The Resolution on January 30, 1919, contained the following:

"2. For similar reasons (freedom and security of all nations), and more particularly because of the historical misgovernment by the Turks of subject peoples and the terrible massacres of Armenians and others in recent years, the Allied and Associated Powers are agreed that Armenia, Syria, Mesopotamia, Palestine and Arabia must be completely severed from the Turkish Empire. This is without prejudice to the settlement of other parts of the Turkish Empire."

The Commissioners make the following observation about the Resolution:

The Resolutions clearly assert several things: (1) that in settling the issues of the Turkish Empire, account may rightfully be taken of any "menace" to "the freedom and security of all nations"; (2) that "the historical mis-government by the Turks of subject peoples and the terrible massacres of Armenians and others in recent years constitute a special reason for separation of territory, but "without prejudice to the settlement of other parts of the Turkish Empire"; (3) that this separation of territory should be taken as a special opportunity to apply "the principle that the well-being and development of subject peoples form a sacred trust of civilization and that the securities for the performance of this trust should be embodied in the constitution of the League of Nations"; (4) that this principle should be carried out through the mandatory system, which the remaining resolutions carefully define.

The Instructions then continue: "And it is agreed that the administration of these mandates shall be in the spirit of the following document which was formally presented to the President of the United States on behalf of the Government of Great Britain and France":

The aim which France and Great Britain have in view in prosecuting in the East the war let loose by German ambition is the complete and final liberation of the peoples so long oppressed by the Turks and the establishment of national governments and administrations deriving their authority from the initiative and free choice of the native populations.

In order to give effect to these intentions, France and Great Britain have agreed to encourage and assist the establishment of native governments and administrations in Syria and Mesopotamia already liberated by the Allies, and in the territories which they are proceeding to liberate, and they have agreed to recognize such governments as soon as they are effectively established. So far from desiring to impose specific institutions upon the populations of these regions, their sole object is to ensure, by their support and effective assistance, that the governments and administrations adopted by these regions of their own free will shall be exercised in the normal way. The function which the two Allied Governments claim for themselves in the liberated territories is to ensure impartial and equal justice for all; to facilitate the economic development of the country by encouraging local initiative; to promote the diffusion of education; and to put an end to the divisions too long exploited by Turkish policy.

This is as admirable a statement of the spirit in which mandates should be administered as could be asked, and reflects honor on the two great Allies from whom it originally came.

Taken as a whole, the actions of the Peace Conference, in which all the Allies have shared, reflected in the forming of the Commission on Mandates and embodied in the Instructions to the Commission, form a solid basis for the policy to be adopted in Asia Minor. It is no sentimental program; but it is just on the one hand, and considerate on the other. If the Conference proceeds, in its further dealings with Turkey, honestly and strongly and consistently to build on the foundations so prepared, essential justice will be done to all the peoples concerned, rankling wrongs will be set right, and the purposes of the Allies will be just so far vindicated.

But that situation, and similar situations among the best in all the Allies, can be changed only by some clear demonstration that somewhere and on a large and impressive scale, the often asserted high and unselfish aims of the Allies have been honestly carried out. That would come like an invigorating breeze out of the North, bringing new faith in men and in the genuineness of human ideals and endeavor.

That opportunity is offered, in a peculiar degree, in the righteous settlement of the problems of the Turkish Empire. No namby-pamby, sickly sentimental treatment is called for here. There are great and lasting wrongs in Turkey which must be set right. And there are world relations and interests honestly to be recognized and permanently to be satisfied. For the sake of justice to Turkey herself and to all her subject peoples; for the sake of the honor of the Allies and the renewed confidence of men in them; for the stemming of the tide of cynicism and selfish strife; for a fresh and powerful demonstration of moral soundness in the race; the Allies should recognize the grave dangers of all selfish exploitation of Turkey, and turn their backs on every last vestige of it.

After condemning the "policy of selfish exploitation in Turkey" which "in its entirety is not the deliberate aim of any power," the Commissioners inquire into "a proper division of the Turkish Empire."

Let us read the Report.

But if a selfishly exploiting division of the Turkish Empire is not justified it may be asked: Why is it necessary to divide Asia Minor, at least, at all? For such a division there are at least two great reasons: first, the hideous mis-government and massacres of the Turkish rule; and second, Turkey's utter inadequacy to the strategic world position in which she is placed.

1. In the first place, there cannot be left out of account the hideous mis-government of Turkey for centuries, even for citizens of the Turkish race.

(1) One may recognize fully the agreeable and attractive personal qualities of the Turks that commonly make them the best liked, probably, of all the peoples in the Empire, and that almost unconsciously turn most foreigners who stay long in the country into pro-Turks. One may recognize, too, that there has long been in the Turkish Government a kind of negative, indolent tolerance of other peoples, that allowed them much of the time to go on in their own ways, though constantly despised, robbed, oppressed. It may be granted, also, that the Turks have been successful in keeping, through long periods, widely scattered areas together and giving them a sort of unity, by the method of "divide and rule", of leaving regional governments pretty largely to themselves so long as the Turkish revenues were obtained; and of using other races very largely as officials. It is only fair, also, to remember the very considerable amount of demoralization caused by the perpetual intriguing of European powers in Turkish affairs.

(2) But while all this may be freely admitted, it must still be clearly seen, that the Government of the Turkish Empire has been for the most part a wretched failure, in spite of

generally good laws. For that Government has been characterized by incessant corruption, plunder, and bribery. It might almost be called a government of simple exploitation. So that Ramsay, who judges the Turk leniently, feels obliged to say: "The Turk is not naturally a good officer or a good official" . . . .[13] "Bribery is the universal rule."[14] And he speaks of the deep-seated mingled hatred and fear on the part even of the Turkish peasantry for government officials. In fact it is hardly too much to say that Turkish history shows gross neglect of the most ordinary and essential duties of a government in the Empire as a whole.

(3) And the treatment of the other subjects has been still worse than that of the Turks. For them nothing has been secure—whether property, lives, wives, or children. To all this have been added the horrible massacres of the Armenians, especially since Abd-ul-Hamid's time, and somewhat similar deportations of the Greeks. Both races have proved themselves abler, more industrious, enterprising, and prosperous than the Turks, and so have made themselves feared and hated, doubtless not altogether without some provocation on their part in certain cases. And these massacres have been due to deliberate and direct government action, in which the Turkish people themselves have been too willing to share. They have not been crimes of the passion of the moment. And they have involved cruelties horrible beyond description.

For it must not be forgotten that this thing was not done in a corner. The evidence for few events in history has been more carefully gathered, sifted and ordered. The Bryce report upon *The Treatment of Armenians in the Ottoman Empire, 1915–16*,[15] leaves no room for doubt of the essential facts. It is idle to attempt to deny it, or appreciably to mitigate its force.

Lord Bryce, himself a trained historian, says of the report: "Nothing has been admitted the substantial truth of which seems open to reasonable doubt." And in estimating the value of the evidence, he calls attention to these facts: (1) "Nearly all of it comes from eye witnesses"; (2) "the main facts rest upon evidence coming from different and independent sources"; (3) "facts of the same, or of a very similar nature, occurring in different places, are deposed to by different and independent witnesses",—including Danish and German witnesses; (4) "the volume of this concurrent evidence from different quarters is so large as to establish the main facts beyond all question"; (5) "in particular is it to be noted that many of the most shocking and horrible accounts are those for which there is the most abundant testimony from the most trustworthy neutral witnesses. None of these cruelties rest on native evidence alone." And he adds: "A recollection of previous massacres will show that such crimes are a part of a long settled and often repeated policy of Turkish rulers" . . . . "The attempts made to find excuses for wholesale slaughter and for the removal of a whole people from its homes leave no room for doubt as to the slaughter and the removal. The main facts are established by the confession of the criminals themselves . . . ."[16] The disproval of palliations which the Turks have put forward is as complete as the proof for the atrocities themselves."

Mr. Moorfield Storey, ex-President of the American Bar Association, records the natural verdict of one skilled in the weighing of evidence, when he writes to Lord Bryce: "In my opinion, the evidence which you print is as reliable as that upon which rests our belief in many of the universally admitted facts of history, and I think it establishes beyond all reasonable doubt the deliberate purpose of the Turkish authorities practically to exterminate the Armenians, and their responsibility for the hideous atrocities which have been perpetrated upon that unhappy people."

It is not pleasant to call these dark facts to mind, but unfortunately there is only the slightest evidence that the Turkish Government or people as a whole have recognized or repudiated the crime of the Armenian massacres, or done anything appreciable to set them right. Some small groups of Turks have characterized these crimes aright, but there is almost nothing to show repentance or the fruits of repentance on the part of the great majority of the people or of their leaders, or to give reasonable hope that the massacres might not be repeated; though there is doubtless some excuse for the comparative indifference with which these massacres have been regarded by the Turks, because of a certain amount of revolutionary activity on the part of the Armenians in some cases, and because of the widespread wretchedness and want and sufferings of the whole Turkish population in ten years of war and disorder.

Now these crimes—black as anything in human history—cannot be simply forgotten and left out of account in seeking a righteous solution of the Turkish problem. If the rankest conceivable wrongs are not to be passed over in silence, it is inevitable that any just solution of the Turkish problem must contain that small measure of justice which it is now possible to render in this case.

It is strange that Lord Bryce in reviewing all the evidence concerning the Armenian massacres of 1915–16 should feel compelled to say: "The record of the rulers of Turkey for the last two or three centuries, from the Sultan on his throne to the district Mutessarif, is, taken as a whole, an almost unbroken record of corruption, of injustice, of an oppression which often rises into hideous cruelty . . . ."[17] Can anyone still continue to hope that the evils of such a government are curable? Or does the evidence contained in this volume furnish the most terrible and convincing proof that it cannot longer be permitted to rule over subjects of a different faith"? Is it strange that he should be unable to shake off the conviction that these facts are inevitably knit up with a proper solution of the problem of Turkey: "It is evidently desirable", he writes, "that the public opinion of the belligerent nations —and, I may add, of neutral peoples also—should be enabled by knowledge of what has happened in Asia Minor and Armenia, to exercise its judgment on the course proper to be followed when, at the end of the present war, a political resettlement of the Nearer East has to be undertaken".

Surely the Peace Conference was justified in its resolution:

"more particularly because of the historical mis-government by the Turks of subject peoples and the terrible massacres of Armenians and others in recent years, the Allied and Associated Powers are agreed that Armenia . . .[18] must be completely severed from the Turkish Empire".

That the formation of a separate Armenian State is the deliberate intention of the Peace Conference seems further indicated in the later actions of the Conference concerning Armenia, like the appointment of Colonel Haskell as High Commissioner in Armenia on behalf of the four Great Powers, and the appointment of Major General Harbord by President Wilson to investigate conditions in Armenia. Many incidental things also indicate the general expectation on the part of the Allies that an Armenian State will be formed.

(4) The great and primary reason for this decision by the Peace Conference, is undoubtedly to be found in the Armenian massacres which have just been reviewed. But it might still be asked whether the situation created by the massacres could be met only by the formation of a separate Armenia. For such a separation, it must be admitted, involves very difficult problems. Why, then, is it necessary to set off an Armenian State? What are the reasons?

The only possible substitute for a separated Armenia is a general mandate by one of the Great Powers over all Asia Minor, which should ensure equal rights to all elements of the population,—to all races, and to all religions. If such a mandate were honestly carried out, we should certainly hope for a far better government on modern lines. But under the proposed mandatory system of the League of Nations, it is intended that the mandate shall be for a limited period. Even if that period were considerably prolonged, what would happen when the Mandatary withdrew? It is impossible to be sure, if the Turks still constituted the majority, that the state would not slump back into many of its old evils, including oppression of other races. The history of the Turks, unfortunately, gives all too small reason to hope for more.

The reasons for a separate Armenia, then, may be said to

be: because of the demonstrated unfitness of the Turks to rule over others, or even over themselves; because of the adoption of repeated massacres as a deliberate policy of State; because of almost complete lack of penitence for the massacres, or repudiation of the crime—they rather seek to excuse them; because practically nothing has been done by the Turks in the way of repatriation of Armenians or of reparations to them—a condition not naturally suggesting a repetition of the experiment of Turkish rule; because, on the contrary, there is evidence of intense feeling still existing against the Armenians, and implicit threatening of massacre; because there has been sufficient proof that the two races cannot live peaceably and decently together so that it is better for both that they have separate states; because of complete failure of the strong clauses of the Treaty of 1878[19] to protect the Armenians; because the most elementary justice suggests that there must be at least some region in Turkey where Armenians can go and not have to live under Turkish rule; because nothing less than that could give to the Armenians any adequate guarantee of safety; because, consequently, nothing less will satisfy the conscience of the world upon this point; because in this day of opportunity for small nations under the League of Nations, the Armenians have surely earned the right, by their sufferings, their endurance, their loyalty to principles, their unbroken spirit and ambition, and their demonstrated industry, ability and self-reliance, to look forward to a national life of their own; because such a separate state would probably make more certain decent treatment of Armenians in other parts of Turkey; and because there is no adequate substitute for such a state. In the interests of the Armenians, of the Turks, and of the peace of the world alike, the formation of a separate Armenian State is to be urged.

The Commissioners discuss at length the age-old Eastern Question which has plagued Europe for centuries and has caused concern and anxiety to many European statesmen. They consider various possibilities for a "righteous division" of Turkey which "is held by a people whose incompetence to convert nature's gifts into use or profit is historically patent" (Dominian, Frontiers of Language and Nationality in Europe, p. 236).

The problem of the control of Constantinople and the Straits is widely discussed by the Commissioners and the feasibility of establishing a Constantinopolitan State does seem possible and desirable. ". . . it is certainly better for Turkey herself," they assert, "to be delivered from this intolerable responsibility, and to have her own government taken out of the midst of what has been, through the centuries, a center of boundless intrigue. The common people of Turkey would lead a much happier life in a state freed from outreaching imperialism, and at liberty to devote itself to the welfare of its own citizens."

The Commissioners deal with the various problems of a separate Armenia, an international Constantinopolitan State, a continued Turkish State, the Greeks and other minority races. We are here concerned solely with the problem of a separate Armenia as presented by the Report as follows:

(1) The reasons why it is necessary that a separate Armenian State should be set up, have already been fully given. They need not be restated.

(2) The conception of such a State. It is well to have in mind the exact nature of the State proposed in this report, in order to prevent misunderstandings on any side.

It is not proposed in such a state to establish the rule of a minority of Armenians over a majority of other peoples. That would inevitably seem to the Turks to be very unjust, and would at once excite resentment and unremitting opposition. Moreover, such an arrangement would be unfair to the Armenians as well, for it would place them from the start in a false and untenable position. It would put them, too, under great temptation to abuse of power. And it would be no fair trial of a truly Armenian State. It would, of course, also make any mandate mean little or nothing, if not make it entirely impossible.

But such a separated State should furnish a definite area into which Armenians could go with the complete assurance, that there they would never be put under the rule of the Turks. It should be also a region in which Armenians could gradually concentrate, and from which the Turkish population might tend increasingly to withdraw; though no compulsion should be put on any people.

All this necessitates a strong Mandatory Power. The State could not even start without such help. This separated State should be therefore a state definitely under the rule of a Mandatory Government, organized on modern lines to do justice to all elements of the population: and a state from which the Mandatory should not withdraw, until the Armenians constituted an actual majority of the entire population, or at least until the Turks were fewer than the Armenians. This would necessarily mean that full Armenian self-government would be long delayed. And that fact should be definitely faced as inevitable. The conditions are such that there is no defensible alternative.

(3) The term of the Mandate is practically involved in the conception of the State, which is forced upon us. It cannot be a short-term mandate, not because of any reluctance to withdraw on the part of the Mandatary, but because under the peculiar circumstances, a true Armenian State cannot be established in a brief period of time, however ardent the desires of both the Armenians and the Mandatory Power. For the Armenians cannot safely undertake the government independently, until they constitute an actual majority. There is also the added consideration of the natural need of considerable time for the amalgamation and consolidation of the Armenian people, as against some tendency to split up into fragments. The mandate must be long enough, too, to make the people thoroughly ready for both self-government and self-protection, through an increasing use of Armenians in the government even from the beginning.

(4) An American Mandate Desired. It seems universally recognized that the Armenians themselves desire an Ameri-

can Mandate. And this choice is apparently generally approved by America's Allies. The Turks, too, though not wishing any separate Armenian State, would probably favor an American Mandate for Armenia, if there must be an Armenia at all.

(5) The Conditions upon which America would be justified in taking the mandate for Armenia may be said to be: the genuine desire of the Armenians; the cordial moral support of the Allies in carrying out the mandate; willingness on the part of the Armenians to bear with a pretty long mandatory term, for the reasons already stated, and to give up all revolutionary committees; that Armenia should have territory enough to ensure a successful development; and that the peculiarly difficult mandate for Armenia should not be the only mandate given America in Turkey. None of these conditions, perhaps, call for comment, except the last, which will come up for later consideration.

(6) The Extent and Boundaries of the Armenian State. The General Adviser, Dr. Lybyer, has expressed so exactly the convictions of the Commissioners concerning the extent and boundaries of the Armenian State, that his statement may well replace any other discussion of this question:

1. The Armenians should be provided with a definite territory, and organized as soon as practicable into a self-governing independent state. Otherwise the questions of their safety and of their ceasing to be a center of world-disturbance cannot be answered.

2. This area should be taken from both Turkish and Russian territory. The wars of the 19th century divided the proper Armenian land between these two empires.

3. The Armenians are entitled to an amount of Turkish territory which takes into account their losses by the massacres of 1894–6, 1908–9, and 1915–16. These losses may be estimated at one million.

4. They should not be given an excessive amount of Turkish territory, if their state is to be practicable.

   a. The Turks, Kurds, and other races should not be left

with a just grievance, since that would solidify their traditional hostility, and embitter them against the League of Nations.

b. It has been questioned, even by many of themselves, whether the Armenians are ready for self-government at present; certainly an imperial rule by them over other peoples should not be thought of for the present or the future.

c. It is too much to ask of the League of Nations or a mandatory power that they undertake to hold down and perhaps squeeze out a large majority, in order that a small minority may have time to multiply and fill the land.

d. There is a limit beyond which the project of ever producing an Armenian majority is actually not feasible; that is to say, if the Armenians are assigned too large an area, they will never be able to occupy and hold it.

e. The idea has been suggested that Armenia should be developed as a wall of separation or a buffer state between the two Moslem areas occupied by Turks and Arabs. This might be done by a compact, homogeneous state with considerable population and resources, but it is a burden which the Armenian state cannot be expected to bear within a conceivable time.

5. The proposed large Armenia, to extend from the Black Sea to the Mediterranean, is probably impossible of realization, and therefore should not be planned for. It encounters all the objections previously mentioned.

a. In 1914 and before 1894 the Armenians were in a small minority in such an area, probably never exceeding twenty-five per cent. If they should be given the control, the majority populations would be injured, in violation of all "Wilsonian principles" and war aims. With allowance for the estimated million who perished, and assuming that all these could have been gathered into the territory, the Armenians would still now number only about one-third of the total population.

b. There never was an Armenia which ruled all this territory. The real Armenia, as maps and records show, was a highland country, which at one time reached the Caspian Sea, which came near to the Black Sea without reaching it, and which never came near the Mediterranean Sea. The Lesser Armenia of the Middle Ages in the Cilician region was the result of the expulsion and flight of Armenians from further east, —a process which scattered them over a large area, in which they have ever since been in a minority almost everywhere. The demand for both areas is therefore an imperialistic claim, based historically upon an overstrained interpretation of facts.

c. The Armenians are reduced, allowing for the return of survivors, to about ten per cent of the population in the large area proposed. Assuming an optimistic amount of migration of other Armenians into, and of Turks and Kurds out of the land, the Armenians would still constitute only about one-fourth of the population. The situation of a mandatory power would be extremely difficult in defending this minority, which would as future owners and rulers of the land, be much more obnoxious to the majority than at present.

d. No European power will undertake so difficult a task, and it must therefore be left to the United States. If the American people should be induced to begin the process, and this should turn out to be fundamentally unjust, they would modify their intention. The chances are considerable that the large Armenia would never become an Armenian State at all, but a mixed State, composed of minorities of Armenians, Turks, Kurds, etc., which could not maintain internal order or security against external aggression without the support of a strong mandatory power. This would disappoint both the Armenians, who could never control the government, and the mandatory power, which could never leave the country.

6. On the contrary, an Armenia reduced to the Armenian highlands in both Turkey and Russia, with an outlet on the Black Sea, would have a good chance of establishment and continuance. The Turkish area which the Russians held in 1917 may be taken approximately as the Turkish portion of this "Small Armenia", and the present territory of Russian Armenia as the remainder. Engineers could overcome the physical obstacles to internal and external communication.

　　a. The Turks and Kurds could not rightfully complain of such an area, because it is the historical Armenia, and because if the million dead Armenians could be restored and brought into the land, the Armenians would have about one-half the population. Migration of Turks and Kurds from this area can be more easily accomplished than from the larger land, inasmuch as a considerable proportion of them fled before the Russians, and thus are in a dislocated condition.

　　b. The Armenians might become the majority of the actual population within a few years, and with that in view, and with the smaller area, they could be given a larger share in administration from the start, and trained more rapidly to self-government.

　　c. The duration of the mandate would be materially shortened, with a soldier [*solider?*] ethical foundation and a more compact area. The Mandatory would need far fewer troops, and would be put to much less expense.

　　d. The doubts as to the possibility of erecting an Armenian State in the larger area, are reduced for the smaller land. The mandatory power could with a prospect of success, keep in mind the giving of control to the Armenians, since they would after a time not be a minority, causing trouble by incessant pushing for special privileges of an economic and political nature, but a majority with a just right to a larger place.

  e. This land having secure frontiers, as was tried out thoroughly during the Great War, gives promise of self-defensibility. A state reaching to the Mediterranean is a far more difficult matter, with its long frontiers, containing each a number of vulnerable spots, and its permanent difficulties of international communication, due to the broken configuration of the land. Its very existence might moreover be regarded by the Turks and Arabs as a provocation.

  f. The economic opportunity of an Armenia on this basis would be ample; all essentials for food, fuel, and shelter can be obtained locally, and surpluses are easily to be produced which can be exchanged for other wares.

      i. In Turkish Armenia the Armenians were able to live and often to prosper, and yet they paid considerable taxes and were subject to frequent robbery.

      ii. In Russian Armenia the Armenians have thriven greatly, under only moderately favorable conditions.

      iii. This area is crossed by commercial routes of immemorial importance, notably through Erzingan and Erzerum between Anatolia and Persia and Trans-caucasia, and through Trebizond toward the Persian Gulf. This guarantees the importance of several towns at nodal points, such as Kars, Erivan, Erzerum, Mush, and Van, and suggests valuable possibilities in the direction of transportation, trade, and manufacture for export.

7. All this is argued with the best interest of the Armenians in mind, on the basis of genuine friendliness toward

them, and of concern to give them a real and not an illusory opportunity. They are in genuine danger of grasping at too much and losing all.

If they establish themselves securely in the more restricted area, and if Anatolia fails to develop as a well knit and successful state, there is no reason why the question should not be resumed later of connecting Cilicia with Armenia.
(Abstracted from "Papers Relating to the Foreign Relations of the United States—*The Paris Peace Conference 1919*, Volume XII.)

(f) *Recognition of the Armenian Republic,* January 19, 1920. Quoted in *La Société des Nations et les Puissances devant Le Problème Arménien,* by Andre N. Mandelstam:

"In the beginning of 1920," writes M. Mandelstam, "the principals of the Allied powers recognized the Armenian State as a *de facto* government. And on January 27th the General Secretariat of the Peace Conference informed the President of the Delegation of the Armenian Republic that the Supreme Council in its session of January 19, 1920 had made the following decisions:

" '1. That the government of the Armenian state shall be recognized as *de facto* government.

" '2. That this recognition will not prejudice the question of eventual boundaries of that State.' "[20]

(g) *The Treaty of Sevres,** August 10, 1920

The adoption of the final draft of the Turkish Treaty was delayed until March 1920 when it failed to get a majority vote in the U.S. Senate. When the Allied Powers began to draft the provisions of the Turkish Treaty without the help of America, President Wilson, even though paralyzed and unable to write ordered Secretary of State Colby to send a message to the

* See Appendix B, Chapter 6, for the articles of the treaty that pertained to an Armenian settlement.

Allied Powers. The following two paragraphs of that message, dated March 24, 1920 are pertinent to our cause:

> The genuine interest of the Government of the United States in the plan for Armenia cannot be questioned, and the Government are convinced that most liberal treatment for that unfortunate country is both expected and demanded by the civilized world. Armenia's boundaries, therefore, should be fixed in such a way as to recognize all the legitimate claims of the Armenians, and to secure for them unencumbered and easy access to the sea. . . . Taking into consideration that Trebizond always has been the termination of the trade routes across Armenia, and that M. Venizeles, speaking on behalf of the Turks of that district, has expressed their preference for connection with Armenia rather than Turkey, it is hoped that the Powers will agree to grant Trebizond to Armenia. (*Memoirs of the Peace Conference,* by David Lloyd George. p. 839)

(h) *The London Conference*

The attitude of the Western Powers in favor of Turkey became apparent in the London Conference, in February 1921. The Sevres Treaty had lost its meaning because of disagreements between triumphant allies.

> "Armenia was the first," writes M. Mandelstam, "to suffer. The errors committed, because the four vilayets for which President Wilson had made his arbitration, had become the cradle of Turkish nationalism, the center of Kemalist movement. The Armenian independence from then on was fatally destined to become the first sacrifice which the Allies, weary of struggle and desiring general peace, offered to the Turks of Angora. That independence unfortunately was not deemed a political necessity to the Allies; they did not take into account the services which a strong Armenia would have been able to render to civilization in the struggle against an invading pan-turanism. Then again, the international moral considerations were such that the solemn promises made to the Armenians during the war no longer appear to weigh in the balance of the Allies as at the time when the Treaty of Sevres was concluded. In sitting around the green table of the London Conference the diplomats of vanquished Turkey had a very clear view of

the new state of mind of the victors, and with a perfect competency they made sure that their conduct would conform to that situation. In the notable diplomatic successes which they gained in the course of their struggle for the recognition of the Turkish national pact, the abandonment of the Armenian independence by the Allies had granted them almost without restraint, as the first natural consequence of the new general situation, brought about by the faults and weaknesses of some and the energy of others.[21]

(i) *Proposal to the Turkish Delegation* by Lloyd George on behalf of the Allied Powers, March 12, 1921; quoted in *The Lausanne Treaty, Turkey and Armenia:*

"Turkey to recognize the rights of Turkish Armenians to a national Home on the eastern frontiers of Turkey in Asia, delimitation of the frontiers to be decided by a commission appointed by the Council of the League of Nations."[22]

(j) *The Lausanne Treaty,* July 24, 1923

"At the conference of Lausanne," writes M. Mandelstam, "which ended with a peace treaty, signed on July 24, 1923, the Turks not only figured as conquerors of the Greeks, but conquerors of the Allies as well."

(1) *Lord Curzon's Plea*

Not a word was said about the Armenian Question in spite of the plaintive plea of Lord Curzon. Here is what he said about the Armenians:

> I now come to the Armenians. They deserve special consideration not only because of cruel sufferings they have sustained and which have provoked sympathy and horror in the civilized world, but because of the special assurances given them about their future. In the old Russian province of Erevan which now forms a Soviet Republic, there supposedly exists an Armenian State which contains, I am told, about a million and a quarter inhabitants, but which is already so cramped by refugees from everywhere that it cannot receive a population so large.
> Besides, the Armenian population of Kars, Ardahan, Van,

Bitlis and Erzeroum has practically disappeared. When the French evacuated Cilicia the Armenian population of that province, overcome by panic, followed them, and is now dispersed in the cities of Alexandretta, Aleppo, Beyrouth and along the frontiers of Syria. There remain, I think, about 130,000 Armenians in Turkey in Asia out of a population that formerly counted about three million souls. Hundreds of thousands have been scattered in the Caucasus, Russia, Persia and the neighboring regions.

Since I arrived at Lausanne I have learned that the government of Angora, convinced that it has suffered by the disappearance of that intelligent and capable race, is disposed to encourage the Armenians to return and settle again in Anatolia. In my opinion such an attitude shall be of great advantage to Turkey and I will be happy to have the Turkish delegation give us certain assurances about that point. However, in the future Turkish state, in Asia Minor as well as in Europe, there will be a large number of Armenians for whose security and protection certain special clauses ought to be inserted in the treaty.

I should now refer to the well-known demand presented both by Armenians and their friends in all parts of the world, aiming for the creation of an Armenian National Home. It is natural for a people of such a strong individualism, with a history so remarkable and yet so tragic, with a national spirit so fundamental, to aspire to live in its own land. Should one state that there is already a place in the Republic of Erevan, it should be answered that that area is very poor and over-populated and that the regime there is strongly repugnant to many Armenians.

That is why the demand is made, that is why it has been repeated many times that Turkey find for the Armenians, in some parts of its territory in Asia, be it in the North-Eastern provinces or the South-Eastern part of Cilicia and Syria, where they could gather as a group.

The circumstances may have rendered the realization of that hope more difficult than ever before, but we will be happy to hear the views of the Turkish delegation on this subject.[23]

(2) Ismet Inonu's Reply

In response to Lord Curzon's suggestion, the head of the Turkish delegation totally rejected the idea of a Home for

Armenians on Turkish territory and ended his speech as follows:

In conclusion the Delegation of the Grand Assembly of Turkey is of the opinion:

1. That the amelioration of the condition of minorities in Turkey depends first of all on the exclusion of any sort of foreign intervention and any possibility of provocation from the outside.

2. That that purpose can only be attained by proceeding before anything with exchange of Turkish and Greek populations.

3. That the best guarantees for the security and progress of minorities, remaining outside the application of measures for reciprocal exchange, shall be those that the laws of the country as well as the liberal policy of Turkey can furnish to all communities the members of which do not get away from their duty as Turkish citizens.[24]

REFERENCES

1. pp. 179–181.

2. Andre Mandelstam, p. 141.

3. p. 297.

4. Vol. I, p. 28.

5. *Ibid.*, p. 816.

6. Gidney, pp. 81–82.

7. *Ibid.*, p. 90.

8. *Ibid.*, p. 91.

9. *Ibid.*, p. 156.

10. *Ibid.*, p. 202.

11. *Ibid.*, pp. 162–163.

12. *Ibid.*, p. 164.

13. Omission indicated in the original report.

14. W. M. Ramsay, *Impressions of Turkey* (New York: G. P. Putnam's Sons, 1897), pp. 164 and 165.

15. Great Britain, Cd. 8325, October 1916.

16. Omission indicated in the original report.

17. Omission indicated in the original report.

18. See *Foreign Relations*, 1919, vol. II, pp. 824ff; *ibid.*, The Paris Peace Conference, 1919, vol. VII, pp. 28 and 43; *ibid.*, vol. IX, p. 167.

19. *Foreign Relations*, 1878, p. 306.

20. Mandelstam, *op. cit.*, p. 64.

21. *Ibid.*, p. 179.

22. *Ibid.*, p. 200.

23. *Ibid.*, pp. 269–270.

24. *Ibid.*, p. 274.

Chapter 7

The Genocide Goes Unpunished

That Turkey would be held accountable for her crimes was taken as a matter of course well before the War was over, and that the most salient feature of her reparations would be the establishment of an Armenian homeland was universally assumed. Newspapers quoted here from as early as 1916 affirmed these assumptions explicitly, and even the callously pro-Turkish writer, Pierre Loti, yielded to his conscience sufficiently to recommend the creation of an Armenian homeland.

How, then, did it happen that by 1923 the Armenian cause was lost, its just claims ignored, the support of the United States and other great powers withdrawn or flouted?

There were many reasons, all of them discreditable to the one-time friends of Armenia. The defeats of Woodrow Wilson and the United States rejection of membership in the League of Nations; the dilatoriness of President Harding; the dissension among the victorious Allies; the defeat and massacre of the Greek forces (and of course civilians) by Ataturk and his consequent rise to power—all of these events conspired unhappily to betray the rights of the surviving remnant of the Armenian nation.

It is only proper to review some of the authoritative opinions preceding the Great Betrayal in the following pages and

249

to establish that Turkey's crime was a true genocide as defined by the General Assembly of the United Nations.

Post-Standard, Syracuse, New York; editorial of February 1, 1917, quoted in *The New Armenia,*

> There can be no peace that does not wreak vengeance upon him who has gained new title to the appellation 'unspeakable.' There can be no just claim that the war against Germany is a war for civilization unless it is a war to deprive the Turk of all power in government. There can be no reform of conditions in the Turkish Empire short of elimination of the Empire. . . The Allies' profession that they are warring for civilization is a farce if they lay down their arms without imposing conditions that shall shear Islam for all time of its power thus to butcher the hapless Christians within its dominion, with whom it is not at war. More than that the United States, if it is to have any part in the negotiations for peace, may justly demand that the world shall be guaranteed against any repetition of this medieval madness. We have, to be sure, no interest excepting that of humanity, but if ever intervention was ordered by humane consideration alone, it is warranted by the atavism of Turkey to-day. (p. 43)

Arnold J. Toynbee—*The Murderous Tyranny of the Turks,* Hodder & Stoughton, London, 1917.

In the section entitled "The Armenian Atrocities of 1915" Prof. Toynbee writes:

> Only a third of the two million Armenians in Turkey have survived, and that at the price of apostatising to Islam or else of leaving all they had and fleeing across the frontier. The refugees saw their women and children die by the roadside, and apostacy too, for a woman, involved the living death of marriage to a Turk and inclusion in his harem. The other two-thirds were 'deported'—that is, they were marched away from their homes in gangs, with no food or clothing for the journey, in fierce heat and bitter cold, hundreds of miles over rough mountain roads. They were plundered and tormented by their guards and by subsidised bands of brigands, who descended on them in the wilderness, and with whom their guards fraternised. Parched with thirst, they were kept away from the water

with bayonets. They died of hunger and exposure and exhaustion, and in lonely places the guards and robbers fell upon them and murdered them in batches—some at the first halting place after the start, others after they had endured weeks of this agonising journey. About half the deportees—and there were at least 1,200,000 of them in all —perished thus on their journey, and the other half have been dying lingering deaths ever since at their journey's end; for they have been deported to the most inhospitable regions in the Ottoman Empire: the malarial marshes in the Province of Konia; the banks of the Euphrates where, between Syria and Mesopotamia, it runs through a stony desert; the sultry and utterly desolate track of the Hedjaz Railway. The exiles who are still alive have suffered worse than those who perished by violence at the beginning.

This wholesale destruction, which has already overtaken two of the subject peoples (Armenians and Arabs) in Turkey, and threatens all that 60 per cent of the population which is not Turkish in language, is the direct work of the Turkish government. The "Deportation Scheme" was drawn up by the central government at Constantinople and telegraphed simultaneously to all the local authorities in the Empire; it was executed by the officials, the Gendarmerie, the Army, and the bands of brigands and criminals organised in the government's service. No State could be more completely responsible for any act within its borders than the Ottoman State is responsible for the appalling crime it has committed against its subject peoples during the War.[1] pp. 15–17

Christian Science Monitor, Editorial entitled "Armenia and Peace," January 4, 1917, quoted in *The New Armenia*, January 15, 1917:

"Consequently, in the days when nations talk of peace, these nations should be thinking of what can be done to punish the perpetrators of the Armenian atrocities in the past, and to protect the Armenians against further atrocities in the future. The latter is the more important question, and the solution seems to be found unquestionably in an autonomous Armenia, approximating as nearly as possible to the old Kingdom of Armenia, and placed under a European guarantee." (p. 28)

Viscount James Bryce, article entitled "Armenian Martyrs," published in *The New Armenia*, March 15, 1917:

In the history of the early Christian Church there are no figures so glorious, none which have continued to be so much honoured by the Church, all through its later days, as those of the martyrs, men and women who from the time of Nero down to that of Diocletian sealed with their blood the testimony of their faith, withstanding every lure and every threat in order to preserve their loyalty to their Lord and Master, Christ.

In our times we have seen this example of fidelity repeated in the Turkish Empire and it is strange that the Christians of Europe and America should not have been more moved by the examples of courage and heroic devotion which the Armenian Christians have given.

It is not religious fanaticism that led the present rulers of Turkey to seek to root out Christianity. So far from being fanatics, most of these men, though nominally Mohammedans, have no religion whatever. Their aim was political. They wanted to make the whole Turkish Empire Mohammedans, with only one creed, in order to make it uniform. They saw that the Christian part of the population, suffering under constant oppressions and cruelties, continued to turn its eyes Westward and hope for some redress from the Christian nations; so they determined to eliminate Christianity altogether.[2]

Pierre Loti is a poet in prose, but always a poet, and as such he has all the privileges of poets, who are understood to ignore the facts. . . . At the moment of this writing we have before us a book of more than 800 pages which throws a sinister glimpse on the "poor Turks" as Loti calls them ingeniously. This is the official report, presented to the English Parliament about *The Treatment of the Armenians in the Ottoman Empire.* It contains direct and legally verified proof of the massacres and deportations of Armenians and other oriental Christians of Asia Minor; Armenia and the north-western part of Persia which was invaded by Turkish troops. The major part of the evidence was given by those who suffered the cruelty and bestiality of the Turks. One can also find in that book depositions of foreigners who know a great deal more than Loti about the old conditions of existence in the Ottoman Empire, which, fortunately, no longer continue. . . . Pierre Loti apparently considered the extermination of hundreds of thousands of Armenians a matter which does not deserve long consideration. But the bad treatment inflicted upon one Turk arouses his compassion and puts to play his most pathetic eloquence. He exaggerates more than reasonable, even for a poet. He also forgets that "these poor Turks," "these brave defenders of their country" are still at war with France.[3]

Pierre Loti (Julien Viaud), *Les Massacres d'Armenie,* Paris, 1918.

Notwithstanding his great love for the Turks and his reservations about the Armenians, even though Pierre Loti tries very hard to put the blame of the atrocities committed by the Turks against the Armenians on the Armenians themselves, he is unable to justify the attempt to exterminate an entire nation. Let us see what he says:

> But could all these griefs (caused by the Armenians)— and so many others as well—give enough of a reason to exterminate them (the Armenians)? God forbid that such a thought had crossed my mind for an instant. On the contrary, if my humble voice could ever be heard, I would beseech Europe, but it is too late already, I would beg her to intervene, to protect the Armenians and to *isolate* [Emphasis ours—D.H.B.] them; since for centuries there has existed between them and the Turks a *mutual* [Emphasis ours—D.H.B.] hatred absolutely irreducible. A certain territory in Asia may be designated as Armenian land where they could be their own masters, where they could correct their faults acquired in servitude, and to develop in peace the qualities which they still possess—since these qualities are theirs; I admit that they are industrious, persevering, that a certain patriarchal side of their family life commands respect. And, finally, which may be secondary, they have physical elegance, which in the west has become weakened more and more by excessive instruction, intellectual overwork, deadly factory work and alcohol; I cannot think, without special sadness, about the slaughtered woman, who for the most part without doubt, had admirable eyes of velvet . . .[4]

The League of Nations

(a) *Mandates*—Covenant of the League of Nations, adopted April 28, 1919, published in *League of Nations,* Vol. II:

Article XXII—entitled "Control of Colonies and Territories" provides in part as follows:
"4. Certain communities formerly belonging to the Turkish Empire have reached a stage of development where their existence as independent nations can be provisionally recognized subject to the rendering of administrative advice and assistance by a mandatory until such time as they are able to stand alone. The wishes of these communities must be a principal consideration in the selection of the mandatory."[5]

(b) *Mandatory System*—*Treaty of Peace with Germany,* published in the *League of Nations,* special number, Vol. II, June 1919:

In accord with Wickersham's stated principle the *Official Summary* of the *Treaty of Peace with Germany* presented to the German Delegates by the Allied and Associated Powers in Versailles on May 7, 1919, contains the following provision under the subtitle *The Mandatory System*:
"The tutelage of nations not yet able to stand by themselves will be intrusted to advanced nations who are best fitted to undertake it. The Covenant recognizes three different stages of development requiring different kinds of mandatories—
"(a)—Communities like those belonging to the Turkish Empire which can be provisionally recognized as independent subject to advice and assistance from a mandatory, in whose selection they would be allowed a voice."[6]

(c) *Colonial Mandates,* proposed by George W. Wickersham, published in the *League of Nations,* Vol. II, No. 3, June 1919:

George W. Wickersham, in a letter to the League of Nations on the subject of Colonial Mandates, wrote in part:

"In the case of communities formerly belonging to the Turkish Empire, which have reached a stage of development where their existence as independent nations can provisionally be recognized, subject to the general assistance and control of a mandatory, it is declared that the wishes of those communities should be the principal consideration in the selection of a particular mandatory."[7]

(d) *Resolution*, November 20, 1920, quoted in *The New Armenia*, November–December, 1920:

"The French Foreign Office, speaking through M. Viviani, endeavored to strengthen the position of Mustapha Kemal [Ataturk], its protege, with a view to a revision of the Turkish Treaty, to deprive the Armenians even of the circumscribed Armenia created at Sevres. M. Viviani also plainly indicated that France herself was anxious to be the mediator when he declared:

" 'You express doubts as to whether Kemal will listen to arbitration. I will take on myself the responsibility that he will.'

" 'How can you negotiate with a chief of brigands?' was the retort of Mr. Balfour, according to G. H. Ferris, in a dispatch to The New York *Times*, on November 26.

"The League of Nations sent, on November 25, to the United States as well as the League members an invitation to volunteer, not for 'negotiating' with Mustapha Kemal which M. Viviani had clearly and repeatedly urged, but for mediating between him and Armenia. The Telegram to President Wilson reads:

" 'The Assembly of the League of Nations voted the following resolution on November 22:

" 'The Assembly being anxious to co-operate with the Council in order to end, in the shortest possible period, the horrors of the Armenian tragedy, requests the Council to arrive at an understanding with the governments with a view to entrusting a Power with the task of taking necessary measures to stop hostilities.

" 'The Council of the League has, after consideration, decided to transmit this request to the governments of all the members of the League and to the United States Government in order to find a Power to use its good offices to end the present terrible tragedy as speedily as possible.'

"The proposal does not involve a repetition of the request to accept a mandate. While the Council does not wish to suggest that America should assume unwelcome duties, it felt bound to offer it an opportunity to undertake this humanitarian task, as the fate of Armenia had always aroused special interest among the American people and as their president had already agreed to delimit Armenia's boundaries. As the matter is one of great urgency, the Council ventures to ask for a reply with the shortest possible delay.

(e) *General Assembly of the League of Nations,* unanimous resolution, September 21, 1921:

"Whereas the first Assembly, on November 18, 1920, entrusted to the Council the task of safeguarding the future of Armenia; and

"Whereas the Council, on February 25, 1921, realizing the impossibility of taking any affirmative action to meet the situation in Asia Minor requested the Secretariat to follow the course of events in Armenia, so as to enable the Council to take ultimately new decisions; and

"Whereas in the meantime, the Supreme Council (Allied) in view of the probable revision of the Sevres Treaty, has proposed the creation of a National Home for the Armenians; and

"Whereas there exists an imminent possibility of a Treaty of peace being made between the Allied Powers and Turkey;

"Therefore be it

"Resolved that the Assembly invites the Council, at once, to press upon the Supreme Council (Allied) the necessity of making provisions in the Treaty, safeguarding the future of Armenia, and, further, insuring for the Armenians a National Home, wholly independent of Turkish rule." (*The Lausanne Treaty, Turkey and Armenia,* 1923, p. 202)

(f) *Unanimous Resolution,* September 18, 1922:

(1) The First Resolution, presented by Lord Cecil, not adopted;

(2) The Second Resolution, expressing a desire for an Armenian National Home, unanimously adopted;

(3) Comments by Andre N. Mandelstam. (Note: Items (1), (2) and (3) quoted in *La Societe des Nations et les Puissances Devant le Probleme Armenien.*)

On September 18, 1922 only a few weeks before the Lausanne Conference Lord Robert Cecil presented the following draft resolution to the Assembly of the League of Nations:

"The Assembly takes notice of the resolutions of the Council pertaining to Armenia and declares that *in its opinion* [Emphasis by DHB] one of the essential conditions for total peace with Turkey ought to be the concession to the Armenians of a National Home. The Assembly calls upon the Council to take all measures it deems *necessary* to that effect."[8]

The Assembly, however, unanimously adopted the following amended resolution:

"The Assembly takes notice of the resolutions of the Council pertaining to Armenia and *expresses the desire* [Emphasis ours—DHB] that in the negotiations of a peace treaty with Turkey, one should not lose sight of the need to establish a National Home for the Armenians. The Assembly calls upon the Council to take all measures it deems *useful* to that effect."[9]

M. Mandelstam makes the following comment:

"The Third Assembly of the League of Nations unanimously voted the proposal of the Sixth Commission. But the hopes of the League in the moral force of its wishes were destined to suffer, for the third time, a severe test."[10]

Justice Russell, Supreme Court of Nova Scotia, article: "The Verdict of Civilization," quoted in *The New Armenia*, October 1, 1916:

> It is to be hoped that the counsel to be adopted when the allied nations get together at the end of the war will be . . . that Turkey will utterly cease to be a national power either in Europe or in Asia and that it shall be reduced to a condition of nullity and consequent harmlessness. Nothing short of this will be sufficient to avenge the wrongs that Turkey has inflicted on Armenia, a country which has surely by its sacrifices, its sufferings, and its sorrows earned the right of an independent national existence. It is the hope of all right-thinking persons that the aspirations of the Armenian people for this assured status among the nations of the world will be cordially supported by the allies who profess to be warring for the liberation of the small nations . . . It is inconceivable that the generous and humane impulses that will insist on justice being done to Belgium should become dulled and quiescent in the face of the equal or greater sufferings of Armenia.

The reason for rejecting the Armenian mandate appears in the following short paragraph from *The Peace Negotiations* by Robert Lansing:

". . . there was a sustained propaganda—for it amounted to that—in favor of the United States assuming mandates over Armenia and the municipal district of Constantinople, both of which, if limited by boundaries which it was then proposed to draw, would be a constant financial burden to the Power accepting the mandate, and, in the case of Armenia, would require that Power to furnish a military force estimated at not less than 50,000 men to prevent the aggression of war-like neighbors and to preserve domestic order and peace."[11]

On September 21, 1918 Mr. Lansing had prepared a memorandum "of my views as to the territorial settlements which would form, not instructions, but a guide in the drafting of instructions for the American Commissioners."

The memorandum contained the following article:

"*Seventeenth.* Armenia and Syria to be erected into protectorates of such Government or Governments as seem expedient from a domestic as well as an international point of view, the guaranty being that both countries, will be given self-government as soon as possible and that an 'Open Door' policy as to commerce and industrial development will be rigidly observed."[12]

Stephen Bonsal, American delegate at Paris in 1918–1919, during the Peace Conference, summed up the situation in *Suitors and Suppliants*, © 1946 by Stephen Bonsal, published by Prentice-Hall, Inc., Englewood Cliffs, New Jersey. This book is a compilation of selected portions of daily entries made by the author in his diary. We make direct quotations from Chapter XII, entitled "Armenian Disaster":

March 15, 1919
A long talk with Nubar Pasha (the ranking delegate of the Egyptian-Armenian contingent) today. He takes me back to the cradle of his unfortunate people. He says the Armenians are closely related to the Hittites . . . Skipping many epochs and ignoring many national vicissitudes, I bring Nubar down to date, or almost, and I am rewarded by facts that will have a bearing on the settlement of the question, if one is reached. He concedes that in many districts of Anatolia in Turkey before the war the Armenians had sizeable majorities—which were indeed before the massacres of 1896 overwhelming majorities—but that they are now minorities. 'But,' he argues, 'should our people lose their homes and their lands because they have—that is, so many of them—lost their lives?' (pp. 187–188)

Today (March 8) Boghos Nubar Pasha had his hour in court, and while his statement of the Armenian case was somewhat rambling, all agreed that he acquitted himself well. He first spoke in impeccable French for Mr. Clemenceau, and then in High Church English for the benefit of President Wilson and Mr. Balfour. Right at the beginning he pitched into the middle of things.

It would be shameful, he announced, to leave us under the domination of the Turks. We are as deserving of liberty and independence as are the Greeks, the Arabs, and the Zionists, although, I admit, not more so. Indeed, we have the same aspirations and pursue the same high ideals. Nothing can divide us from these noble peoples who have suffered similar hardships and vicissitudes— not even the question of Trebizond—although of course Armenia to survive must have an outlet on the Black Sea. Between people of our culture this problem can and will be adjusted. To negotiate with a noble man like M. Venizelos is a very different affair from negotiating with Abdul Hamid and those who have come after him, who have only changed their names but who pursue the same diabolical objectives.

I trust that no one here will seek to restore the Turkish Empire even on a reduced scale. It has been kept alive for generations by the unhappy rivalries of the European Powers with the result that it has generated wars and revolutions, rebellions and massacres without end. Turkey was given a chance to reform and to survive in 1914. Had she not joined the Central Powers, had she remained at least neutral in the struggle, something might be said today in her behalf; but she joined up against civilization and by her action prolonged the war for at least two years. Had she remained neutral, Bulgaria in all probability would not have entered the struggle or, in any event, could have been easily and quickly crushed. How many millions of dead is she responsible for? The flower of our generation is gone!

There can be no mistake about it. Civilization must not permit non-Ottoman peoples to remain under the yoke of Turkish oppression. The extinction of Turkey is essential to world peace. Otherwise it will prove an idle dream and indeed a cruel one for which thousands will have died in vain.

We deserve independence on another score: We have fought for it. We have poured out our blood for it without stint. Our people have played a gallant part in the armies that have won the victory.

I disagree with those who assume that in the hour of triumph the suffering and the blood shed by my people, our contribution to the common victory, is to be forgotten, and I shall be precise in telling you what we expect at your hands. It is an independent Armenia embracing Cilicia and the six Armenian vilayets of Turkey; and to these must be joined the Armenian provinces of Russia whose inhabitants, numbering over two million and having the advantage of forming a compact body, have already been successful in forming an independent government of their own. This reunited and independent Armenia, we think, should be placed under the collective protection of the Christian nations, or under that of the League, which is to us the hope of the world. We also ask for the particular guidance of any one of these nations to stand by us in the transition period we are entering upon. It is clear that this aid and guidance will be indispensable to us as we begin the reconstruction of our devastated country, now reduced to ashes, blackened fields, and heaps of rubble by the Turks in retaliation for our unflagging devotion to the cause of the Allies.

Nubar's statement and his appeal were much more eloquent than would appear from the scrappy notes which I here recall. He was listened to with sympathetic attention by the great men who today hold the balance of power. But there was a faraway look in their eyes and no promises were made. That, indeed, is the trouble. Armenia *is* far away, and other problems nearer at hand and hence thought more urgent are coming home to roost.[13]

A prophecy concerning the betrayal of Armenia is clearly seen in the following entry made by Stephen Bonsal:

"May 2, 1919

"Colonel (Edward M.) House told me that President had decided to send a fact-finding mission to Armenia and he will ask General Pershing to designate a competent officer to head it. He will publish the report and then await popular reaction at home on its findings; Poor Nubar! Poor Aharonian! Unfortunate Armenians! Our promises are out the window, and the reconstituted Armenian state has not a Chinaman's chance."[14]

Washington, January 1922:

In this entry Col. Bonsal refers to the San Francisco Democratic National Convention of 1920, to which Carter Glass, Secretary of the Treasury under Wilson, was a delegate.

As Glass was leaving, the President said, handing him a slip of paper, 'I wish you would get this into the platform.' On the train the Senator from Virginia told me, 'I read the paper and found it to be a declaration for an Armenian mandate to be assumed by the United States.' Written by the President himself on his typewriter and initialed 'W.W.,' the suggested plan read:

'We hold it to be the Christian duty and privilege of our Government to assume the responsible guardianship of Armenia, which now needs only the advice and assurance of a powerful friend to establish her complete independence and to give her distracted people the opportunities for peaceful happiness which they have vainly sought for through so many dark years of suffering and hideous distress.'

This was hardly a clarion note, but when it came back from the drafting committee, largely through the opposition of Senator Walsh of Montana, it sounded like the squeak of a penny whistle. As placed in the platform, the President's resolution reads:

'We express our deep and earnest sympathy for the unfortunate people of Armenia, and we believe that our Government, consistent with its Constitution and principles, should render every possible and proper aid to them in their efforts to establish and maintain a government of their own.'

After a bitter struggle in the Committee Glass secured the approval of the Treaty and the Covenant that is written in the party platform; but, as he admits, the opposition to the President's original Armenia policy was overwhelming.[15]

Leonard Leese, *Armenia and the Allies*, a pamphlet published by The British Armenia Committee, London, 1920.

In Section IV entitled *"Methods of Liberation"* the author writes in part:

"It is hardly possible here to give more than a summary of the main projects which have been put forward for the solution of the (Armenian) problem. They are roughly four in number:

"(1) An American mandate for a united Armenia.

"If this is not feasible, the ambition of France to hold Cilicia will doubtless prevail, in which case the alternatives for the government of the other Armenian provinces are: —

"(2) A British mandate.

"(3) A small Power mandate—Holland, Switzerland, or Denmark—perhaps with American financial assistance as suggested by Lord Bryce in the *Contemporary Review* of January, 1920.

"(4) An independent and enlarged Republic of Erivan under the protection of the League of Nations or of France.

"An American mandate would be by far the best solution in every respect. . . .

"Britain and France, however, have no right to disown responsibility, if the United States should decline to shoulder a burden which it had no part in creating and which nothing beyond the common cause of humanity calls upon it to assume. We, above all, must be prepared to do our part, as our statesmen have pledged—and rightly pledged —both during the war and since the Armistice that we should. From the past comes the cry of two generations of misery and massacre, and from the future the call for peace, security, and order, which we must help the peoples of the Middle East to establish both in their interests and in our own. But however we discharge the task, we must do it in spirit, not of imperialism, but of humanity. Speaking upon the Treaty of Berlin in 1878, Gladstone said: 'Those provinces of the Turkish Empire, which have been so cruelly and unjustly ruled, ought to be regarded as existing, not for the sake of any other Power whatsoever, but for the sake of the populations by whom they are inhabited. The object of our desire ought to be the development of those populations on their own soil, as its proper masters, and as the persons with a view to whose welfare its destination ought to be decided.' Forty years later these words still ring true; it remains for the British people to insist that they are now applied.[16]

Dr. Henry C. King and Charles R. Crane report, January 30, 1919, quoted in *The Great Betrayal*, by E. H. Bierstadt, 1924:

The reason for a separate Armenia, then, may be said to be because of the demonstrated unfitness of the Turks to rule over the others, or even over themselves; because of the adoption of repeated massacres as a deliberate policy of State; because of almost complete lack of penitence for the massacres, or repudiation for the crime—they rather seek to excuse them; because practically nothing has been done by the Turks in the way of repatriation of Armenians or of reparation to them—a condition not naturally suggesting a repetition of the experiment of Turkish rule; because, on the contrary, there is evidence of intense feeling still existing against the Armenians, and implicit threatening of massacre; because there has been sufficient proof that the two races cannot live peaceably and decently together, so that it is better for both that they have separate states; because of the complete failure of the strong clauses of the Treaty of 1878 to protect the Armenians; because the most elementary justice suggests that there must be at least some region in Turkey where Armenians can go and not have to live under Turkish rule; because nothing less than that could give to the Armenians any adequate guarantee of safety, consequently, nothing less will satisfy the conscience of the world upon this point, because in this day of opportunity for small nations under the League of Nations, the Armenians have surely earned the right, by their sufferings, their endurance, their loyalty to principles, their unbroken spirit and ambition, and their demonstrated industry, ability and self-reliance, to look forward to a national life of their own; because such a separate state would probably make more certain decent treatment of Armenians in other parts of Turkey; and because there is no adequate substitute for such a state. In the interests of the Armenians, of the Turks, and of the peace of the world alike, the formation of a separate Armenian state is to be urged.[17]

Georges Clemenceau, an answer to the Memorandum presented by the Ottoman Delegation, June 25, 1919, published in *Réponses à Pierre Loti—Ami des Massacreurs.*

On June 17, 1919 Damad Ferid (Sherif) Pasha, Grand Vizier, and president of the Turkish Delegation, delivered to the Council of Ten a memorandum which, in substance, put all the blame for the entry of Turkey into the war and the atrocities committed by the Turkish Government during the war on the Committee of Union and Progress; absolved the Sultan and the Government which the Turkish Delegation represented of all responsibility, and advocated that the territorial integrity of Turkey should be preserved.

The Allied and Associated Powers replied to Ferid Pasha

on June 25, 1919. That reply, which follows, was signed by Georges Clemenceau, President of the Peace Conference, but it is generally believed to have been the work of President Woodrow Wilson. It is considered as the greatest document ever penned in condemnation of the Turkish rule:

The Council of the principal Allied and Associated Powers has read with the most careful attention the memorandum presented to them by your Excellency on June 17, and in accordance with the promise then made, desires now to offer the following observations upon it:

In your recital of the political intrigues which accompanied Turkey's entry into the war and of the tragedies which followed it, your Excellency makes no attempt to excuse or qualify the crimes of which the Turkish Government was then guilty. It is admitted directly or by implication, that Turkey had no cause of quarrel with the Entente Powers, that she acted as the subservient tool of Germany, that the war, begun without excuse and conducted without mercy, was accompanied by massacres whose calculated atrocity equals or exceeds anything recorded in history.

But it is argued that these crimes were committed by a Turkish Government for whose misdeeds the Turkish people were not responsible, that there was in them no element of religious fanaticism, that Moslems suffered from them not less than Christians, that they were entirely out of harmony with the Turkish tradition as historically exhibited in the treatment by Turkey of subject races, that the maintenance of the Turkish Empire is necessary for the religious equilibrium of the world, so that the policy not less than justice, requires that its territories should be restored undiminished, as they existed when the war broke out.

The council can neither accept this conclusion nor the arguments by which it is supported. It does not, indeed, doubt that the present Government of Turkey profoundly disapproves of the policy pursued by its predecessors. Even if considerations of morality did not weigh with it—as doubtless they did—consideration of expediency would be conclusive. As individuals, its members have every motive, as well as every right, to repudiate the actions which have proved so disastrous to their country.

But, speaking generally, a nation must be judged by the Government which rules it, which directs its foreign policy, which controls its armies. Nor can Turkey claim any relief from the legitimate consequences of this doctrine merely because her affairs, at a most critical moment in her history, had fallen into the hands of men who, utterly devoid of the principle of pity, could not even command success.

It seems, however, that the claim for complete territorial restoration put forward in the memorandum is not based really on the plea that Turkey should not be required to suffer for the sins of her Ministers. It has a deeper ground. It appeals to the history of Turkish rule in the past and to the conditions of affairs in the Moslem world.

Now, the council is anxious not to enter into unnecessary controversy or to inflict needless pain on your Excellency and the delegates who accompany you. It wishes well to the Turkish people and admires their excellent qualities. But it cannot admit that among those qualities are to be counted capacity to rule over alien races. The experiment has been tried too long and too often for there to be the least doubt as to its results.

History tells us of many Turkish successes and of many Turkish defeats—of nations conquered and nations freed.

The memorandum itself refers to the reductions that have taken place in the territories recently under Ottoman sovereignty. Yet in all these changes there is no case to be found, either in Europe, or Asia, or Africa, in which the establishment of Turkish rule in any country has not been followed by a diminution of material prosperity and a fall in the level of culture. Nor is there any case to be found in which the withdrawal of Turkish rule has not been followed by a growth in material prosperity and a rise in the level of culture.

Neither among the Christians of Europe, nor among the Moslems of Syria, Arabia and Africa has the Turk done other than destroy, wherever he has conquered. Never has he shown himself able to develop in peace what he has won by war. Not in this direction do his talents lie.

The obvious conclusion from these facts would seem to be that, since Turkey has, without the least excuse or provocation, deliberately attacked the Entente Powers and been defeated, she has thrown upon the victors the heavy duty of determining the destiny of the various populations in her heterogenous empire. This duty the council of the principal Allied and Associated Powers desire to carry out as far as may be in accordance with the wishes and permanent interests of the populations themselves.

But the council observes with regret that the memorandum introduces in this connection a wholly different order of consideration based on opposed religious rivalries. The Turkish Empire is, it seems, to be preserved unchanged, not so much because this would be to the advantage of the Moslems or of the Christians within its borders, but because its maintenance is demanded by the religious sentiment of men who never felt the Turkish yoke or have forgotten how heavily it weighs on those who are compelled to bear it.

But surely there never was a sentiment less justified by facts. The whole course of the war exposes its hollowness. What religious issue is raised by a struggle in which Protestant Germany, Roman Catholic Austria, Orthodox Bulgaria and Moslem Turkey banded themselves together to plunder their neighbors?

The only savor of deliberate fanaticism perceptible in these transactions was the massacre of Christian Armenians by the order of the Turkish Government. But your Excellency has pointed out that, at the very same time and by the very same authority, unoffending Moslems were being slaughtered, in circumstances sufficiently horrible and in numbers sufficiently large, to mitigate, if not wholly to remove, any suspicion of religious partiality.

During the war, then, there was little evidence of sectarian animosity on the part of any of the Governments and no evidence whatever, so far as the Entente Powers were concerned. Nor has anything since occurred to modify this judgment; every man's conscience has been respected, places of sacred memory have been carefully guarded, the States and peoples who were Mohammedan before the war are Mohammedan still.

Nothing touching religion has been altered, except the security with which it may be practiced, and this, wherever Allied control exists, has certainly been altered for the better.

If it be replied that the diminution in the territories of a historic Moslem state must injure the Moslem cause in all lands, we respectfully suggest that in our opinion this is an error. To thinking Moslems throughout the world the modern history of the Government enthroned at Constantinople can be no source of pleasure or pride.

For reasons we have already indicated the Turk was there attempting a task, for which he had little aptitude and in which he has consequently had little success. Set him to work in happier circumstances, let his energies find their chief exercise in surroundings more congenial to his genius, under new circumstances less complicated and difficult, with an evil tradition of corruption and intrigue severed, perhaps forgotten, why should he not add lustre to his country and thus indirectly to his religion, by other qualities than that of course and discipline, which he has always so conspicuously displayed.

Unless we are mistaken your Excellency should understand our hopes. In an impressive passage of your memorandum you declare it to be your country's mission to devote itself to an intensive economic and intellectual culture.

No change could be more startling or impressive; none could be more beneficial. If your Excellency is able to initiate this great process of development in men of the Turkish race you will deserve and will certainly receive all the assistance we are able to give you.

Despite the universal demand that Armenia be granted a home, as recognized in the Paris Peace Conference, President Wilson's plan for the Armenian boundaries, the terms of the Treaty of Sevres, the Allies with unspeakable weakness and callousness to the call of their consciences, acceded to the Treaty of Lausanne, thereby leaving what Arnold Toynbee himself called a genocide unpunished.

The United States did not sign the Lausanne Treaty because technically she had not been at war with Turkey. A review of the events culminating in the Lausanne Treaty and the text of the U.S.-Turkish Treaty follow.

The Turko-American Treaty, 1923

(Digest of the terms of the treaty concluded by the United States after the signing of the Lausanne Treaty between the Allies and Turkey):

(a) *Statement of U. S. Department of State*

Immediately after the signing of the treaty of amity and commerce between the United States and Turkey the State Department at Washington issued the following statement and with it a summary of the terms of the treaty:

'Diplomatic relations between the United States and Turkey were severed on April 20, 1917. Although no declaration of war followed, there have been no official relations between the two countries from that date. Since 1919 the interests of the United States have been protected by an American High Commissioner at Constantinople. Peace negotiations between the allied powers and Turkey were instituted early in 1920 and resulted in the signing of the Treaty of Sevres on August 10, 1920. This treaty was not ratified by Turkey. The United States was not a party to the treaty.

'The allied powers subsequently invited Turkey to a conference which assembled at Lausanne on November 20, 1922, for the purpose of establishing peace in the Near East and to revise the Treaty of Sevres. The Governments of Great Britain, France and Italy, having informed this Government that they would welcome American representation at the conference, this Government sent to Lausanne Richard Washburn Child, the American Ambassador at Rome; Rear Admiral Mark L. Bristol, the American High Commissioner at Constantinople, and Joseph C. Grew, the American Minister at Berne. The American representatives followed the proceedings of the conference and expressed this Government's position in matters of direct American interest and of general humanitarian concern. As the United States had not been at war with Turkey and was not negotiating a treaty of peace with that country, this Government did not become a party to the allied treaty.

'On February 4, 1923, the conference was suspended owing to the rejection by the Turkish delegates of certain clauses in the proposed allied treaty. A second session of the Lausanne Conference began on April 23, 1923, and continued until July 24, when a treaty of peace between the allied powers and Turkey was signed. During this second part of the conference Minister Grew was the American representative.

'The prospective conclusion of peace between the principal allied powers and Turkey made it appear advisable, in order to appropriately protect American interests, that the relations between the United States and Turkey be regularized at an early date. This appeared all the more necessary in view of the fact that in the course of the allied negotiations with Turkey the abrogation of the capitulations had been agreed to.

'On May 5, 1923, Ismet Pasha, the principal Turkish delegate at the Lausanne Conference, wrote to Minister Grew proposing the negotiation of a treaty of amity and commerce. The Department of State thereupon authorized Mr. Grew to begin informal conversations with the Turkish delegates to ascertain whether a proper basis for negotiations could be found. Those conversations were followed by formal negotiations, and full powers were sent to Mr. Grew. A treaty of extradition was also negotiated.

'After almost three months of negotiation, the department, on the afternoon of August 2, authorized Mr. Grew to sign the treaty of amity and commerce and the treaty of extradition. The department is now informed that these treaties were signed at Lausanne on Monday, August 6, 1923.

'A summary of the treaty of amity and commerce, which comprises thirty-two articles, and which assures to the United States and its nationals in Turkey treatment as favorable as that accorded to any other nation, is given below. The extradition treaty contains the usual provisions of such treaties and calls for no special comment.

'Ismet Pasha has also communicated to Mr. Grew copies of the Turkish declaration with regard to the designation by the Turkish Government of foreign judicial advisers and a communication with regard to foreign schools and institutions in Turkey, assuring to such American institutions the same treatment as enjoyed by the like institutions of any foreign power, and defining in some detail the rights and privileges to be accorded these institutions.'

SUMMARY OF THE TREATY

PREAMBLE—The purpose of the Treaty is to regulate the conditions of intercourse between the United States and Turkey and to define the rights of their respective nationals in the territory of the other in accordance with the principles of international law and on the basis of reciprocity.

ARTICLE 1—Most-favored-nation treatment is accorded to the diplomatic officers of the two countries.

ARTICLE 2—Provides for the abrogation of the capitulation relating to the regime of foreigners in Turkey, both as regards conditions of entry and residence and as regards fiscal and judicial questions.

ARTICLE 3—Nationals of the High Contracting Parties have full liberty of entry, travel and residence upon conforming to the laws of the country, and shall enjoy protection in conformity with international law. Their property shall not be taken without due process of law or without indemnity. They may, under the local laws and regulations in force, engage in every kind of profession, commerce, &c., not forbidden by laws to all foreigners. They shall have the right to possess and dispose of all kinds of movable property on a footing of equality with the nationals of the country. As regards immovable property, the nationals of each country shall, in the territory of the other, enjoy the treatment generally accorded to foreigners by the laws of the place where the property is situated, subject to reciprocity. They may own, lease and construct buildings for residential purposes or any other purpose permitted by the present treaty. Upon conforming to the laws they shall enjoy liberty of conscience and worship and shall, equally with the nationals of the country, have free access to the tribunals.

ARTICLE 4—Commercial, industrial and financial companies and associations, organized under the laws of the United States and Turkey and maintaining head offices in the country in which they are organized, shall be recognized by the other country provided they pursue no aims contrary to its laws. They shall be entitled to the same protection as that accorded to nationals in Article 3. Subject to the applicable laws they shall have free access to the courts. Such companies and associations shall, subject to the laws in force in the country, have the right to acquire, possess and dispose of every kind of movable property. As regards immovable property and right to engage in commerce and industry, such companies shall enjoy, on condition of reciprocity, the treatment generally accorded by the laws in the locality where such companies are instituted. They shall be able freely to carry on their activities subject to the requirements of public order.

ARTICLE 5—Domiciliary visits and searches of dwellings, warehouses, factories, et cetera, of nationals or companies, as well as the inspection of books, accounts, et cetera, shall take place only under the conditions and in the form prescribed by the laws with respect to the nationals of the country.

ARTICLE 6—The nationals of one country in the territory of the other shall not be subject to military service, and both individuals and companies shall be exempt from forced loans or other exceptional levies on property.

ARTICLE 7—The nationals of each country shall be accorded, in the territory of the other, the same treatment as natives in all matters concerning the collection of taxes, imposts and other charges. The companies mentioned in Article 4 shall, on condition of reciprocity, enjoy the same treatment as any similar foreign company. But this Article does not apply to exemption from taxes, &c., accorded to State institutions or to concessionaires of a public utility.

ARTICLE 8—In matters of personal status and family law (e.g., marriage, divorce, dowry, adoption, &c.), and, as regards movable property, the law of succession, liquidation, &c., citizens of the United States and Turkey shall be subject exclusively to the jurisdiction of the tribunals and other national authorities of the United States sitting outside of Turkey. This does not affect the special rights of consuls in matters of civil status under international law, or special agreements, nor does it preclude the Turkish tribunals from requiring proof regarding matters coming within the competence of the national tribunals of the interested parties. Turkish tribunals may also have jurisdiction in the above-mentioned cases, provided all interested parties submit thereto in writing.

ARTICLE 9—provides for freedom of commerce and navigation between the two countries upon most-favored-nation treatment subject to sanitary, police and customs regulations. The merchant ships of the two countries shall not be subjected to higher tonnage dues or port charges than national vessels. However, this Article and other provisions of the Treaty do not apply to the coastwise trade.

ARTICLE 10—Merchant and war vessels and aircraft of the United States enjoy complete liberty of navigation and passage in the Dardanelles, the Sea of Marmora and the Bosporus on a basis of equality with similar craft of the most favored nation, subject to the rules relating to such navigation and passage of the Straits Convention of Lausanne of July 24, 1923.

ARTICLE 11—Most-favored-nation treatment as regards import duties is accorded to articles exported from one country to the other, and no export duty is to be levied higher than that imposed upon similar articles exported to any other foreign country. No prohibition or restriction shall be imposed upon the importation or exportation of an article which is not equally applied to those of the most favored nation. Vessels and goods of the two countries shall be accorded the same facilities accorded to those of a third country, irrespective of any favors granted to the third State in return for special treatment. This Article does not apply to the commerce between the United States and Cuba and the Panama Canal Zone, nor to special arrangements between Turkey and the countries detached from the Ottoman Empire since 1914.

ARTICLE 12—Most-favored-nation treatment is provided as regards the collection of consumption, excise, octoi and other local taxes on merchandise.

ARTICLE 13—Most-favored-nation treatment is accorded all merchandise as regards transit warehousing, drawbacks, &c.

ARTICLE 14—No dues for tonnage, harbor, pilotage, &c., shall be levied on any vessel which are not equally levied on national vessels.

ARTICLE 15—Any vessel carrying papers required by its laws shall be deemed to be a vessel of the country whose flag it flies.

ARTICLE 16—Most-favored-nation treatment is accorded regarding patents, trademarks, &c.

ARTICLES 17 to 26 define in detail the rights and duties of consular officers.

ARTICLE 27 provides for the protection of shipwrecked vessels and the operation of salvage.

ARTICLE 28—For the purpose of the present treaty the territories of the two countries are considered to comprise all land, water and air over which sovereignty is exercised, except the Panama Canal Zone.

ARTICLE 29—No taxes are to be collected from American citizens for any taxable periods prior to the fiscal year 1922–1923 which, under the laws in force on August 1, 1914, were not applicable to them. Any taxes collected after May 15, 1923, on periods prior to the fiscal year 1922 will be returned, but no taxes collected before May 15, 1923, for periods prior to May 15, 1923, will be returned.

ARTICLE 30—All previous treaties between the United States and Turkey are abrogated. A new Extradition Treaty is to replace the one of 1874.

ARTICLE 31—The Treaty shall come into force two months after the exchange of ratifications. Articles 1 and 2 shall be permanent. Articles 3, 4, 5, 6, 7, and 8 shall be for the duration of seven years, while Articles 9 to 28 shall remain in force for five years. If neither country notifies the other six months before the expiration of these periods of its intention to denounce any of the Articles in question, they shall remain in force until the expiration period of six months from the date on which they shall have been denounced.

ARTICLE 32—The French, English and Turkish text of this treaty shall be ratified. In case of differences the French text shall prevail. Ratifications are to be exchanged at Constantinople as soon as possible.

"An agreement was not reached with regard to the manner of settlement of claims against the respective Governments. Mr. Grew exchanged communications with Ismet Pasha which provided for further considerations of this question at an early date, and reserved the right of the two Governments to withhold ratification of the treaties until an accord on the point has been reached." (Reprinted From *Current History*, October, 1923)

The following analysis of the Turko-American treaty of 'Amity and Commerce' which was negotiated at Lausanne is taken from a statement appearing over the signature of

Ambassador James W. Gerard issued on behalf of the American Committee for the Independence of Armenia. The statement is not given in full.

AMERICAN INTERESTS IN TURKEY: On October 30, 1922, the Department of State, in the identic note which it addressed to our Ambassadors, accredited to the Principal Allied Powers, set down seven subjects in which America was interested in respect of Turkey, namely: 1. Maintenance of Capitulations; 2. Protection of American philanthropic institutions; 3. Indemnity for damages suffered by Americans; 4. Freedom of the Straits; 5. Opportunity for archeological research; 6. Open Door; 7. Protection of Minorities.

1. *Capitulations.* We have abandoned them. The comment which the *New York Times* makes on the subject in its excellent editorial, headed 'Amity and Commerce,' is illuminating. It says:

'. . . According to the dispatches from Lausanne, the Treaty clarifies the hitherto equivocal position created by Turkey's abolition of the capitulations. So it does. The equivocal position consisted in the fact that Turkey had abolished the capitulations, although Mr. Hughes declared that Turkey could do no such thing without our consent. We have now given our consent, so the situation is clarified.

. . . Under the capitulations Americans who were accused of crimes in Turkey were tried by American Consular courts. Now the jurisdiction of Consular courts is ended. Americans may be arrested by Turkish police and tried by Turkish courts . . . .

2. *Our missionary institutions in Turkey,* which engage the support of millions of Americans, are now made subject to Turkish laws. Ismet Pasha, by a letter to our Observer at Lausanne, promised them protection. They have always been entitled to protection, but, frequently, have failed to receive it . . . . The seeming cordiality of the Turks to our missionary organizations during the Conference at Lausanne was manifestly induced by their hope to use the good-will of these representatives to secure American diplomatic support. The known fact is, however, that the Turks have no respect either for our missionaries or for Christianity. Our missionaries, during the last 92 years, have prosecuted their educational and religious activities in

Turkey almost wholly among the non-Moslems. Owing to
the Koranic law, which prescribes death to an apostate
from Islam, they have made no converts among the Turks;
and their schools have been attended almost entirely by
Armenians and Greeks, already Christians. In 1914, there
was only 1 Turk in Robert College, and up to 1910 there
were none for several years . . . .

3. *The question of indemnity for damages suffered by
Americans* "through arbitrary and illegal acts" has been
left for later discussion . . . . . Americans have suffered
damages through the burning of Smyrna, through confisca-
tion and destruction of missionary property during the
war, and through flagrant denials of justice by the Ottoman Government, of all which the State Department has
voluminous records. Ismet characterized the burning of
Smyrna as an "incident" of war, and the Turkish Government has called on the European insurance companies to
"idemnify" it for the destruction of the Armenian and
Greek sections of Smyrna (the Turkish section was not
touched by the fire), just as it attempted in 1915 to cash in,
according to Ambassador Morgenthau, on the life insurance policies of the Armenians who were murdered by its
order.

4. *Freedom of the Straits.* Here we secured an illusory
concession of a right which we have always possessed. We
are not represented on the Commission of Control of the
Straits, but our merchant vessels may go through the
Dardanelles, as in the past, in times of peace or war—providing the Turks do not close them, as they did in 1914.

5. *Archeological research.* We have secured, as *The
Times* well puts it, the same rights for archeological research that are enjoyed by Turkish archeologists. But since
there are no Turkish archeologists, we shall be compelled
to wait indefinitely before we enjoy any nominal rights in
this most important matter. Meanwhile, through Turkish
ignorance, carelessness and even willful vandalism, the
rapid destruction will continue of all traces of the great
cities and supreme civilizations which flourished in these
regions before the long night of Turkish barbarism descended upon them. While scholars wait eagerly for the
concession to make researches, the evidences which they
seek are being destroyed through the reckless habits of a
nomad and half savage race. Year by year countless sculp-
tures and beautiful carvings are burned to make lime for

Turkish hovels. Year by year, through the repulsive and improvident habits of the Turkish peasantry, fire and flood take toll of the priceless antiquities which even within our time were to be found on every hand. Year by year even the face of nature is changed and her fruitfulness destroyed by these same improvident hands which pull up the roots of the olive tree and the vine that firewood may be had; heedless that the floods inevitably follow and the soil is carried into the sea.

6. *Open Door*. Under the Lausanne Treaty, we have the privilege to trade with and invest in Turkey—as in the past. But, what opportunities are there in Turkey for American capital? In 1913, our exports to Turkey amounted to $3,313,821. At that time, Turkey had an estimated population of 17,500,000, and an area of 694,960 sq. miles. She now has an estimated population of 5,000,000 to 6,000,000, and an area of 300,000 sq. miles. Arabia, Mesopotamia and Syria, with an estimated population of 6,000,000, have been severed from her. Over 4,000,000 Armenians and Greeks—except possibly 300,000—who were the principal producers and consumers, and who, according to the Annuaire de Commerce, (a French publication), controlled 66% of her commerce, have been expelled from Turkey. (The Turks controlled only 12%, the remaining 24% being in the Hands of Syrians, Jews, Levantines, Arabs, and foreigners). The indolent and illiterate Turkish peasant has a primitive standard of living—he wants almost nothing that we produce. His country has no industries, and its agriculture is archaic. . . .

7. *Protection of minorities*. This is generally conceived as a humanitarian interest only, but, as a matter of record, we have fixed moral and legal responsibility to the Armenian people, evolving from the formal pronouncements and acts of the President and Government of the United States; and it was our clear duty to do our utmost—at least as much as we did in behalf of oil—to discharge that responsibility.

Ambassador Gerard, letter to President Harding, dated November 8, 1922, quoted in *The Great Betrayal,* by E. H. Bierstadt, 1924, whereby he accuses the United States of having broken its promises to render substantial help to the Armenians. Here are a few extracts:

". . . on September 5, 1919, the Secretary of State informed me that, 'with the cordial approval of this Government, France has agreed to send immediately ten to twelve thousand troops into the Caucasus to replace the British troops.'

"On September 8, 1919, Senator Williams offered a Resolution in the Senate, authorizing the President to send troops to Armenia, and to furnish equipment for an Armenian army, etc. This Resolution was consolidated with the Lodge Resolution, and hearings were held by a sub-Committee under your Chairmanship.

"In view of this action of the Senate, France held back the dispatch of troops to Armenia, and Great Britain refrained, for a similar reason, from furnishing arms and munitions.

"With the conclusion of the hearings on October 10, 1919, you, Mr. President, as Chairman of the sub-Committee of the Senate, informed me that, realizing as you did the desperate character of the situation in Armenia, you would report at once, and, further, specified the recommendations which you were disposed to make. Then months elapsed and no action was taken.

"Consequently, by numerous letters and telegrams, I conveyed to you information showing that the conditions in Armenia were growing worse from day to day; that the Turks were deriving comfort and encouragement from our delay; that the Armenians were defenseless, and could not get help elsewhere pending the disposition of your Committee's Resolution, and that we would be responsible for the consequences of our dilatory policy.

"You acknowledged the justice and force of these arguments, but, owing to the Presidential primaries in which you were engaged, you did not make your report for seven months, or until May 13, 1920, and your report did not contain the recommendation which you said you would make.

"The delay of one and one-half years which we imposed upon the Allies deprived the Armenians of the opportunity of looking for help elsewhere; offered some of the Allies the opportunity to intrigue among themselves, and made it possible for the Turks to organize themselves with the active aid of two of the Allies and of Moscow.

"The destruction of the independence of Armenia; the

slaughter, at the hands of the Turks, of 300,000 additional Armenians, and the present terrible plight of the Armenian people are the logical consequences of the policy of procrastination which we pursued.

"On December 17, 1920, after your election, when Mr. Jessup and I had the honor of conferring with you on this matter, you expressed yourself as being in favor of the Department of State addressing identic notes to the Allies, insisting that they carry out the Armenian provisions of the Sevres Treaty. Thus, you recognized then our duty and right to speak for Armenia to the Powers.

"In the light of our responsibility for the plight of Armenia and of your own pledges to Armenia, some of which I have mentioned, I now express the most earnest hope that you may direct the Department of State to take the step which you favored on December 17, 1920."

In reply to my letter, the President said that

"'. . . everything which may be done will be done in seeking to protect the Armenian people and preserve to them the rights which the Sevres Treaty undertook to bestow.'

"On December 10, 1922, Lord Curzon informed the Turkish Delegation at Lausanne that the Allies would insist on the erection of a State or National Home for the Armenians. On December 30, 1922 our Chief Observer spoke, 'in principle,' in favor of assigning a 'refuge' to the Armenians; and, the following day, our Delegation displayed an official notice on the billboard of the Conference Building that its statement of the previous day for Armenia was made 'unofficial' only. The role which our Observers played may be best gleaned from a telegram which the Lausanne correspondent of VAKIT, a Turkish daily of Constantinople, sent to his paper. He 'learned from a highly placed personage that the American Delegation, under the pressure of religious organizations, may find itself in the necessity of speaking, in a perfunctory way, for the Armenians.' And VAKIT, in an editorial article, complimented Rear-Admiral Mark L. Bristol, one of our Observers at Lausanne and American High Commissioner at Constantinople, for his 'unvarying efforts in behalf of the Turks,' and expressed 'gratitude to America for the *benevolent* attitude of her representatives at Lausanne.' Indeed, as I stated in my letter to Secretary Hughes, dated April 14, 1923, '. . . The Turkish press of Constantinople commended our representatives for the services which they rendered the Turks at Lausanne, and their services included, no doubt, the part which they played towards the burial of the Armenian case.'

Mr. Gerard continues: *Tevhidi* (Tefkira) *Efkiar*, another Turkish daily in Constantinople, said that,

". . . Had the Western Powers earnestly desired the protection of the Armenians, they would have insisted upon the setting up of an Armenian Home, and, if need be, they would have been prepared to break up the Conference on that issue, as they threatened to do on matters which they were intimately interested in . . . ."

The weakest feature of the Turkish case was its Armenian part. Had we joined the Allies, firmly and honorably, in insisting on securing some measure of justice for Armenia, the Turks might have, and according to some competent opinion, would have, made—as ultimately they must make—some fair concessions to the Armenians. But as the *New York Evening Post* well observes:

'In dealing with Turkey we made no vigorous effort to prevent the two great blots which deface the agreements between the Powers and the Angora Government—the provisions for a compulsory exchange of populations and the abandonment of Armenia. We refused to associate ourselves with the Allies or to act with vigor. . . . Our principal display of energy was in asserting certain American commercial rights which struck Europe as showing that the open-door policy can be made to cover a wonderfully wide field. . . .'

Our Government not only failed to make any honest effort to fulfill our commitments to Armenia, and thus to interpret the sentiment of the American people, but its platonic and perfunctory expressions of interest, formally declared to be 'unofficial' only, quite naturally encouraged the Turks to persist in their intransigeant attitude, and thus allowed the Allies to escape from their own responsibility. The Administration was insistent in its demand for opportunities in the oil fields of Mosul for a few privileged syndicates, on the ground that 'America contributed to the defeat of Turkey'; but it failed to speak earnestly for the rights of outraged humanity, on the ground that 'America did not declare war on Turkey.'[18]

Stanley Baldwin and Herbert A. Asquith, a joint proposal, September 26, 1924, quoted in *Armenia and the Near East*, by Fridtjof Nansen.[19]

On September 26, 1924 former Prime Minister Stanley Baldwin and Herbert A. Asquith, the leader of the Liberal Party, presented a memorial to Ramsay MacDonald, the head of the Government, to grant an aid for the resettlement of the Armenian refugees, such grant to be administered by the Lord Mayor's Fund, giving the following principal reasons:

1.—Because the Armenians were encouraged by promises of freedom to support the Allied cause during the War, and suffered for this cause so tragically;

2.—Because during the War and since the Armistice statesmen of the Allies and Associated Powers have given repeated pledges to secure the liberation and independence of the Armenian nation;

3.—Because in part Great Britain is responsible for the final dispersion of the Ottoman Armenians after the sack of Smyrna in 1922;

4.—Because the sum of £5,000,000 (Turkish gold) deposited by the Turkish Government in Berlin in 1916, and taken over by the Allies after the Armistice, was in large part (perhaps wholly) Armenian money;

5.—Because the present conditions of the refugees are unstable and demoralizing, and constitute a reproach to the Western Powers.

We recognize, the document went on, with deep regret that it is impossible now to fulfill our pledge to the Armenians . . . But there is open to us another method of expressing our sense of responsibility and of relieving the desperate plight of the scattered remnants of the Turkish Armenians. The most appropriate territory for their settlement would surely be in the Russian Armenia. Facilities are offered by the local Government . . .

It is our opinion the duty of Great Britain to give substantial support to this scheme. We desire to express our view that, as some compensation for unfulfilled pledges is morally due to the Armenians, the British Government should forthwith make an important grant . . .

Signed H. A. Asquith
Stanley Baldwin

In *The Great Betrayal*, Edward H. Bierstadt, sums up the situation as of 1924 as follows:

1. The Allies, both severally and jointly, pledged themselves to:

> (a) The relief of the Armenians from Turkish oppression;
> (b)The establishment of an autonomous Armenian State;

2. France expressed through her spokesmen her willingness to accept a mandate over Armenia.

3. The United States expressed through her statesmen her willingness to accept a mandate over Armenia.

4. Thereafter Armenia turned to the United States.

5. At the request of the United States the Allies postponed a final settlement with Turkey, pending the active cooperation of America.

6. The United States did nothing for one and a half years.

7. That delay directly resulted in:

> (a) the complete resurrection of Turkish power;
> (b)the massacre and expulsion of all Armenians in Turkey;
> (c) the overwhelming victory of Turkey at Lausanne.[20]

On Genocide

It is remarkable how precise a description of genocide is contained in many of the documents relating to the Armenian massacres. In such an account as the great Dr. Lepsius's, nothing is lacking but the word itself, not yet coined.

Since World War II, however, the word *genocide* has come to be explicitly applied to the Turkish campaign of extermination, notably by Arnold Toynbee, who even in his youth was an authority on Turkish misrule and Armenian suffering.

In addition, a Polish writer, Bohdan Gebarski, in his remarkable "Letter to my Turkish Friend" reproduced here, specifically equates the Turkish actions with those of the Nazis. It is appropriate that this should be done, for it is a neglected truth that needs recognition. In order to clarify the importance of gaining that recognition on a broad scale, we

have included the official definition of genocide as formulated
at Nuremberg after World War II.

Dr. Johannes Lepsius: sworn testimony at the trial of Sog-
homon Tehlirian in Berlin, for the assassination of Talaat
Pasha, June 2, 1921; from the transcript of the record.

Dr. Lepsius, appearing as a witness for the defense at the
trial testified as follows under oath:

> The Committee of Young Turks determined the total de-
> portation, Talaat Pasha as Minister of the Interior (with
> Enver Pasha as the Minister of War) gave the command
> and the decision was carried out with the help of the Com-
> mittee of the Young Turk Organization. The deportation
> and exile, which had been already decided in April 1915,
> was directed against the entire Armenian population, with
> a small exception which I shall tell. Before the war there
> lived in Turkey 1,850,000 Armenians. Of course, there is
> no exact census in a country like Turkey. That figure we
> have taken from statistics which agree with census taken
> by the Armenian Patriarchate. The Armenian population
> before the war was spread over Turkey in Europe (Con-
> stantinople, Adrianople, Rodosto) and over Turkey in Asia
> (Anatolia, Cilicia, the northern Assyria and Mesopotamia).
> The great majority of the Armenians lived in the eastern
> Anatolia on the mountainous heights of Armenia, the an-
> cient home of the Armenian nation, in the six vilayets,
> Garin, Van, Paghesh, Diarbekir, Sepastia, and Kharpert; a
> strong part of the people in the western Anatolia lived
> across Constantinople on the southern shores of the sea of
> Marmora. On the southern Anatolia—Cilicia—with the
> steppes of the Taurus mountains and with the land around
> the Gulf of Alexandria, bordering Assyrian lands on the
> north—was a part of the ancient Armenian fatherland.
> The entire Armenian population of Anatolia was de-
> ported, by a supreme command, to the northern and east-
> ern boundaries of the Mesopotamian desert—Der El Zor,
> Racca, Meskeneh, Rass-ul-ain, up to Mousoul.
> Approximately 1,400,000 Armenians were displaced.
> What is the meaning of this deportation?
> In one of the orders signed by Talaat the following phrase
> is found. 'The place of exile is extinction.' This order was
> carried out with great care. Only 10% of the people de-

ported from the eastern Anatolian provinces reached their places of exile. The remaining 90% were killed on route, aside from the women and girls sold by the gendarmes and seduced by the Kurds. The rest died of starvation and exhaustion. The Armenians who were driven to the desert from western Anatolia, Cilicia and northern Assyria, gradually reached in concentration camps, numbered hundreds of thousands. The great majority of these also were later eliminated by a systematic starvation and periodical massacres. As soon as the concentration camps were filled and there was no room for the new arrivals, they were dispatched to the desert in groups and killed outright. The Turks have said that the idea of concentration camps was taken from the British treatment of the Boers in South Africa: Officially it was declared that the exiles were intended to serve as precautionary measures, but men in authority were overtly stating that the aim was to eliminate the Armenian people.

My testimony is based on documents which I received from the archives of Imperial Embassies and the Ministry of Foreign Affairs and published, especially the reports of German Consuls and German Ambassadors in Constantinople.

You heard the testimony of Tehlirian and Mrs. Terzibashian about what they suffered and what they witnessed during the deportations. Hundreds of such stories, in greater details, all of which bear the print of personal experiences, have been published, mostly in German and partly in American and English publications. The facts are irrefutable. The methods of implementation everywhere are similar to those described to us here by Tehlirian and Mrs. Terzibashian. Otherwise it might have been necessary to ask: how could millions of persons be killed in such a short time? That was possible in the most ruthless manner, as has been proven by the speeches made during the trial of Talaat Pasha and his colleagues before the Court Martial in Constantinople. The Court Martial was formed by the commander of an Army Corps, as president, 3 generals, among whom were known generals from the war front, and a captain. The first of the five counts of the indictment referred to the Armenian massacres. By the decision of the Court Martial on July 6, 1919, Talaat, Enver, Jemal and Dr. Nazim, the principal authors of the crime, were sentenced to death.

The carrying out of the plan to exterminate the Armenians was assured by an order from Constantinople to the *Valis, Mutesarifs,* and *Kaimakams.* That is to the top governors, the heads of the government and the councillors of the state. Officials who disobeyed were removed. For instance, the governor of Aleppo, Jelal Pasha, refused to carry out the deportation order. He was dismissed by Talaat and was transferred to Konia. His actions in his new post were the same as in Aleppo; he protected the Armenians who had not yet been deported and placed under his protection the deportees who had reached there. The result was that he was again dismissed without being assigned to another post. He was one of the most famous and righteous governors (Valis) in Turkey. Another Vali, Rashid Bey, in Diarbekir caused the death at the hands of ruthless killers two *kaimakams* (mayors) who had refused to carry out the order of deportation. Among the Turkish people those who were unwilling to accept the orders of the government were subjected to harsh treatment, even civil officials and military men. The commander of the Third Army Corps issued an order whereby any Turk who renders help to Armenians would be slain in front of his home and his home would be burned. Officials who would commit the "crime" of helping Armenians would be dismissed from office and court-martialed.

From the original 1,850,000 Armenians 1,400,000 were deported. There remained 450,000. From these about 200,-000 living in Constantinople, Smyrna and Aleppo were not deported. In saving the Armenians of Aleppo from deportation the German Consul Roessler played a great role; that was the man who was accused in the Allied press as having organized the massacres. In Smyrna General Liman von Sanders, from whom you will hear in person, prevented the deportation of the Armenians. Grand Marshall von der Goltz acted in the similar manner. When he went to Baghdad he learned that the Armenians had been deported to Mousoul and from there with the Armenians of Mousoul would be deported towards the River Euphrates, which meant towards death. Von de Goltz announced to the Vali of Mousoul that he prohibited any deportation. When the Vali received a new order for deportation, von der Goltz presented his resignation. Enver Pasha yielded but in his note to von der Goltz he said that "his (Goltz') authorities as commander-in-chief do not give him the right to interfere in the internal affairs of the Turkish State."

The ambassadors in Constantinople prevented the deportation of Armenians from that city. Allow me to make a passing comment. We often read the Armenian massacres are due to the fact that the Armenian merchant class has robbed the Turks and the infuriated Turkish people spontaneously stood up against the Armenians. First it has been proven that neither the massacres of 1895–96 nor the recent massacres were originated from innate popular disturbances. At both instances the executive orders of the Turkish government were being carried out. The truth is that the Armenian merchants in the principal businesses in Constantinople, Smyrna and Aleppo were spared at both times, partly because they were able to buy their freedom. Conversely the entire rustic people of Anatolia, 80% of which were Armenians, together with all the tradespeople, most of them Armenians, were sent to the desert and perished.

The rest of the Armenian population, about 250,000 from eastern vilayets, were saved from deportation by the Russian occupation of the neighboring territories, and took refuge in the Caucasus. At that time Russian armies reached the western shore of the Sea of Van. When they retreated, they took the Armenians with them, not because they loved the Armenians. The fact is that when the Russians again advanced in these territories, they did not allow Armenian families to return to their homeland. Nicholas Nicholayevitch's chief of staff, Janoushgevitch, who was the Army commander in the Caucasus at the time, announced that Russia would establish communities of Kurds and Kazaks in the depopulated (Armenian) lands, instead of Armenians. Mutukov, the chief of Russian cadets, in the Duma, strongly criticized the government for doing what the Turks had done and for wanting to have 'an Armenia without Armenians.' The Russian advance, however, saved the lives of 350,000 Armenians, and the Russian retreat deprived them of their homeland. Even now they (Armenians) live in a very poor land and for years they suffered starvation and great hardship.

One involuntarily asks oneself: how could such happenings become possible historically? I shall try to give a concise answer to that question.

Armenian Question is not a self-produced plant, but the

off-spring of European diplomacy. The Armenian nation is the victim of opposing political interests of Russia and England. The enmity between these two states has its origin in the Crimean War, the Berlin Conference. In the game of chess between London and Petersburg the Armenian was the pawn, sometimes pushed forward, sometimes sacrificed. The humanitarian causes, 'protection of Christians,' were pretexts. When in 1895 Abdul Hamid was forced to sign the plan of reforms presented by England, Russia and France, he had already set in motion a number of Armenian massacres. Lord Salisbury, announced that as far as England was concerned, the Armenian Question had ceased to exist. Prince Lobanov indicated to the Sultan that he had nothing to worry about because Russia pays no attention to the execution of reforms. The Sultan drew his own conclusions. . . . The massacre of Sassoun in 1894, which created the occasion for the plan of reforms, had cost the lives of 1,000 Armenians, the massacres of 1895–96, which followed the plan, took the lives of 100,000 Armenians. The massacres of 1915–18, which had been preceded by the plans of reforms of 1913, raised the number of victims to one million. This staircase of 1894, 1895, and 1915, with its respective victims of 1,000–100,000–1,000,000 represents a horror which in history of the massacres of the world hardly has a parallel; There is also the in between period of 1909 when 25,000 Armenians were killed in Cilicia.

(Editor's Note: Authoritative evidence has proved beyond any doubt that the figures quoted above by the distinguished friend of the Armenians are not accurate. The following figures are much closer to the truth: in 1894, 5,000 Armenians were killed in Sassoun; in 1895–1896, 300,000 Armenians were massacred; in 1915–1918, 1,500,000 Armenians lost their lives; in 1909, 30,000 were slaughtered in Cilicia.)

In spite of Article 61 of the Berlin Treaty which was signed by six states, in spite of the Cyprus Convention of 1878 which provided that England was to insure the protection of Christians and the implementation of the Armenian reforms, in spite of the fact that the Sultan had signed the plan of reforms prepared by England, Russia and France, none of these great powers raised a finger to save their proteges or at least to have the murderers punished. Until now Armenians have only been means to an end in the political play of England, Russia and France. The publication of documents shall prove that, since the Berlin Conference Germany has shown a friendly and sane attitude toward the Armenian Question, and in spite of that she has been accused in all the world as a government which supported all the wicked deeds of the Sultan and the Turkish government. It was the political game England and Russia played which convinced the Sultan and the Young Turks to consider the Armenians as the most dangerous racial group in Turkey.

Abdul Hamid reached this conclusion: 'Because of European intervention in favor of Bulgaria, I lost Bulgaria. Now they join the Armenians to take the eastern Anatolia away from me, so as to separate it from Turkey piece by piece.' Hence the madness in massacring and persecuting the Armenians.

But the Armenian reforms still remain in the political design of the powers. In 1913 they again were put on the agenda. Russian and German ambassadors were conducting negotiations. England remained aloof. These negotiations resulted in a program of reforms, which was signed by the (Sublime) Porte and which was satisfactory to the Armenians. The supervision of the reforms was delegated to two European General Directors. The matter did not reach the stage of supervision. War was declared and the two reformers were called back. I was in Constantinople in 1913. During the negotiations the Young Turks were very much enraged by the fact that the question of Armenian reforms still occupied the powers, and they were doubly embittered when the question was settled according to the wishes of the Armenians by the agreement between Germany and Russia. The Young Turks then freely commented: 'If you Armenians do not withdraw from reforms, something will happen which will make the massacres perpetrated by Abdul Hamid seem like child's play.'

Young Turks and Armenians had brought about the revolution. The leaders fraternized and helped each other during elections. During the first months of the war everything seemed peaceful between them. Then suddenly during the night of April 24–25, 1915, to the bewilderment of the entire Constantinople 235 of the topmost Armenian intellectuals were arrested, jailed and transferred to Asia

Minor. On the following days several hundred others were added to that list, 600 all told. Only 15 of these remained alive. It was the Armenian intelligentsia of Constantinople. Vartkes, the Armenian member of the parliament and Talaat's personal friend was still alive. He went to Talaat to inquire about what was happening. Talaat said to Vartkes: 'During the days of our weakness you jumped at our throats and stirred up the question of Armenian reforms, and for that reason now we will take advantage of our favorable situation and disperse your nation in such a way that you will be unable to think about reforms for 50 years.'

'Then you intend to continue Abdul Hamid's work,' retorted Vartkes, and Talaat answered 'Yes.'

As was the threat so was the act. According to the report of 'Journal Officiel,' the court-martial trials furnished the evidence that the Young Turks' Committee has decided the deportation and that Talaat Pasha, the soul of the Committee and its most influential person, has ordered the extermination (of the Armenians) and has done nothing to prevent it. This can be proven officially in writing, based on German and Turkish documents.

My words intended to show that the political game of the powers arrived at a point when first Abdul Hamid and then the Young Turk became so suspicious about the Armenians that they reached this conclusion: that extermination was the only thing to be done to Armenians. The eyewitness testimonies given at this trial about thousands and tens of thousands of acts of extermination, prove that point.

Bohdan Gebarski, "A Letter to my Turkish Friend," November 26, 1961; published in the *Polish Kiernuki*, translated by Matthew Callender from the Armenian translation and published in *The Armenian Mirror-Spectator*, June 30, 1962. (Editor's Note: The Armenian translation from the original text in Polish was made by a contributor to *Nairi*, published in Beirut, Lebanon.)

Excerpts:

. . . I had reason to be interested in your country from an additional point of view. I simply felt a necessarily unavoidable urge to look into the eyes of a man who should have felt the responsibility towards the most horrible crime in human history. In the simple language of the time (and that happened in the days of the First World War) the word was crime. Today, alas, we already know the name of that crime—GENOCIDE.

. . . Twenty-five years have passed since that conversation. . . However, since there is not the slightest mention in your letter about the subject, it appears that we did not even cover the subject during our conversation. I did surmise, though, reading between the lines, that you fully recalled the subject of our conversation when you wrote me about the unprecedented acts of Eichmann and call them a crime. Do you know that Eichmann was only a diligent pupil of yours? All that Eichmann did to the Jews during 1942–1944 was the repetition, on a larger scale, of exactly that which your countrymen inflicted on the Armenians in the year 1915. And that happened, please don't forget, for the first time in history, organized and executed with scientific precision and system—the organized extermination of a people!

That massacre, which was carried out and executed to its last detail, had no similarity with those random exploits of one Abdul Hamid during the years 1895–1896 when the savage bands of Kurds and the scum of the Turkish rabble were provoked against the Armenians culminating in "moderate" results—hardly half a million Armenians massacred.

. . . According to reliable statistics that have reached us, the authorities issued orders for all Armenians to leave their native habitations usually within two hours "for the purpose of reaching new quarters." They were allowed to take with themselves only light articles which they could carry by hand, leaving their entire property to the Turkish population. It was strictly forbidden to use any means of conveyance. No exception was made for the aged, the sick, the children, even in case of pregnant women. Under the scorching summer sun of Asia Minor the caravans on foot were accompanied by gendarmes, armed with rifles and and whips. If any sympathetic Muslim were tempted to give water to the Armenians, he was instantly whipped or even shot there and then on the spot.

If any of the prisoners fell exhausted (which happened every moment in that death caravan from its beginning) gendarmes killed the fallen or kicked with their boots. Hordes of *tchetchens* and rover bandits, who followed the caravans, denuded the bodies of the dead with insolent abuse, with the tacit consent and permission of the gendarmes. They immediately seized and carried away young women and girls who had fallen down or straggled a few paces behind the caravan. After raping them repeatedly, they murdered them in the most atrocious manner. Among others, that also was being done according to secret orders issued to the gendarmes, which meant that those who were being exiled were to be slaughtered en route.

. . . The number of the dead exceeded ten thousand each day. . . . Deportation embraced within its folds all the persons of that unfortunate people, from the Bulgarian frontier to that of Persia. . . .

The continuation of the onslaught took on an entirely different aspect. Those Armenians who had somehow escaped deportation were subjected to a ruthless massacre. Attention was first directed to those who had saved their lives by means of self-defense in a few isolated spots of resistance, where besieged Armenians received occasional help from the French, the British or the Russians. That was the case, for example, in Cilicia and around Lake Van.

. . . Let me say in parenthesis that the territories occupied by you were of no benefit to you. About two years ago, while I was passing along the boundaries between Armenia and Turkey, during two hours of my travel I did not see a single living soul on your side of the frontier. You have converted the thickly populated territory into a desert, dead and ghastly, like a forgotten and desecrated graveyard. Did you massacre the rightful owners of that territory, contrary to all divine and human laws, so as to call that land "Turkey" and scorch it?

. . . Every century has its own true image. The 20th century differs from those that preceded it in that it is the century of greatest crimes and greatest retributions. The greatest crimes of the 20th century are the massacres, that is the attempts to exterminate an entire people by torture and murder, attempts which fortunately never succeeded by one-hundred percent.

The first attempt at such a crime, which was successful in sixty percent, was made during the first part of our century, in the beginning of the spring of 1915. That was called "the complete solution of the Armenian Question."

. . . I am neither Turk nor Armenian, therefore, I cannot consider it my duty to evaluate the manifest means of retribution which the Armenians demand from you. But I know that during this historic era of ours, in this era of self-obtained freedom by the persecuted and tortured peoples, the Armenian Question also will undoubtedly arise.

Arnold Toynbee—*Experiences*, New York and London, Oxford University Press, 1969

There has not, so far as I know, been any previous age in which the common humanity of all human beings, just in virtue of our all being human, has been so widely recognized and acted upon as it is today. The famous and moving sentiment 'homo sum, humanum nihil a me alienum puto',* which the Roman playwright Terence put into the mouth of one of his characters, is actually more characteristic of the present-day world than it was of the Graeco-Roman World of the second century B.C. Yet the age through which I have lived has also seen the moral implications of mankind's common humanity repudiated in outrageous doctrines that have served as excuses for atrocious acts.

Human beings have occasionally massacred each other unconstitutionally—apart from the hallowed ritual form of massacre in war—since the earliest times of which we have surviving records. But in our time we have had to coin a new word, 'genocide', to describe a new kind of massacre. The distinguishing marks of our twentieth-century genocide are that it is committed in cold-blood by the deliberate *fiat* of holders of despotic political power, and that the perpetrators of genocide employ all the resources of present-day technology and organization to make their planned massacres systematic and complete. I am old enough to remember the horror at the massacre of Armenian Ottoman subjects in the Ottoman Empire in 1896 at the instigation of the infamous Sultan 'Abd-al-Hamid II. But this act of genocide was amateur and ineffective compared with the largely successful attempt to exterminate the Ottoman Armenians that was made during the First World War, in 1915, by the post-Hamidian regime of 'The Committee of Union and Progress,' in which the principal criminals were Tala't and Enver. The Second World War was accompanied by the Nazis' genocide of the Jews both in Germany and in the other European countries that were temporarily

---

* "I am a human being, so there is nothing human that I do not feel to be my concern" (Terence, Heautontimorumenus, line 77).

overrun and occupied by the German military forces. Since the general level of technological and organizational efficiency in Germany during the dozen years of the Nazi regime was considerably higher than it had been in Turkey during the ten years of the C. U. P. regime, the German genocide of the European Jews was still more effective than the Turkish genocide of the Ottoman Armenians had been. . . .

To be massacred is a worse fate than to be evicted from one's native land and to be robbed of one's home and property. The refugee has ransomed his life at this price, and, so long as he remains alive, he can cherish at least a forlorn hope of eventual repatriation and restitution, or alternately of compensation and re-settlement in some new habitat that will be congenial enough to make it possible for him to strike fresh roots there. All the same, the eviction of entire populations, or even of diasporas, is a recent relapse, in the present age, into a barbarous practice that was occasionally followed in past times, but in those times less remorselessly and less thoroughly.[21]

The genocide committed against the Armenians in the Ottoman Empire in 1915 and against the Jews in Germany and in the German-occupied non-German parts of Europe during the Second World War was carried out, in both cases, under the cloak of legality, by cold-blooded government action. These were not mass-murders committed spontaneously by mobs of private people. The responsibility of the private citizens of the Committee of Union and Progress's Turkey and Hitler's Germany was, of course, grave, but it was a sin of omission. Private citizens in general did not summon up in themselves the public spirit and the readiness for self-sacrifice that are required of a human being by his conscience (a daunting requirement) when his conscience condemns the acts of people in power who are acting in his name as representatives of the government of the country of which he is a citizen.[22]

The Greatest Crime in the History of Mankind—Genocide

1. The word *genocide* did not exist at the time the Turks planned and carried out the total extermination of the Armenian people. It was coined by Rapael Lemkin in 1944, after Hitler's attempt to exterminate the Jews in Germany.

Only a year after the termination of the global war, the General Assembly of the newly formed United Nations in its resolution 96 (I) dated December 11, 1946, declared that "genocide is a crime under international law, contrary to the spirit and aims of the United Nations and condemned by the civilized world and agreed upon a set of principles which is called Convention on the Prevention and Punishment of the Crime of Genocide." On December 9, 1949 the General Assembly at its 179th plenary meeting by resolution 260 (III) approved the Convention and proposed for signature and ratification or accession. Pertinent articles of the Convention are hereinafter set forth:

CONVENTION ON THE PREVENTION AND PUNISHMENT OF THE CRIME OF GENOCIDE

The Contracting Parties,

Having considered the declaration made by the General Assembly of the United Nations in its resolution 96 (I) dated 11 December, 1946, that genocide is a crime under international law, contrary to the spirit and aims of the United Nations and condemned by the civilized world;

Recognizing that at all periods of history genocide has inflicted great losses on humanity; and

Being convinced that, in order to liberate mankind from such an odious scourge, international co-operation is required;

Hereby agree as hereinafter provided.

ARTICLE I

The Contracting Parties confirm that genocide, whether committed in time of peace or in time of war, is a crime under international law which they undertake to prevent and to punish.

ARTICLE II

In the present Convention, genocide means any of the following acts committed with intent to destroy, in whole or in part, a national, ethnical, racial or religious group, as such:

(a) Killing members of the group;

(b) Causing serious bodily or mental harm to members of the group;

(c) Deliberately inflicting on the group conditions of life calculated to bring about its physical destruction in whole or in part;

(d) Imposing measures intended to prevent births within the group;

(e) Forcibly transferring children of the group to another group.

ARTICLE III

The following acts shall be punishable:
(a) Genocide;
(b) Conspiracy to commit genocide;
(c) Direct and public incitement to commit genocide;
(d) Attempt to commit genocide;
(e) Complicity in genocide.

ARTICLE IV

Persons committing genocide or any of the other acts enumerated in Article III shall be punished, whether they are constitutionally responsible rulers, public officials or private individuals.

ARTICLE V

The Contracting Parties undertake to enact, in accordance with their respective Constitutions, the necessary legislation to give effect to the provisions of the present Convention and, in particular, to provide effective penalties for persons guilty of genocide or any of the other acts enumerated in Article III.

ARTICLE VI

Persons charged with genocide or any of the other acts enumerated in Article III shall be tried by a competent tribunal of the State in the territory of which the act was committed, or by such international penal tribunal as may have jurisdiction with respect to those Contracting Parties which shall have accepted its jurisdiction.

ARTICLE VII

Genocide and the other acts enumerated in Article III shall not be considered as political crimes for the purpose of extradition.

The Contracting Parties pledge themselves in such cases to grant extradition in accordance with their laws and treaties in force.

ARTICLE VIII

Any Contracting Party may call upon the competent organs of the United Nations to take such action under the Charter of the United Nations as they consider appropriate for the prevention and suppression of acts of genocide or any of the other acts enumerated in Article III.

ARTICLE IX

Disputes between the Contracting Parties relating to the interpretation, application or fulfillment of the present Convention, including those relating to the responsibility of a State for genocide or any other acts enumerated in Article III, shall be submitted to the International Court of Justice at the request of any of the parties to the dispute.

(Articles X, XI, XII and XIII omitted)

ARTICLE XIV

The present Convention shall remain in effect for a period of ten years as from the date of its coming into force.

It shall thereafter remain in force for successive periods of five years for such Contracting Parties as have not denounced it at least six months before the expiration of the current period.

Denunciation shall be effected by a written notification addressed to the Secretary-General of the United Nations.

ARTICLE XV

If, as a result of denunciations, the number of Parties to the present Convention should become less than sixteen, the Convention shall cease to be in force as from the date on which the last of these denunciations shall become effective.

ARTICLE XVI

A request for the revision of the present Convention may be made at any time by any Contracting Party by means of a notification in writing addressed to the Secretary-General.

The General Assembly shall decide upon the steps, if any, to be taken in respect to such request.

ARTICLE XVII

The Secretary-General of the United Nations shall notify all the members of the United Nations and the non-member States contemplated in Article XI of the following:

(a) Signatures, ratifications and accessions received in accordance with Article XI;

(b) Notifications received in accordance with Article XII;

(c) The date upon which the present Convention comes into force in accordance with Article XIII;

(d) Denunciations received in accordance with Article XIV.

(e) The abrogation of the Convention in accordance with Article XV;

(f) Notifications received in accordance with Article XVI.

ARTICLE XVIII

The original of the present Convention shall be deposited in the archives of the United Nations.

A certified copy of the Convention shall be transmitted to all members of the United Nations and to the non-member States contemplated in Article XI.

ARTICLE XIX

The present Convention shall be registered by the Secretary-General of the United Nations on the date of its coming into force.

The first genocide of the twentieth century was committed by Turkey and the Turks against the Armenians to destroy the entire nation. Each and every act specified in Article II of the Convention was committed in the most gruesome, ruthless, inhuman and horrible manner, as has been shown in innumerable testimonies by persons whose reputation and integrity cannot be questioned.

The parallels between the Nazi and Turkish genocides are by no means confined to the systematic devastation inflicted upon two unarmed and innocent peoples. The constructive talents of both Jews and Armenians have been dramatically demonstrated since the disasters that decimated them: in Israel, even the most hostile of anti-Jewish factions freely admit that the Jews have worked wonders.

In Soviet Armenia, the accomplishments of the Armenians —a pitiful remnant of a great people half a century ago— although little known, have been spectacular. One wonders, indeed, what might have been the glorious destiny of Turkey itself, had the Armenians been the dominant rather than the exploited element there. But the Armenians, courageous as they have shown themselves on innumerable occasions, are a peaceable, constructive people.

Because of their constructive impulses and their manifold gifts, the Armenians could, in a short time, convert their rightful homeland into a comparative paradise, to the benefit, and not at the expense, of the Turks themselves. They could create in Turkish Armenia, a center of enlightenment and productivity to rival Israel, and there could be no nation— the Turks themselves excepted—which would not rejoice in what they did.

With such a development, justified as it is by history, tradition, solid promises, international law, property rights, and the reality of the crime of genocide, Asia Minor could enter upon a phase of achievement brilliantly in contrast to her dark and tortured past.

REFERENCES

1. pp. 15–17.

2. p. 85.

3. pp. 63–64.

4. p. 35.

5. p. 488.

6. p. 437.

7. p. 159.

8. Mandelstam, *op. cit.*, p. 255.

9. *Ibid.*, p. 255.

10. *Ibid.*, p. 257.

11. p. 159.

12. pp. 195–196.

13. pp. 189–191.

14. *Ibid.*, p. 196.

15. *Ibid.*, pp. 196–197.

16. pp. 14–16.

17. p. 305.

18. Bierstadt, *op. cit.*

19. pp. 321–323.

20. Bierstadt, *op. cit.*, pp. 184–185.

21. pp. 241–242.

22. *Ibid.*, p. 341.

Chapter 7

Epilogue

The title of this book, *Armenia: The Case For A Forgotten Genocide*—fully expresses the purpose which inspired its preparation. The more than six hundred conscientiously and scrupulously gathered and classified documents contained in the volume constitute a mere fragment of thousands of authentic statements which reveal the magnitude of the Turkish persecutions of Armenians over the centuries.

The quotations, which establish fully the right to the independent existence of Armenia and the Armenian people, include parts of international treaties between great powers as well as pledges by responsible leaders of various states (Kings, Presidents, Prime Ministers, Secretaries of State, Senators, etc.), the official reports and unbiased testimonies of ambassadors and consuls, and of well-known public figures and missionaries.

All these documents, which supplement each other, prove two conclusive and undisputed facts:

First: That the Armenian provinces, occupied and exploited by Turkey, have from time immemorial formed an indivisible part of the historic homeland of the Armenian people, factually and juridically. The designation A R M E N I A on authentic maps prepared by Europeans and even by Turks, as well as factual information recorded in the history books of many nations, have formed the basis of negotiations between

Ottoman Sultans and European Statesmen for the liberation
of Armenia from Turkey and the granting to Armenians an
independent state similar to those in the Balkan and Arab
countries, which were also under Ottoman misrule.

As late as August, 1920, when the Turks had already massacred or deported more than half of the Armenian people,
the victorious Allies in a peace conference with Turkey,
where the Armenians were legally represented, imposed a
treaty on the vanquished enemy which contained provisions
for the liberation of several provinces in Western Armenia.
President Wilson was requested and empowered to determine
the boundaries of Armenia. Acting under such a mandate
President Wilson did in fact designate certain territories
which were to be ceded to the Armenians.

By the Treaty of Sevres the Allies affirmed the free status
of Armenia. By signing the Treaty Turkey admitted that the
Western Armenian provinces, which she had unlawfully held
for centuries, formed an integral part of the Armenian homeland. Unfortunately, however, the provisions of the treaty, so
solemnized by the Allies, were never enforced.

Second: Succeeding administrations of the Ottoman Empire, whether under the aegis of Sultans, Young Turks or
Kemalists, planned and carried through the first genocide in
the twentieth century. Their main purpose was the extermination of the Armenian people and the elimination of the
Armenian Question once and for all, so that the retention of
all the territories of Armenia might become permanent and
irrefutable. Carrying out their threat methodically and mercilessly, the Turks massacred more than one million and a half
innocent and defenseless Armenians—men, women and children—and deported at least another million to the deserts of
Arabia, there to perish by starvation, disease, exposure, and
murder, all within a period of twenty-five years, 1895–1920.
The plan to exterminate the Armenians began in April, 1915,
when over two hundred Armenian intellectuals, professionals, scientists, merchants, and clergymen were arrested and

deported to unknown destinations, many of them to be murdered on the way. That was followed by the general deportations.

The Allied powers, engaged in a relentless war, were powerless to stop the murderous hands of the Turks—government leaders, the army and the mob. Consequently a million and a half Armenians lost their lives by murder, rape, strangulation, and other physical tortures; more than a million were exiled and scattered over all parts of the world; the western Armenian provinces were laid waste and destroyed; all personal properties, worth millions of dollars, were confiscated; and all real estate, of immeasurable value, was expropriated.

After their attempt to exterminate the Armenian people the Turks felt secure in their domination of the country which had belonged to the Armenians for more than three thousand years. Whenever there was a demand for restitution they claimed that possession of the land for about five hundred years vested its ownership in them permanently.

Nevertheless, the history of mankind and the liberation of many enslaved peoples refute entirely the Turkish attempt to justify expansionism. In the course of history, mighty empires have at one time or another invaded countries far and wide, subjugated the native races and peoples, and ruled over them for five hundred or even a thousand years; but when their military power weakened, subject nations shook off the bonds of tyranny, repossessed their homeland, and reinstated their independence.

In the last few decades several empires have been eliminated and about fifty nations have regained their independence either with or without bloodshed. Poland, like Armenia, had been divided into several parts and for centuries had suffered under the heels of various tyrannies, but she never lost her identity. For about nine hundred years Great Britain ruled over the neighboring Ireland, but in 1922 that numerically small but brave people won their freedom. France granted independence to all her colonies in Africa and signed treaties of friendship and mutual defense, with a promise to give them generous assistance. But Algeria was not accorded similar privileges. She was considered an integral part of France and for over eight years waged bitter war to establish her domination over that territory. And France, after spending enormous sums of money, suffering great loss of prestige and shedding priceless blood, realized that freedom-loving peoples and countries cannot be forever enslaved—not by arbitrary proclamations, not even by fire and sword. Algeria insisted upon her identity and finally won her freedom as an independent nation.

The experiences of the Armenian people have not been different. For more than three thousand years the land between the River Kur and the mountain ranges of Taurus has been recognized as the Armenian homeland, with the biblical Mt. Ararat as its symbol of identity. It constituted and was known as historic Armenia, with intermittent periods of independence noted for remarkable progress and achievement. Because of its location, however, it was a natural highway between East and West, for military expeditions and bloody encounters on Armenian soil. And following in the footsteps of Alexander the Great, Persians, Romans, Byzantines, Arabs, Tartars, Seljuks, and Turks have trampled over Armenia and dominated her territories.

The Armenian plateau was captured and ruled over by some of these tyrants for hundreds of years. They plundered and devastated the country and slaughtered and enslaved its people periodically. But in spite of this devastation Armenia still remained the homeland of the Armenians. Moreover, Persian Kings, Roman Caesars, Byzantine Emperors, Arab Khalifs, and Tartar Khans recognized the rights of their Armenian subjects to exist as a free people and to live on their native land. History has recorded incidents when a power ruling over Armenia has offered a crown to an Armenian prince, made him a king and concluded a treaty with him.

The last foreign tyranny to subjugate the Armenian people and rule over their motherland was the Ottoman Empire. Even now its successors are holding it in captivity. But the

Armenians were not the only people to suffer the ravages caused by the Turkish sword.

After the occupation of Constantinople, the Ottomans expanded the frontiers of their country from the Crimea and the Persian Gulf to the Balkans and the gates of Vienna, and from Cilicia to the Red Sea and the shores of the Atlantic. They excelled their predecessors in ferociousness by destroying, plundering, butchering and slaying. They built nothing, created nothing and improved nothing over the lands they occupied. They expropriated everything produced by the sweat, blood and skill of their subjects; and wherever they passed they spread misery and destruction, brutally persecuting and killing Christian Greeks, Serbs and Bulgars, and especially Armenians. Moreover, with the same indiscriminate barbarity they massacred Mohammedan Arabs, Albanians and Kurds.

The destructive spirit which incited the Turks to perpetrate so many atrocious crimes was a major cause of the collapse of the Ottoman Empire. During one century, from 1818 to 1918, Greece, Bulgaria, Bosnia, Montenegro, Hungary, Rumania, the Crimea, Georgia, Syria, Lebanon, Palestine, Cyprus, Iraq, Jordan, Hejaz, Yemen, Egypt, Tripoli, Tunisia, and Algeria all gained their freedom from the Turkish yoke, either by internal revolution or as a result of wars between Turkey and another power. It does seem, therefore, rather cruel and contrary to the ideals of justice and the conscience of mankind that the only territory that still remains under a forced occupation is the Armenian homeland, now laid waste, devastated and depopulated. Can it be inferred that the maintenance of the status quo is intended to absolve Turkey of the crime of genocide committed against the Armenians?

Had the Turks succeeded in their ruthless plan of extermination, the ownership of the Armenian homeland would have fallen permanently into their hands and no one would have been left to demand its return. But the Armenian people refused to die and refused to be entombed. During the period from 1915 to 1920, although ill-equipped, they defended themselves in heroic struggles against Turkish hordes, from Eastern Armenia to Cilicia and Musa Dagh, the valiant defense of which was immortalized by the renowned novelist Franz Werfel in *The Forty Days of Musa Dagh*.

A great number of the survivors, scattered in various Near Eastern and European countries, continued to live in deprivation and misery as exiles. Others, impoverished though they were, found refuge in that portion of Eastern Armenia where in 1918 an independent government was established and duly recognized by European governments and the United States of America. In 1920 the tottering Armenian government, under threats of annihilation by Kemalist hordes and the pressure exerted by Communist Russia surrendered the reins of the government to the Armenian Communists and Armenia became one of the Republics of the Soviet Union. With the establishment of permanent peace and the total elimination of external dangers, the Armenians increased their number, improved their economy and within less than half a century reached a lofty standard in scientific, educational, cultural, and industrial achievements.

The number of Armenians in the world today has almost reached five million, more than half of whom now reside in present Soviet Armenia, part of their historic homeland. The remaining half constitute the Armenian diaspora, scattered in many lands from the Caucasus and the Middle East to the most distant parts of the globe. Hundreds of thousands are immigrants without a country, subject to a depressed economy and political insecurity.

In the last quarter of a century about 150,000 displaced Armenians migrated to and settled in Soviet Armenia, there to find work, security and national identity. During the last ten or more years 4000 to 5000 Armenians have found shelter annually in that country. That small number of repatriates, however, cannot appreciably effect a change in the situation of those remaining behind or reduce the potential of their growth, because the ratio of births exceeds by far the number of repatriates.

Moreover, Armenia today consists of a small territory, more than half of which is unfit for cultivation because of its mountainous character, whereas the Turkish provinces of Armenia are blessed with fertile fields and rich farmlands, with rivers for irrigation and forests for lumber. These sparsely populated, barren and uncultivated provinces still remain under Turkish occupation.

These indisputable historical facts form the legal, equitable and moral basis for the claim of the Armenian people against Turkey.

The Armenian cause is further strengthened by the fact that during the two global wars—1914–1918 and 1939–1945 —several hundred thousand Armenians served in the Allied armies, far beyond what might have been justified by the total number of the Armenian people. They contributed to the Allied victory by enormous sacrifices on various battlefields; they remained steadfastly loyal to the ideals of freedom, and millions suffered incredible torments and martyrdom.

While the free nations were drawn together into a solemn pact to fight against tyranny, oppression and imperialist aggression, and to "save the world for democracy," Turkey became an active ally of Germany in World War I, and her role in the struggle against Nazism and Fascism in the second global war was less than honorable. Under the guise of neutrality she secretly expressed her sympathies for the cause of the Axis Powers, rendered them material aid and prayed for their victory. It was only after the Allied forces had decisively triumphed over their foe that Turkey was forced to declare war against Germany, so that she might be allowed to become a member of the United Nations.

The Armenian people, in freedom or in subjugation, during the course of their history have created and developed a rich culture—a language and alphabet of their own and a literature which has inspired many generations by its grandeur. They have demonstrated great skill, ingenuity and originality in architecture, music, miniature painting, sculpture, and other forms of the arts and sciences. The powers that ruled over them, such as Rome, Byzantium and Turkey were enriched by their skill. Temples, palaces, churches, and mosques designed and built by Armenians have enhanced the architectural and artistic values of their respective countries.

In spite of the horrible crime of Armenocide in 1915, the Armenian people presented to the world an extraordinary phenomenon. With half of their total number brutally destroyed, they succeeded in achieving a miraculous renaissance—physical, mental and spiritual—and from the orphans surviving the crime emerged hundreds of renowned scientists, educators, artists, professionals and industrialists, who have received universal acclaim by their extraordinary skill. They have made notable contributions to all efforts of mankind to make life richer and more radiant, happier and more benevolent.

The Turks, on the other hand, as evidenced by their history—whatever country they have invaded, whatever people they have subjugated—spread in their wake only death, destruction and misery. Even when they were victorious in their military exploits they continued to subject the peoples they conquered to plundering and persecution and to the terrors of savage tyranny and slavery. Since the occupation of Constantinople the Ottoman Turks have been residing side by side with the remarkable civilization created by European countries, for more than five hundred years. Yet they failed substantially to contribute to the progress and culture of mankind, nor have they shown consistent intelligence, any sustained creative talent in their fine arts, or any substantial creative skill. They have lived on the products of the talent, sweat and blood of such subject races as the Armenians, Greeks, Arabs, and Jews, who furnished intellectuals and professionals, artisans and tillers of the soil, merchants and manufacturers, slaves and martyrs.

The bloody nature of the Turks and their obsessive savagery have been most aptly described by the great novelist and poet Victor Hugo in a poem of 1829:

"Les Turcs ont passé là. Tout est ruine et deuil."

("The Turks have passed by there. There is ruin and desolation everywhere.")

As an aftermath of the genocide perpetrated against Armenians, Turkey confiscated the enormous wealth of her victims numbering about three million—rich cities and towns, invaluable personal belongings, business establishments, etc., the monetary worth of which reached the stupendous figure of several billion dollars. The Turks claimed ownership and retained possession of about 300,000 square miles of territory, 85 percent of which consists of abundantly fertile valleys and fields.

But in spite of that enormous wealth the Turks have not been able to extricate themselves from the clutches of poverty. Basic commodities for a bare livelihood, such as sugar, meat, grain, or other nutriments, are sorely lacking. Present day Turkey, the disenchanted successor of the Ottoman Empire, became a subsidized country, a veritable pauper. In the years after 1920 she received all manner of help from the countries that were her enemies. Meanwhile she received material and military aid from Nazi Germany in return for a secret hideout to spy on the Allies. Moreover, since 1947 she has received billions of dollars from the United States, based on her threat to side with the enemy if refused. Even today Turkey, with her inexhaustible natural wealth and with enormous material help from the West, lives in want and deprivation.

Directly across her borders lies Soviet Armenia, with barely 11,000 square miles of mountainous territory. In 1920 it was the home of abandoned and naked orphans and half-starved natives and immigrants, destitute and forlorn. But within that same half century the people in Armenia have become well-fed, and self-sufficient, and the country an acknowledged center of science with a modern industry and a resplendent culture. Today Armenia produces and manufactures most of the needs of her people; she exports to fifty different countries, from India to South America, a variety of scientific, electrical and industrial machinery and equipment.

Such evidence must strongly fortify the rights of the Armenian people and justify their demands for consideration by all civilized nations. We believe that their appeal, suppressed for a long time, will find an echo in the souls and consciences of responsible leaders in every civilized nation, who must surely remember the solemn promises of their predecessors to establish a greater Armenian homeland by the union of the western Armenian provinces with the independent territory of Armenia. We sincerely believe and hope that all small nations which have suffered a similar fate in persecution and servitude and which eventually gained their freedom, will participate in all efforts to accord justice to the Armenians. We believe that the solution of the Armenian case can be expedited, if it is maintained in its simple character, free from international involvement and disputes. Moreover, the principles adopted by the United Nations, recognizing and protecting the basic rights of all peoples, offer the best guide for such a solution.

The crime of genocide committed by any power against a subject people or community is vehemently condemned by the United Nations and every people. The act of murdering a nation is a crime against humanity, and such action is not exempted by a statute of limitations. Under the humanitarian concept of the United Nations those guilty of genocide, as well as their successors, cannot be allowed to retain the wealth, the property and the homeland of their victims.

At the Nuremberg trials after World War II these moral principles accorded the victorious Allies the authority to bring the leaders of Nazi Germany to the bar of justice as war criminals and to accuse them of the wholesale murder of about six million Jews residing in Germany and in the countries occupied by Germany, as well as millions of Russians, Poles, Yugoslavs, Greeks, Czechoslovaks, and others. The International Court found the accused guilty and sentenced them to death or imprisonment.

The Nuremberg trials did not deal with the punitive aspect of the law only. Justice required far more than the imprisonment or death of a few criminals. There was the matter of retribution which involved billions of dollars, and the new German government wisely accepted its share of the responsibility in the crime and conviction and agreed to partly compensate the monetary losses suffered by the Jews, with payment in cash or material to the newly organized State of Israel, an amount reaching many millions of dollars in value.

The claims of the Armenian people are based on similarly incontrovertible legal grounds. The concept of justice is the same in both the Jewish and Armenian cases, and the law providing for redress cannot be applied in one instance and withheld in another. The evidence compiled in this volume proves beyond reasonable doubt that Turkey committed the *first* crime of genocide in the twentieth century by attempting to exterminate a whole nation. During two decades more than two million Armenian men, women and children were brutally murdered by the Turks and more than one million suffered in exile, with the loss of all their wealth in money, valuables and property.

The crime committed by the Turks is rendered more heinous by the fact that the Armenians were massacred on or deported from their own native land. They were not foreign subjects. The land upon which they lived had been theirs for three thousand years. They were not invaders to be disposed of at an opportune time. . . . [The Turks] must now be called before an international tribunal to answer for their crime.

It is understandable, of course, that the real perpetrators of the crime of Armenocide cannot be brought to justice and be sentenced as at Nuremberg, because the principal criminals have since died and disappeared. The right of retribution, however, is very much alive and must be recognized by the leaders of present day Turkey which is a member of the United Nations and as such has solemnly agreed to abide by its code of justice.

The Nuremberg trials confirmed a precedent which in essence has always existed, that no person or government shall remain unpunished for the crimes committed by him or them. The United Nations has adopted that principle and has codified sanctions against wrongdoing nations. The present government of Turkey, therefore, cannot be absolved from responsibility for a crime against humanity committed by their predecessors.

Beyond punishment, however, Turkey should be made to satisfy the Armenian demands which are not confined solely to the property rights of individuals, but include the restoration to the Armenians of the Western Provinces, which have constituted the Armenian homeland for thousands of years.

Such a reasonable solution by the United Nations and its acceptance by Turkey will be an act of supreme justice. It will restore the faith of small nations that their inherent rights are fully recognized and will be protected against molestation. Such a solution will also be a decisive warning to those who might be tempted to expand their territories by genocidal acts.

About one week before the beginning of World War II, while Hitler was admonishing his military commanders to carry out mercilessly the plan to exterminate the Jews, Poles and Slavs, one of the generals suggested that some day Nazi leaders might be called to an accounting for their crimes, whereupon Hitler gave the following characteristic assurance: "Who, after all, speaks today of the annihilation of the Armenians? The world believes in success only." (*What About Germany?* by Louis Lochner, New York, 1942).

The consequences of genocidal acts have been clearly determined by the decisions of the Nuremberg Tribunal, which may serve as a safeguard against any individuals in their official capacity to plan, influence, or perpetrate such a crime. If the victorious Allies in 1918 had subjected the Turkish officials to such trials and punishment, six million Jews and millions of other victims of the Nazis might have been saved from wholesale murder.

Article II of the "Convention on the Prevention and Punishment of the Crime of Genocide," as adopted by the United Nations clearly defines genocide to mean "acts committed with intent to destroy, in whole or in part, a national, ethnical, racial or religious group." Article III enumerates the following acts to be punishable: (a) Genocide; (b) Conspiracy to commit genocide; (c) Direct and public incitement to commit genocide; (d) Attempt to commit genocide; (e) Complicity to genocide. And Article IV provides: "Persons committing genocide or any other acts enumerated in Article III shall be punished, whether they are constitutionally responsible rulers, public officials or private individuals."

These principles adopted by the United Nations and confirmed by the International Tribunal at Nuremberg can have a fundamental and everlasting value if applied in all cases of genocide, free of all political considerations. And if so applied, the demands of the Armenian people will be given international recognition worthy of a just and honorable solution. A positive determination will mean that the government of Turkey shall have no right to claim and retain the ownership of a territory the real owners of which were victimized by massacres and deportations.

Some of the survivors of these massacres and deportations found refuge in a territory wherein was established an autonomous republic. They have now become a thriving, visionary, enthusiastic, and dynamic people, united in spirit and determined never to stop demanding their lost territories as their rightful heritage. No Armenian, in his native land or in the dispersion, will ever accept or sanction the permanent retention by Turkey of the Western Armenian Provinces. Armenia would not be complete without Ani and Kars, without the sacred Mt. Ararat and its valleys, without the glorious Van and Daron, and without the territories consecrated by the sweat, toil and blood of her people who dreamed about, struggled and yearned for freedom and for a peaceful future.

For 500 years or more the Armenians suffered persecution, torture and massacres. They lived in the clutches of a savage tyranny. Notwithstanding that the Armenians of today seek no revenge. Three thousand years of intermittent freedom and slavery, of glory and humiliation, of victory and defeat have taught them to be realistic and noble, always sustained by a profound love for freedom and an unquenchable desire for progress. They recognize the fact that geography has placed the two countries side by side; that they are neighbors and their mutual interests make it necessary for them to co-exist in harmonious relationship. But, of course, such a desirable dream can only be realized if the Turks express their willingness to make amends for the crimes committed by them or their predecessors. Concessions made by one side only cannot be expected to bear fruit; solutions not based on justice and equity are bound to fall apart. A confession of guilt, however, cleanses the soul and facilitates forgiveness by the injured party.

The demands of the Armenians are not unreasonable. They seek no unjust enrichment. All they want is a piece of land solemnized by a treaty to which Turkey was a signatory, the territory delineated by President Woodrow Wilson. Such a concession to the Armenians would still leave in Turkish hands a fertile land of a very large area barely cultivated, with a great potential in producing immense quantities of grain, fruits, vegetables, timber and a notable area for pasturage and forests. There will be immense possibilities for mutual assistance between Armenia, as an industrial country, and Turkey, as an agricultural state. Old wounds may be healed, leaving no perceptible scars and an association on a high level might create a relationship for the mutual benefit of both countries.

The purpose of this volume, therefore, is not to encourage a desire for vengeance, nor to inflame the hatred existing between the two neighboring peoples, but to bring to the attention of the civilized world the need for an equitable adjustment. The justice of the Armenian claims can no longer be thwarted.

We believe that the voice of truth and the call of justice will find an awakened conscience and an unwavering attitude in the hearts and minds of all peoples, great or small, within or without the organizational unit of the United Nations. We appeal to them all to seek and procure a just solution for these claims, with a determination that is sincere and strong, so that at least a portion of the Armenian homeland solemnized by a treaty may be restored to its rightful owners.

Such a restoration will be the vindication of the often promised justice to the Armenians for the endless persecutions and martyrdom suffered by them.

We further believe that such a solution of the problem may prove beyond doubt that co-existence in harmony and peace between two unfriendly peoples is not impossible.

APPENDIX A

Chapter 1

The extermination orders of Talaat Bey and Enver Pasha quoted in Chapter 1 are only a small part of the authenticated correspondence involving Talaat, Enver, and Dr. Nazim Bey. In the interests of accuracy, a considerable number of documents of the 1915–1916 period are reproduced here.*

Orders of Deportation and Massacres

The diabolical plan to exterminate an entire nation is depicted in the orders communicated by letters, ciphered telegrams, etc. as herein set forth:

February 28, 1915

To delegate Jemal Bey of Adana:

The only force in Turkey able to frustrate the policies of Ittihad and Terakki, are the Armenians. Periodic news arriving from Cairo recently indicate that Dashnagtzoutiun (The Armenian Revolutionary Federation) is preparing a decisive attack upon the Jemiyet (Union and Progress Committee).

If we examine all the historical events in detail we shall see that all the agitators which have obstructed Jemiyet's patriotic efforts have been the result of seeds of turbulence sown by the Armenians.

Dr. Nazim Bey writes: "If the Armenians cease to exist, with only a small signal from Ittihad and Terakki, I can guide Turkey into the desired path."

Jemiyet has decided to free the fatherland from the covetousness of this accursed race and to bear upon their shoulder the stigma that might malign the Ottoman history.

Unable to forget the disgrace and bitterness of the past, filled with vengeful episodes, Jemiyet, hopeful about its future, has decided to exterminate all Armenians living in Turkey, without allowing a single one to remain alive

* Most of these documents were compiled by Aram Andonian from the *Memoirs of Naim Bey*, pp. 26ff., 1919.

and to this regard has given the Government extensive authority.

The Government shall give all necessary instructions to the governors (of Vilayets) and the commanders of the Army about the arrangements concerning massacres. All delegates of the Ittihad and Terakki will be engaged about this matter in their respective localities.

All properties left behind will, for the time being, be seized and kept in the manner deemed best by the government, with the understanding that they will be sold later for the expansion of the organization of the Jemiyet and for (other) patriotic purposes.

Whenever deemed necessary, you may receive financial accounting from Committees formed for that purpose. Should you find any evidence of misappropriation (of funds), you shall make appropriate report to the governors and to us. (*The Great Crime,* Andonian, pp. 129–133. The exact photocopy of this original in Turkish appears on pages 116 and 117.)

(Signature unknown)

March 25, 1915

To Jemal Bey, Delegate of Adana

It is the duty of all of us to realize in a wide range and free from political interventions our intention to wipe out of existence the known elements (Armenians) who have obstructed the political progress of our State for centuries. Assuming the consequences, whatever they may be in that regard, we must accept the full responsibility, and fully appreciating that the government has entered the global war with a great sacrifice, we must strive to carry to success all the activities that have been undertaken.

As it had been stated in our letter of February 18, 1915 the Jemiyet has decided to destroy from their foundation and to annihilate various opposing forces that have obstructed our ways for years, and to that effect it is obliged, unfortunately, to resort to bloody means. Rest assured that we are also affected by the thought of these horrible means; but Jemiyet finds no other way to secure its eternal existence.

Ali Riza is criticizing us and appeals for compassion. This degree of naivete is stupidity. Go to Aleppo, try to convince him and work together if you can. Should that be impossible we will find a suitable place to play on his heart-strings. Until the successful completion of the activities undertaken for the known people (Armenians), It would not be right to bother ourselves for the *others* (Greeks, Arabs, Syrians). For the time being it has been deemed proper to punish the notables by legal means; this will be the starting point of our future actions.

I wish to remind you again about the abandoned properties. It is very essential. Their disposition should be under your very eyes. Examine the accounts and means of performances at all times. Let us also know of the date of your departure. (Andonian; pp. 134–5)

(Signature unknown)

An order for the total annihilation of the Armenians was found in the archives of the secret documents of the Director-General of the Refugees. We deem it essential to produce a translation of that document, the date of which we were unable to ascertain. It seems quite certain, however, that it had reached Aleppo during the time Jelal Bey was the governor of the province. Here it is:

> Although it was previously intended to exterminate the Armenian element which had for centuries wanted to destroy the firm foundation of our State and appeared to be a great peril to our government, but the exigencies of the times made it impossible to realize that sacred intention. Now that all obstacles have been removed and the time has come to save our country from that dangerous element, we urgently recommend that you not be influenced by compassion, because of their miserable plight, and, by putting an end to them all, do your very best to obliterate the Armenian name from Turkey. See to it that the officials, who are to be entrusted to realize that purpose, be patriotic and trustworthy men.

All instructions from the Central authorities were directed to one basic purpose: the elimination of the Armenian people. The following two telegrams prove that contention; both are addressed to the Government of Aleppo. The first telegram reads:

> It has come to our attention that some officials have been brought before the military tribunal (court martial) under the accusation that they have committed acts of

severity and extortion against certain known individuals
(Armenians). Even though this may be a formality but it
may lessen the confidence of other officials. For that reason I command you not to allow such examinations.

Minister of the Interior

Talaat

The following is the second telegram:

To give consideration to the complaints and claims of
certain people (Armenians) about all sorts of personal
matters, will not only delay their dispatch (to the desert)
but will open the door to a series of actions which, in all
probability, may create political inconveniences. For that
reason these appeals must be disregarded, and orders must
be given to this effect to all officials concerned.

Minister of the Interior

Talaat

(*Editor's Note:* The actual dates of the two preceding telegrams have not been reported.)

On April 15, 1915 the Union and Progress Committee circulated the following order:

To the Excellent Governors, Honorable Mayors, and Re-
spectful Town Authorities:

You are familiar with the cruel political reasons which
forced the mighty Ottoman Empire and the great Turkish
people to enter the war with Germany and Austria against
"The Triple Alliance." In order to emerge victorious from
this fateful war, we repeat, every Mohammedan and Turk,
whom the same holy providence is urging forward, should
stand together as one man against our monstrous and infidel enemies and become a support to our valiant and
wise leaders and to our army which gives a heroic defense
on sea and on land waging a victorious war against the
treacherous foes.

Irrespective of the nature and the outcome of this war,
be it favorable or unfavorable for us, diplomacy has determined and proved historically, that one or the other of Russian and English governments, who have united to wage
war against us in the first instance, has joined us against
the other in order to defend our land, for us. Because the

occupation of Constantinople the queen of the seas and the eastern provinces that open the land route to India, is fatal to one or the other, especially to England.

In the event of victory they may agree upon a third competent inheritor, by finding a people that could serve their interests, so that they might converse with each other in the home of that people.

And that third inheritor can only be the Armenian people. May God save us, but in the event of our defeat during peace negotiations, will come to the fore that 'Armenian Question,' which for more than half a century has received an international character and has pierced our bosom threateningly.

Therefore, in order to protect our country, our nation, our government and our religion against the possibility of such a danger, the government which represents the Islam and Turkish people, and the Committee of 'Union and Progress', whatever may happen, intending to forestall the presentation of the Armenian Question in any place and in any matter, taking advantage of the freedom which the war has granted us, has decided to end that question once for all, by deporting the Armenians to the deserts of Arabia, exterminating that spurious element, in accordance with the secret order given us.

The following serve as an excuse to implement that plan:

(a) The Armenian voluntary forces, serving in the enemy armies;

(b) The existing (Armenian) parties in the interior of the country, which have been organized to give a body blow to our Army;

(c) The unaccountable number of firearms and war material discovered and confiscated everywhere in the country.

With that excuse we, the government and the Central Committee of Ittihad appeal to you and to your patriotism and command you to assist with all the means at your disposal the local organs of the "Union and Progress" Party, who at the sunrise of April 24th will undertake the implementation of the order, in conformity with secret instructions.

Any official or a special individual, who opposes this sacred and patriotic work and fails to discharge the duties imposed on him or protects or hides this or that Armenian in any way, shall be branded as an enemy of the country and religion and shall be punished accordingly.

The Minister of Interior   and   Minister of War
Talaat   Enver

The Executive Secretary of the Union
and Progress Committee

Dr. Nazim

Secret Telegram #303   April 17, 1331 (1915)

To the Police Commissioner of the Vilayet (Province) of Adana—

As a supplement to the order of April 15, 1915, and in compliance with the telegram of the Minister of the Interior, it is requested that the names of the members of the Committee (Armenian?) and the names of those who are to be arrested, or have already been arrested and deported, as well as any bomb and prohibited firearms and as many photographs as possible, be sent to us.

The Governor of Adana

Paul de Veou, in the preface of his book *La Passion de la Cilicie 1919–1922* (page 13), reproduces the following telegram:

It has been previously communicated that the government by the order of the Assembly (Jemiet) has decided to exterminate entirely all the Armenians living in Turkey. Those who oppose this order can no longer function as part of the government. Without regard to women, children and invalids, however tragic may be the means of transportation, an end must be put to their existence.

May 15, 1915   Minister of the Interior, Talaat

The inhuman attitude of the perpetrators of the crime of genocide is clearly shown by the following telegrams:

No. 502   September 3, 1915

To the Government of Aleppo:

We recommend that the operations which we have ordered you to perform shall first be carried out involving certain people (Armenians) and that you shall subject *women and children* [Emphasis ours—D.H.B.] to the same fate also. Appoint trustworthy persons for that work.

Minister of the Interior

Talaat

September 9, 1915

To the Government of Aleppo:

All rights of the Armenians to live and work on Turkish soil have been completely cancelled, and the Government having assumed all responsibility has commanded that *even babes in the cradle are not to be spared* [Emphasis ours—D.H.B.]. The results of carrying out this order have been seen in some provinces. In spite of that, for reasons unknown to us, exceptional measures are taken regarding certain people, and these people instead of being sent straight to the place of exile are left in Aleppo, whereby the Government becomes involved in an additional difficulty. Without accepting any of their reasoning, remove them thence—women or children, whatever they may be, even if they are unable to move—and do not let them be protected by the people who through ignorance place material gains higher than patriotic feelings, and cannot appreciate the great policy of the Government in that regard. Because instead of the indirect measures of extermination used in other places—such as violence, haste (in carrying out the deportations), difficulties of travelling and misery—direct measures can be safely used there; therefore work wholeheartedly, without wasting time. General Orders have been communicated from the War Office to all the Commanders of the Army that they are not to interfere in the work of deportation.

Tell the officials assigned this task that they must act to put into execution our real intent, without being afraid of responsibility. Please send ciphered reports of the results of your activities every week.

Minister of the Interior

Talaat

For the sake of preventing the spread of contagious diseases the authorities in Aleppo made an attempt to establish an orphanage and gave refuge to many homeless children who swamped the streets. The Central Authorities having heard of that activity hastened to send the following telegram:

September 21, 1915

There is no need of such an orphanage. This is not the time to give way to your emotions in order to feed them (the orphans) and prolong their lives. Send them away (to the desert) and inform us.

Minister of the Interior

Talaat

(1) Nazim Bey reports that the Central Authorities forbade marriages between Moslems and Armenian women; hence the following telegram:

No. 537   September 29, 1915

Cipher telegram to the administration of Aleppo.

We are informed that individuals from the (Turkish) people and officials marry Armenian women. We forbid that strictly and urgently recommend that these women be separated and sent away (to the desert).

Minister of the Interior

Talaat

It has been stressed many times that the extermination of the Armenians was considered "a sacred patriotic duty" of the Turks. The following telegram is one of the many proofs in that regard:

No. 544   October 3, 1915

Cipher telegram to the administration of Aleppo.

The reason why the Sandjak of Zor has been chosen as the place of deportation was explained in our secret order No. 1843 of September 2, 1915. Since all the crimes committed against the known individuals (Armenians) serve the purpose desired by the government, there shall be no legal proceedings for such acts. Necessary instructions have already been transmitted to the authorities of Zor and Ourfa.

Minister of the Interior

Talaat

(Andonian, p. 203)

In various places Turkish families gave refuge to a number of Armenian children above the ages of five years. The government, unable to tolerate such acts of benevolence, sent the following telegram:

No. 603   November 5, 1915

We are informed that certain Moslem families have adopted or taken in as servants the orphaned children of the known persons (Armenians) who were deported from Sivas, Mamuret-ul-Aziz, Diarbekir and Erzeroum, and died en route. We are hereby advising you to collect, in your province, all the children of that category, dispatch them to places of deportation (the deserts) and give necessary circular instructions to the people.

Minister of the Interior

Talaat

The Turkish government made every effort to conceal the truth about their program of deportations and massacres and about its implementation, and being afraid of an adverse reaction in the Christian world, sent the following telegram:

November 18, 1915

From the intervention of the Embassy in Constantinople upon the instructions of the American government, it appears that in certain localities American consuls have secured information through secret means. Although in reply to their inquiries it has been stated that the deportation (of Armenian refugees) is being conducted in safety and comfort, but because that has not been sufficiently convincing, take care that the deportation from cities, towns and central localities shall not create events that may attract attention. From the point of view of the present policy it is necessary for the foreigners in such localities to be convinced that the transfer (of refugees) is solely for the purpose of relocation. For that reason, it is necessary, for the time being, that the deportees be afforded gentle treatment and the known methods be applied only in the most suitable places. We urgently advise you to arrest the informants and to hand them over to military authorities for trial.

Minister of the Interior
Talaat

"When I was in the desert," writes Naïm Bey, "Armenians from the six Armenian vilayets were searched for. The persecution against them never ceased." The following telegram bears that out.

No. 691   November 23, 1915

As and when the Armenians from the eastern provinces are delivered to your hands, destroy them by secret means.

Minister of the Interior
Talaat

In order to comply with the order of the Minister of the Interior, that no orphanages are needed, the Deputy Director of Refugees sent the following telegram to the Director of Relocation in Constantinople:

No. 31   November 26, 1915

Four hundred boys are now found in the orphanage; they will all be joined to the caravans and dispatched to the places of deportation.

Deputy of the General Director
Abdulahad Nouri

Naïm Bey reports in his memoirs that sometime in November 1915 the Minister of the Interior, while caravans of refugees were being driven without rest and to unknown destinations, said:

"The purpose of sending away these known persons (Armenians) is to assure the welfare of our country; because wherever these people are located they will not refrain from their accursed idea; we must try to reduce their numbers as much as possible."

"While I was in Aleppo," writes Naïm Bey, "The following cipher telegrams came to the Governor of Aleppo:"

December 1, 1915

In spite of the fact that it is necessary above all to work for the extermination of the clergy of the known people (Armenians) we have learned that they are being sent to such questionable places as Syria and Jerusalem. Such indulgence is an unpardonable sin. The place for such agitators is annihilation. I suggest that you act accordingly.

Minister of the Interior
Talaat

(Andonian, page 102)

It being the intention of the Turkish government to exterminate the Armenians "to the last man," their settlement in and around Aleppo could not be acceptable. Hence the following cipher telegram addressed to the administration of Aleppo:

No. 723   December 3, 1915

You must send without delay to places of deportation all Armenians who have been settled around Aleppo, and advise as to that effect.

Minister of the Interior
Talaat

(Andonian, p. 89)

It was natural for some Armenians to complain and protest, whenever they had the opportunity, against the horrible treatments given them on their way to death. The following telegram clearly shows how futile these protests were:

No. 745, cipher telegram dated December 9, 1915 and addressed to the administration of Aleppo:

There is nothing improper in receiving telegraphic complaints and protests by certain known persons (Armenians) against government officials for their mistreatment. But it would be a waste of time to examine them. You may inform the complainants to pursue their lost claims in their place of exile.

Minister of the Interior

Talaat

In order to put a stop to any leakage of information to foreign consular authorities concerning the persecution of Armenians on their way to exile, the following telegram was sent to the administration of Aleppo:

December 11, 1915

We are informed that a few correspondents to American newspapers, traveling in your areas, have formed a file with photographs and papers depicting tragic episodes and delivered it to the American consul of your locality. Arrest such dangerous persons and destroy them.

Minister of the Interior

Talaat

Realizing that children of tender age could be raised as Turks and become useful citizens, the Minister of the Interior sent the following telegram:

No. 830   December 12, 1915

To the administration of Aleppo:

Gather and feed only those orphans who do not remember the disaster their parents suffered. Send away all the rest with the caravans.

Minister of the Interior

Talaat

In certain localities Armenians were advised that if they renounced their religion and accepted Mohammedanism their lives would be spared. Numerous instances proved that even conversion to Islamism would not save the individual. Knowing full well that the Armenians would not be allowed to live even after reaching their place of exile, the Minister of the Interior advised the Governor of Aleppo in a telegram that follows:

No. 762

To the administration of Aleppo:

Answer to your telegram dated December 2, 1915.
Inform the Armenians, who wish to convert to Islamism
that in order to escape deportation, they should become
Mohammedans in their places of exile.

Minister of the Interior

Talaat

It was generally known that the majority of the officials
in railroad construction were Armenian. In order to escape
any serious inconvenience, the government ordered the deportation of these officials as shown by the following telegram:

No. 801   December 26, 1915

It has been decided to deport all Armenians employed
generally in all establishments, such as railroads and
other construction works, and the war ministry has informed the commanders of the Army to this effect. Inform
us of the result.

Minister of the Interior

Talaat

In apprehension of the possible, unfavorable reaction that
might be created by the reports of foreign correspondents,
the government hastened to send the following cipher telegram:

No. 809   December 29, 1915

It has come to our attention that foreign officers are
photographing corpses of known persons (Armenians)
piled up over the length of the roads. We strongly urge
you to dispose of these corpses by burying them immediately.

Minister of the Interior

Talaat

Fearing that some of the Armenians en route to exile,
might escape while passing through populated centers, the

following specific order was given for their safe transfer to their destination:

No. 820   January 4, 1916

To the Administration of Aleppo:

I strongly urge that all Armenians coming from the north hereafter be sent directly to their places of exile, without passing through a city or town.

Minister of the Interior

Talaat

That all orders from the Central Government were being carried out meticulously, is shown by the following telegram:

No. 57   January 10, 1916

To the Director-General of the settlement of refugees:

After investigation it has been confirmed that ten percent of the Armenian deportees have reached their place of exile. The rest have perished on the way by starvation and natural illness. You are informed that similar results will be accomplished by employing severe means against the survivors.

Deputy Director-General

Abdulahad Nouri

Suspecting that there were in the area of Roum-Kale a number of men and women originally from the Eastern (Armenian) provinces, Governor Moustapha Abdulhalile sent the following telegram to the Mayor of Aintah:

January 11, 1916

We are informed that Armenians from Sivas and Harpout are found in your district. Do not give them an opportunity to settle in that area, and do whatever is necessary, *according to the methods previously reported*, [Emphasis ours—D.H.B.] and inform us about the results.

Governor

Moustapha Abdulhalile

Only one week later the Mayor of Aintah replied to the above cipher telegram of January 11, 1916 as follows:

January 18, 1916

To the Governor of Aleppo:

It has been ascertained that only 500 persons from the said provinces were found in the area of Roum Kale. The Kaimakam (burgomaster) of Roum Kale informs us that women and children comprise the great majority of that group, and that they were sent away in *the manner imparted to us,* [Emphasis ours—D.H.B.] with Kurds as their guide, never to return.

Governor

Ahmed

The Turkish Government constantly feared that an impressive number of Armenian orphans might be collected and settled in orphanages. Numerous orders were sent out to that effect, of which the following is a typical example of barbarous nature of the Turks:

January 15, 1916

To the Governor of Aleppo:

We are informed that the children of certain people (Armenians) are also being admitted in the orphanages recently opened. Since the government considers their existence dangerous, the care of these children and the effort to prolong their lives, or to show them mercy, whether due to a failure to understand the true purpose or to scorn such purpose, are entirely opposed to the wishes of the government. I recommend that such children be refused admittance in the orphanage, and no attempts be made to establish orphanages for them.

Minister of the Interior

Talaat

Severely criticizing the humanitarian compassion shown by Djemal Pasha and the Railroad Director Kairi Bey towards a multitude of refugees in the proximity of the railroad lines, the Minister of the Interior dispatched the following telegram:

No. 840   January 16, 1916

To the Governor of Aleppo:

We are informed that 40-50,000 Armenians, mostly women and children are found along the railroad line extending from the regions of Intilli and Airan. Those persons who cause the concentration of misery on locations which are exceedingly important for military transportation shall be very severely punished. Therefore, after negotiating with the government of Adana, send these Armenians on foot to their places of exile (the desert), without allowing their approach to Aleppo. I anxiously await the result of your action within one week.

Minister of the Interior

Talaat

Realizing that something important was left out of the telegram just sent, the following supplement was dispatched:

January 16, 1916

To the Governor of Aleppo:

A Supplement to Telegram No. 840, dated January 16, 1916:

Do not send away those Armenians, found on location in the region of Intilli and Airan, who work on the railroad construction projects, until the work is finished. But as they are not allowed to live with their families, give them suitable temporary quarters in the vicinity of Aleppo. Send away (to the desert), without delay, the remaining derelict women and children, in accordance with the previous instructions.

Minister of the Interior

Talaat

The Office of the Deputy Director General for the settling of refugees was very important, as noted by previous communications. The orders sent out by him were comparable to the orders given by the Minister of the Interior. The following communication, addressed to Mouharrem Bey, the officer in charge of deportations in Bab, is proof of his authority:

No. 344   January 20, 1916

You certainly appreciate the importance of the work entrusted to you from our office, based on the confidence which the Governor of our province has in you. No Armenian should be allowed to remain in Bab. The severity and swiftness alone shown by you in the dispatch of refugees can insure the purpose which we pursue. You must, however, see to it that no corpses are left exposed on the ways. You inform us of the full amount of remuneration paid to the persons engaged by you for that work.

Do not try to find means of transportation. The refugees can go on foot just as well.

The weekly list of deaths sent to us these days is not satisfactory. That indicates that these people (Armenians) are living very comfortably there.

The sending of the refugees must not be like a journey. Pay no attention to protests and lamentations. The office of the Governor has sent all necessary information to the Kaimakam as well. Make every effort.

Abdulahad Nouri

The Minister of the Interior, considering any amount spent for the support of Armenian children a waste of money, has sent the following cipher telegram to the Governor of Aleppo:

No. 853   January 23, 1916

At a time when there are thousands of destitute Moslem refugees and widows of martyrs it is not proper to waste money for the support of the children of a certain people (Armenians), who would serve no purpose other than become dangerous in the future. In accordance with our instructions all these (children), together with those who have been fed till now, must be removed from the (your) province and sent to Sivas.

Minister of the Interior

Talaat

The Turkish Government tried every means to conceal the horrible atrocities perpetrated by it, and to find ways to justify its actions. The following cipher telegram is intended for that purpose:

February 3, 1916

To the Government of Aleppo:

A commission headed by Moustapha Nail Effendi has been dispatched to Ourfa with the duty to investigate and secure documentary evidence concerning the provocative ideas and actions of a certain people. The commission, after discharging its duty (in Ourfa) shall conduct investigations in Aintah and Kilis within your jurisdiction. Therefore, you are to secretly inform wherever necessary to take the best measures to facilitate their efforts and make them fruitful.

Minister of the Interior

Talaat

The need for manpower in construction works behind the lines, necessitated the use of the Armenians who had not yet been deported and who had become of age. The following telegram is intended to find a way to utilize these Armenians, even though their wives and children were not to be spared:

February 20, 1916

To the Government of Aleppo:

The military authorities have indicated that those of a certain people (Armenians) who have become of age are needed for military service. Since it will be impossible to send them to war zones and their remaining in the city is not tolerated, we authorize you to employ them in road building or other construction work out of the city, provided that their families shall be sent away with the rest of the deportees. The Ministry of War has sent specific instructions to Army Commanders, to that effect. Therefore, communicate with them and act according to their instructions.

Minister of the Interior

Talaat

The plan of exterminating all Armenians was being carried out satisfactorily according to the following telegram:

February 26, 1916

To the Executive Director for the settling of Refugees and Ashirets:*

I report for your information that, with the exception of those who *were sent to Syria as craftsmen,* barely one-fourth of the Armenians sent away (to the desert) to this date, have reached the places of exile. The rest have died on

* Ashirets are Kurdish chieftains.

the way from natural causes. Measures have been taken to dispatch swiftly those who have so far remained in Aleppo for various reasons.

Deputy General Director

Abdulahad Nouri

(*Editor's Note:* We have italicized the words "were sent to Syria as craftsmen" to explain one fact: After the Armenians were deported, the Turkish government realized life in Turkey had become very difficult. With the deportation of all craftsmen or artisans the country was left without tailors, without shoemakers, without blacksmiths, without bakers, without carpenters, without masons, without jewelers (silversmiths, goldsmiths, etc.). The only way the government could partly rectify its mistakes was to stop the deportation of craftsmen at the tail end of the plan.)

The story of the cipher telegram which we are about to reproduce is almost incredible. It appeared only after the Armenian Question had been almost settled in Turkish minds. It was in Damascus where a Turkish major named Neshat Bey in a drunken stupor showed a copy of the telegram to an Armenian. Copies were made and circulated soon after. Here it is:

February 27, 1915

A cipher telegram from the Ministry of War addressed to all the Military Commanders:

In view of the present situation the total extermination of the Armenian race has been decided by an Imperial order. The following operations are to be performed to that effect:

1. All Ottoman subjects over the age of five years bearing the name Armenian and residing in the country should be taken out of the city and killed.

2. All Armenians serving in the Imperial armies should be separated from their divisions, without creating incidents, taken into solitary places, away from the public eyes, and shot.

3. All Armenian officers in the army should be imprisoned in their respective military camps until further notice.

Forty-eight hours after the above instructions are transmitted to the commanders of the army specific orders will be issued for their execution. Aside from preliminary preparations no action should be taken in that regard.

Deputy Commander General and
Minister of War

Enver

In their places of exile, such as Res-ul-ain, Racca, Der-el-Zor, wherever the Armenians remained for several months, they built homes for themselves. On the line from Meskene to Der-el-Zor they built armories, hospitals, hotels, etc. But even then they were not wanted; massacres arrived shortly and put an end to their creative work. The following telegram indicates the extent of the loss of lives:

No. 76   March 7, 1916

To the Executive Director for the Settling of Refugees and Ashirets:

It is understood from the reports received that altogether 95,000 (100,000) Armenians have met death from various causes, as follows: 35,000 in the areas of Bab and Meskene; 10,000 in the center of departure in Aleppo (Kadlik); 20,000 in the district of Dipsi, Abuharrar and Hamam and 35,000 in Res-ul-ain.

Deputy Director-General

Abdulahad Nouri

The Central Government could not tolerate any attempt to give the least amount of subsistence to Armenian orphans. The following cipher telegram is intended to put a stop to such benevolence:

March 7, 1916

By the order of the Ministry of War, collect all the children of certain people (Armenians who have been gathered and cared for, on the pretext that they will be taken care of by the refugee offices, take them away in a group, without arousing suspicion, destroy them and report.

Minister of the Interior

Talaat

Of all the Turkish officials bent on the extermination of the Armenians, the most impatient and inhuman official was Zeki Bey, the Governor of Der-el-Zor. He was ambitious, and craving for recognition by the higher-ups for his homicidal acts. The following telegram is an indication of the vicious character of the man if one assumes, as is reasonable, that his references to a "changed dwelling place" refers in fact to etxermination:

July 31, 1916

Cipher telegram to the Government of Aleppo:

In accordance with the order sent to me from the Ministry, the *dwelling place of the Armenians living here will be changed* [Emphasis ours—D.H.B.] after the deportation of the Armenian refugees from Aleppo is somewhat abated. Therefore, please advise how long the deportation of the refugees is to last.

Governor
Zeki

APPENDIX B
Chapter 1

There was only one advanced nation that might have effectively aided the Armenians in 1915–1916, and that was Germany. German influence in Turkey was so strong that many observers spoke of the nation as a mere German dependency. It is therefore all the more shocking that the Kaiser and his Ambassador, von Wangenheim, chose to give the Turks a free hand in their ruthless plan of genocide. Wangenheim indeed often sounded as rabidly anti-Armenian as any Turkish zealot.

Those Germans who were genuinely moved by the plight of the Armenians were too few and lacked authority. It is true that Wangenheim's successor, Count Wolff-Metternich, was a humane man, but the extermination was already well under way when Wangenheim died in 1915.

During the terrible months of May to August, 1915, a number of Germans in Turkey attempted to intercede on behalf of the Armenians. Of these, the clergyman Johannes Ehman, was outstanding.

The following are telegraphic communications between Rev. Johannes Ehman, the Director of the German school in Harpout-Meziré and the German Ambassador von Wangenheim, and his successor, Count Wolff-Metternich:

May 15, 1915

To Wangenheim:

"During the last few days strict searches are being made in Christian homes, persons who are considered suspicious in the eyes of the government are being arrested and Christians are ordered to surrender their arms. For that reason the entire Christian population is subject to an awful terror, fearing worst consequences. On the basis of the truthful reports

337

made during my experience of 18 years in this country, I
would have liked to invite your attention to the fact that the
absolute majority of the population of this province is obedient to the government and the idea of insurrection against it
crossed nobody's mind. From 20 to 45 year old males were
conscripted without any difficulty. The Christian population
did everything possible to meet the demands of the government in surrendering all military materials, so that in the
name of human decency I plead with you to seek compassion
and protection for the Christian population of this province:
The Governor-General assured me that he would take all
measures to put this matter in order peacefully. He himself
is convinced of the peaceful nature of the Christian population in this place. There is, however, the danger that strong
and influential elements, who hate the Armenians, might become dominant and take the most wicked measures; for that
reason I beg your Excellency in the name of human interest
to take all necessary measures to enlighten the Central Authorities about the conditions and situation of this place."

Ehman

Pera, May 19, 1915, Be. No. 3010

I have received your correspondence of the 15th inst, and
the telegram of the 17th in due time. I am content to learn
from your writing that the situation where you are does not
give cause for concern at the present time, and I am hoping
that wise elements will succeed in the future to prevent dire
occurrences. It is natural and understandable that the government, in consequence of the deplorable happenings in Van,
take precautionary measures and on such an occasion the
peaceful people may suffer as well. On every occasion I shall
invite attention on your detailed reports, and on the other
hand I ask you to utilize your relations with the authorities
and the people by pacifying means. With this in mind I
should like to note especially that, in spite of the understandable irritations of present times and in spite of certain mischievous acts, no wholesale undertakings and lootings, etc.

have taken place. I am waiting for detailed information in the future with special interest and pleasure.

Wangcnhcim

A telegram to Wangenheim: June 18, 1915

Christians surrendered their arms. The politically innocent form the overwhelming majority. The protestant community of this city is entirely detached from and has no part in political activities. I plead with your excellency to especially intercede with the Turkish Central authorities to spare the politically innocent and the protestant community of this city from what seems probable deportation and other punishments.

Ehman

The answer to the telegram of June 18

June 19, 1915, Pera

According to the information given by the ministry of the interior affairs, the deportation of the Armenian population of your locality has not been thought of.

Wangenheim

Telegram   June 25, 1915

I am deeply gratified by the contents of your telegram of June 19. But the situation and the state of affairs here prove just the contrary (to your assertion), the situation is desperate. I confirm and reiterate the entire contents of my telegram of June 18, and repeat my humble plea.

Ehman

Telegram   June 27, 1915

To His Excellency von Wangenheim

German Embassy

After so much of anxious difficulties in the last few days it is now ordered to subject the entire Christian population of the province and city to forced deportation. In the name of humanitarian principle I beg of you to plead the cause of the innocent, the weak and the aged so that they may be treated with compassion. Aside from that I beg your excellency to protect and defend our institutions and all their employees.

Ehman

Telegram   June 27, 1915

To His Excellency von Wangenheim

German Embassy

The Governor-General of the province informs me that the order of deportation concerns all local Christians without exception and without racial differences. In his opinion it is possible to save our orphans, widows and employees, if your excellency should be willing to secure from Turkish Central Authorities a permit which will allow the employees of the institutions to remain here. I implore your excellency to take all necessary measures in that regard, because the deportation will commence 4 days later.

Ehman

An answer to Ehman's first telegram of June 27, 1915

Your telegraphic request of June 27 has been submitted to the consideration of the Ministry.

Wangenheim

An answer to Ehman's second telegram of June 27, 1915
Pera, July 1, 1915

It is not possible to retract the decision to deport the Armenians of your locality. As to your missionary institutions the Ministry of the Internal Affairs telegraphed special instructions yesterday.

Wangenheim

Telegram, July 10, 1915, translated from French

To His Excellency von Wangenheim

German Embassy

My most profound gratitude for having secured protection for our institutions. Relying on the next to last paragraph of your excellency's letter of May 19, this very last minute I earnestly implore your excellency in the name of humanitarian principles to take interceding steps so that, on the occasion of His Majesty the Sultan's joyful recovery (from his illness), protection and clemency be extended, by an Imperial proclamation of compassion, to the aged, the women, the children and a small number of the remnants of families who have been deported.

Ehman

Answer   Pera, July 14, 1915

Alas, the Ministry of the Interior rejected the request in a most painful manner, stating that the widowed, the sick and the crippled, without exception, will not be deported.

Wangenheim

Letter, July 17, 1915

To His Excellency von Wangenheim

German Embassy

In view of the most rigid implementation of the deportation order for the last two weeks, and the resultant confusing situation, the next to the last statement of your excellent letter No. 3010, dated May 19, resulted unfortunately in altogether and entirely adverse result. It is regrettable that it is no longer possible to do much against the existing facts. Should, however, it be possible, with the efforts of your Excellency, to put in a good word for the small remnants, so that they may be granted protection of their person and belongings, even that would be a very valuable work and accomplishment.

Ehman

Telegram   July 21, 1915

To Prince Hohenlohe

German Embassy

I humbly beg of your Highness to consider graciously my letters and telegrams sent to his excellency von Wangenheim.

Ehman

Telegram   August 12, 1915

To Prince v. Hohenlohe

The German Embassy, Constantinople

Whereas the remnants of the Catholic-Armenians have escaped deportation, I pray your majesty to intercede before the Central Government of Turkey, so that the small number of the remnants of the protestant community in this city be granted the same privilege.

Ehman

The reply   August 22, 1915

According to the latest decision of the Sublime Porte the protestant Armenians have also been freed from deportation. As to your institutions special instructions are yet to be forwarded.

Hohenlohe

Telegram   September 6, 1918 (5)

Prince Hohenlohe

The German Embassy

The worthy results obtained through the efforts of your highness for the saving of protestant Armenians from deportation encourages me to request humbly, in the name of justice and humanity, to intercede before the central authorities of Turkey to grant the same privileges to the (Gregorian) Armenians. It is often very difficult to distinguish Catholics and Protestants from Gregorians from the lists which carry the general heading "Christians."

Ehman

The reply   September 8, 1915

The Christians who have been officially designated as protestants can take advantage of this privilege when they furnish a statement in writing from their religious authorities
that they separated and moved out of the Gregorian community. Referring to my telegram of September 5, please inform
me whether the schools of Houlpbund (the missionary association of Frankfurt) are still functioning and whether any
Armenian teachers and students are left in there.

Prince (Duke) Hohenlohe

Telegram   August 19, 1915

Duke Hohenlohe

The German Embassy

I wish to express my humble and profound gratitude for
your success in obtaining permission allowing the rest of the
protestant Christians to remain here. Since it is politically
expedient as yet, with the consent of the Governor, I beg of
your Excellency to intercede so that the protestant Christians,
even though they have been moved out of their homes, but
are still found in areas close to the province, may benefit by
this privilege and be allowed to return.

Ehman

(Editor's Note: The foregoing communications have been
translated from German to Armenian and published in the
Hooshamadyan, pp. 393–396. The present translation to
English is from Armenian.)

Germany's presence in Turkey was so strong during World
War I that she was often coupled with her as a twin bar-
barian. The precise degree of German responsibility is not
easy to determine, but in the following extracts it is clear
that even the best German reactions to the massacres were
not implemented with effective action. At worst, as in the
case of Count Reventlow, the Turkish actions were positively
approved, with only a shallow attempt at justification by a

totally fabricated charge of Armenian treason and revolt.

After the war, the German writer and photographer, Armin T. Wegner, addressed a long and very moving letter to President Wilson on the subject of the terrible things he had witnessed in Turkey. This masterful document sums up and forms a fitting close to the material relating to Germany in this Appendix.

1. *Baron von Wangenheim*

(a) Report to the German Chancellor, dated July 17, 1915, quoted in an article entitled "Germany, Turkey and the Armenians," by J. Ellis Barker, published in the *Quarterly Review*, April, 1920:

> It is obvious that the banishment of the Armenians is due not solely to military considerations. Talaat Bey, the Minister of the Interior, has quite frankly said to Dr. Mordtmann of the Embassy, that the Turkish Government intended to make use of the World War and deal thoroughly with its internal enemies, the Christians in Turkey, and that it meant not to be disturbed in this by diplomatic intervention from abroad. The Armenian Patriarch told the same gentleman (a member of the Embassy) a few days later (that) the Turkish Government did not intend merely to make the Armenians temporarily innocuous but to expel them from Turkey or rather to exterminate them.

(b) Message to Bethmann-Hollweg, July 16, 1915, quoted in the *Quarterly Review*, April, 1920:

> . . . . Notwithstanding our repeated pressing representations, the Turkish Government continues to deport the Armenians and to expose them to destruction by settling them in barren districts. We cannot prevent them in this, but we must leave to Turkey the responsibility for the economic and political consequences.

(c) Protest to Turkish Government, August 9, 1915, quoted in a leaflet entitled "Armenia," published by the American Committee for Armenian and Syrian Relief, February 21, 1916:

The German Embassy regrets to have to realize that, according to information received from impartial and reliable sources, acts of violence, such as massacres and plunders, which could not be justified by the aim that the Imperial Government was pursuing, instead of being checked by the local authorities, regularly followed expulsion of Armenians, so that most of them perished before reaching their destination. It is chiefly from the provinces of Trebizond, Diarbekir, and Erzeroum that these facts are reported; in some places, as in Mardin, all Christians, without distinction of race or religion had the same fate. At the same time the Imperial Government has thought it right to extend the measure of expatriation to the other provinces of Asia Minor, and very recently the Armenian villages of the district of Izmit, near the capital, have been evacuated under similar conditions. Under such circumstances the German Embassy, by order of its Government, is obliged to remonstrate once more against these acts of terror.

2. *Prince Hohenlohe*, telegram to German Consulate, Aleppo, August 2, 1915, quoted in the *Quarterly Review*, April, 1920:

" 'All our representations have been of no avail in the presence of the government's determination to rid itself of the native Christians from the eastern provinces."

3. *Mehmed Cherif Pasha*, letter to the editor of *Journal de Geneve*, published in the *New York Times*, September 21, 1915:

The New York Times reported in its issue of September 21, 1915 that Mehmed Cherif Pasha, former Turkish Minister to Sweden, who had fled from Turkey, wrote a letter to the editor of Journal de Geneve, in which he branded "the Armenian atrocities perpetrated under the present regime as surpassing the savagery of Genghis Khan and Tamerlane." The letter continues: "To be sure, the state of mind of the Unionists was not revealed to the civilized world until they had openly taken sides with Germany; but for more than six years I have been exposing them in the *Mecheroufiette* (his newspaper, published first in Constantinople, then in Paris) and in different journals and reviews warning France and England of the plot against them and against certain nationalities within the Ottoman borders, notably the Armenians, that was being hatched.

"If there is a race which has been closely connected with the Turks by its fidelity, by its services to the country, by the statesmen and functionaries of talent it has furnished, by the intelligence which it has manifested in all domains— commerce, industry, science, and the arts—it is certainly the Armenians. . . .

"Alas! At the thought that a people so gifted, which has served as the fructifying soil for the renovation of the Ottoman Empire, is on the point of disappearing from history— not enslaved, as were the Jews by the Assyrians, but annihilated—even the most hardened heart must bleed; and I desire, through the medium of your estimable journal, to express to this race which is being assassinated, my anger toward the butchers and my immense pity for the victims."

Editor's Note: Mehmed Cherif Pasha was the son of Said Pasha, who was one of the chief advisers of Abdul Hamid and the first Grand Vizier under the new constitution.

4. *Archbishop of Canterbury,* letter read in a meeting held in Newport, England, and quoted in *The New Armenia,* January 15, 1916. The letter said in part:

> If we as a belligerent power are unable to take effective action in the matter, we can at least do our utmost to secure that nonbelligerent nations shall be awakened to those fearful realities. We want not merely to render impossible the continuance of the present horrors, we want to prevent their recurrence in years to come. To that end every effort that we can make is worth while. I shall take every opportunity of calling attention to the subject and of bidding men and women weigh the true meaning of these vast and organized iniquities perpetrated by Turkish hands and apparently with the connivance of their German Allies.

5. *James Bryce,* letter to Aneurin Williams, dated September 18, 1915, and published in The *New York Times* of September 20, 1915:

Dear Mr. Williams:

You are right in thinking that the civilized world, and especially that the American people ought to know what horrors have been passing in Asiatic Turkey during the last few months, for if anything can stop the destroying hand of the Turkish Government, it will be an expression of the opinion of neutral nations, and especially of the judgment of humane America.

Soon after the war between Turkey and the Allies broke out, the Turkish Government formed, and has ever since been carrying out with relentless cruelty, the plan of extirpating Christianity by killing off the Christians of Armenian race. The Armenian population, peaceable peasants and artisans in Eastern provinces of Turkey, were remaining quiet. They had not rebelled. They were unarmed. Many of them were serving in the Turkish army. But they were Christians and the Government doubtlessly supposed that they were not in sympathy with rulers who had oppressed and robbed them for generations, and who in 1895–6, and again six or seven years ago, had massacred many thousands of them without provocation.

The massacres of this year have, however, gone far beyond even those of 1895–6. The accounts which have now found their way to Western Europe—accounts coming from different sources, but agreeing with one another, and as to whose substantial truth there can be do doubt—prove that over the whole of Eastern and Northern Asia Minor and Armenia the whole Christian population is being deliberately exterminated. The men of military age have been killed. The younger women have been seized for Turkish harems; compelled to become Mohammedans, and kept, sometimes with their children, also forcibly converted, in virtual slavery.

The rest of the inhabitants, old men, women, and children, have been torn from their homes and driven away under convoys of Turkish soldiers, largely composed of released criminals, some into unhealthy parts of Asia Minor, some into the deserts between Syria and the Euphrates. Many die, or are murdered, on the way; all perish sooner or later. Lest any should, if they escaped, try to regain their homes, Muslims have been brought in from other places to occupy the houses and farms from which the Christians had been expelled.

No greater injury could be done to the country than to destroy the most intelligent and industrious and educated part of its population, but for that the reckless and ruthless men who now control Turkey do not care. In Trebizond, a city where the Armenians numbering more than 10,000 persons, had dwelt in peace with their Muslim neighbors, orders came from Constantinople to seize all the Armenians. Many of these kindly neighbors tried to hide or protect them, but in vain. The troops hunted them all out, drove them to the shore, placed them in sailing boats, took them out to sea, threw them overboard and drowned them all—men, women, and children. Resistance was impossible, for younger men had been carried off to the Army and the rest were unarmed. This was seen and is described by the Italian Consul.

How many have perished over the whole country no one can tell. Some seem to have saved their lives by professing to accept Islam, and about 250,000 are said to have escaped across the frontier into Russian territory. But a far greater number, perhaps 500,000, have been slaughtered or deported, and the deported are fast dying of ill-treatment, disease, and starvation, while the massacres still go on.

Christianity, after maintaining itself in Armenia for seventeen centuries against the attacks first of the Persian fire worshippers and then of Saracens and Turks, is now being completely routed out of these countries. The roads and hills, says one account, are strewn with corpses, the corpses of innocent peasants.

The story of these horrors must surely touch every American heart, whatever its racial origin, whatever may be its sympathies with one or other party, in the present war. No man in whom any pity lives can fail to feel for the helpless victims of the ferocity of their own Government. What can be done? We can all, of course, try to send aid to the miserable refugees now in Russian territory. But what can stop the massacres? Not the Allied Powers at war with Turkey. Only one power can take action for that purpose. It is Germany. Would not an expression of American public opinion, voicing the conscience

of neutral nations, lead Germany to exert her influence to
check the Turkish government before their ghastly work
is complete?

I am, faithfully yours,

Bryce

Aneurin Williams, Esq. M.P.

6. *Count von Reventlow*, military writer for the *Deutsche
Tageszeitung*, has been reported to have made the following
comments about the Armenian atrocities:

(a) Dispatch from Amsterdam, via London, October 7,
(1915), published in the *New York Times*, referring to the
request of the American Government that the German Ambassador at Washington use his influence with the German
Government in behalf of the Armenians in Turkey, the
Count says:

"There can be no question of meddling at the instigation
of a third party with the affairs of our Turkish ally. If the
Turkish authorities believe it opportune to take vigorous
measures against unreliable, bloodthirsty Armenian elements, is not only their right but their duty to do so."

(b) An article entitled *"The Uproar about 'The Armenian
Atrocities' begins,"* published in the *Tageszeitung* and reported by the *New York Times*, October 9, 1915. The Count
says in part:

> If Turkey considers it necessary that the Armenian up-
> risings and other intrigues be suppressed with all means
> possible, so that a repetition be impossible, that does not
> constitute massacres or atrocities, but simply a measure
> of a justified and necessary character, the more justified
> and the more necessary for the fact that the Turkish Em-
> pire is in its hardest fight for existence and has enough
> foreign enemies. To demand that it shall also nourish an
> internal enemy in its bosom, because that would suit the
> British and the Americans, is to demand a great deal . . .
> We Germans have to give an account neither to enemies
> nor to neutrals of what the Turks do with Armenians or
> what the German consuls say about it. The place of the

German Empire and of every individual German is at the side of our Turkish ally, and that without criticism.

7. *Professor Albert Bushnell Hart*, in an article entitled "German Influence in Turkey," published in *The New Armenia*, March 25, 1916, writes in part:

> They (the Germans) are at this moment practically masters of Turkey. The Turkish government may do some things without asking their permission, but quickly undoes everything to which the Germans object. Hence the clear and awful responsibility of the Germans for the Armenian massacres. They have denied the truth of the statements of American missionaries and consuls, eye-witnesses of the horror; they have supported the preposterous theory that the Armenian old men, women and children were revolting against the Turks! They have refused to utter the warning which would have stopped the massacres within twenty-four hours, and would have restored the unhappy victims to the homes which had already been bestowed upon their enemies.

8. *Count Wolff-Metternich*, report to German Chancellor, December 7, 1915, quoted in the *Quarterly Review*.

Count Wolff-Metternich was appointed Ambassador after von Wangenheim's death. The new Ambassador recognized that "paper protests and warnings and verbal admonitions were worse than useless." Therefore, on December 7, 1915 he wrote to the Imperial Chancellor as follows:

> . . . . Colonel von Kress, Djemal's Chief of Staff, tells me that the misery of the Armenians is indescribable and is far greater than we have been told. At the same time, the rumour was spread about that the Germans desired to see Armenians massacred. I have employed extremely sharp language. Protests are useless, and the Turkish assertions that no further deportations will take place are worthless . . . In order to have success in the Armenian Question we must instil into the Turkish Government the fear of consequences. If, for military reasons, we may not dare to act firmly, it is useless to protest any longer. Mere protests rather annoy than are useful; and if we cannot act, we must look on while our ally continues his policy of massacre . . .

9. *Count Wolff-Metternich,* telegram to the German Chancellor, Bethmann-Hollweg, dated July 10, 1916, quoted in *Deutschland und Armenien,* by Dr. Johannes Lepsius and reproduced by Andre N. Mandelstam in the *La Societe des Nations et les Puissances devant le Probleme Armenien,* Paris, A. Pedone, 1925.

"In its attempt to carry out its purpose to resolve the Armenian question by the destruction of the Armenian race, the Turkish Government has refused to be deterred neither by our representations, nor by those of the American Embassy, nor by the delegate of the Pope, nor by the threats of the Allied Powers, nor in deference to the public opinions of the west representing one-half of the world." (p. 50).

10. *Von Scheubner-Richter,* report dated December 4, 1916, quoted in an article entitled "The Armenian Question," by Dr. Johannes Lepsius, published in *The Moslem World,* October, 1920:

"A great part of the Young Turkish Committee seems to take the point of view that the Turkish Empire can only be built upon a purely Mohammedan pan-Turkish foundation. The population which is neither one nor the other must either become Turkish and Mohammedan or must be completely destroyed."

11. *Armin T. Wegner,* A German writer and an eye-witness to the genocide of the Armenians, who photographed more than 8000 horrible and ghastly scenes of tragic episodes and fiendish acts. Upon his return to Berlin he showed these pictures to thousands of people congregated in various auditoriums. In January, 1919, Mr. Wegner wrote a lengthy and comprehensive letter to President Woodrow Wilson. We quote that letter in its entirety.

Berlin, January, 1919

MR. PRESIDENT:

In your message to Congress of January 8, 1918, you made a demand for the liberation of all non-Turkish peoples in the Ottoman Empire. One of these peoples is the Armenian nation. It is on behalf of the Armenian nation that I am addressing you.

As one of the few Europeans who have been eye-witnesses of the dreadful destruction of the Armenian people from its beginning in the fruitful fields of Anatolia up to the wiping out of the mournful remnants of the race on the banks of the Euphrates, I venture to claim the right of setting before you these pictures of misery and terror which passed before my eyes during nearly two years, and which will never be obliterated from my mind. I appeal to you at the moment when the Governments allied to you are carrying on peace negotiations in Paris, which will determine the fate of the world for many decades. But the Armenian people is only a small one among several others; and the future of greater States more prominent in the world's eye is hanging in the balance. And so there is reason to fear that the significance of a small and extremely enfeebled nation may be obscured by the influential and selfish aims of the great European States, and that with regard to Armenia there will be a repetition of the old game of neglect and oblivion of which she has so often been the victim in the course of her history.

But this would be most lamentable, for no people in the world has suffered such wrongs as the Armenian nation. The Armenian Question is a question for Christendom, for the whole human race.

The Armenian people were victims of this war. When the Turkish Government, in the Spring of 1915, set about the execution of its monstrous project of exterminating a million Armenians, all the nations of Europe were unhappily bleeding to exhaustion, owing to the tragic blindness of their mutual misunderstanding, and there was no one to hinder the lurid tyrants of Turkey from carrying on to the bitter end those revolting atrocities which can only be likened to the acts of a criminal lunatic. And so they drove the whole people—men, women, hoary elders, children, expectant mothers and dumb sucklings—into the Arabian desert, with no other object than to let them starve to death.

For a long time, Europeans had been wont to regard Siberia as one of the most inhospitable regions in the world; to be condemned to live there was regarded as a most severe punishment. And yet, even in that place, there are fertile lands and, despite the cold of its winters, the climate is healthy. But what is Siberia compared with the Mesopotamian Steppes? There we find a long tract of land without grass, without trees, without cattle, covered with stunted weeds, a country where the only inhabitants are Arab Bedouins, destitute of all pity; a stretch of grey limestone plains several miles in extent, bare wastes of rock and stone, ruined river banks, exposed to the rays of a merciless sun, ceaseless autumn rains, and frosty winter nights, leaving sheets of ice behind them. Except its two large rivers there is no water. The few small villages scarcely suffice to feed a handful of Bedouins, who, in their wretched poverty, regard any traveller as a welcome prey. From the dwellings which their race had held for more than two thousand years, from all parts of the Empire, from the stony passes of the mountain region to the shores of the Sea of Marmora and the palmy oases of the South, the Armenians were driven into this desolate waste, with the alleged purpose of forcibly transplanting them from their homes to a strange land—a purpose which, even had it been the real one, is repugnant to every human feeling. The men were struck down in batches, bound together with chains and ropes, and thrown into the river or rolled down the mountain with fettered limbs. The women and children were put on sale in the public market; the old men and boys driven with deadly bastinadoes to forced labour. Nor was this sufficient; in order to render indelible the stain on their criminal hands, the captors drove the people, after depriving them of their leaders and spokesmen, out of the towns at all hours of the day and night, half-naked, straight out of their beds; plundered their houses, burnt their villages, destroyed the churches or turned them into mosques, carried off the cattle, seized all the vehicles, snatched the bread out of the mouths of their victims, tore the clothes from off their backs, the gold from their hair. Officials—military officers, soldiers, shepherds—vied with one another in their wild orgy of blood, dragging out of the schools delicate orphan girls to serve their bestial lusts, beat with cudgels dying women or women close on childbirth who could scarcely drag themselves along, until the women fell down on the road and died, changing the dust beneath them into bloodstained mire. Travellers passing along the road turned away their eyes in horror from this moving multitude, driven on with devilish cruelty—only to find in their inns new-born babes buried in the dung-heaps of the court-yards, and the roads covered with severed heads of boys, who had raised them in supplication to their torturers. Parties which on their departure from the homeland of High Armenia consisted of thousands, numbered on their arrival in the outskirts of Aleppo only a few hundreds, while the fields were strewed with swollen, blackened corpses, infecting the air with their odours, lying about desecrated, naked, having been robbed of their clothes, or driven, bound back to back, to the Euphrates to provide food for fishes. Sometimes gendarmes in derision threw into the emaciated hands of the starving people a little meal which they greedily licked off, merely with the result of prolonging their death-agony.

Even before the gates of Aleppo they were allowed no rest. For incomprehensible and utterly unjustifiable reasons of war, the shrunken parties were ceaselessly driven barefooted, hundreds of miles under a burning sun, through stony defiles, over pathless steppes, enfeebled by fever and other maladies, through semi-tropical marshes, into the wilderness of desolation. Here they died—slain by Kurds, robbed by gendarmes, shot, hanged, poisoned, stabbed, strangled, mowed down by epidemics, drowned, frozen, parched with thirst, starved—their bodies left to putrify or to be devoured by jackals.

Children wept themselves to death, men dashed themselves against rocks, mothers threw their babes into the brooks, women with child flung themselves, singing, into the Euphrates. They died all the deaths on the earth, the deaths of all the ages.

I have seen maddened deportees eating as food their own clothes and shoes, women cooking the bodies of their new-born babes.

In ruined caravanserais they lay between heaps of corpses and half-rotted bodies, with no one to pity them, waiting for death; for how long would it be possible for them to drag out a miserable existence, searching out grains of corn from horse-dung or eating grass? But all this is only a fraction of what I have seen myself, of what I have been told by acquaintances or by travellers, or of what I have heard from the mouths of the deportees.

Mr. President, if you will look through that dreadful enumeration of horrors compiled by Lord Bryce in England and by Dr. Johannes Lepsius in Germany with regard to these occurrences, you will see that I am not exaggerating. But I may assume that these pictures of horrors of which all the world has heard except Germany, which has been shamefully deceived, are already in your hands. By what right, then, do I make this appeal to you?

I do it by the right of human fellowship, in dutiful fulfilment of a sacred promise.

When in the desert I went through the deportees' camp, when I sat in their tents with the starving and dying, I felt their supplicating hands in mine, and the voices of their priests, who had blessed many of the dead on their last journey to the grave, adjured me to plead for them, if I were ever in Europe.

But the country to which I have returned is a poor country; Germany is a conquered nation. My own people (the Germans) are near starvation; the streets are full of the poor and wretched. Can I beg help of a people which perhaps will soon not be in a condition to save itself for a people (the Armenians) which is an even more evil case?

The voice of conscience and humanity will never be silenced in me, and therefore I address these words to you.

This document is a request. It is the tongues of a thousand dead that speak in it.

Mr. President, the wrong suffered by this people is immeasurable. I have read everything that has been written about the war. I have carefully made myself acquainted with the horrors in every country on this earth, the fearful slaughters in every battle, the ships sunk by torpedoes, the bombs thrown down on the towns by air-craft, the heart-rending slaughters in Belgium, the misery of the French refugees, the fearful sickness and epidemics in Roumania. But here is a wrong to be righted such as none of these peoples has suffered—neither the French nation, nor the Belgian, nor the English, nor the Russian, nor the Serbian, nor the Roumanian, nor even the German nation, which has had to suffer so much in this war. The barbarous peoples of ancient times may possibly have endured a similar fate. But here we have a highly civilized nation, with a great and glorious past, which has rendered services that can never be forgotten to art, literature and learning; a nation which has produced many remarkable and intellectual men, profoundly religious, with a noble priesthood; a Christian people, whose members are dispersed over the whole earth, many of whom have lived for many years in your country, Mr. President. Men acquainted with all the languages of the world, men whose wives and daughters have been accustomed to sit in comfortable chairs at a table covered with a clean white cloth, not to crouch in a cave in the wilderness. Sagacious merchants, distinguished doctors, scholars, artists, honest prosperous peasants who made the land fruitful, and whose only fault was that they were defenceless and spoke a different language from that of their persecutors, and were born into a different faith.

Every one who knows the events of this war in Anatolia, who has followed the fortunes of this nation with open eyes, knows that all those accusations which were brought, with great cunning and much diligence, against the Armenian race, are nothing but loathsome slanders fabricated by their unscrupulous tyrants, in order to shield themselves from the consequences of their own mad and brutal acts, and to hide their own incapacity for reconciliation with the spirit of sincerity and humanity.

But even all these accusations were based on the truth, they would never justify these cruel deeds committed against hundreds of thousands of innocent people.

I am making no accusation against Islam. The spirit of every great religion is noble, and the conduct of many a Mohammedan has made us blush for the deeds of Europe.

I do not accuse the simple people of Turkey, whose souls are full of goodness; but I do not think that the members of the ruling class will ever, in the course of history, be capable of making their country happy, for they have destroyed our belief in their capacity for civilisation.

Turkey has forfeited for all time the right to govern itself.

Mr. President, you will believe in my impartiality if I speak to you on this subject, as a German, one of a nation which was linked with Turkey in bonds of close friendship, a nation which in consequence of this friendship has most unjustly been accused of being an accomplice in these murderous man-hunts. The German people knows nothing of this crime. The German Government erred through ignorance of the Turkish character and its own preoccupation with solicitude for the future of its own people. I do not deny that weakness is a fault in the life of nations.

But the bitter reproach of having made possible this unpardonable deportation does not fall on Germany alone.

In the Berlin Treaty of July 1878, all the six European Great Powers gave most solemn guarantees that they would guard the tranquility and security of the Armenian people. But has this promise ever been kept? Even Abdul Hamid's massacres failed to bring it to remembrance, and in blind greed the nations pursued selfish aims, not one putting itself forward as the champion of an oppressed people.

In the Armistice between Turkey and your Allies, which the Armenians all over the world awaited with feverish anxiety, the Armenian question is scarcely mentioned. Shall this unworthy game be repeated a second time, and must the Armenians be once more disillusioned?

The future of this small nation must not be relegated to obscurity behind the selfish schemes and plans of the great states. Mr. President, save the honour of Europe.

It would be an irremediable mistake if the Armenian districts of Russia were not joined with the Armenian provinces of Anatolia and Cilicia to form one common country entirely liberated from Turkish rule, with an outlet of its own to the sea. It is not enough, Mr. President, that you should know the sufferings of these people. It is not enough that you should give them a state in which the houses are destroyed, the fields laid waste, the citizens murdered. The exhaustion of this country is such that by its own strength it cannot rise again. Its trade is ruined; its handicrafts and industries have collapsed. The asset of its annihilated population can never be restored.

Many thousands of Armenians were converted to Islam by force, thousands of children and girls kidnapped, and thousands of women carried away and made slaves in Turkish harems. To all these must be given perfect assurance of their return to freedom. All victims of persecution who are returning to their homes after spending two years and more in the desert must be indemnified for the wealth and goods that they have lost; all orphans must be cared for. What these people need is love, of which they have so long been deprived. This is, for all of us, a confession of guilt.

Mr. President, pride prevents me from pleading for my own people (the Germans). I have no doubt that, out of

plentitude of its sorrow, it will gain power by sacrifice to
co-operate in the future redemption of the world. But, on
behalf of the Armenian nation, which has suffered such
terrible tyranny, I venture to intervene; for if, after this
war, it is not given reparation for its fearful sufferings,
it will be lost forever.

With the ardour of one who has experienced unspeakable, humiliating sorrows in his own tortured soul, I utter
the voice of those unhappy ones, whose despairing cries
I had to hear without being able to still them, whose cruel
deaths I could only helplessly mourn, whose bones be-
strew the deserts of the Euphrates, and whose limbs once
more become alive in my heart and admonish me to speak.

Once already have I knocked at the door of the American people when I brought the petition of the deportees
from their camps at Meskene and Aleppo to your Embassy
at Constantinople, and I know that this has not been in
vain.

If you, Mr. President, have indeed made the sublime
idea of championing oppressed nations the guiding principle of your policy, you will not fail to perceive that even
in these words a mighty voice speaks, the only voice that
has the right to be heard at all times—the voice of humanity. (Originally printed by Richard Clay & Sons, Ltd.,
London)

Sir Edwin Pears, in his *Forty Years in Constantinople,*
1916, writes:

"The story of the massacre of the Armenians requires little
explanation here. Travellers have recognized for centuries
that the Armenian population of Turkey, numbering about
two millions, is a most valuable element in the country. The
people, like ourselves, belong to the Indo-European race. A
large portion of them occupy a mountainous country, and
the men are usually stalwart and industrious. Their country
was civilised and prosperous in the time of Christ, and I
cannot doubt that the general average intelligence of Armenians is due to the fact that they are the descendants of
parents who have been civilised for centuries, and possibly
even millenniums. Armenia was the first country to establish Christianity as the religion of the State. Their great

Christian teacher and national saint is Gregory the Illuminator." (p. 149)

Sir Edwin describes in detail the important role the Armenians played in Turkey, even after the accession of Abdul Hamid. But their unquenchable desire for education did not "sit quietly under Turkish or other misrule."

> The Turks, [writes Sir Edwin,] amongst whom the Armenians are generally dispersed, resented this desire for instruction and closed the schools. It did not occur to them for many years to open Turkish schools, even in districts where the Armenians spoke only Turkish. I had learnt that such districts were not uncommon through having to work up a case regarding an alleged Armenian estate dating back to about 1780. A large number of undoubtedly genuine Armenian letters of that date had been preserved in a monastery and had to be translated. I then saw not only that the Armenians were bitterly persecuted, but that they were forbidden to speak their own language, under the penalty of having their tongue cut out if they did so. (pp. 151–152)
>
> The condition of disorder in Armenia had gradually become worse instead of better. Then Abdul Hamid seems to have determined to try his own hand at statesmanship. Men were arrested on the slightest pretext and thrown into prison. I remember one instance, simple but typical, which Sir Philip Currie told me of at the time it occurred. A Turk had been murdered in a large village in Armenia. Had it been a Christian no one except perhaps members of his own family would have taken any notice of the occurrence. The majority of the inhabitants were Armenians and every man was immediately thrown into prison. Many of them were subjected to torture of the most hideous kind, one of the commonest forms indeed being such as I cannot describe. Our Consul made a representation of the facts to Sir Philip and he immediately determined to do what he could to save the miserable victims. I saw him the day after he had made a visit on the subject to the Sultan. He told me how he had described the tortures, His Majesty answered, "But a Moslem has been killed," leaving the impression on Sir Philip that of course in such case the authorities were justified in arresting all the Armenians in order to find out who was the culprit. (p. 153)

It was quite natural for the Armenians to resent this highly provocative treatment and to think of rebelling against this tyrannical rule. The author of this book, however, contends, perhaps with logical reasoning, that any attempt to "raise a rebellion" may be futile and "purely mischievous," since no intervention by European governments was probable. "Lord Salisbury had publicly declared that as he could not get a fleet over the Taurus he did not see how England could help the Armenians, as much as she sympathised with them."

The result of the failure of these attempts was that Abdul Hamid determined once and for all to make revolt impossible. It was commonly said that he had made up his mind to exterminate the Armenian population. It may well be doubted whether he deliberately contemplated a step so difficult. But he and some of his creatures organised a series of massacres such as had not been seen in any European country for upwards of a century. In making his preparations he took all steps he could devise to prevent the truth becoming known. Every letter sent to or coming from Asia Minor was opened, and when delivered was intentionally left open. Foreigners as well as Turkish subjects were forbidden to go into the provinces where Armenians abounded. The system of local passports had already become so strict that no person was allowed to travel in the country, even from one village to another, without possessing one. . . .

When all arrangements had been made for preventing news coming from Armenia, Abdul Hamid set about the task which he called giving the Armenians a lesson. Emissaries were sent into the provinces. The Moslems were invited to assemble in the mosques, were informed of the Sultan's plan, and told that they were at liberty to take their neighbours' goods and to kill them if any resistance was made.

In one or two cases—lamentably rare, I am afraid—the emissary was opposed in the mosque by the man who would correspond to the parish priest. One brave fellow rose to speak after the emissary had proclaimed his mission and boldly stated that he did not believe that the Padishah had sent such orders, but if he had done so he would still oppose their execution. 'You know me,' said the venerable old man, 'as a good Moslem. The teaching of Islam is that we are not permitted to kill unbelievers unless they are in rebellion. There is not a man among you who dare say that the Armenians in this town are rebels. Therefore, if even the order come from the Padishah, I say that I will not be party to their execution, and that in the day of judgment I will accuse anyone who kills his Armenian neighbour, and let it be known that it was done after my warning that it was unlawful to do so.' Nevertheless a great massacre took place in that city next day.

The precautions that Abdul Hamid had taken to prevent news being transmitted of his devilish work were largely successful. Very few private letters were smuggled into Constantinople from the area of the massacre, the fullest account of the early stages having been sent by way of Russia to the *Daily Telegraph*. The lowest serious estimate that has been made of the victims killed is 100,-000. Sir William Ramsay's estimate of a quarter of a million of victims is probably not too high, if to the number of those actually killed are added those who died of starvation and other consequential causes. (pp. 155–157)

The most cruel outrage in the Armenian massacres took place in the Armenian cathedral at Urfa, on Sunday, December 29, 1896. The Christians had been deceived by a Moslem mob into believing that they would be unmolested in the great church; and, on the Sunday morning, at least 3,000 persons had been assembled. When Mr. Fitzmaurice saw it he was able to read on one of the pillars of the church a record by the priest that he had administered last communion to 1,800 members of his flock. These, with other Armenians, were intentionally burnt to death in the cathedral.

When the mob broke in with a rush they killed all who were on the ground floor, these being nearly all men, the women and children being in the gallery. They mockingly called on Christ to prove that He was a greater prophet than Mahomet. In the meantime, while revolver and other shots were being discharged against the occupants of the gallery, native mattresses, *yorghans* or *duvets*, the straw matting which covered the floor, and other combustibles were piled up for a big fire. Thirty cans of petroleum were poured over them and fire set to the mass. Abdul Hamid had avenged himself, and a deed of devilry had been done, worse in its extent than even the slaughter of Batak in Bulgaria in 1876. (p. 161)

It might be appropriate to add here that it was Sir Edwin's dispatches from Bulgaria in 1876, when he was a correspondent for the *Telegraph,* which awakened the civilized world to Turkish brutality.

APPENDIX A

Chapter 2

The first few years of Abdul Hamid's reign were of uncommon interest both as to the internal relations between Turks and Armenians and for the international consequences of the Russian victory over Turkey. The Treaty of San Stefano (San Stefano is a suburb of Istanbul/Constantinople) is of central interest in any discussion of Turkish-Armenian relations, and, since it was largely disregarded by Abdul so far as Armenian rights were concerned, foreign reaction to the treaty and Turkish violations of it are deserving of some attention. In the following pages we have attempted by quotation and commentary to capture some of the crucial importance of the early Hamidian years.

In 1876–77 there was a general discontent in Turkey. An organization called Young Turkey "demanded the carrying out of the Hatt of 1877, establishing a constitution and parliament." A constitutional government was officially proclaimed in Turkey. Midhat Pasha, the Grand Vizier, conceived the plan which was formally approved by the Sultan. A constitution was promulgated. A parliament, consisting of a Senate and an elective assembly was created, and its first session was opened by Abdul Hamid in person on March 19, 1877.

The new constitution* had hardly been declared the supreme law of the land, in practice as well as in theory, when, before the end of the same year "one designing politician managed to get parliament involved in a corrupt job, and then, to avoid investigation, persuaded the Sultan to issue a decree abrogating the constitution and abolishing parliament! It was a coup d'etat, and it was successful; thanks largely to the indifference of the Powers, and especially to England."

---

* It has been authoritatively asserted that the author of the Constitution was Krikor Odian, a well-known Armenian statesman, who was serving as secretary to Midhat Pasha.

Bleeding Armenia, by Rev. A. W. Williams. Midhat Pasha, the author of the constitution, suffered martyrdom.

The Treaty of San Stefano, March 3, 1878.

An international conference, which met in Constantinople in the last days of 1876, adopted certain resolutions regarding the nomination of an international commission to investigate the state of the European provinces in Turkey, and the appointment by the sultan, with the approval of the powers, of governors-general for five years. These resolutions were rejected by the Porte. This led to war between Russia and Turkey which was declared on April 24, 1877.

In about nine months the hostilities came to an end with the defeat of Turkey. The agreement for an armistice signed at Adrianople on January 31, 1878 made no mention of the Armenians. When Patriarch Nerses Varjabedian learned that the proposed treaty contained no provisions for the Armenians, he personally appealed to Grand Duke Nicholas, but was told that it was too late to insert any further provisions in the treaty. Count Ignatieve, who was a good friend of the Armenian Patriarch, interceded. Whereupon Grand Duke Nicholas proposed to the Turkish delegation an additional paragraph in the treaty. The Turks protested, but were obliged to give in. Hence Article 16 of the treaty, signed on March 3, 1878.

Article 16: "As the evacuation by the Russian troops of the territory which they occupy in Armenia, and which is to be restored to Turkey, might give rise to conflicts and complications detrimental to the maintenance of good relations between the two countries, the Sublime Porte engages to carry into effect, without further delay, the improvements and reforms demanded by local requirements in the provinces inhabited by the Armenians, and to guarantee their security from Kurds and Circassians."

It should be noted that the San Stefano Treaty makes certain facts evident: (a) that there is a country known as "Armenia"; (b) that local conditions in that country demand

improvements and reforms; (c) that the Armenians are being mistreated by Kurds and Circassians; (d) that Turkey
promises "to carry into effect, without further delay", such
improvements and reforms as are necessary.

"To this treaty", writes M. G. Rolin-Jaequemyns, "belong
the honour and merit of being the first international compact
which mentions Armenia."

England was not pleased with that treaty. Russia's sole
supervision over the implementation of the terms of the
treaty by Turkey was considered detrimental to the interests
of Great Britain. Diplomatic negotiations began between the
two great Powers, resulting in a memorandum signed at London on May 30, 1878, by Marquis of Salisbury and Count
Schouvaloff, which specified the points on which an understanding had been arrived at relative to Article 16 of the
treaty.

Item Number 7 of the memorandum provides:

"The promises respecting Armenia, stipulated in the preliminary Treaty of San Stefano, must not be made exclusively
to Russia, but to England also."

The Armenians now had two powerful protectors neither
of whom was free or willing to exercise sufficient force to
become protector in fact, rather than on paper only.

The Anglo-Turkish (Cyprus) Convention

Even the Memorandum signed on May 30, 1878, did not
satisfy Great Britain. She wanted a stronger hold on Turkey,
as the protector of Christian minorities as well as the defender of Turkey against Russia and against any other Power
that might try to interfere with the internal affairs of Turkey.

It did not require much pressure to persuade Turkey to
cede Cyprus to England as evidence of her good faith in in-
troducing measures which would guarantee the security of
her Christian subjects. On June 4, 1878, Turkey and England
signed the so-called Cyprus Convention which contained the
following Article:

"*Article 1.* If Batoum, Ardahan, Kars, or any of them shall be retained by Russia, and if any attempt shall be made at any future time by Russia to take possession of any further territory of His Imperial Majesty, the Sultan, in Asia, as fixed by the Definitive Treaty of Peace, England engages to join His Imperial Majesty, the Sultan, in defending them by force of arms.

"In return, His Imperial Majesty, the Sultan, promises to England to introduce necessary reforms, *to be agreed upon later between the two Powers,* into the Government and for the protection of the Christian and other subjects of the Porte in these territories; and in order to enable England to make necessary provisions for executing her engagements, His Imperial Majesty, the Sultan, further consents to assign the island of Cyprus to be occupied and administered by England."

The underlined clause—*to be agreed upon later between the two Powers*—leaves not doubt that there had been no definite understanding about the kind of reforms and improvements Turkey was supposed to introduce for the protection of the Armenians who constituted the great majority of the Christians in Turkey.

The Duke of Argyll, one of England's greatest statesmen, made the following significant remark in the House of Commons: "In no part of the world has our policy been dictated by such immoral and senseless considerations."

The Berlin Conference

It should be noted that while the Cyprus Convention was being negotiated, England sought the intervention of the other European powers to reexamine and modify the San Stefano Treaty by amending or annulling some of its provisions. Article 16 of that treaty, pertaining to Armenia, was one of the principal topics on the agenda of the conference convened in Berlin on June 13, 1878, with the participation of all the great powers of Europe and presided over by Prince Bismarck of Germany.

Armenian Proposals to the Berlin Conference

An Armenian delegation, headed by Archbishop Mugurditch Khrimian, the former Patriarch of Constantinople, presented to the President of the Conference a Memorandum containing "proposals for the formulation of certain rules pertaining to Turkish Armenia" and accompanied by a map.

That memorandum deserves a reproduction:

I.

"In conformity with the chart attached hereto Turkish Armenia comprises Vilayets of Erzeroum and Van, the northern part of the Vilayet of Diarbekir, that is, the eastern part of the Sandjak of Kharpout (bounded on the west by the Euphrates river), the Sanjak of Arghana and the northern part of the Sandjak of Segherte, all of which form that part of Turkey known as Armenia Major, including the port of Rizi between Trebizonde and Batoum to facilitate commerce and exports.

"Armenia shall be administered by an Armenian Governor-General appointed by the Sublime Porte, with the consent of the guarantor powers. He shall reside in Erzeroum.

"The Governor-General shall be vested with all the prerogatives of an executive power; he shall safeguard the maintenance of order and the security of the people throughout the province; he shall collect taxes and shall appoint administrative agents responsible to him; he shall appoint judges and shall summon the General Council to a meeting and shall preside over such meeting; and he shall supervise over the entire administrative functions of the province.

"Invested with such authority for a period of five years the Governor-General shall not be removed by the Sublime Porte, except with the consent of the Guarantor Powers.

"There shall be a Central Administrative Council, under the presidency of the Governor-General, which shall be composed of the following:

1. The Director of Finances
2. The Director of Public Works
3. A legal Advisor
4. The Commander of the Armed Forces,
5. The Superintendent of Christian schools, and
6. The Superintendent of the Musulman schools, who shall be named by the Governor-General upon the recommendation of the Chief of the Judiciary of the *Cheri* in the province.

"The province shall be divided into *Sandjaks*, which in turn shall be subdivided into *cazas*. The Governors of *Sandjaks* and the Deputy Governors of *cazas* shall be appointed by the Governor-General.

"The governors and deputy-governors are the representative agents of the governor-general of the province and represent him in all the subdivisions of the province. They are assisted in their administration by two advisors appointed by the Governor-General.

II.

"The maintenance of order and public safety being the responsibility of the administration of the province, a sum equivalent of 20% of the general revenue of the province shall be paid annually to the Minister of Imperial Finances.

"From the rest of the revenues of the province the necessary expenses of civil and judicial administration and for the maintenance of the gendarmerie and the militia will be paid first and the remainder shall be used as follows:

"1. 80 % (of such remainder) shall be devoted to the construction and maintenance of roads and other public utilities.

"2. 20% shall be used for the establishment and maintenance of schools. Certain amounts shall be set aside for high schools and the rest shall be distributed, in form of subsidy between Musulman and Christian schools in proportion to the settled population of each religious group.

III.

"There shall be a chief Musulman magistrate, appointed by His Majesty the Sultan, who supervises over all the Courts of the *Cheri* functioning in the province. (The *Cheri* tribunals shall only deal with contests between Musulmans.)

"All the civil, criminal and commercial proceedings among Christians and between Christians and Musulmans shall be tried in ordinary tribunals. Each of these tribunals shall consist of three judges, one of whom acts as the presiding justice. The governor-general shall appoint the judges and shall designate the presiding justices of these tribunals.

"The justice of peace is named by the Deputy-Governor of the *caza* and his advisors.

"Specific rules shall determine the number, the competence and the qualifications of the members of *Cheri* tribunals and ordinary tribunals and the justices of peace. One civil and one criminal code shall be adopted to conform with the modern principles of justice in Europe.

IV.

"There shall be a complete freedom of worship.

"Each community shall be responsible for the support of the clergy and for the needs of religious institutions.

V.

"The Armed Forces of the province shall be supported by:

1. A gendarmerie
2. A militia.

"The militia shall be composed of:

1. Armenians
2. Non-Armenian elements having resided in the province for five consecutive years.

"Kurds, Circassians and other nomadic races are excluded from the militia.

"The gendarmerie shall be responsible for the maintenance of order and security throughout the province.

"It shall be under the command of a chief named by the governor-general as proposed by the commanding officer of the armed forces of the province and subject to his immediate orders.

"The militia shall be placed under the command of the Commanding General of the armed forces and shall have for its mission the support of the gendarmerie, in case of need.

"Under ordinary circumstances 4,000 men under arms in active service shall compose the militia, without prejudice to the garrison of regular troops which the Imperial Government may wish to place in the forts and strongholds of the province, at its own expense.

VI.

"The Council General shall be formed in the following manner:

"Each *caza* shall send two delegates, one Musulman and one Armenian, elected respectively by the Musulman and Christian population of the *Caza*.

"These delegates shall meet in the principal locality of the *Sandjak* and shall elect two councillors to represent the *Sandjak,* one Christian and one Musulman.

"The electors and those eligible shall be of two classes:

1. All the inhabitants of the province, over 25 years of age, who own property or pay tax of some sort;
2. The clergy and the ministers of different religious groups;
3. Professors and school masters. The chiefs of recognized religious communities shall be, by right, members of the said council, one for each religion.

"The General Council shall meet in session once a year at the principal place of the province, to examine and verify the budget of the province and determine the apportionment of the taxes. The governor-general shall submit to the council an annual financial accounting.

"The method of collecting and apportioning taxes may be modified with the view of facilitating the development of the riches of the country.

"The governor-general and the general council shall fix, with mutual understanding for all five years, the sums of money to be remitted to the Sublime Porte in accordance with the dispositions hereinabove stated.

VII.

"An international commission shall be appointed by the Guarantor Powers, for a period of one year, to supervise the implementation of these rules, which shall be put into effect within three months from the signing of the Protocol."

It can be assumed that copies of the above memorandum was circulated among all the delegates of the conference, but no one seems to have paid any attention to it.

The Treaty of Berlin

After a month's deliberation the Conference agreed upon a treaty on July 13, 1878, which nullified Article 16 of the San Stefano Treaty and substituted therefor the following articles:

"*Article 61:*—The Sublime Porte undertakes to carry out, without further delay, the amelioration and reforms demanded by local requirements in the provinces inhabited by the Armenians, and to guarantee their security against the Circassians and Kurds. It will make known periodically the steps taken to this effect to the Powers, who will superintend their application." (July 13, 1878)

"*Article 62:*—The Sublime Porte having expressed the wish to maintain the principle of religious liberty, to give it the widest scope, the contracting parties take note of this spontaneous declaration. In no part of the Ottoman Empire shall difference of religion be alleged against an individual as a ground for exclusion or in capacity as regards the discharge of civil and political rights, admission to the police service, functions and honors, and the exercise of the different professions and industries. All persons shall be admitted without distinction of religion to give evidence before the tribunals. Liberty and outward exercise of all forms of worship are assured to all, and no hindrance shall be offered either to hierarchial organizations of the various communions or their relation with their spiritual chief. The right of official protection by the diplomatic and consular agents of the powers in Turkey is recognized both as regards the above mentioned persons and their religions, charitable and other establishments in the holy places."

Comments on the Aftermath of the Treaty of Berlin

1. Dr. Fridtjof Nansen, in his excellent book *Armenia Under the Turks*, 1928, writes:

> In the Armenian people's long tale of woe the most woeful chapters are concerned with the time when the Armenians were under Turkish rule. To their Mohammedan 'masters' the Christians were slaves and chattels, whom the Allah had given to the faithful, and who were quite outside of the pale of the law. The evidence of an infidel— i.e. a Christian—against a Moslem was invalid in the law courts; nor could he defend himself against violence and robbery, because no Christian was allowed to carry arms; this of course gave the kurds and other marauders a pretty free hand. As Christians could not do war-service for Allah, every male between the ages of eight and sixty had to pay a specially heavy tax in addition to all the other taxes and dues. Furthermore, there was the "boy tax" which the Sultan exacted from the infidels; this consisted in taking every year thousands of boys, aged between four and eight, from Christian families, in order that they might be circumcised and brought up as Moslems to form the standing army of Janissaries which for long was Turkey's most formidable weapon against the Christians.

After making special reference to the various solemn proclamations which the Sultans issued as far back as 1839, after the Crimean War in 1856, again in 1876 (the year of the

Bulgarian atrocities), and later promising all subjects, irrespective of race and religion, equal rights, equality in the sight of the law, religious freedom "without compulsion of any sort" and "much beside" and after mentioning "the Russo-Turkish war in 1877–1878, which naturally raised such strong hopes in the breasts of the Armenians in Turkey, or the devious diplomatic negotiations of the subsequent peace conference at Berlin, in 1878, which approved the sultan's promises to give the Armenians better conditions," Dr. Nansen wrote:

"All this paper, all these fine promises, meant so many victories for West-European diplomacy and European justice and philanthropy which the diplomatists could exhibit to the world although they knew perfectly that the Turks had no intention of keeping their word."

"For the Armenians in the Turkish Empire," continues Dr. Nansen, "this was worse than nothing. It raised false hopes, and actually made things worse for them. It is the tragic truth that they would have been better off if the nations of Europe and their governments and diplomatists had never pleaded their cause at all. By their alleged sympathy with the Armenians and their representatives and notes demanding better treatment for them—demands which they *never once* made any serious sacrifice to try to enforce—they merely irritated the Turks, at the same time showing that they did not mean business."

After describing the looting by the Kurds of a number of villages in the district of Sassun, and the killing of thousands of Armenians, in which "several regiments and mountain artillery took part," Dr. Nansen wrote: "These outrages made public opinion uneasy, especially in England; but France and Russia, who were now allies (of Turkey), would do nothing. On the initiative of the Powers, however, a Turkish (!) commission was sent in January 1895 to 'investigate the criminal acts of the Armenian brigands.' In the end the consular officers also went to Sassun, and made it clear that the Armenian population were not to blame."

2. *Henry Morgenthau* makes the following comments about the consequences of the Treaty of Berlin in *All In A Lifetime*, 1927:

> This Congress could have freed all the subject peoples and solved the Eastern question, but again civilized Europe threw away the opportunity. At this Congress England, in the person of Disraeli, became the Sultan's advocate, and again the Sultan came out victorious. Certain territories he lost, it is true, but Constantinople was left in his hands and a great area of the Balkans and a larger part of Asia Minor. As for the Armenians, the Syrians, the Greeks, and the Macedonians, the world once more accepted from Turkey promises of reform. Thus Gladstone and the most enlightened opinion in England lost their battle, and British authority again became the instrument for preserving that "terrible oppression, that multitudinous crime which we call the Ottoman Empire."
>
> Had it not been for the Congress of Berlin it is possible that we should never have had the world war. . . . By leaving Turkey an independent sovereignty, with its capital on the Bosphorus, it made possible the intrigues of Germany for a great Oriental empire. No wonder Gladstone denounced it as an "insane covenant" and "the most deplorable chapter in our foreign policy since the peace of 1815." (p. 431)

3. *An Identical Note by the Powers:*

On June 11, 1880, an identical note of the great powers demanded the execution of different clauses of the Treaty of Berlin, which had hitherto remained in suspense. The note among other things reminded the Porte that by Article 61 of the treaty it "undertook to carry out without further delay the improvements and administrative reforms demanded by local requirements in the provinces inhabited by the Armenians and to guarantee their security against the attacks and the violence of Circassians and Kurds, and periodically to make known the steps taken to this effect to the powers who are to superintend their application," and complained that "nothing has been done by the Sublime Porte to make known the measures which it may have taken in order to meet the stipulations of Article 61 of the Treaty of Berlin, nor have any measures been adopted by the Porte for the superintendence to be exercised by the Powers."

4. *The Turkish Reply and the Collective Note of the Ambassadors:*

On July 5th, the Turkish Foreign Minister, Abeddin Pasha, replied to that note lengthily, but his answers and explanations were not considered satisfactory by the ambassadors of the great powers. "A careful study," said the reply, "of this document has proved to them that the proposals made by the Ottoman Government do not meet either the spirit nor the letter of this Article." This collective note of the ambassadors dated September 7, 1880, contained the following, concluding paragraphs:

"It is absolutely necessary to carry out, without loss of time, the reforms intended to secure life and property of the Armenians; to take immediate measures against the incursions of the Kurds; to carry out at once the proposed system of finance; to place the gendarmerie provisionally on a more satisfactory footing; and, above all, to give the governors-general greater security of office and a more extended responsibility.

"In conclusion, the powers once more recall to the Sublime Porte the essential fact that the reforms to be introduced into the provinces inhabited by the Armenians are, by Treaty engagements, to be adapted to local wants, and to be carried out under the supervision of the Powers." (Signed) Hatzfeldt, Novikow, G. J. Goschen, Corti, Tissot, Calice.

5. *Protest and Complaints Rejected by the Turks:*

In spite of the collective demands of the Great Powers the Sublime Porte acted on its own and paid no attention to these demands. The appointments of *mudirs* and various other functionaries in the formation of communes were "ridiculous." In one district only one *mudir* out of seventeen could read and write Turkish. Protests against these appointments were of no avail. On the contrary, the Turkish authorities considered such protests contemptible and ridiculous.

6. *Captain Everett,* dispatch dated December 16, 1880, in Blue Book, Turkey, No. 8, 1881, page 293, quoted in *Armenia, the Armenians and Treaties:*

"If a year ago there was little security for life and property, now there is still less; if there was poverty, it is greater; if there was injustice, so there is at present; while the crimes of oppression and corruption have increased proportionately with the impoverished state of the Empire."

7. *A. N. Mnatzukanian,* in his book *The Tragedy of the Armenian People,* writes:

"According to published sources in the years from 1820–1890 93,000 Armenians, Greeks and Bulgars have been massacred in Turkey of the Sultans. An English author, McCool, has written that the 'outrage had been long premeditated.' He tells about the partial massacres of Armenians in 1822, in 1828–1867, and in 1877. One of the chapters of his book is entitled 'The Massacres of Christians were being carried out periodically.' "

The Great Powers Lose Interest in Armenian Affairs

Scarcely two years had gone by when the Great Powers began to lose interest in the Armenian reforms. On January 12, 1881 Earl Granville instructed the Ambassadors of Her Majesty at Paris, Berlin, Vienna, St. Petersburg and Rome to tell those governments of the state of affairs in Armenia.

The circular, addressed to each of the Great Powers, stated in part: "The way in which the Porte is dealing with its offer of reforms would appear to furnish grounds for remonstrance on the part of the representatives, and Her Majesty's Government would be glad if the – – – – – – – Government would instruct their Ambassador at Constantinople to join with his colleagues in a representation to the Sublime Porte on the subject."

Mr. Rolin-Jaequemyns comments:

If any Power at any time had considered it compatible with its interests to reply frankly to the English proposal, it would have said to Earl Granville: 'Our isolated demands have not been listened to; our Identical Note was answered evasively; our Collective Note has not been answered at all—in fact, no notice has been taken of it. The situation is such that if Armenia does not at once rebel, it is because the reign of terror and extermination which oppresses her, deprives her of the strength to do so. What, therefore, do you expect from a fresh Collective Note, if the Turkish Government is not convinced that, in case it continues to act in violation of Article 61 of the Berlin Treaty, Europe will carry it into effect of its own accord? If, as is right, you ask for deeds and not words, begin by proving yourself that you are ready to pass from threats to actions.' (p. 98)

But no power made such a reply. All answers were evasive. Russia and Italy agreed to join the representatives of other signatory powers. Austria found no "sufficient occasion" for a collective representation. France replied that "Prince Bismarck expressed the opinion that there would be serious inconvenience in raising the Armenian Question before the definitive settlement of the Greek Question," so she was not sure that the present was "opportune" for "the line of action" as recommended by Her Majesty's Government. Prince Bismarck did really express the opinion that "it was better to concentrate the representatives of the Powers on one question at a time."

The enforcement of sanctions unanimously adopted by the Great Powers was set aside indefinitely and sentenced to die a natural death. "Christian and civilized Europe was more occupied with its internecine quarrels and jealousies than its collective duties," as these other excerpts show:

1. *Clifford Lloyd*, dispatch dated October 2, 1890, addressed to the British Foreign Office and published in the Blue Book, Turkey, No. 1, 1890–91, Mr. Lloyd (Her Majesty's Consul at Erzeroum) writes in part:

"It is admitted by everyone that a change is necessary in the system of government now being applied to the Christian population of Kurdistan, i.e. the Armenian people. Their sufferings at present proceed from these direct causes:

"1. The insecurity of their lives and properties owing to their habitual ravages by the Kurds.

"2. The insecurity of their persons, and the absence of all liberty of thought and action (excepting the exercise of public worship).

"3. The unequal status held by the Christians as compared with the Musulmans in the eyes of the government."

2. *Edward C. Little,* Congressman from Kansas, in a speech delivered before the House of Representatives, on February 7, 1918, makes the following comment on the Berlin Treaty:

In 1878, when Beaconsfield and Bismarck held the great Berlin conference that was supposed to settle the destiny of Europe forever, Mugurditch Khurimian, long the Armenian Patriarch of Constantinople, with three others, appeared to represent the Armenian people at this congress of Berlin. They secured an agreement in that great treaty that the Armenians should hereafter have justice from the Turkish Government, an agreement guaranteed by all the great powers of Europe. This was never carried out by the Turks, was never sustained by the guarantors, and the continued persistence of the Armenians in demanding its enforcement had much to do with the terrible massacres to which they have been subjected since. They actually stood up for their rights under the law, just as an American would, something no Turk could endure from a Christian, and especially from an Armenian.

3. *William Gladstone,* "The Berlin Treaty and the Anglo-Turkish Convention," a speech in the House of Commons, July 30, 1878:

I have not, Sir, however, gone through the whole work of the Congress. We have had most important engagements undertaken by the whole of assembled Europe with respect to Armenia. The noble Lord appears to be under the impression that although Russia has acquired a new frontier for herself in Armenia that is all which has occurred, and that with the exception of that single change, the entire field of Asiatic Turkey has been left open to us by the Treaty of Berlin. The noble Lord must have overlooked that article of the Treaty which refers to the future conditions of Armenia. It is not a field left open to us. The whole of the Powers of Europe have required from the Porte the information—which means the transformation—of the government of Armenia. They have obtained from the Porte a Treaty stipulation to that effect. That Treaty stipulation has been concluded by Turkey, not only with all the Powers, but with each Power. In the Treaty of Paris, in 1856, the Powers made provision against the single action within the Turkish Empire of any among them. There is no such settlement in the Treaty of Berlin. The covenants of Turkey are covenants with all, and are likewise covenants with each, and each Power with which the engagements have been contracted would be entitled to call Turkey to account for the breach of those engagements. There is, therefore, a most important provision made for the future intervention of Europe in the internal affairs of that portion of Asiatic Turkey which borders upon the Russian frontier. It must, however, Sir, revert to Turkey in Europe, with which I have not yet completely finished.

4. *Sir Tilford Vaugh*, the author of *Turkey, Yesterday, To-Day and To-morrow*, 1930. In Chapter I, entitled "The Days Before Yesterday," Lord Vaugh makes the following comment:

The equality between Moslem and Christian, proclaimed in 1839, had in no way been realized. It was found necessary to reaffirm the principle in a further edict, known as the 'Khat i Humayun,' which was solemnly read at the Sublime Porte on February 18th, 1856. It contained twenty articles, one of which provided for the admission of all Turkish subjects to military service. The European Powers took note of this Firman in article 9 of the Treaty of Paris. Equality between Moslems and Raya necessarily involved equal liabilities, and this proved the stumbling-block. The Christians themselves were unwilling to be enrolled in Moslem regiments, and the Government had no confidence in the fidelity of exclusively Christian regiments. The problem remained insoluble, even when the Union and Progress Revolution of 1908 proclaimed its grand principle of liberty, equality, fraternity and justice; and its solution was ultimately found in the extermination of the Christians in Turkey by massacre and forced exchange of population.

5. *William E. Gladstone*, a letter dated April 20, 1895 to Rev. Frederick D. Greene, author of the book entitled *The Rule of the Turk and the Armenian Crisis*, 1897:

"Dear Sir:

"I am glad to hear that your book is about to (be) published.

"I believe it will materially assist in arousing public attention to the recent outrages in Armenia which almost pass description and have inflicted indelible disgrace on the Sultan of Turkey and on his officers and soldiers concerned in perpetrating, in denying, and in shielding them.

"I remain, dear Sir,

Your very faithful and obedient"

W. E. Gladstone

6. *Rev. Edwin M. Bliss*, in the concluding Chapter XXX of his book *Turkey and the Armenian Atrocities*, reproduces a letter from "one of the largest cities in the empire," from which the following excerpts are presented here:

Do they (Christian nations) know that, horrible and revolting as was the savagery of the recent massacres, they have been narrow in effect and tame in cruel barbarity compared with the deliberate, malicious and unrelenting, crushing and grinding process to which the remnant of the Armenian people are being subjected? . . . Overcrowded dungeons, unfit for men to stay in, the most violent and offensive insults, beatings and torture till the victim faints, are not uncommon; live coals put upon the naked bodies of men, sodomy forced upon an Armenian priest, are among amusements in which Turkish jailers have been freely indulging.

These are only *specimens of classes of facts* [Emphasis ours—D.H.B.] of which I have the most unimpeachable evidence; and what is more, these things are part of a *plan* [Emphasis ours—D.H.B] which is being carried out in the end of this nineteenth century by a government in treaty with Christian nations, and under the most solemn pledges and obligations to secure special privileges to its Christian subjects.

Dr. Bliss ends his book with the following quotation:

"Though the mills of God grind slowly, yet they grind exceedingly small; Though with patience He stands waiting, with exactness grinds He all."

7. *William Willard Howard*, writes in his *Horrors of Armenia*, 1896:

As a result of the Sultan's promises of reform three thousand villages are in ruins, fifty thousand persons are dead, half a million are naked and hungry, all business is at an end, and an industrious, peaceful people are on the verge of utter extermination.

True prophecy: The future is as plain as the past. Even without a renewal of wholesale massacres in obedience to orders from the 'Shadow of God on Earth' there will be the same raping and ravishing of women and girls, the same beating and torturing of men, and the same skinning and burning of priests as in the recent past. In the event of general massacres men will be burned alive in pits in the ground, and the earth will be trampled down upon their writhing bodies. Other living men will be bound hand and foot and corded up in rows, one row upon another, with brushwood between. The kerosene oil will be poured upon the squirming mass and set on fire. Moslem fiends will dance about this awful funeral pile until the bodies of these Christian men have burned to ashes. These things will be done, because they have been done in Armenia within the past two years.

That the Sultan of Turkey has a tangible reason for putting Christians to death in this wholesale way there can be no doubt. He says that he is suppressing revolutionary uprising, but that is ridiculous. There is no revolutionary uprising . . . The real reason for the massacres is to be found in this Mohammedan prayer: (p. 42)

(Editor's Note: That prayer is more fully quoted by Rev. Frederick D. Greene, in his book *The Rule of the Turk*, on page 75, as follows):

"I seek refuge with Allah from Satan, the accursed. In the name of Allah the Compassionate, the Merciful! O Lord of all creatures! O Allah! Destroy the infidels and polytheists, thine enemies, the enemies of the religion! O Allah! Make their children orphans, and defile their abodes! Cause their feet to slip; give them and their families, their households and their women, their children and their relations by marriage, their brothers and their friends, their possessions and their race, their wealth and their lands, as booty to the Moslems, O Lord of all Creatures!"

8. *Rev. James Wilson Pierce*, author of the *Story of Turkey and Armenia*, 1896. In Chapter IX of his book Dr. Pierce reproduces verbatim a speech by William E. Gladstone on August 6, 1895, discussing the claims of the Armenians in Turkey. The following are extracts from that speech:

> Now, it was my fate, I think some six or more months ago to address a very limited number . . . of Armenian gentlemen and gentlemen interested in Armenia, on this subject, and at that time I ventured to point out that one of our duties was to avoid premature judgments. There was no authoritative and impartial declaration before the world at that period on the subject of what is known as the Sassoun Massacre; that massacre to which the noble duke (of Westminster) has alluded and with respect to which, horrible as that massacre was, one of the most important witnesses in this case declares that it is thrown into the shade and has become pale and ineffective by the side of the unspeakable horrors which are being enacted from month to month, from week to week, from day to day in the different provinces of Armenia. It was a duty to avoid premature judgment, and I think it was avoided. There was a great reserve, but at last the engine of dispassionate inquiry was brought to bear, and then it was found that another duty, very important in general in these

cases, really in this particular instance had no particular place at all, and though it is a duty to avoid exaggeration, a most sacred duty, it is a duty that has little or no place in the case before us, because it is too well known that the powers of language hardly suffice to describe what has been and is being done, and that exaggeration, if we were ever so much disposed to it, is in such a case really beyond our power. . . .

The whole substance of the situation may be summed up in four awful words—plunder, murder, rape and torture. Every incident turns upon one or upon several of those awful words. Plunder and murder you would think are bad enough, but plunder and murder are venial by the side of the work of the ravisher and the work of the torturer, as it is described in these pages, and as it is now fully and authentically known to be going on . . . In all ordinary cases when we have before us instances of crime, perhaps a very horrible crime—for example, there is a sad story in the papers today of a massacre in a portion of China—we at once assume that in all countries unfortunately, there are malefactors, there are plunderers whose deeds we are going to consider. Here, my Lord Duke, it is nothing of the kind; we have nothing to do here with what are called the dangerous classes of the community; it is not their proceedings which you are asked to consider; it is the proceedings of the government of Constantinople and its agents.

There is not one of these misdeeds for which the government at Constantinople is not morally responsible. Now, who are these agents? . . . They fall into three classes. The first have been mentioned by the noble Duke, namely, the savage Kurds, who are, unhappily, the neighbors of the Armenians, the Armenians being the representatives of one of the oldest civilized Christian races, and being beyond all doubt one of the most pacific, one of the most industrious and one of the most intelligent races in the world. These Kurds are by them; they are wild, savage clans . . . These the Sultan and the government at Contantinople have enrolled, though in a nominal fashion.

. . . When I say that a case of this kind puts exaggeration out of question, I am making a very broad statement, which would in most cases be violent, which would in all ordinary cases be unwarrantable. But those who will go through the process (of examining the documents) I have described, or even a limited portion of the process, will find that words are not too strong for the occasion.

Dr. Pierce reproduces in his book an abridged version of an article by E. J. Dillon, entitled "The Condition of Armenia," originally published in the *Contemporary Review*, January 1896. We quote the following from that article:

> Turkey's real sway in Armenia dates from the year 1847, when Osman Pasha gave the final *coup de grace* to the secular power of the Kurdish *Derebeks* (chieftains) in the five southeastern provinces (Van, Bitlis, Moush, Bayazid and Diarbekir). During that long spell of nearly fifty years we can clearly distinguish two periods: one of shameful misgovernment (1847–1891), and the other (1892–1894) of frank extermination.
>
> This plain policy of extermination has been faithfully carried out and considerably extended from that day to this, and unless speedily arrested will undoubtedly lead to a final solution of the Armenian problem. But a solution which will disgrace Christianity and laugh civilization to scorn.
>
> The massacre of Sassoun itself is now proved to have been the deliberate deed of the representatives of the Sublime Porte, carefully planned and unflinchingly executed....
>
> An eminent foreign statesman, who is commonly credited with Turcophile sentiments of uncompromising thoroughness, lately remarked to me in private conversation that Turkish rule in Armenia might be aptly described as organized brigandage, legalized murder and meritorious immorality.
>
> There is no redress whatever for a Christian who has suffered in property, limb, or life at the hands of Mohammedans; not because the law officers are careless or lethargic, but because they are specially retained on the other side. And the proof of this, if any proof were needed, is that the complainants themselves are speedily punished for lodging an information against their persecutors. But whenever a Kurd or a Turk is the victim of a "crime," or even an accident, the energy of the government officials knows no bounds.
>
> The Armenians are naturally peaceful in all places; pas-

sionately devoted to agriculture in the country, and wholly absorbed by mercantile pursuits in the towns. Lest their inborn aversion to bloodshed, however, should be overcome by the impulse of duty, the instinct of self-defense, or deep-rooted affection for those near and dear to them, they are forbidden to possess arms, and the tortures that are inflicted on the few who disregard this law would bring a blush to the cheek of a countryman of Confucius. They must rely for protection exclusively upon the Turkish soldiers and the Turkish law.

English people have not even a remote notion of the extent to which young married women and girls were outraged all over Armenia by Turkish soldiers, Imperial Zaptiehs, Kurdish officers and brigands—and outraged with such accompaniments of nameless bestiality that their agonies often culminate in a horrible death. Girls of eleven and twelve—nay, of nine—are torn from their families and outraged in this way by a band of "men" whose names are known, and whose deeds are approved by the representatives of law and order.

9. Rev. George H. Filian, in his book entitled *Armenia and Her People,* quotes E. J. Dillon's article published in *The Contemporary Review,* January 1896. We quote the first paragraph:

"If a detailed description were possible of the horrors which our exclusive attention to our own mistaken interests let loose upon Turkish Armenians there is not a man within the Kingdom of Great Britain whose heart-strings would not be touched and thrilled by the gruesome stories of which it would be composed."

10. *Rev. Ohan Gaidzakian,* in *Illustrated Armenia,* 1898, quotes from the Dillon article:

During all those seventeen years, written law, traditional custom, the fundamental maxims of human and divine justice were suspended in favor of a Mohammedan Saturnalia. The Christians, by whose toil and thrift the Empire was held together, were despoiled, beggared, chained, beaten and banished or butchered. First their movable wealth was seized, then their landed property was confiscated, next the absolute necessaries of life were wrested from them, and finally honor, liberty and life were taken with as little ado as if these Christian men and women were wasps or mosquitoes.

. . . . Human hatred, and diabolical spite, combined with the most disgusting sights and sounds, and stenches, with their gnawing hunger and their putrid food, their parching thirst and the slimy water, fit only for sewers, rendering their agony maddening. Yet these were not criminals nor alleged criminals, but upright Christian men who were never even accused of an infraction of the law. No man who has not seen these prisons with his own eyes, and heard these prisoners with his own ears can be expected to conceive, much less realize, the sufferings inflicted and endured. The loathsome diseases whose terrible ravages were freely displayed; the still more loathsome vices which were continuously and openly practiced, the horrible blasphemies, revolting obscenities, and ribald jests which alternated with cries of pain, songs of vice, and prayers to the unseen God, made these prisons in some respects, nearly as bad as the Black Hole of Calcutta, and in others infinitely worse. In one corner of this foul fever-nest a man might be heard moaning and groaning with the pain of a shattered arm or leg; in another, a youth is convulsed with the death spasms of cholera or poison; in the centre, a knot of Turks, whose dull eyes are fired with bestial lust, surround a Christian boy who pleads for mercy with heart-rending voice while the human fiends actually outrage him to death.

. . . . Nights were passed in such hellish orgies and days in inventing new tortures or refining upon the old, with an ingenuity which reveals unimagined strata of malignity in the human heart. The results throw the most sickening horrors of the Middle Ages into the shade. Some of them cannot be described nor *even* hinted at. The shock to people's sensibilities would be too terrible. And yet they were not merely described to, but endured by men of education and refinement, whose sensibilities were as delicate as ours.

. . . . In the homes of these wretched people the fiendish fanatics were equally active and equally successful. Family life was poisoned at its very source. Rape and dishonor, with nameless accompaniments, menaced almost every girl and woman in the land. They could not stir out of their houses in broad daylight to visit the bazaars, or to work in the fields, nor even to lie down at night in their own homes, without fearing the fall of that Damocles' sword ever suspended over their heads. Tender youth, childhood itself, was no guarantee . . . A bride would be married in church yesterday, and her body would be devoured by the beasts and birds of prey tomorrow,—a band of ruffians, often officials, having within the intervening forty-eight hours seized her and outraged her to death.

11. *Dr. Johannes Lepsius,* author of *Armenia and Turkey: An Indictment,* English translation, London, Hodder & Stoughton, 1897, gives a detailed account of the massacres in the Armenian provinces, during the years 1895–1896 and makes the following indictments against Turkey in Chapter I of his book, entitled *The Truth about Armenia:*

All such proofs of the guilt of the authorities, both civil and military, could be multiplied indefinitely, but we think that no further representation is needed to convince our readers, and we therefore condense our indictments against the Turkish authorities of the Armenian provinces under the following heads:

I. The civil and military authorities have in no way obstructed the preparation for the massacres on the part of the Mohammedan population, either by their spontaneous action, or even in response to appeals from the chief Armenians of the districts or from the consuls.

II. The civil and military authorities have themselves organized these preparations by taking the following measures before each outbreak:

1. They enforced, in a thorough and systematic manner, the disarming of the Armenian population.

2. They left the Mohammedan population in possession of their arms.

3. They even went beyond this and supplied the Turkish and Kurdish population with an abundance of weapons partly taken from the military depots.

4. Certain *valis* and military commanders made tours in the vilayets in order to incite the population to plunder, to distribute weapons, and to invite the tribes of Kurds and Circassians to the assault of Armenian villages and quarters, giving them special instruction how to proceed.

5. They deceived the Christian population by assuring

them of protection, and by quartering soldiers on them and calling out the Reserves, which ostensibly were placed there for the preservation of order, while in fact they were instructed to take part in the massacre and loot.

6. They made the assault and plundering of bazaars possible by obliging the townspeople, who in view of the threatening massacre had closed their shops and withdrawn into their houses, to open them again and resume business. This they did either by raising illusive hopes that peace was soon to be restored, or by absolute commands and violent coercion.

III. The civil and military authorities made themselves responsible in many ways for the massacre, by personal co-operation with the highest officials in the plunder, and forced conversions, since

1. They fixed the exact time for the outbreak of the massacres;

2. They arranged a definite period of days and hours, during which liberty to murder and plunder with impunity was given to the Kurds, the mob, and the soldiery;

3. The massacres were begun and closed with the sound of a trumpet or some other signal;

4. The Christian population who sought help were repulsed or the supplicants arrested;

5. Appeals for help and telegraphic petitions to the highest authorities, especially the Sultan, were stopped;

6. Before, during and after the massacres countless arrests of Armenians took place, the majority of whom without the formality of legal proceedings languish still in prisons, and many have suffered most horrible tortures;

7. The military, the Redifs, the Kurds, and the Circassians were commanded to take part in the massacres;

8. They secured to themselves a share of the booty by means of the troops or police placed under their command.

IV. The civil authorities attempted to hide or excuse the fact of the massacres and plunder when all was over.

1. They falsely accused the Armenians of instigating them;

2. By imprisonment, by threats of death or fresh massacres, they extracted from the chief Armenians declarations that the Armenians had been the cause of the outbreaks,

and that, thanks to the measures taken by the authorities, order was again restored;

3. They sought, as far as was practicable by a systematic disposal of the corpses, to do away with all trace of the devastation;

4. They prevented transmission of intelligence by opening the letters of the victims, by hindering emigration, and by refusing admission to foreign correspondents;

5. Here and there they ordered an apparent restoration of stolen property, in which only the most worthless things, only indeed one-hundredth part of what had been lost, were restored;

6. They made proclamations prohibiting massacres, plunder, and compulsory conversions, without seeing that these were enforced.

V. The authorities did nothing to avert the inevitable consequences of the massacres from the inhabitants whose property had been thoroughly plundered.

1. Any support given to the suffering people from the government was ridiculously inadequate, and was stopped again in a few days;

2. The pains taken by the European committees of relief to relieve the misery were baulked in every imaginable fashion, and it was only at the energetic initiative of the English Ambassador, as the president of the international relief committee, that any change was effected in this respect;

3. Nothing was done for the rebuilding of houses, for the recultivation of the land, or the protection of the sufferers in view of the coming winter;

4. The emigration of the sufferers was stopped.

5. No care of any sort was taken of the hundreds of thousands of widows, orphans, sick and helpless;

6. The last remnants of the property of the sufferers were generally taken from them by rigorous taxation, and in the same way they were even robbed of the money which they had received for their support.

VI. No obstacle to a repetition of the massacres or to an attack on districts as yet unaffected by them must be expected even now from the authorities. On the contrary, as the latest massacres (June 1896) in Van, Egin and

Niksar, and the disturbances in Trebizond in August last (1896), as well as the forced conversions everywhere abundantly prove, the annihilation of the Armenian people is still being systematically completed.

VII. The originators and accomplices of the wholesale murder, plunder, and forced conversions remain unpunished.

12. *Frank Maloy Anderson and Amos Shartle Hershey*, in their *Handbook for the Diplomatic History of Europe, Asia, and Africa* provide an accurate summary of the period of Abdul Hamid's rule:

THE ARMENIAN QUESTION, 1878–1897

1. *Treaties of San Stefano and Berlin, 1878*

The Armenian question may be said to have arisen after the close of the Russo-Turkish War of 1877–1878. By article 16 of the Treaty of San Stefano, Turkey had agreed to "carry into effect, without further delay, the improvements and reforms made necessary by local needs in the provinces inhabited by the Armenians, and to guarantee their security against the Kurds and Circassians."

This provision was superseded by article 61 of the Treaty of Berlin, which stipulated in addition that the Sublime Porte should "give notice periodically of the measures taken to this end to the Powers, who will watch over their application." It should be noted particularly that the obligation undertaken by Turkey at Berlin was to the powers, whereas in the Treaty of San Stefano it had only been to Russia.

(After citing Article 62 of the Treaty of Berlin, which is intended "to maintain the principle of religious liberty", the authors continue:)

Though the Armenians are not specifically mentioned in this article, they were entitled to claim the benefit of its provisions.

By the Cyprus Convention of June 4, 1878, the Sultan also promised Great Britain to introduce necessary reforms "for the protection of the Christians and other subjects of the Porte" in the Turkish territories in Asia. . . .

2. *Failure of Policy of Enforcement, 1878–1882.*

It soon became evident that there was to be no attempt to carry out the provisions of the treaties on the part of the Turkish Government. In April, 1879, Lord Salisbury laid it down that "the Sultan is bound not only to promulgate new and better laws, but to actually introduce reforms." In November, 1879, the English Government went to length of ordering an English squadron to the Archipelago for the purpose of a naval demonstration. This brought nothing but fair promises.

On June 11, 1880, an identical note of the great powers demanded the execution of different clauses of the treaty of Berlin, including that of article 61. (British and Foreign State Papers, vol. 72, pp. 469–470.) The Ottoman Government replied in a note of July 5, indicating certain so-called executed and intended reforms. (Ibid., pp. 1197–1200.) The powers replied in a collective note, dated September 7, 1880, severely censuring the so-called reforms and proposing others. (Ibid., pp. 1201–1207.) To this collective note of the powers, the Sublime Porte did not even deign to reply; but assuming a haughty tone, merely notified the powers of what it intended to do in a note dated October 3, 1880.

In a circular of January 12, 1881, Earl Granville instructed the British ambassadors at Paris, Berlin, etc., to call the attention of the Governments to which they were accredited to the state of affairs in Armenia. He said:

The way in which the Porte is dealing with its offer of reforms would appear to furnish food for remonstrance, and her Majesty's Government would be glad if the Governments would instruct their ambassadors at Constantinople to join with his colleagues in a representation to the Sublime Porte on the subject.

Austria declined to act in concert with the other powers, and Bismarck expressed the opinion that it was better for the powers to concentrate on one question at a time. "When the Greek question is over, it will be the moment to begin the Armenian question," he said. France hid herself behind the refusal of Germany. Only Italy and Russia gave a conditional assent. It was, indeed, evident that the policy of enforcement by the powers was a failure.

3. *Period of European Indifference, 1882–1889.*

There followed a period of European indifference to reform in Armenia. The consequence of this indifference and neglect was the rise of a nationalist movement in Armenia and the formation of revolutionary societies. London was a center of propaganda, and the Sultan became very much alarmed. The Russian Government was also alarmed lest the revolutionary and nationalistic movement spread to Russian Armenia. During this period Anglo-French rivalry in Egypt was intense, and France showed a disposition to support Russian intrigue in the Near East, whereas Germany supported Austria. The foundation and rise of German influence in Turkey, which certainly did not favor the Armenians, can be traced to this period.

4. *Period of Agitation in England, 1889–1893.*

In 1890 there was formed the Anglo-Armenian Association, and an increasing agitation in behalf of Armenia began to manifest itself in England. An active propaganda was also carried on in Turkish Armenia, but was strongly opposed by the Armenian clergy and the American missionaries.

5. *Massacres of 1894–1896.*

In August–September, 1894, occurred the brutal Sassoun massacres, in which Turkish soldiers took part. In November, 1894, a Turkish commission of enquiry, accompanied by the consular delegates of Great Britain, France, and Russia, was sent to Armenia. It elicited the fact that there had been no attempt at revolt to justify the action of the Turkish authorities. Throughout the year 1894 the British Government, supported in lukewarm fashion by France and Russia, urged administrative reforms in Armenia.

On May 11, 1895, Great Britain, France, and Russia presented to the Sultan a complicated scheme of reforms. Great Britain alone favored coercion. The Sultan delayed his reply, and finally appealed to France and Russia against England.

While these negotiations had been going on, disturbances arose at Tarsus, Armenians were murdered, and the life of the patriarch threatened. On October 1, 1895, a riot occurred in Constantinople in which a number of Armenians and some Moslems were killed.

The British ambassador now pressed the scheme of reforms upon the Sultan, who accepted it on October 17. Meanwhile there had been a massacre at Trebizond on October 8, in which armed men from Constantinople took part. Finding there was to be no coercion, the Sultan refused to publish the scheme of reforms he had accepted, and organized massacre followed massacre until the summer of 1896. The number of those who perished in these massacres during this period has been variously estimated at from 20,000 to 50,000.* Many were forced to embrace Mohammedanism.

6. *Final Failure of the European Concert, 1896–1897.*

In August, 1896, the powers again demanded action by the Sultan and (on September 2) sent him a collective note reviewing the entire situation. On October 20 Lord Salisbury once more proposed a joint reform program to be followed by coercive measures in case of refusal by the Sultan. On December 26, 1896, a conference of ambassadors met at Constantinople to discuss matters. It ended on February 10, 1897, without accomplishing any real result. By 1898, when the German Emperor visited Jerusalem and Damascus (See article, The Journeys of William II to the Near East), it had become evident that Germany was becoming the power behind the Sultan's throne and that so far at least as Armenia was concerned the treaties of 1878 had long been dead, if, indeed it may be claimed that they were ever alive. (pp. 216–219)

The documents we have presented in this Appendix to Chapter 2 reveal that the conditions of the Armenians under Abdul Hamid were not only intolerable but also were impossible of alleviation because of the apathy and conflicting interests of the great powers. That they could have become worse after Abdul would have then seemed inconceivable, but the ultimate tragedy was still to come.

* The authenticated number of persons perished during that period is closer to 300,000.

APPENDIX A

Chapter 4

It is no part of this book's purpose to present a catalogue of horrors, but it is important to present as fully as space permits those documents which attest to the actual suffering of the victims of Turkish brutality. If their suffering were to go down in history merely as additional evidence of man's inhumanity to man, many of them would be omitted here. The fact is, however, that to bring before the reader the testimony of reliable, skilled, and humane observers and commentators, documents the grievances of the Armenian people.

Grievances have been common in the checkered history of the human race, but grievances of the dimensions of 1915–1916 in Turkey have been rare, in the Western world unprecedented until World War II. If there is any validity to the ideal of "redress of grievances," which a chastened Germany acknowledged freely after World War II, there can never be too much reliable documentation.

The sufferings of the Armenians at the hands of the Turks form a large part, though not by any means all, of the Armenian demand for a homeland. Theft alone demands redress. When it is combined with every conceivable variety of murder, torture, and rape, it cries aloud to be heard as a part of the record.

The accounts of Armenian suffering are often harrowing, and many of them testify to the precision and skill of the observers, while others merely show the simple humanity of outraged spectators. In this appendix, they form an overwhelming testimony to the Armenian cause.

Viscount James Bryce compiled many documents under the title of *The Treatment of Armenians in the Ottoman Empire, 1915–19*, a remarkable volume containing 149 documents, most of which are from non-Armenian sources. We regret that it will not be possible for us to reproduce all of these documents, but we feel confident that the following will sufficiently describe the horrors to which the Armenian people were subjected so ruthlessly by their persecutors, who were bent upon exterminating an entire nation.

Lord Bryce, through whose efforts this great volume came to light, confidently writes: "Life will assuredly spring up again when the ashes are cleared away, for attempts to exterminate nations by atrocity, though certain of producing almost infinite human suffering, have seldom succeeded in their ulterior aim." (pp. 594–595)

Here are extracts from reports published by Viscount Bryce:

(a) *An authoritative source at Constantinople*, letter dated 2/15 August, 1915, says in part:

It is now established that there is not an Armenian left in the provinces of Erzeroum, Trebizond, Sivas, Harpout, Bitlis and Diyarbekir. About a million of the Armenian inhabitants of these provinces have been deported from their homes and sent southwards into exile. These deportations have been carried out very systematically by the local authorities since the beginning of April last. First of all, in every village and every town, the population was disarmed by the gendarmerie, and by criminals released for this purpose from prison. On the pretext of disarming the Armenians, these criminals committed assassinations and inflicted hideous tortures. Next, they imprisoned the Armenians *en masse,* on the pretext that they had found in their possession arms, books, a political organisation, and so on—at a pinch, wealth or any kind of social standing was pretext enough. After that, they began the deportation. And, first, on the pretext of sending them into exile, they evicted such men as had not been imprisoned, or such as had been set at liberty through lack of any charge against them; then they massacred them—not one of these escaped slaughter. Before they started, they were examined officially by the authorities, and any money or valuables in their possession were confiscated. They were usually shackled—either separately, or in gangs of five to ten. The remainder—old men, women and children—were treated as waifs in the province of Harpout, and placed at the disposal of the Moslem population. The highest official, as well as the most simple peasant, chose out the woman or girl who caught his fancy, and took her to wife, converting her by force to Islam. As for the children, the Moslems took as many of them as they wanted, and then the remnant of the Armenians were marched away, famished and destitute of provisions, to fall victims to hunger, unless that were anticipated by the savagery of the brigand-bands.

(b) *Statement of a German eye-witness of occurrences at Moush* (abstracts):

Towards the end of October (1914), when the Turkish war began, the Turkish officials started to take everything they needed for the war from the Armenians. Their goods, their money, all was confiscated. Later on, every Turk was free to go to an Armenian shop and take out what he needed or thought he would like to have. Only a tenth was really for war, the rest was pure robbery. . .

Towards the middle of April (1915) we heard rumours that there were great disturbances in Van. . . All villages inhabited by Armenians were burnt down. At the beginning of June we heard that the whole population of Bitlis had been got rid of. . . . In Moush itself, there are 25,000 Armenians; in the neighborhood there are 300 villages, each containing about 500 houses. In all these not a single male Armenian is now to be seen, and hardly a woman either, except for a few here and there. . . Every officer boasted of the number he had personally massacred as his share in ridding Turkey of the Armenian race.

We left for Harpout. Harpout has become the cemetery of the Armenians; from all directions they have been brought to Harpout to be buried. There they lie, and the dogs and the vultures devour their bodies. Now and then some man throws some earth over the bodies. In Harpout and Mezre the people have had to endure terrible tortures. They have had their eye-brows plucked out, their breasts cut off, their nails torn off; their torturers hew off their feet or else hammer nails into them just as they do in shoeing horses. This is all done at night time, and in order that the people may not hear their screams and know of their agony, soldiers are stationed round the prisons, beating drums and blowing whistles. It is needless to relate that many died of these tortures. When they die, the soldiers cry: 'Now let your Christ help you.' . . .

Early in July, 2,000 Armenian soldiers were ordered to leave for Aleppo to build roads. The people of Harpout were terrified on hearing this, and a panic started in town. The Vali sent for the German missionary, Mr. Ehemann, and begged him to quiet the people, repeating over and over again that no harm whatever would befall these soldiers. Mr. Ehemann took the Vali's word and quieted the people. But they had scarcely left when we heard that they had all been murdered and thrown into a cave. Just a few managed to escape, and we got the reports from them. It was useless to protest to the Vali.

Already by November (1914) we had known that there would be a massacre. The Mutessarif of Moush, who was a very intimate friend of Enver Pasha, declared quite openly that they would massacre the Armenians at the first opportune moment and exterminate the whole race. Before the Russians arrived they intended first to butcher the Armenians, and then fight the Russians afterwards. Towards the beginning of April, in the presence of a Major Lange and several other high officials, including the American and German consuls, Ekran Bey quite openly declared the Government's intention of exterminating the Armenian race. All these details plainly show that the massacre was deliberately planned.

In a few villages destitute women come begging, naked and sick, for alms and protection. We are not allowed to give them anything, we are not allowed to take them in, in fact we are forbidden to do anything for them, and they die outside. If only permission could be obtained from the authorities to help them! If we cannot endure the sight of these poor people's sufferings, what must it be like for the sufferers themselves?

It is a story written in blood.

(c) Rev. Robert M. Labaree of the American Mission Station at Tabriz. Report, dated March 1, 1915, describes the exodus from Urmia in January, 1915, and says in part:

I doubt whether the story of that awful flight can ever adequately be told. Few tales that I have ever heard can compare with it in heart-rending interest. The whole northern section of the Urmia plain learned of the departure of the Russian troops about ten o'clock on the night of Saturday, the second January (1915). By midnight the terrible exodus had begun, and by morning the Christian villages of that district were practically deserted. People left their cattle in the stables and all their household goods in their homes, just as they were, and hurried away to save their lives. If anyone possessed a horse or a donkey or any other beast of burden he was fortunate, and if he happened to have ready cash in his home he was even more so; but, well-to-do as a man may be, cash is not always on hand in the villages, and so many who, according to the standards of the country, were rich, started on their long journey with a mere pittance, and the vast majority of men and women and children were on foot. . .

I have wondered time and again whether this panic-stricken flight was not some horrible mistake, and whether the people had not better stayed at home and cast themselves on the mercies of the Kurds and their Moslem neighbors; but as the stories of the sufferings of those who remained behind begin to reach us—stories of bloodshed and forced apostacy, and of women and girls carried off to a life worse than death—I have revised my judgment. Even all this untold misery by the way and in a strange land is better than the fate of those who remained at home. (pp. 107–108, Doc. No. 28)

(d) Comm. G. Gorrini, then Italian Consul-General at Trebizond, extracts from an interview published in the newspaper *Il Messaggero*, Rome, 25th August 1915:

As for the Armenians, they were treated differently in the different vilayets. They were suspect and spied upon everywhere, but they suffered a real extermination, worse than massacre, in the so-called 'Armenian vilayets.' There are seven of these, and five of them (including the most important and most thickly populated) unhappily for me formed part of my own Consular jurisdiction. These were the vilayets of Trebizond, Erzeroum, Van, Bitlis and Sivas.

In my district, from the 24th June onwards, the Armenians were all 'interned,'—that is, ejected by force from their various residences and dispatched under the guard of the gendarmerie to distant, unknown destinations, which for a few will mean the interior Mesopotamia, but for four-fifths of them has meant already a death accompanied by unheard-of cruelties.

The official proclamation of internment came from Constantinople. It is the work of the Central Government and the 'Committee of Union and Progress.' The local authorities, and indeed the Moslem population in general, tried to resist, to mitigate it, to make omissions, to hush it up. But the orders of the Central Government were categorically confirmed, and all were compelled to resign themselves and obey.

The Consular Body intervened, and attempted to save at least the women and children. We did, in fact, secure numerous exemptions, but these were not subsequently respected, owing to the interference of the local branch of the 'Union and Progress Committee,' and to fresh orders from Constantinople.

It was a real extermination and slaughter of the innocents, an unheard-of-thing, a black page stained with the flagrant violation of the most sacred rights of humanity, of Christianity, of nationality. The Armenian Catholics, too, who in the past had always been respected and excepted from the massacres and persecutions, were this time treated worse than any—again by the orders of the Central Government. There were about 14,000 Armenians at Trebizond—Gregorians, Catholics and Protestants—*they had never caused disorders or given occasion for collective measures of police.* [Emphasis ours; D.H.B] When I left Trebizond, not a hundred of them remained. Document No. 73 (pp. 290–292)

(e) Miss A. A., a foreign traveller in Asiatic Turkey, describes a journey from X to Z, August 10th to September 6th, 1915. We reproduce the concluding paragraphs of her report:

Our findings in regard to what we have witnessed, are as follows:

I. The Armenians have been deported practically universally from these six vilayets. Many of them have been killed by order of the Government and many have died by the way, but many also are enduring months of travel, and are approaching the borders of the great Arabian desert, where help must be gotten to them. A large plan of relief is absolutely necessary. It must emanate from the capital and there receive authority.

II. Orders given from Constantinople are often made void by other private orders; so anything that is promised must be written, and put in the hands of the people authorised to carry it out in co-operation with the Government. Only official seals will be recognized.

III. The orders about Protestants are only partially acknowledged by a few authorities, and in most cases all Protestants have either gone into exile or have been terrorized into becoming Mohammedans. Some order providing for relief for them, either where they are this winter or after they return to their plundered homes, is necessary if any real help is to be given them.

IV. Permission for the recantation of the recently 'turned' Protestants would be of the greatest help to the country, for their condition is most pitiable. They are neither one thing nor the other, and are afraid to engage in any real business, for all they possessed is soon required of them in bribes by different officers.

V. Bribe-taking has been enormous in some places, notably in X.; many have paid 2,000 liras to save their lives and then been sent into exile practically without a para.

VI. Forcible Mohammedanizing has been universal, in the assurance that death on the road is the only available alternative. Many, for the sake of trying to save wife and children, a little while, have so changed their faith. The best of the Turks, however, only emphasise the national side of this change and not the religious.

VII. The Turkish houses are full of Christian children, girls and women. They are usually early registered Mohammedans and an Imam comes and teaches them some of the prayers. After a while their 'nufus teskeriés' are called for and a Turkish one given in their place, and so their nationality is lost. . . .

IX. What has become of the men is a profound mystery, but I am increasingly certain that the large majority of them have been killed. The soldiers are still most of them alive, I believe, though all say that in the end they will also be killed. I talked with one who had managed to crawl to the Z. hospital wounded. He was one of ten men who had escaped, when all the rest of their company of 200 had

been shot by the gendarmes in a defile of the mountains.
Doc. No. 89 (pp. 356–363)

(f) *Narrative by a physician of foreign nationality,* resident of Turkey, for ten years, travelling through Asia Minor
during the deportation of the Armenians. (Abstracts) (Doc.
104, pp. 409–413):

At the first large station a sight burst upon my view
which, although I knew and was prepared for it, was nevertheless a shock. There was a mob of a thousand or more
people huddled about the station and environs, and long
strings of cattle-trucks packed to suffocation with human
beings. It was the first glimpse of the actual deportation of
the Armenians. Our train drew up to the station, but there
was no confusion, no wailing, no shouting, just a mob of
subdued people, dejected, sad, hopeless, past tears—looking backward to abandoned homes, to husbands, fathers,
brothers, who had been torn from them; looking forward
to a death in the desert, or to a living death in the hands
of captors who were compelled, "by political and military
necessity," to free their land of the curse of a nation which
had grown powerful while they themselves stagnated.
There were guards everywhere among the people, making
communication with them impossible. The advent of a for-
eigner among them was the sign for eager enquiring looks
from some, as if to say: "Can it be that he brings deliverance for us;" while others seemed to accept their lot in
settled despair. (p. 409)
   This general plan of deportation I saw carried out in several towns. Such animals and carriages as were available
were loaded with goods and sent to the outskirts of the
town, where they waited until all were ready; then they
were joined by the crowds on foot and all went off together.
It was pitiful enough as they set out, but I met group after
group on the road "on the march"—and these travel-
stained, worn and haggard—on and on, and on to their
death. Ah, yes, one can stand almost any hardship if hope
fills the breast and home and friends are at the journey's
end. (p. 412)
   If the events of the past year demonstrate anything, they
show the practical failure of Mohammedanism in its struggle for existence against Christianity—in its attempt to

eliminate a race, which, because of Christian education, has been proving increasingly a menace to stagnating Moslem civilisation. We may call it political necessity or what not, but in essence it is a nominally ruling class, jealous of a more progressive Christian race, striving by methods of primitive savagery to maintain the leading place. (p. 413)

Dr. Martin Niepage, an accredited Representative of Germany and a higher grade teacher in the German Technical School at Aleppo, in a pamphlet entitled "The Horrors of Aleppo," includes a letter dated October 8, 1915, addressed to the Imperial German Ministry of Foreign Affairs at Berlin. We shall make a few extracts from the pamphlet and will reproduce the report in its entirety as it appears therein.

When I returned to Aleppo in September, 1915, [writes Dr. Niepage,] from a three months' holiday at Beirut, I heard with horror that a new phase of Armenian massacres had begun which were far more terrible than the earlier massacres under Abd-ul-Hamid, and which aimed at exterminating, root and branch, of the intelligent, industrious, and progressive Armenian nation, and at transfering its property to Turkish hands.

Such monstrous news left me at first incredulous. I was told that, in various quarters of Aleppo, there were lying masses of half-starved people, the survivors of so-called "deportation convoys." In order, I was told, to cover the extermination of the Armenian nation with a political cloak, military reasons were being put forward, which were said to be necessary to drive the Armenians out of their native seats, which had been theirs for 2,500 years, and to deport them to the Arabian deserts. I was also told that individual Armenians had lent themselves to acts of espionage.

After I had informed myself about the facts and had made enquiries on all sides, I came to the conclusion that all these accusations against the Armenians were, in fact, based on trifling provocations, which were taken as an excuse for slaughtering 10,000 innocents for one guilty person, for the most savage outrages against women and children, and for a campaign of starvation against the exiles which was intended to exterminate the whole nation.

Horrified by the spectacle witnessed by him for several days, Dr. Niepage wrote the following report which was signed by "my colleague, Dr. Greater (higher grade teacher), and by Frau Marie Spiecker, as well as by myself."

The Report was also signed by "The head of our institution, Director Huber, who added "a few words in the following sense: 'My colleague Dr. Niepage's report is not at all exaggerated . . .' ":

> As teachers in the German Technical School at Aleppo, we permit ourselves with all respect to make the following report:
>
> We feel it our duty to draw attention to the fact that our educational work will forfeit its moral basis and the esteem of the natives, if the German Government is not in a position to put a stop to the brutality with which the wives and children of slaughtered Armenians are being treated here.
>
> Out of convoys which, when they left their homes on the Armenian plateau, numbered from two to three thousand men, women and children, only two or three hundred survivors arrive here in the south. The men are slaughtered on the way; the women and girls, with the exception of the old, the ugly and those who are still children, have been abused by Turkish soldiers and officers and then carried away to Turkish and Kurdish villages, where they have to accept Islam. They try to destroy the remnant of the convoys by hunger and thirst. Even when they are fording rivers, they do not allow those dying of thirst to drink. All the nourishment they receive is a daily ration of a little meal sprinkled over their hands, which they lick off greedily, and its only effect is to protect their starvation.
>
> Opposite the German Technical School at Aleppo, in which we are engaged in teaching, a mass of about four hundred emaciated forms, the remnant of such convoys, is one of the *hans* (inns). There are about a hundred children (boys and girls) among them, from five to seven years old. Most of them are suffering from typhoid and dysentery. When one enters the yard, one has the impression of entering a mad-house. If one brings them food, one notices that they have forgotten how to eat. Their stomach, weak-

ened by months of starvation, can no longer assimilate nourishment. If one gives them bread, they put it aside indifferently. They just lie there quietly, waiting for death.

Amid such surroundings, how are we teachers to read German Fairy Stories with our children, or, indeed, the story of the Good Samaritan in the Bible? How are we to make them decline and conjugate irrelevant words, while around them in the yards adjoining the German Technical School their starving fellow-countrymen are slowly succumbing? Under such circumstances our educational work flies in the face of all true morality and becomes a mockery of human sympathy.

And what becomes of these poor people who have been driven in thousands through Aleppo and the neighbourhood into the deserts, reduced almost entirely, by this time, to women and children? They are driven on and on from one place to another. The thousands shrink to hundreds and hundreds to tiny remnants, and even these remnants are driven on till the last is dead. Then at last they have reached the goal of their wandering, the 'New Homes assigned to the Armenians,' as the newspapers phrase it.

'Ta'alim el aleman ("the teaching of the Germans") is the simple Turk's explanation to everyone who asks him about the originators of these measures.

The educated Moslems are convinced that, even though the German nation discountenances such horrors, the German Government is taking no steps to put a stop to them, out of consideration for its Turkish Ally.

Mohammedans, too, of more sensitive feelings—Turks and Arabs alike—shake their heads in disapproval and do not conceal their tears when they see a convoy of exiles marching through the city, and Turkish soldiers using cudgels upon women in advanced pregnancy and upon dying people who can no longer drag themselves along. They cannot believe that their Government has ordered these atrocities, and they hold the Germans responsible for all such outrages, Germany being considered during the war as Turkey's schoolmaster in everything. Even the *mollahs* in the mosques say that it was not the Sublime Porte but the German officers who ordered the ill-treatment and destruction of the Armenians.

The things which have been passing here for months under everybody's eyes will certainly remain as a stain on Germany's shield in the memory of Orientals.

In order not to be obliged to give up their faith in the character of the Germans, which they have hitherto respected, many educated Mohammedans explain the situation to themselves as follows: 'The German nation,' they say, 'probably knows nothing about the frightful massacres which are on foot at the present time against the native Christians in all parts of Turkey. Knowing the German love of truth, how otherwise can we explain the articles we read in German newspapers, which appear to know of nothing except that individual Armenians have been deservedly shot by martial law as spies and traitors?' Others again say: 'Perhaps the German Government has had its hands tied by some treaty defining its powers, or perhaps intervention is inopportune for the present.'

I know for a fact that the Embassy at Constantinople has been informed by the German Consulates of all that has been happening. As, however, there has not been so far the least change in the system of deportation, I feel myself compelled by conscience to make my present report. (pp. 5–9)

The following remarks by Dr. Niepage deserve consideration:

What we saw with our own eyes here in Aleppo was really only the last scene in the great tragedy of the extermination of the Armenians. It was only a minute fraction of the horrible drama that was being played out simultanenously in all the other provinces of Turkey. Many more appalling things were reported by the engineers of the Bagdad Railway, when they came back from their work on the section under construction, or by German travellers who met the convoys of exiles on their journeys. Many of these gentlemen had seen such appalling sights that they could eat nothing for days. (p. 11)

Dr. Niepage firmly believes that Germany could have prevented the deportation and massacres of the Armenians, if she so desired. Here are his own words:

The author of the present report considers it out of the question that, if the German Government is seriously determined to stem the tide of destruction even at this eleventh hour, it would find it impossible to bring the Turkish Government to reason. If the Turks are really so well inclined to us Germans as people say, cannot they have it pointed out to them how seriously they compromise us before the whole civilised world, if we, as their Allies, have to look on passively while our fellow-Christians in Turkey are slaughtered in their hundreds of thousands, their women and daughters violated, their children brought up as Mohammedans? Cannot the Turks be made to understand that their barbarities are reckoned to our account, and that we Germans will be accused either of criminal complicity or of contemptible weakness, if we shut our eyes to the frightful horror which this war has produced, and seek to pass over in silence facts which are already notorious all over the world? If the Turks are really as intelligent as is said should it be impossible to convince them that in exterminating the Christian nations in Turkey, they are destroying the productive factors and the intermediaries of European trade and general civilisation? If the Turks are as far-sighted as is said, can they blind themselves to the danger that, when the civilised States of Europe have taken cognisance of what has been happening in Turkey during the war, they may be driven to the conclusion that Turkey has forfeited the right to govern herself and has destroyed once for all any belief in her tolerance and capacity for civilisation? (pp. 17–18)

Dr. Niepage makes the following characteristic observation in his pamphlet:

If anyone enquires into the motives which induced the Young Turkish Government to decree and carry out these frightful massacres against the Armenians, one might give the following explanation: —
The Young Turk has the European ideal of a united national state always floating before his eyes. He hopes to Turkify the non-Turkish Mohammedan races—Kurds, Persians, Arabs, and so on—by administrative methods and through Turkish education, reinforced by an appeal to their common interests as Mohammedans. The Christian nations—Armenians, Syrians and Greeks—alarm him by their cultural and economic superiority, and he sees in their religion an obstacle to Turkifying them by peaceful means. They have, therefore, to be exterminated or converted to Mohammedanism by force. The Turks do not suspect that, in doing this, they are sawing off the branch on

which they are sitting themselves. Who is to bring progress to Turkey if not the Greeks, Armenians and Syrians, who constitute more than a quarter of the population of the Empire. (p. 20)

Rene Pinon, *La Suppression des Armeniens*, 1916, writes:

When the whims of Germany precipitated Turkey into the combat, not only the Armenian and non-Turk populations, but a very great number of Turkish patriots suffered profound pain. The Armenians of the Caucasus, who had found refuge on Russian soil since the massacres of 1895, requested in unison entry into the Army of the Tsar for the deliverance of their oppressed brothers. The Armenians of the Ottoman Empire maintained a sad but loyal attitude. Without murmur they allowed themselves to be skinned by the government which demanded from them monetary contributions three times higher than what they were legally bound to pay. . . According to the law only persons from 20 to 35 years of age from among Christian populations could be called to serve under the flag; but by an arbitrary measure—which reveals the intention already decided upon to deprive the Armenian people of all able-bodied men in order to exterminate it without resistance—Armenians from 18 to 48 years of age were conscripted. Labor detachments were formed without being given arms and they were assigned to the most menial jobs and subjected to insults and maltreatment by their superiors and their Turkish comrades; it was already difficult to say if these unfortunates were soldiers called to defend a country which had done nothing to gain their confidence, or they were held as hostages, almost condemned. (pp. 20, 21)

Fayez El Ghosein, in *The Massacres in Turkish Armenia*, 1917, gives a vivid description of his experiences in Turkey during the period of Armenian massacres in Turkey. Here are a few paragraphs:

One day I went to church to find out for myself the manner in which the goods belonging to Armenians were being disposed of. That was one scene I should have never seen, because one's heart becomes depressed when one sees in the hands of a Kurd a magnificent wedding gown and one thinks that the beautiful young lady, for whom this expensive garment was destined, might be subjected to a frightful attack. (p. 28)

Who can describe the emotions which crush the spectator's heart when he ponders over this unfortunate and heroic nation, which astonished the world by its courage and intrepidity, which only yesterday was the most virile and progressive of the nations which inhabit the Ottoman Empire and which to-day is only a memory of the past. Its schools which once were filled with students are now deserted; its most precious books now serve as wrapping paper for cheese. . . (pp. 28, 29)

Kurds and gendarmes have violated a large number of young girls. Those who resisted were killed, and these wild beasts satisfied their animal passion even upon those who were breathing their last. (p. 32)

Should one ask for the reasons for which the Turkish Government massacred the Armenians—men, women and children—and subjected their honor and their goods to violence and pillage, they will answer that the Armenians have killed Musulmans in Van, have concealed forbidden arms and explosive material, as well as insignias of an Armenian state, such as flags and others; all this clearly indicates that this community (Armenian) pursued its intrigues, waiting for a favorable occasion to foment trouble and to massacre Musulmans, aided by Russia, the enemy of Turkey. (pp. 50–51)

Such are the allegations of the Turkish Government.

But I have studied this question at most authoritative sources; I have learned from these inhabitants and officials of Van who were found in Diarbekir and my inquiries have proved to me that the Armenians have not killed one single Musulman, neither at Van nor in the surrounding localities; the fact is that the government ordered the inhabitants to leave the city long before the Russians arrived there, where not a single person had been killed. The government also demanded of the Armenians to surrender their arms, but they refused because of their fear of the Kurds and the government itself which also demanded that the leaders of the (Armenian) community be delivered as hostages. This appeared to be reasonable. (p. 5)

All this took place while the Russians were marching on Van, but in the rest of the province the government gathered the Armenians and dispatched them to the interior where they were all put to death, without one official, one

Kurd or one Turk having been killed by them (Armenians).
(p. 51)

Henry Barby, in *Au Pays de l'Epouvante—l'Armenie martyre*, 1917, writes:

The most dreadful massacres in the memory of man
cannot be compared with the massacres that are taking
place once more to stain with blood Armenia whose population almost entirely has been the victim of ferocious
mass murder.
Everlasting infamy will become attached to the history
of two peoples associated in crime: The Turks and the
Germans. (p. 3)

In describing the blood-curdling events of Erzeroum,
Henry Barby quotes the words of Rev. Robert S. Stapleton,
the American consul:

The Vali (Governor) told me, explained to me, at my
request, that the decision of his government not only
aimed at the deportation of the Armenians but, for military reasons, the evacuation of the city by all people, without race distinction. This statement was false, as the
subsequent events demonstrated.
The first group of emigrants, comprising about forty
families, left the city on June 16. I know that from this
group only *one man and about forty women arrived at
Kharpout.*
The great mass of the exiles left on June 19. They
formed a large convoy of carts and Turkish gendarmes
escorted each group.
On July 28 the Armenian archbishop, Sempad Sahatjian, the Catholic archbishop and the Protestant minister
were, in their turn, forced to leave the city with the last
caravan of deportees.
It was not until the month of September, he told me,
that for the first time I received news from the exiles. Singularly it was the women who wrote to me. They were
asking me what had happened to their husbands from
whom they were separated and of whom they had heard
nothing. Most of them informed me of the massacre of
their entire family. All these women were directed toward
Seroudy, Ourfa, Aleppo and Rakka. The exiles were to be
sent to Erzindjian and Kharpout. At Erzindjian all their

means of transportation were confiscated. (pp. 31–33)

I do not know which scenes of murder or sadism to choose from among so many nameless horrors in order to give you a complete picture of the horrible martyrdom of the Armenian people. . . . Mothers are placed in line and before their very eyes their babies are disemboweled and the bodies hung on the wall in bloody clusters, like in a butcher shop. The mothers in distress, screaming with terror and grief, are whipped away, while the bodies of the babies, still pulsating, are abandoned to the vultures. (p. 86)

Henry Morgenthau, quoted from the *Secrets of the Bosphorus*, 1918:

In Chapter XXIII, entitled "The 'Revolution' at Van," Mr. Morgenthau describes the volatile conditions in Van and the dangerous situation the Armenians found themselves in because of the suspicions, threats and accusations ever increasing day by day, especially after the replacement of Tahsin Pasha, the conciliatory governor of Van, by Djevdet Bey, a brother-in-law of Enver Pasha, who "hated the Armenians and cordially sympathised with the long-established Turkish plan of solving the Armenian problem." So, when Djevdet Bey entered upon the discharge of his duties as Governor of Van, his first demand from the Armenians was to furnish 4,000 soldiers, his purpose being "merely to massacre them, so that the rest of the Armenians might have no defenders." The demand was rejected by the Armenians, whereupon "Djevdet began to talk aloud about 'rebellion' and his determination to 'crush' it at any cost." " 'If the rebels fire a single shot' he declared, 'I shall kill every Christian man, woman and child up to here,' pointing to his knee."

On April 20th, a band of Turkish soldiers seized several Armenian women who were entering the city; a couple of Armenians ran to their assistance and were shot dead. The Turks now opened fire on the Armenian quarters with rifles and artillery; soon a large part of the town was in flames and a regular siege had started. The whole Armenian fighting force consisted of only 1,500 men; they had only 300 rifles and a most inadequate supply of ammunition, while Djevdet had an army of 5,000 men, completely equipped and supplied; yet the Armenians fought with utmost heroism and skill. They had little chance of holding off their enemies indefinitely, yet they knew that a Russian army was fighting its way to Van, and their utmost hope was that they would be able to defy the besiegers until these Russians arrived.

As I am not writing the story of sieges and battles, I cannot describe in detail the numerous deeds of individual heroism, the co-operation of the Armenian women, the ardour and energy of the Armenian children, the self-sacrificing zeal of the American missionaries—especially Dr. Ussher and his wife and Miss Grace H. Knapp—and the thousands of other circumstances that make this terrible month one of the most glorious pages of modern Armenian history. The wonderful thing about it is that the Armenians triumphed. (pp. 196, 197)

In Chapter XXIV, entitled "The Murder of a Nation," Mr. Morgenthau describes in gruesome details how the extermination of the Armenian people was perpetrated ruthlessly and with beastly savagery. One paragraph will suffice to give the reader an idea about the enormity of the crime of genocide:

And thus, as the exiles moved, they left behind them another caravan—that of dead and unburied bodies, of old men and women in the last stages of typhus, dysentery, and cholera, of little children lying on their backs and setting up their last piteous wails for food and water. There were women who held up their babies to strangers begging them to take them and save them from their tormentors, and failing this, they would throw them into wells or leave them behind bushes, that at least they might die undisturbed. Behind was left a small army of girls who had been sold as slaves—frequently for a *medjidie*, or about eighty cents—and who, after serving the brutal purposes of their purchasers, were forced to lead lives of prostitution. A string of encampments filled with the sick and the dying, mingled with the unburied or half-buried bodies of the dead, marked the course of the advancing throngs. Flocks of vultures followed them in the air, and ravenous dogs, fighting one another for the bodies of the dead, constantly pursued them. The most terrible scenes took place at the rivers, especially the Euphrates. Sometimes, when crossing this stream, the gendarmes would push the women into the water, shooting all who attempted to save themselves by swimming. Frequently the women themselves would save their honour by jumping into the river, their children in their arms. (p. 208) . . . It is absurd for the Turkish government to assert that it ever seriously intended to deport the Armenians to new homes; the treatment which was given the convoys clearly shows that extermination was the real purpose of Enver and Talaat. (p. 209)

The renowned author of the *Secrets of the Bosphorus* sadly asserts: "I am confident that the whole history of the human race contains no such horrible episode as this. The great massacres and persecutions of the past seem almost insignificant when compared to the sufferings of the Armenian race in 1915." (p. 211)

In his article entitled "The Greatest Horror in History," *The Red Cross Magazine,* March, 1918, Ambassador Morgenthau asserted:

The final and the worst measure used against the Armenians was the wholesale deportation of the entire population from their homes and their exile to the deserts, with all the accompanying horrors on the way. No means were provided for their transportation or nourishment. The victims, which included educated men and women of standing, had to walk on foot, exposed to the attacks of bands of criminals especially organized for that purpose. Homes were literally uprooted; families were separated; men killed, women and girls violated daily on the way or taken to harems. Children were thrown into the rivers or sold to strangers by their mothers to save them from starvation. *The facts contained in the reports received at the Embassy from absolutely trustworthy eyewitnesses surpass the most beastly and diabolical cruelties ever before perpetrated or imagined in the history of the world.* [Emphasis ours— D.H.B.] The Turkish authorities had stopped all communication between the provinces and the capital in the naive belief that they could consummate this crime of the ages before the outside world could hear of it. But the information filtered through the Consuls, missionaries, foreign travellers, and even Turks. *We soon learned that orders had been issued to the governors of the provinces to send into exile the entire Armenian population in their jurisdiction, irrespective of age and sex.* (Italics in the French text.) The local officers, with a few exceptions, carried out literally those instructions. All the able-bodied men had either been drafted into the Army or been disarmed. The remaining people, old men, women and children, were subjected to the most cruel and outrageous treatment! (p. 9)

After referring to many statements and eye-witness reports, much of which "has already been published in the excellent volume of documentary material collected by Viscount Bryce," Mr. Morgenthau writes:

I have space here to quote from only one document. Strange to say this report was made to me by a German missionary. The statement was made to me personally and put in writing at the Embassy. (Italics in the French text.)
The following are excerpts from that report:
There came an order from the government that we have to hand over to them all our people in the house, big or small. All my requests and petitions were in vain . . . When I pleaded with him (the *Mutesarif*) to at least spare the children, he replied: "you cannot expect the Armenian children to remain alone with the Mohammedans; they must leave with their nation."
. . . It was that very afternoon that I received the first terrible reports, but I did not fully believe them . . . The men had all been tied together and shot outside of town. The women and children were taken to the neighboring village, placed in houses by the hundred and *either burned alive or thrown into the river.* (Italics mine. DHB) (p. 12)
Three weeks later when we left Mush (for Mezreh), the villages were still burning . . . The soldiers who accompanied us showed us with pride *where* and *how* and *how many* women and children they had killed . . . Mamuret-ul-Aziz has become the cemetery of all Armenians; all the Armenians from the various vilayets were sent there, and those who had not died on the way, came there simply to find their graves. (p. 12)

APPENDIX B

Chapter 4

The "Uprising" of Van

The Turks and their friends have on numerous occasions stated that the repressive measures taken against the Armenians, followed by massacres and deportations was due to the rebellion of the Armenians of Van in the spring and summer of 1915 against duly constituted authorities. These accusations have never been substantiated by direct evidence; on the contrary, all the available evidence tends to prove and does prove that *there was no rebellion in Van* other than precautious measures in self-defense.

The two most important on the scene eye-witnesses were Dr. Clarence D. Ussher and Miss Grace Higley Knapp, whose testimony is so valuable that we shall quote from them as well as Ambassador Morgenthau liberally.

Miss Grace H. Knapp, during the troubles in Van wrote several letters to Dr. Barton, dated respectively May 25, June 14, 20 and 22, and July 26, 1915. The following are excerpts from these letters, combined in a report published in *The Treatment of Armenians in the Ottoman Empire,* pages 32 to 47 inclusive:

THE SETTING OF THE DRAMA AND THE ACTORS THEREIN

Van was one of the most beautiful cities of Asiatic Turkey—a city of gardens and vineyards, situated on Lake Van in the centre of a plateau bordered by magnificent mountains. The walled city, containing the shops and most of the public buildings, was dominated by Castle Rock, a huge rock rising sheer from the plain, crowned with ancient battlements and fortifications, and bearing on its lakeward face famous cuneiform inscriptions. The Gardens, so-called because nearly every house had its garden or vineyard, extended over four miles eastward from

415

the walled city and were about two miles in width.

The inhabitants numbered fifty thousand, three-fifths of whom were Armenians, two-fifths Turks. The Armenians were progressive and ambitious, and because of their numerical strength and the proximity of Russia the revolutionary party grew to be a force to be reckoned with. Three of its noted leaders were Vremyan, member of the Ottoman Parliament; Ishkhan, the one most skilled in military tactics; and Aram, of whom there will be much to say later. The Governor often consulted with these men and seemed to be on the most friendly terms with them.

The American Mission Compound was on the southeastern border of the middle third of the Gardens, on a slight rise of ground that made its buildings somewhat conspicuous. These buildings were a church building, two large new school buildings, two small ones, a lace school, a hospital, dispensiary and four missionary residences. South-east, and quite near, was a broad plain. Here was the largest Turkish barracks of the large garrison, between which and the Armenian premises nothing intervened. North and nearer, but with streets and houses between, was another large barracks, and farther north, within rifle range, was Toprak-Kala Hill, surmounted by a small barracks dubbed by the Americans the 'Pepper Box.' Five minutes' walk to the east of us was the German Orphanage managed by Herr Spöerri, his wife and daughter (of Swiss extraction) and three single ladies.

The American force in 1914–1915 consisted of the veteran missionary, Mrs. G. C. Raynolds (Dr. Raynolds had been in America a year and a half collecting funds for our Van college, and had been prevented from returning by the outbreak of war); Dr. Clarence D. Ussher, in charge of the hospital and medical work; Mrs. Ussher, in charge of a philanthropic lace industry; Mr. and Mrs. Ernest A. Yarrow, in charge of the Boys' School and general work; Miss Gertrude Rogers, principal of the Girls' School; Miss Caroline Silliman, in charge of the primary department, and two Armenian and one Turkish kindergarten; Miss Elizabeth Ussher, in charge of the musical department; Miss Louise Bond, the English superintendent of the hospital; and Miss Grisel McLaren, our touring missionary. Dr. Ussher and Mr. Yarrow had each four children; I was a visitor from Bitlis.

BETWEEN THE DEVIL AND THE DEEP SEA

During the mobilization of the fall and winter the Armenians had been ruthlessly plundered under the name of requisitioning; rich men were ruined and the poor stripped. Armenian soldiers in the Turkish army were neglected, half starved, set to digging trenches and doing the menial work; but, worst of all, they were deprived of their arms and thus left at the mercy of their fanatical, age-long enemies, their Moslem fellow-soldiers. Small wonder that those who could find a loophole of escape or could pay for exemption from military duty did so; many of those who could do neither simply would not give themselves up. We felt that a day of reckoning would soon come—a collision between these opposing forces or a holy war. But the revolutionists conducted themselves with remarkable restraint and prudence; controlled their hot-headed youth; patrolled the streets to prevent skirmishes; and bade the villagers to endure in silence—better a village or two burned unavenged than that any attempt at reprisals should furnish an excuse for massacre.

For some time after Djevdet Bey, a brother-in-law of Enver Pasha, minister of war, became Governor General of Van Vilayet, he was absent from the city fighting at the border. When he returned in the early spring, everyone felt there would soon be "something doing." There was. He demanded from the Armenians 3,000 soldiers. So anxious were they to keep the peace that they promised to accede to this demand. But at this juncture trouble broke out between Armenians and Turks in the Shadakh region, and Djevdet Bey requested Ishkhan to go there as peace commissioner accompanied by three other notable revolutionists. On their way there he had all four treacherously murdered. This was Friday, the 16th April. He then summoned Vremyan to him under the pretence of consulting with this leader, arrested him and sent him off to Constantinople.

The revolutionists now felt that they could not trust Djevdet Bey, the Vali, in any way and that therefore they could not give him the 3,000 men. They told him they would give 400 and pay by degrees the exemption tax for the rest. He would not accept the compromise. The Armenians begged Dr. Ussher and Mr. Yarrow to see Djevdet Bey and try to mollify him. The Vali was obdurate. He 'must be obeyed.' He would put down this 'rebellion' at all costs. He would first punish Shadakh, then attend to Van, but if the rebels fired one shot meanwhile he would put to death every man, woman and child of the Christians.

The fact cannot be too strongly emphasized that there was no 'rebellion.' As already pointed out, the revolutionists meant to keep the peace if it lay in their power to do so. But for some time past a line of Turkish entrenchments had been secretly drawn round the Armenian quarter of the Gardens. The revolutionists, determined to sell their lives as dearly as possible, prepared a defensive line of entrenchments. [Emphasis ours—D.H.B.]

Djevdet Bey said he wished to send a guard of fifty soldiers to the American premises. This guard must be accepted or a written statement given him by the Americans to the effect that it had been offered and refused, so that he should be absolved from all responsibility for our safety. He wished for an immediate answer, but at last consented to wait till Sunday noon.

Our Armenian friends, most of them, agreed that the guard must be accepted. But the revolutionists declared that such a force in so central a location menaced the safety of the Armenian forces and that they would never permit it to reach our premises alive. We might have a guard of five. But Djevdet Bey would give us fifty or none. Truly we were between the devil and the deep sea, for, if both revolutionists and Vali kept their word, we should be the occasion for the outbreak of trouble, if the guard were sent; if it were not sent, we should have no official assurance of safety for the thousands who were already preparing to take refuge on our premises. We should be blamed for an unhappy outcome either way. On Monday, when Dr. Ussher saw the Vali again, he seemed to be wavering and asked if he should send the guard. Dr. Ussher left the decision with him, but added that the sending of such a force might precipitate trouble. It was never sent.

Meanwhile Djevdet Bey had asked Miss McLaren and Schwester Martha, who had been nursing in the Turkish military hospital all winter, to continue their work there, and they had consented.

WAR! "ISHIM YOK, KEIFIM TCHOK."

On Tuesday, the 20th April, at 6 a.m., some Turkish soldiers tried to seize one of a band of village women on their way to the city. She fled. Two Armenian soldiers came up and asked the Turks what they were doing. The Turkish soldiers fired on the Armenians, killing them. Thereupon the Turkish entrenchments opened fire. The siege had begun. There was a steady rifle firing all day, and from the walled city, now cut off from communication with the Gardens, was heard a continuous cannonading from Castle Rock upon the houses below. In the evening, houses were seen burning in every direction.

All the Armenians in the Gardens—nearly 30,000, as the Armenian population of the walled city is small—were now gathered into a district about a mile square, protected by eighty "teerks" (manned and barricaded houses) besides walls and trenches. The Armenian force consisted of 1,500 trained riflemen possessing only about 300 rifles. Their supply of ammunition was not great, so they were very sparing of it; used pistols only, when they could, and employed all sorts of devices to draw the fire of the enemy and waste their ammunition. They began to make bullets and cartridges, turning out 2,000 a day; also gunpowder, and after awhile they made three mortars for throwing bombs. The supply of material for the manufacture of these things was limited, and methods and implements were crude and primitive, but they were very happy and hopeful and exultant over their ability to keep the enemy at bay. Some of the rules for their men were: Keep clean; do not drink; tell the truth; do not curse the religion of the enemy. They sent a manifesto to the Turks to the effect that their quarrel was with one man and not with their Turkish neighbours. Valis might come and go, but the two races must continue to live together, and they hoped that after Djevdet went there might be peaceful and friendly relations between them. The Turks answered in the same spirit, saying that they were forced to fight. Indeed, a protest against this war was signed by many prominent Turks, but Djevdet would pay no attention to it.

The Armenians took and burned (the inmates, however, escaping) the barracks north of our premises, but apart from this they did not attempt the offensive to any extent —their numbers were too few. They were fighting for their homes, their very lives, and our sympathies could not but be wholly on their side, though we strove to keep our actions neutral. We allowed no armed men to enter the premises, and their leader, Aram, in order to help us to preserve the neutrality of our premises, forbade the bringing of wounded soldiers to our hospital, though Dr. Ussher treated them at their own temporary hospital. But Djevdet Bey wrote to Dr. Ussher on the 23rd that armed men had been seen entering our premises and that the rebels had prepared entrenchments near us. If, at the time of attack, one shot were fired from these entrenchments, he would be 'regretfully compelled' to turn his cannon upon our premises and completely destroy them. We might know this for a surety. We answered that we were preserving the neutrality of our premises by every means in our power. By no law could we be held responsible for the actions of individuals or organisations outside our premises.

Our correspondence with the Vali was carried on through our official representative, Signor Sbordone, the Italian consular agent, and our postman was an old woman bearing a flag of truce. On her second journey she fell into a ditch and, rising without her white flag, was instantly shot dead by Turkish soldiers. Another was found, but she was wounded while sitting at the door of her shack on our premises. Then Aram said that he would permit no further correspondence until the Vali should answer a letter of Sbordone's, in which the latter had told Djevdet that he had no right to expect the Armenians to surrender now, since the campaign had taken on the character of a massacre.

Djevdet would permit no communication with Miss McLaren at the Turkish hospital, and would answer no question of ours concerning her welfare, though after two weeks he wrote to Herr Spörri that she and Schwester Martha were well and comfortable. Dr. Ussher had known the Vali as a boy and had always been on the most friendly terms with him, but in a letter to the Austrian banker who had taken refuge on the German premises, the Vali wrote that one of his officers had taken some Russian prisoners and cannon and that he would cause them to parade in front of 'His Majesty Dr. Ussher's fortifications, so that he, who with the rebels was always awaiting the Russians, should see them and be content.' This letter ended with the words: 'Ishim yok, keifim tchok' ('I have no work and much fun.') While he was having no work and much fun, his soldiers and their wild allies, the Kurds, were sweeping the countryside, massacring men, women, and children and burning their homes. Babies were shot in their mothers' arms, small children were horribly mutilated, women were stripped and beaten. The villages were not prepared for attack; many made no resistance; others resisted until their ammunition gave out. On Sunday, the 25th, the first band of village refugees came to the city. At early dawn we heard them knocking, knocking, knocking at our gate. Dr. Ussher went out in dressing gown and slippers to hear their pitiful tale and send the wounded to the hospital, where he worked over them all day.

THE MISSION'S FIRST-AID TO THE INJURED

Six thousand people from the Gardens had early removed to our premises with all their worldly possessions, filling church and school buildings and every room that could possibly be spared in the missionary residences. One woman said to Miss Silliman: "What would we do without this place? This is the third massacre during which I have taken refuge here." A large proportion of these people had to be fed, as they had been so poor that they had bought daily from the ovens what bread they had money for, and now that resource was cut off. Housing, sanitation, government, food, relation with the revolutionist forces, were problems that required great tact and executive ability. The Armenians were not able to cope with these problems unaided. They turned to the missionaries for help.

Mr. Yarrow has a splendid gift for organisation. He soon had everything in smoothly running order, with everyone hard at work at what he was best fitted to do. A regular city government for the whole city of thirty thousand inhabitants was organised with mayor, judges, and police— the town had never been so well policed before. Committees were formed to deal with every possible contingency. Grain was sold or contributed to the common fund by those who possessed it, most of whom manifested a generous and self-sacrificing spirit; one man gave all the wheat he possessed except a month's supply for his family. The use of a public oven was secured, bread tickets issued, a soup kitchen opened, and daily rations were given out to those on our premises and those outside who needed food. Miss Rogers and Miss Silliman secured a daily supply of milk, and made some of their school-girls boil it and distribute it to babies who needed it, until 190 were being thus fed. The Boy Scouts, whom thirteen-year-old Neville Ussher had helped organize in the fall, now did yeoman's service in protecting the buildings against the dangers of fire, keeping the premises clean, carrying wounded on stretchers, reporting the sick, and, during the fourth week, distributing milk and eggs to babies and sick outside the premises.

Our hospital, which had a normal capacity of fifty beds, was made to accommodate one hundred and sixty-seven, beds being borrowed and placed on the floor in every available space. Such of the wounded as could walk or be brought to the hospital came regularly to have their wounds dressed. Many complicated operations were required to repair the mutilations inflicted by an unimaginable brutality and love of torture. Dr. Ussher, as the only physician and surgeon in the besieged city, had not only the care of the patients in his hospital, the treatment of the wounded refugees and of the wounded Armenian soldiers, but his dispensiary and out-patients increased to an appalling number. Among the refugees exposure and privation brought in their train scores of cases of pneumonia and dysentery, and an epidemic of measles raged among the children. Miss Silliman took charge of a measles annex, Miss Rogers and Miss Ussher helped in the hospital, where Miss Bond and her Armenian nurses were worked to the limit of their strength, and after a while Mrs. Ussher, aided by Miss Rogers, opened an overflow hospital in an Armenian school-house, cleared of refugees for the purpose. Here it was a struggle to get beds, utensils, helpers, even food enough for the patients. Indeed all this extra medical and surgical work was hampered by insufficient medical and surgical supplies, for the annual shipment had been stalled at Alexandretta.

DARK DAYS

At the end of two weeks the people in the walled city managed to send us word that they were holding their own and had taken some of the government buildings, though they were only a handful of fighters and were cannonaded day and night. About 16,000 cannon balls or shrapnel were fired upon them. The old-fashioned balls sunk into the three-feet thick walls of sun-dried brick without doing much harm. In time, of course, the walls would fall in, but they were the walls of the upper stories. People took refuge in the lower stories, so only three persons lost their lives from this cause. Some of the "teerks" in the gardens were also cannonaded without much damage being done. It seemed the enemy was reserving his heavier cannon and his shrapnel till the last. Three cannon balls fell on our premises the first week, one of them on the porch of the Usshers' house. Thirteen persons were wounded by bullets on the premises, one fatally. Our premises were so centrally located that the bullets of the Turks kept whizzing through, entered several rooms, broke the tiles on the roofs, and peppered the outside of the walls. We became so used to the pop-pop-pop of rifles and booming of cannons that we paid little attention to them in the daytime, but the fierce fusillades at night were rather nerve-racking.

A man escaping from Ardjish related the fate of that town, second in size and importance to Van in the vilayet. The kaimakam had called the men of all the guilds together on the 19th April, and, as he had always been friendly to the Armenians, they trusted him. When they had all gathered, he had them mown down by his soldiers.

Many of the village refugees had stopped short of the city at the little village of Shushantz, on a mountain side near the city. Here Aram bade them remain. On the 8th May we saw the place in flames, and Varak Monastery near by, with its priceless ancient manuscripts, also went up in smoke. These villagers now flocked into the city. Djevdet seemed to have altered his tactics. He had women and children driven in by hundreds to help starve the city out. Owing to the mobilisation of the previous fall, the supply of wheat in the Gardens had been very much less than usual to begin with, and now that 10,000 refugees were being given a daily ration, though a ration barely sufficient to sustain life, this supply was rapidly approaching its limit. The ammunition was also giving out. Djevdet could bring in plenty of men and ammunition from other cities. Unless help came from Russia, it was impossible for the city to hold out much longer against him, and the hope of such help seemed very faint. We had no communication with the outside world; a telegram we had prepared to send to our embassy before the siege never left the city; the revolutionists were constantly sending out appeals for help to the Russo-Armenian volunteers on the border, but no word or sign of their reaching their destination was received by us. At the very last, when the Turks should come to close quarters, we knew that all the population of the besieged city would crowd into our premises as a last hope. But, enraged as Djevdet was by this unexpected and prolonged resistance, was it to be hoped that he could be persuaded to spare the lives of one of these men, women and children? We believed not. He might offer the Americans personal safety if we would leave the premises, but this, of course, we would not do; we would share the fate of our people. And it seemed not at all improbable that he would not even offer us safety, believing, as he seemed to believe, that we were aiding and upholding the "rebels."

Those were dark days indeed. Our little American circle came together two evenings in the week to discuss the problems constantly arising. We would joke and laugh over some aspects of our situation, but as we listened to the volley firing only two blocks away, we knew that at any hour the heroic but weakening defence might be overpowered; knew that then hell would be let loose in the crowded city and our crowded compound; knew that we should witness unspeakable atrocities perpetrated on the persons of those we loved, and probably suffer them in our own persons. And we would sing:

"Peace, perfect peace; the future all unknown!
Jesus we know and He is on the throne,"

and pray to the God who was able to deliver us out of the very mouth of the lion.

On Saturday forenoon a rift seemed to appear in the clouds, for many ships were seen on the lake, sailing away from Van, and we heard that they contained Turkish women and children. We became a "city all gone up to the house tops," wondering and surmising. Once before such a flight had taken place, when the Russians had advanced as far as Sarai. They had retreated, however, and the Turkish families had returned.

That afternoon the sky darkened again. Cannon at the Big Barracks on the plain began to fire in our direction. At first we could not believe that the shots were aimed at our flag, but no doubt was permitted us on that point. Seven shells fell on the premises, one on the roof of Miss Rogers' and Miss Silliman's house, making a big hole in it; two others did the same thing on the boys'-school and girls'-school roofs. On Sunday morning the bombardment began again. Twenty-six shells fell on the premises before noon.

When the heavy firing began Dr. Ussher was visiting patients outside and Mrs. Ussher was also away from home at her overflow hospital, so I ran over from our own hospital to take their children to the safest part of the house, a narrow hall on the first floor. There we listened to the shrieking of the shrapnel and awaited the bursting of each shell. A deafening explosion shook the house. I ran up to my room to find it so full of dust and smoke that I could not see a foot before me. A shell had come through the three-feet-thick outside wall, burst, scattering its contained bullets, and its cap had passed through a partition wall into the next room and broken a door opposite. A shell entered a room in Mrs. Raynold's house, killing a little Armenian girl. Ten more shells fell in the afternoon. Djevdet was fulfilling his threat of bombarding our premises, and this proved to us that we could hope for no mercy at his hands when he should take the city.*

DELIVERANCE

In this darkest hour of all came deliverance. A lull followed the cannonading. Then at sunset a letter came from the occupants of the only Armenian house within the

---

* The shelling of the mission buildings is also described by Mr. Yarrow in an interview published in the *New York Times* 6th October, 1915, the day after his arrival in America:

"For twenty-seven days 1,500 determined Armenians held Van against 5,000 Turks and Kurds, and for the last three days they were shelled with shrapnel from a howitzer brought up by a Turkish company headed by a German officer. I myself saw him directing the fire of the gun. Two days before the Russians came to Van the Turks deliberately fired at the mission buildings. They stood out prominently and could not be mistaken, and also flew five American flags and one Red Cross flag as a protection. The firing was so accurate that the shots cut the signal halyards and brought the flags to the ground."

Turkish lines which had been spared (because Djevdet had lived in it when a boy) which gave the information that the Turks had left the city. The barracks on the summit and at the foot of Toprak-Kala were found to contain so small a guard that it was easily overpowered, and these buildings were burned amidst the wildest excitement. So with all the Turkish 'teerks' which were visited in turn. The Big Barracks was next seen to disgorge its garrison, a large company of horsemen who rode away over the hills, and that building, too, was burned after midnight. Large stores of wheat and ammunition were found. It all reminded one of the seventh chapter of II Kings.

The whole city was awake, singing and rejoicing all night. In the morning its inhabitants could go whither they would unafraid. And now came the first check to our rejoicing. Miss McLaren was gone! She and Schwester Martha had been sent with the patients of the Turkish hospital four days before to Bitlis.

Mr. Yarrow went to the hospital. He found there twenty-five wounded soldiers too sick to travel, left there without food or water for five days. He found unburied dead. He stayed all day in the horrible place, that his presence might protect the terrified creatures until he could secure their removal to our hospital.

On Wednesday, the 19th May, the Russians and Russo-Armenian volunteers came into the city. It had been the knowledge of their approach that had caused the Turks to flee. Some hard fighting had to be done in the villages, however, before Djevdet and his reinforcements were driven out of the province. Troops poured into the city from Russia and Persia and passed on towards Bitlis.

Aram was made temporary governor of the province, and, for the first time for centuries, Armenians were given a chance to govern themselves. Business revived. People began to rebuild their burned houses and shops. We reopened our mission schools, except the school in the walled city, the school-house there having been burned.

THE TABLES TURNED

Not all the Turks had fled from the city. Some old men and women and children had stayed behind, many of them in hiding. The Armenian soldiers, unlike Turks, were not making war on such. There was only one place where the captives could be safe from the rabble, however. In their dilemma the Armenians turned, as usual, to the American missionaries. And so it came to pass that hardly had the six thousand Armenian refugees left our premises when the care of a thousand Turkish refugees was thrust upon us, some of them from villages the Russo-Armenian volunteers were "cleaning out."

It was with the greatest difficulty that food could be procured for these people. The city had an army to feed now. Wheat—the stores left by the Turks—was obtainable, but no flour, and the use of a mill was not available for some time. The missionaries had no help in a task so distasteful to the Armenians except that of two or three teachers of the school in the walled city, who now had no other work. Mr. Yarrow was obliged to drop most of his other duties and spend practically all his time working for our proteges. Mrs. Yarrow, Miss Rogers and Miss Silliman administered medicines and tried to give everyone of the poor creatures a bath. Mrs. Ussher had bedding made, and secured and personally dispensed milk to the children and sick, spending several hours daily among them.

The wild Cossacks considered the Turkish women legitimate prey, and though the Russian General gave us a small guard, there was seldom a night during the first two or three weeks in which Dr. Ussher and Mr. Yarrow did not have to drive off marauders who had climbed over the walls of the compound and eluded the guard.

The effect on its followers of the religion of Islam was never more strongly contrasted with Christianity. While the Armenian refugees had been mutually helpful and self-sacrificing, these Moslems showed themselves absolutely selfish, callous and indifferent to each other's suffering. Where the Armenians had been cheery and hopeful, and had clung to life with wonderful vitality, the Moslems, with no faith in God and no hope of a future life, bereft now of hope in this life, died like flies of the prevailing dysentery from lack of stamina and the will to live.

The situation became intolerable. The missionaries begged the Russian General to send these people out to villages, with a guard sufficient for safety and flocks to maintain them until they could begin to get their living from the soil. He was too much occupied with other matters to attend to us.

After six weeks of this, Countess Alexandra Tolstoi (daughter of the famous novelist) came to Van and took off our hands the care of our "guests," though they remained on our premises. She was a young woman, simple, sensible and lovable. We gave her a surprise party on her birthday, carrying her the traditional cake with candles and crowning her with flowers, and she declared she never had a birthday so delightfully celebrated in all her life. She worked hard for her charges. When her funds gave out and no more were forthcoming and her Russian helpers fell ill, she succeeded where we had failed and induced the General to send the Turks out into the country with provision for their safety and sustenance.

THE PESTILENCE THAT WALKETH IN DARKNESS

Our Turkish refugees cost us a fearful price.

The last day of June Mrs. Ussher took her children, who had whooping cough, out of the pestilential atmosphere of the city to Artamid, the summer home on Lake Van, nine miles away. Dr. Ussher went there for the week-end, desperately in need of a little rest. On Saturday night they both became very ill. Upon hearing of this I went down to take care of them. On Monday Mr. and Mrs. Yarrow also fell ill. Ten days yet remained till the time set for closing the hospital for the summer, but Miss Bond set her nurses to the task of sending the patients away and went over to nurse the Yarrows. This left me without help for five days. Then, for four days more, two Armenian nurses cared for the sick ones at night and an untrained man nurse helped me during the daytime. Miss Rogers had come down on Thursday, the day after commencement, for the cure of what she believed to be an attack of malaria. On Friday she too fell ill. Fortunately, there was at last a really good Russian physician in town, and he was most faithful in his attendance. The sickness proved to be typhus. Later we learned that at about the same time Miss Silliman, who had left for America on her furlough on the 15th June, accompanied by Neville Ussher, had been ill at Tiflis with what we now know was a mild form of the same disease. Dr. Ussher might have contracted it from his outside patients, but the others undoubtedly contracted it from the Turkish refugees.

Mrs. Yarrow was dangerously ill, but passed her crisis

safely and first of all. Miss Bond then came to Artamid, though Mr. Yarrow was still very ill, feeling that the Usshers needed her more on account of their distance from the doctor. Miss Ussher took charge of the Yarrow children up in Van; Mrs. Raynolds managed the business affairs of the mission.

Mrs. Ussher had a very severe form of the disease, and her delicate frame, worn out with the overwork and terrible strain of the months past, could make no resistance. On the 14th July she entered into the life eternal.

We dared not let the sick ones suspect what had happened. Dr. Ussher was too ill at the time and for more than two weeks longer to be told of his terrible loss. For three months preceding his illness he had been the only physician in Van, and the strain of overwork and sleeplessness told severely now. After he had passed his typhus crisis, his life was in danger for a week longer from the pneumonia which had been a complication from the first. Then followed another not infrequent complication of typhus, an abscess in the parotid gland which caused long-continued weakness and suffering, at one time threatened life and reason, and has had serious consequences which may prove permanent. Mr. Yarrow was so ill that his life was quite despaired of. It was by a veritable miracle that he was restored to us.

FLIGHT

Meanwhile the Russian army had been slowly advancing westward. It had not been uniformly successful as we had expected it to be. Indeed, the Russians seemed to fight sluggishly and unenthusiastically. The Russo-Armenian volunteers, who were always sent ahead of the main army, did the heavy fighting. By the last week of July the Russians had not yet taken Bitlis, only ninety miles distant from Van. Suddenly the Turkish army began to advance towards Van, and the Russian army to retreat.

On Friday, the 30th July, General Nicolaieff ordered all the Armenians of the Van province, also the Americans and other foreigners, to flee for their lives. By Saturday night the city was nearly emptied of Armenians, and quite emptied of conveyances. Nearly all our teachers, nurses, employees had left. It was every man for himself and no one to help us secure carriages or horses for our own flight.

We at Artamid, with a sick man to provide for, would have had great difficulty in getting up to the city in time, had not Mrs. Yarrow risen from her sick-bed to go to the General and beg him to send us ambulances. These reached us after midnight.

There was little question in our minds as to our own flight. Our experience during the siege had shown us that the fact of our being Americans would not protect us from the Turks. Had not our two men, Mr. Yarrow and Dr. Ussher, been absolutely helpless we might have debated the matter. As it was, we women could not assume the responsibility of staying and keeping them there, and even if we had stayed we could have found no means to live in a deserted city.

We were fifteen Americans and had ten Armenian dependents—women and children—to provide for. The head nurse of the hospital, Garabed, plucky and loyal little fellow that he was, had sent on his mother and wife and had remained behind to help us get out of the country. Dr. Ussher's man-cook, having been with us at Artamid, when the panic began, had been unable to secure conveyance for his sick wife. We greatly needed his help on the journey, but this involved our providing for a third sick person. We had three horses, an American grocer's delivery cart, really not strong enough for heavy work on rough and mountainous roads, and a small cart that would seat three. Our two other carts were not usable.

We begged the General to give us ambulances. He absolutely refused—he had none to spare. But, he added, he was to be replaced in a day or two by General Trokin; we could appeal to him when he came; the danger was not immediate. Somewhat reassured and not knowing how we could manage without help from the Russians, we made no effort to leave that day. But the next day, Monday, we heard that the volunteers who were trying to keep the road open to Russia would not be able to do so much longer—there was no time to lose. We set to work.

One of our teachers who had not succeeded in getting away before Monday morning, kindly took a small bag of clothing on his ox-cart for each of us. We spread the quilts and blankets we should need on the way on the bottom of the delivery cart, intending to lay our three sick people on these. Garabed, who had never driven a team in his life, must drive two of our horses in this cart. Mrs. Raynolds would drive the third horse harnessed to the small cart, and take the babies and what food there was possibly room for; no provisions could be bought on the way. The rest of us must walk, though Mrs. Yarrow and Miss Rogers were newly risen from a sick bed and the children were all under twelve. We put loads on the cows we must take with us for the sake of the babies and the patients. But the cows were refractory; they kicked off the loads and ran wildly about the yard, tails up, heads down, whereupon the single horse broke loose and "also ran," smashing the small cart.

At this moment, the "psychological moment," two doctors of the Russian Red Cross rode into our yard. Seeing our plight they turned and rode out again. They returned a little later and on *their own responsibility* promised to take us with the Red Cross caravan. Thank the Lord!

We now put our loads on the delivery cart; put the wheels of the smashed cart on the body of a wheelless cart, and now that we might take a little more with us that food and bedding, packed in bags what we felt to be absolutely necessary. What we left behind we should never see again; we felt certain that the Russian soldiers before they left would loot our houses and perhaps burn them to forestall the Turks.

The Red Cross provided us with two ambulances with horses and drivers, and a stretcher carried between two horses for Dr. Ussher. He was usually taken into one of their sick tents when we camped at night; most of the rest of us slept on the ground in the open.

We left on Tuesday, the 3rd August. The Russians appeared to have received news that made them very uneasy, and, indeed, General Trokin himself left Van that very afternoon, as we learned later. The next day at sundown we heard the firing between the Kurds and the volunteers who were so gallantly trying to keep them at bay, to keep the road to Russia open as long as possible. It sounded startlingly clear. We travelled till two a. m. that night in order to reach Bergri, where we should be, not safe, but beyond the line along which the Turks would try to intercept travellers. We were just in time. General Trokin's party, that had left Van only a few hours later than we, were unable to reach Bergri, and had to return and get out by the longer route through Persia. Had we with our slower rate of travel been obliged to do this, we might not have been able to get out at all.

Miss Knapp continues her narration of the journey to Etch-miadzin, thence to Tiflis. Several of her companions were laid to rest in Van and on the way. The remaining members of the group sailed from Christiana on a Danish ship and arrived in New York on October 5, 1915.

Clarence D. Ussher, M.D., an American physician, author of *An American Physician in Turkey,* with Grace H. Knapp collaborating, was an eye-witness to the entire Van episode which the Turks have characterized as a revolt against the government and have cited it as justification for their crimi-nal acts to exterminate the Armenians. The event at Van was, in reality, a life-and-death struggle by the Armenians to de-fend their lives, their homes, their honor, and their property, with the hope that their deliverance by the Russian forces would come before their total destruction.

It is not our intention, nor is it within the scope of this volume, to review in detail the contents of this extremely interesting book wherein the author records in moving terms his experiences in Turkey from the day he "sailed from Bos-ton on S.S. Armenian, May 12, 1898" to the day he and his party left Van on August 3, 1915. We shall select certain passages of the book specifically relating to the episode of Van, where the Armenians "were believed to have rebelled against the Ottoman Government." "It is important," writes Dr. Ussher in the preface to his book, "that the facts of the case should be made widely known, and that their (Arme-nians') actual loyalty, their patience under almost unimagin-able provocation, and their heroism when loyalty and patience proved of no avail, should receive their due share of pub-licity and appreciation."

After attending the annual meeting of the Eastern Turkey Mission at Harput, as delegates from Van, in July, 1914, Dr. Ussher and his co-delegates returned to Van where they "found conscription going on and the people in a panic. . . . All males between the ages of twenty and forty-five were re-quired to register. . . . Many Turks and Kurds and a much smaller proportion of Armenians would not register and were considered deserters. Very many Armenians enlisted willingly, glad of a chance to demonstrate their equality with the Turks, and these became brave and efficient soldiers. At Sarekamish on the Erzeroum front the Russians drove the Turks back to Kupri Keuy, and I was informed by a Turkish officer that they there encountered Armenian regiments which hurled the Russians back across the border, capturing one of their cities. The Turkish general sent a telegram to the Vali of Van congratulating him on the valor of his Armenian troops." (pp. 216–217)

In spite of this irrefutable proof of loyalty shown by the Armenians "a week after this battle orders were received from Enver Bey, Minister of War, to disarm all Armenians in the army. This proceeding led to the desertion of many. The disarmed soldiers, among whom were men of education and refinement, some of them graduates of noted American and English universities, were set to digging trenches and making roads. When the makers of roads had finished their work, their Turkish officers, first circulating a report that they were in revolt, had groups of them surrounded and shot down."

Dr. Ussher attributes "the comparative freedom from disturbance" in Van "during the fall, and winter of 1914 and 1915" to "a strong and liberal-minded Vali" who had been transferred to Erzeroum in February (1915) and was succeeded by Jevdet Bey, brother-in-law of Enver Pasha, Minister of War.

When the Vali returned to Van from the Russian border he was greeted by "a great number of prominent Armenians" with almost royal honors "several miles out of the city." "Descending from his carriage," writes Dr. Ussher, "he embraced Vremyan who had been a classmate of his at a Turkish college. Although he was not aware of it, he had just been saved from assassination at the hand of a justly outraged youth by the intervention of these Tashnagist leaders." (Ibid, p. 234)

Dr. Ussher asserts that the Armenians had "proved their loyalty to the government in many ways" and cites several examples. "In spite of the fact that a special order had been sent from Constantinople a few months earlier permitting all Armenians to pay the exemption fee" the new Vali refused the exemption fee and "demanded four thousand soldiers from the Armenians although all of their race in the army had been disarmed." The Armenians refused that demand and offered to give four hundred.

The situation deteriorated day by day, hour by hour. The rumblings of a volcanic eruption were getting louder and louder, ready to burst forth to spread death and destruction in its catastrophic advance. Let us listen to Dr. Ussher's calm and collected description of the events that led to the "revolt" of the Armenians of Van:

> Before sunrise Tuesday, April 20 (1915), we heard several rifle shots on Varak plain. They were followed by a fusillade. During the night Turkish soldiers had occupied a line of trenches about the Armenian quarter of Aikesdan (the Garden City). Two of them had seized a beautiful young woman, one of our former orphan girls fleeing with her children to the City from Shushantz. Two Armenian men running up to rescue the woman were fired at by the Turkish soldiers and killed. All this took place before the German Orphanage premises and was witnessed by Herr and Frau Sporri. Those few shots had been the signal for a general fusillade by the Turks on all sides, and almost immediately Jevdet Bey opened artillery fire on the Armenian quarter in Aikesdan and also on the Armenian quarter in the walled city.
>
> Massacre had so often threatened Van that the Huntchagist (whose leaders were all in prison), Armenist and Tashnagist leaders had before the Turkish Revolution prepared for such an event. They had trained young men as marksmen and smuggled in a quantity of arms and ammunition. Most of the ammunition had been found and seized by the Government a short time before the Revolution. After the Constitutional government had been established (1908) with 'Liberty, Equality, and Fraternity' as its motto, the Armenians had transformed their revolutionary societies into political parties and had ceased to drill their young men. The mobilization of 1914 had greatly reduced their numbers. The greater part of the ammunition which had escaped seizure in 1908 had been secreted in the near-

by villages with the expectation that in the event of a massacre the peasantry would come to the defense of the city.

But in this spring of 1915 very few men had been left in the villages. Thus it came about that in this crisis there were only about three hundred men armed with rifles, and a thousand armed with pistols and antique weapons, to defend thirty thousand Armenians, an area of over a square mile in Aikesdan, and an area of less than a square mile in the walled city. Their leaders had, however, laid their plans carefully during the week past and now bands of young men at the street corners on the boundaries of the Armenian quarter were ready for the oncoming Turkish mob and a charge of infantry. Their return fire was so utterly unexpected that the infantry sought cover. (pp. 247–249)

The (Armenian Military) Council issued orders to their soldiers not to drink, not to curse the religion of the Turks, to spare women and children, and to report truthfully the actions in which they were engaged. (p. 251)

Speaking about Jevdet Bey, the Vali of the province of Van, Dr. Ussher states:

Jevdet Bey had proved himself past-master of the art of concealment and dissimulation. He had deceived even the Armenians as to his intentions; he had pretended to take counsel with their leaders and to need their help up to the very hour of the murder of Ishkhan." (p. 260)

. . . On Monday, the 19th (of April), while he was assuring the people of Van that there would be no further molestation of Armenians, the sub-governor of Arjish (Aqantz), the next largest town of the province, following his orders, summoned the prominent men of the place to the Government building on the pretense of important business. Then his soldiers collected the rest of the Armenian male inhabitants (two thousand five hundred) and after dark they were taken in groups of fifty with their hands tied behind them to the bank of the river and slain. Three, feigning death, escaped at night from under the bodies of their companions. The women and children and property were divided among the Turks.

That Monday all the villages in the province were attacked by Jevdet Bey's soldiers and by Kurds under his command. Shadakh was unconquerable. Moks was protected by a Kurdish chief. Several villages held out as long as their ammunition lasted, but the rest made no resistance; they had lost most of their men by conscription, had no leaders, and were unable to cooperate. *We have absolute proof that fifty-five thousand people were killed.* [Emphasis ours—D.H.B.] (pp. 264-265)

"There was only one hope for the city;" writes Dr. Ussher. "The coming of the Russians—the coming of the Russians *in time.*" [Emphasis ours—D.H.B.]

And the Russians came. The advance guard of the Russo-Armenian regiment entered the city on May 18, exactly four weeks after the Turks seized the city.

The Russian occupation of the vilayet of Van lasted only ten weeks. A general retreat was ordered on July 31. Russia "was not prepared for the war and needed all her munitions at the German front."

The Armenians of Van, who had repelled all Turkish attacks, had to abandon their homes because of the retreat of the Russian forces. General Nicolaieff's proclamation was unmistakable: all people of the province, foreigners as well as Armenians, were ordered to flee.

> Unceasingly throughout that night could be heard from the highway half a mile distant the sound of a great multitude hastening northward—the peasantry of the region fleeing from their homes. (p. 303)
> Before nightfall (August 3, 1915), having overtaken many of the people who had left Van and the region west of it before us on foot, we had become part of the vast ever northward-flowing stream of humanity, the great multitude plodding along in the dust, their faces strained with terror. Not one of all these but knew, most of them by the witness of their own eyes, what it meant to fall into the hands of their oppressors. This was the Exodus of a nation from the land of their captivity. But, alas! it was their homeland as well—the home of the race for centuries before the Turk subjugated all the eastern world. They were leaving the homes they had built with their own hands and the homes of their ancestors for many generations, the fields they had tilled all their lives, the harvests they had sown a few

months before, and all their possessions except what they could carry with them in hurried flight. (Ibid, pp. 308–309)

In passing through "a narrow gorge commanded by precipitous hills bristling with rocks" the advancing "unarmed multitude hemmed in between hills and river," was fired upon by the Turks and Kurds. "Hundreds threw themselves over the precipice into the river to escape the worse fate of falling into the hands of the Kurds. Fathers and mothers killed their own children to save them from the Turks. But thousands struggled in panting, gasping, for mile after mile. . . . It seemed an eternity of horror. . . ."

"More than a year later," writes Dr. Ussher, "in that long, narrow valley through which we had raced so madly, were found the whitening skeletons of about seven thousand men, women, and children who had come to their death by the hand of the Turk that day."

After describing the tragic events at Van, Dr. Ussher writes:

It is the Turkish Government, not the Turkish people, that has done all this. The Government has tried to deceive its Mohammedan subjects and arouse their hatred against the Christians. Jevdet Bey reported the Van Armenians as in rebellion. The fifty-five thousand slaughtered Armenians in that province were reported as fifty-five thousand Mohammedans massacred by Christians. He described in revolting detail actual atrocities,—women and children, ranging in age from six years to eighty, outraged and mutilated to death,—but made one diabolical change in his description: he said these women were Moslems thus treated by Christians. (Ibid. pp. 328–329)

Thousands of Armenians, after struggling footsore and starving along the road to exile for days, whipped along when exhausted, have been taken into Moslem villages and given their choice: "Now accept Mohammed and you shall have home and food and clothing and fields and implements and seed and a bonus from the Government—everything you need. Refuse and you shall not have a drop of water." With hardly an exception these thousands have turned their backs on all thus offered and have gone into the desert to death, rather than deny Christ. (Ibid. p. 331)

Besides Dr. Ussher and Miss Knapp, who were eyewitnesses to the events at Van, there is the moving account by the noble American Ambassador to Turkey, Henry Morgenthau, who labored with such diligence and anguish on behalf of the Armenians. In his fascinating record of those dreadful days *Ambassador Morgenthau's Story*, he writes in Chapter XXIII:

> The Turkish province of Van lies in the remote northeastern corner of Asia Minor; it touches the frontier of Persia on the east and its northern boundary looks toward the Caucasus. . . The location of this vilayet, however, inevitably made it the scene of military operations, and made the activities of its Armenian population a matter of daily suspicion. . . When the war started, the Central Government recalled Tahsin Pasha, the conciliatory governor of Van, and replaced him with Djevdet Bey, a brother-in-law of Enver Pasha (the Minister of War). This act in itself was most disquieting. . . He (Djevdet) hated the Armenians and cordially sympathized with the long-established Turkish plan of solving the Armenian problems . . . Early in the spring the Russians temporarily retreated . . . Instead of following the retreating foe . . . The Turks' army turned . . . their rifles, machine guns and other weapons upon the Armenian women and children and old men in the villages of Van. Following their usual custom, they distributed the most beautiful Armenian women among the Moslems, sacked and burned the Armenian villages, and massacred uninterruptedly for days. On April 15th, about 500 young Armenian men of Akantz were mustered to hear an order of the Sultan; at sunset they were marched outside the town and every man shot in cold blood. This procedure was repeated in about eighty Armenian villages in the district, north of Lake Van, and in three days 24,000 Armenians were murdered in this atrocious fashion . . . And so when Djevdet Bey, on his return to his official post, demanded that Van furnish him immediately 4,000 soldiers, the people were naturally in no mood to accede to his request . . . Djevdet, acting in obedience to orders from Constantinople, was preparing to wipe out the whole population, and his purpose for calling for 4,000 able-bodied men was merely to massacre them, so that the rest of the Armenians might have no defend-

ers. The Armenians . . . offered to furnish five hundred soldiers and to pay exemption money for the rest; now, however, Djevdet began to talk aloud about "rebellion," and his determination to "crush" it at any cost. "If the rebels fire a single shot," he declared, "I shall kill every Christian man, woman, and' (pointing to his knee) 'every child, up to here." For some time the Turks had been constructing entrenchments around the Armenian quarter and filling them with soldiers and, in response to this provocation, the Armenians began to make preparations for a defense. On April 20th, a band of Turkish soldiers seized several Armenian women who were entering the city; a couple of Armenians ran to their assistance and were shot dead. The Turks now opened fire on the Armenian quarters with rifles and artillery; soon a large part of the town was in flames and a regular siege had started. The whole Armenian fighting force consisted of only 1,500 men; they had only 300 rifles and a most inadequate supply of ammunition; while Djevdet had an army of 5,000 men, completely equipped and supplied. Yet the Armenians fought with the utmost heroism and skill; they had little chance of holding off their enemies indefinitely, but they knew that a Russian army was fighting its way to Van and their utmost hope was that they would be able to defy the besiegers until these Russians arrived. As I am not writing the story of sieges and battles, I cannot describe in detail the numerous acts of individual heroism, the cooperation of the Armenian women, the ardour and energy of the Armenian children, the self-sacrificing zeal of the American missionaries, especially Dr. Ussher and his wife and Miss Grace H. Knapp, and the thousand other circumstances that made this terrible month one of the most glorious pages in modern Armenian history. The wonderful thing about it is that the Armenians triumphed . . . After driving off the Turks, the Russians began to collect and cremate the bodies of Armenians who had been murdered in the province, with the result that 55,000 bodies were burned.

I have told this story of the 'Revolution' in Van not only because it marked the first stage of this organized attempt to wipe out a whole nation, but because these events are always brought forward by the Turks as a justification of their subsequent crimes. (pp. 293–300)

In Chapter XXIV entitled "The Murder of a Nation," after relating the gruesome details of massacres and deportation, Mr. Morgenthau writes:

My only reason for relating such dreadful things as this is that, without details, the English-speaking public cannot understand precisely what this nation is which we call Turkey. I have by no means told the most terrible details, for a complete narration of the sadistic orgies of which these Armenian men and women were victims can never be printed in any American publication. Whatever crimes the most perverted instincts of the human mind can devise, and whatever refinements of persecution and injustice the most debased imaginations can conceive, became the daily misfortunes of this devoted people. I am confident that the whole history of the human race contains no such horrible episode as this. The great massacres and persecutions of the past seem almost insignificant when compared with the sufferings of the Armenian race in 1915. (pp. 321–322)

APPENDIX A

Chapter 5

As in the case of the Nazis' treatment of the Jews, the idea of reparations appeared even before the worst was over. Similarly, the idea of an Armenian homeland, roughly comparable in purpose to that of Zionism, emerged as early as 1916 among the enlightened sympathizers with the Armenian people. Either as tradition or as partial redress of grievance, an Armenian homeland made sense. In addition, such a homeland could only tend toward the domestic improvement of Turkey itself, a thesis almost self-demonstrating and soon to be proved in abundance with the establishment of Soviet Armenia.

As early as the fall of 1916, then, and for a number of years thereafter, the cause of an Armenian homeland found its champions in America, Britain, France and other countries. It appeared for a time to be an irresistible movement, and its legitimacy was taken for granted at the Paris Peace Conference after the War. It is interesting to trace its genesis, just as it is depressing to analyze its betrayal in after years.

A large number of documents urging the Armenian cause, ranging from the spontaneous to the official, appear in the following pages.

1. *W. Llew. Williams*, in an article entitled "The Great Opportunity," quoted in *The New Armenia*, November 15, 1916:

Supposing, however, Armenia is cruelly defeated in her hopes. Supposing, and the supposition is not an impossible one, that no help came to Armenia from Europe. It may be that at the Peace Congress the assembled statesmen of Europe in hammering out terms of peace may see fit once again to sacrifice Armenia and the Armenians to their own apparent interests—that, despite all their high-sound-

441

ing declarations, at the last moment they may ignore them, not discerning where their true interests, the interests of peace lie. Once before Armenia in her sore need turned to Europe, sought from the Christian Powers aid against the advancing Moslem hordes, and found no response. They were utterly subdued, and for centuries lay forgotten beneath the yoke of the oppressor. That has not destroyed the people, nor extinguished their 'obstinate nationality,' nor weakened their persistent demand to be free. If Europe decrees that Armenia must be dealt with as a pawn in the diplomatic game, be moved hither and thither, given to this Power or the other, that will not end the Armenian Question. It will still remain to be faced. . . . The interests of peace after this world war will be supreme. The nations will need a prolonged period to recover, heal the wounds inflicted, repair the incalculable damage wrought. Peace can only be established on Righteousness. Justice and Right demand that Armenia shall be satisfied—shall, after the centuries of darkness and sorrow, know a new day of light and joy.

2. *Prof. Arnold J. Toynbee*, article entitled "The Position of Armenia," published in *The New Armenia*, October 15, 1917:

"The claim of Armenia to national independence is three-fold—the sanction of the Berlin Treaty, the wrongs Armenia has endured, and the capacity of her people to hold their own in the world, which they have proved by their miraculous survival."

3. *David Lloyd George*, speech in the House of Commons, December 21, 1917:

"Some say that the Government has not fully stated the objects of the war . . . I stated them quite clearly at Glasgow. . . .

"In the second place the question of Mesopotamia must be resolved by the Peace Conference, with the clear understanding, however, that neither that region nor Armenia can ever be put back under the blighting dominion of the Turks."

4. *Stephen Pichon,* speech in the French Chamber of Deputies, December 27, 1917:

"The allies in their reply of January 10, 1917 to President Wilson stated that it was far from their purpose to annex or incorporate alien territories . . . the policy of the rights of nationalities is the honour of our traditions and history . . . and it applies to the Armenians."

5. *Anatole France,* (pseud. of Jacques Anatole Thibault), speaking at a protest mass-meeting at the Sorbonne, Paris, said in part:

> When we saw in Turkey that unfortunate victim, who has looked to us full of hope we finally understood that our sister was dying in the East. That she was dying solely because she is our sister. Her only crime was that she shared our sentiments. She loved what we have loved, she thought as we thought, she believed as we have believed, and like us she has acquired wisdom, poetry and art. Her crime is only that. . . . (Translated from the Introductory Chapter written by H. Kotzhar, for the book entitled *The Tragedy of the Armenian People,* by A. N. Mnatzakanian, 1965)
>
> After the victory of our armies, which are fighting for justice and liberty, the Allies will have great duties to fulfill; and the most sacred of them will be to bestow life again on the martyred nations—on Belgium and Serbia. They will also insure the safety and independence of Armenia. Turning to her, they will say 'Sister, arise! Suffer no longer; Thou art henceforth free to live in accordance with thy genius and thy faith. (Reproduced from *The New Armenia,* December 1917, p. 346)

6. *David Lloyd George,* speech, January 5, 1918, addressed to the Trade Unions and quoted in *La Societe des Nations et les Puissances devant le Probleme Armenien,* by Andre N. Mandelstam:

"Almost simultaneously with the proclamation of the (President Wilson's) fourteen points on January 5, 1918 Mr.

Lloyd George, in a speech addressed to the Trade Unions, declared that . . . Arabia, Armenia, Mesopotamia, Palestine, and Syria in England's view, were entitled to recognition of their separate national conditions."

7. *Lord A. J. Balfour,* answering Ramsay MacDonald in the British House of Commons, July 11, 1918; quoted in a pamphlet entitled "Armenia's Charter," 1918:

> The following is a full report of the question put in the House of Commons on Thursday, July 11, 1918 by Mr. Ramsay MacDonald, and the answer given by Mr. Balfour:
> Mr. Ramsay MacDonald asked the Secretary of State for Foreign Affairs if he is following the resistance which the Armenians are offering to the Turkish army seeking to overthrow the Armenian Republic in consequence of the declaration of that Republic that it will not accept the provisions of the Brest-Litovsk Treaty regarding Armenia; and whether the Allied Governments pledge themselves to do everything in their power when the settlement after the war comes to be made that the future of Armenia will be decided upon the principle of self-determination?
> Mr. Balfour: Yes, Sir; His Majesty's Government are following with earnest sympathy and admiration the gallant resistance of the Armenians in defence of their liberties and honour, and are doing everything they can to come to their assistance. As regards the future of Armenia, I would refer the Hon. Member to the public statements made by leading statesmen among the Allied Powers in favour of a settlement upon the principle he indicates.

8. *David Lloyd George,* addressing a group of Armenians, Manchester, England, September 11, 1918, quoted in "Armenia's Charter":

> Gentlemen: I am honoured and touched by your address. The spirit of confidence which breathes through your words is a striking demonstration of the unconquerable resolve of your stricken nation. The cry of Armenia is both piteous and compelling, but that which gives her the greatest claim to the unqualified support of those who are fighting for the liberties of mankind is that her sons never falter in their determination to achieve their pur-

pose. In spite of persecution and disaster, and of ruthless and scientific repression, Armenia still claims justice from the world and disdains to crave for mercy from her oppressors.

I ask you to believe, gentlemen, that those responsible for the government of this country are not unmindful of their responsibilities to your martyred race. (p. 9)

9. *Rene Pinon*, article entitled "L'Independence de l'Armenie," published in *La Voix de l'Armenie*, December 15, 1918:

> Since the beginning of the war the Armenians have been actual belligerents; they have suffered for the Allied cause to which they have been steadfastly loyal to the end. In France, in Palestine, in the Caucasus they have fought against the enemies of the Allies for the cause of oppressed peoples. It is just that they reap their part of the victory in form of independence. Besides, there is no race in the world which has given, for many centuries the most extraordinary proofs of its vitality; it has preserved its character, its language and its religion intact through all the vicissitudes of its often glorious, but always tragic, history. (p. 864)

10. *Raymond Poincare*, letter to Msgr. Paul Pierre, Feb. 16, 1919, quoted in *The Lausanne Treaty, Turkey and Armenia"*:

"The Government of the Republic (of France) does not consider that it has already accomplished the task that devolves upon it with regard to the Armenian people. It knows full well that Armenia, and particularly noble Cilicia, expect it to help them so that it may be possible for them to enjoy in security the benefits of peace and liberty. I may assure your Beatitude that France shall respond to the faith that has been reposed in her." (p. 197)

11. *Camille Mauclair,* letter to the editor, published in *La Voix de l'Armenie*, December 1, 1918, and in *Reponses A Pierre Loti—Ami des Massacreurs:*

My dear Colleague:

I consider it my duty as a Frenchman and as a writer to lodge an indignant protest against the article in *l'Echo de Paris,* where M. Pierre Loti reiterates his fantastic love for the Turks and dares to insult the heroism of the Armenians by lending the prestige of his name to the false assertions concerning the events at Bakou—even after the authoritative refutation by Lord Cecil, which he (Loti) could not have ignored.

The genuine admiration which I have always had for Mr. Loti's talents as a novelist has nothing to do with my absolute denial of such erroneous assertions to which my conscience opposes. At the hour when Turkey, the enemy of France, is capitulating, giving publicity to such fables intended to injure Armenia, a friend and ally of France, is more than an unbecoming conduct on the part of a Frenchman and a French officer.

I am sure that many writers have read, like me, that article of Mr. Loti, with astonishment and chagrin. (p. 7)

Mr. Mauclair ends his letter thus:

"Long live autonomous Armenia, co-belligerent, a valiant ally and a very much loved friend." (p. 8)

12. *Viscount Herbert E. Gladstone,* speech in Westminster, June 19, in *Armenia & the Settlement,* 1919:

Armenia for generations has been spoken of, written of, sympathized with; there have been floods of sympathy. But until the time of war little else. The time for action on her behalf has now arrived, and I ask you whether the case of Armenia is not a conclusive argument for the League of Nations? We know the difficulties, great difficulties,—difficulties at present, perhaps, insuperable in some respects. But, it is inconceivable that any association of Great Powers, organized for the purpose of guaranteeing the peace and safety and liberty of the weaker nations of the world, should not be enabled to rescue the Armenians from the hideous state of oppression and brutality under which they have laboured for so many years. (p. 15)

13. *Viscount James Bryce,* speech in Westminster, June 19, 1919, *Armenia & the Settlement,* 1919:

Now at last we rejoice to know that the Powers at Paris appear to have finally decided that Turkish rule is to vanish for ever from all the Armenian regions. (Applause)

I think, and probably you think, that the Turks had too much indulgence shown them in the armistice. The armistice terms ought to have been more stringent. The abominable Turkish Government ought to have been made to realise that they were not only beaten, but that they had committed crimes much too atrocious to entitle them to any consideration whatsoever."

I want to submit to you that an Armenian State must include all Armenia. (Applause) It must include Cilicia on the south, it must include the valley of those gallant mountaineers who for so many centuries maintained at Zeitun their independence against the Turks. The Armenian state must have access to the sea, in order that its commerce may have the development it is entitled to demand. So also Armenia must include that which was the Russian territory in the Caucasus. In that quarter there has already been established an Armenian Republic, which has received a certain measure of recognition from the Powers as being *de facto* independent. (pp. 17–19)

14. *Aneurin Williams,* speech in the same hall, June 19, 1919, *Armenia & the Settlement,* 1919:

We have all striven to do our duty to your (Armenian) people, recognising that the British nation owed a debt to Armenia—owed a debt because unfortunately it has stood in the way, more than once, of her liberation; once pre-eminently when the Russian people would have freed Armenia from the yoke of the Turk. But the time has come when we believe that liberation has come, and we believe that it will be a blessing, not only to the Armenian people but to the Turks who were their oppressors.

15. *Noel Buxton,* speech in the same hall, June 19, 1919, *Armenia & the Settlement,* 1919:

We look to many fruits of liberty to grow out of the great War. But, undoubtedly, to my mind, there is no fruit of liberty among them all which ought to give us such pride and glory as the liberation of Armenia.

Few would have said, I believe, before the War began that there were crying grievances for which it would be worth while to make a War. But there was one exception to this: There were people—and the Duke of Argyll, the great conservative statesman, was one of them—who said deliberately that for such a cause as the liberation of Armenia we must not shrink from the great arbiter of War.

This is a moment when the citizens of the world might reflect that a ghastly horror has for long ages resulted from the want of charity and sympathy of the world, and partly from its want of energy in organizing the suppression of evil. But for us Britons there is something more than that to reflect upon. It is for us a moment when we may reflect upon the tragic part we have played, the enormous debt we owe to the Armenian race, we who are told even by a conservative statesman like the Duke of Argyll that "we have kept these people under a barbaric despotism." (pp. 32–33)

16. *Alexandre Millerand,* speech in Spa, July 16, 1920, quoted in *The Great Betrayal,* by E. H. Bierstadt:

The Allies see clearly that the time has come to put an end to Turkish domination over other races. During the past twenty years Armenians have been massacred with unexampled brutality. During the war, the exploits of the Turkish Government, in massacres, deportations and bad treatment of prisoners of war, exceeded in ferocity its former misdeeds. Not only has the Government failed to protect its subjects against murder and pillage, but it itself has organized and perpetrated these outrages. The Allies are determined to liberate from Turkish rule the regions inhabited by non-Turks.

17. *Morris Gilbert,* letter to the editor, *Manchester Guardian,* November 1920, quoted in *The New Armenia,* November-December, 1920:

France, without question, has failed in Cilicia. It would, I believe, have been easier and more profitable in the long run not to fail than to have adopted the long process of diminishing control, power, and prestige which we have witnessed. A policy similar to the British civil policy in

the country—that is, in short, a light hand on the reins—
might have staved off the conclusions which began to be
tried last January. Success in combatting the accusation
of corrupt dealing would have had value. A strong position, not tinged with so-called pro-Turk sentiment, would
have had a salutary effect both on Christian and Moslem.

In the last analysis, France has failed because, when
the crisis came, she was unwilling to throw sufficient force
into the field to hold the balance. Force, I should judge, is
what no Allied nation will spend in Cilicia—and force is
probably the only thing that can help Cilicia. But I am
convinced that it is both bad morals and bad policy not
to help Cilicia. Historically, Cilicia belongs to the Armenians; in population it belongs to Christianity; in the matters of justice and development it belongs to civilization.
In none of these attributes is the province related to the
Moslem or to the brigands who to-day are dictating to the
Western Powers what is to be done with the Near Eastern
world.

18. *President Woodrow Wilson:*

(1) Letter to Rabbi Stephen S. Wise, June, 1917, wherein
he wrote in part:
"When the war shall have ended, there are two lands that
will never go back to the Turkish Apache. One is Christian
Armenia; and the other, Jewish Palestine." (*The New Armenia,* March-April 1924, p. 21)
(2) Letter to Rt. Rev. Philip M. Rhinelander, dated November 11, 1918, wherein he wrote in part:
"Let me assure you of my profound interest in everything
that affects the Armenian people. I hope with all my heart
that it may be possible for me to serve them in some substantial way." (Ibid, p. 22)
(3) Speech in Boston, Massachusetts, February 24, 1919,
wherein he stated in part:
"Have you thought of the sufferings of Armenia? You
poured out your money to help succor the Armenians after
they suffered; now set your strength so that they shall never
suffer again." (Ibid, p. 22)

19. *Everett P. Wheeler,* in an article entitled "Armenian Independence," published in *The New Armenia,* September 15, 1917, wrote in part:

"The only remedy for Armenian wrongs is Armenian independence. Give to that brave and loyal people freedom and security and they will make Asia Minor a fertile field, as it was when Rome held sway; and will give to our citizens there that just treatment which has been so long denied." [Emphasis ours—D.H.B.] (p. 276)

20. *Senator Henry Cabot Lodge,* resolution introduced in the United States Senate on December 10, 1918, and quoted in *The New Armenia,* January-February 1925.

"Resolved, that in the opinion of the Senate, Armenia (including the six vilayets of Turkish Armenia and Cilicia, Russian Armenia, and the northern part of the Province of Azerbaijan, Persian Armenia) should be independent, and that it is the hope of the Senate that the peace conference will make arrangements for helping Armenia to establish an independent republic." (p. 7)

21. *Henry Morgenthau,* in an article entitled "The Greatest Horror in History," published in *The Red Cross Magazine,* March, 1918, ends his article with the following significant words:

I wonder if four hundred millions of Christians, in full control of all the governments of Europe and America, are going to again condone these offences by the Turkish Government! Will they, like Germany, take the bloody hand of the Turk, forgive him and decorate him, as Kaiser Wilhelm has done, with the highest orders? Will the outrageous terrorizing—the cruel torturing—the driving of women into the harems—the debauchery of innocent girls —the sale of many of them at eighty cents each—the murdering of hundreds of thousands and the deportation to and starvation in the deserts of other hundreds of thousands—the destruction of hundreds of villages and cities—will the wilful execution of this whole devilish scheme to annihilate the Armenian, Greek and Syrian Christians of Turkey—will all this go unpunished? Will the Turks be permitted, aye, even encouraged by our cowardice in not striking back, to continue to treat all Christians in their power as "unbelieving dogs?" Or will definite steps be promptly taken to rescue permanently the remnants of these fine, old, civilized Christian peoples from the fangs of the Turk? (p. 15)

22. *Herbert Adams Gibbons,* in an article entitled "The Armenians at the Peace Conference," published in *La Voix de l'Armenie,* December 1, 1918:

No small nation has greater rights to the Gratitude of the Allied Powers than Armenia. (p. 810) [All capitalized by the author]
No small nation has greater rights to the Sympathy of the Civilized World than Armenia. (p. 811) [All capitalized by the author]
The request of the Armenians is reasonable; how can one, in effect, decide their future, the future of the territories inhabited by them, in conformity with the principles proclaimed by the Allied Powers, without having their voice heard?
Restitutions, reparations and guarantees—are these not due to and also necessary for the Armenians, same as to other belligerents? And can we assume a lasting peace in the world without considering the demands and the wishes —from the mouth of their qualified representatives—of small nations which suffered during this war? We cannot ignore, we cannot omit or leave behind any plan whatever of these nations. (p. 811)

23. *The New York Times,* editorial entitled "Armenia," February 16, 1919, published in a pamphlet "America as Mandatory for Armenia":

Inasmuch as the Armenians furnished many of the ablest administrators and statesmen of the Ottoman Empire, in view of the executive capacity which Armenians have displayed in foreign countries where their abilities were given free rein, it would be rash to say that Armenia is not even now capable of full self-government. One thing is to be made secure—that there is to be no Armenian irredenta in so far as the overlapping of populations may make it possible. Armenia has earned the right to full national liberty. According to the last Turkish statistics, nearly 30 percent of the Armenians of the empire, outside of Constantinople, lived in Cilicia, on the Mediterranean. Cilicia is within the sphere of influence alloted to France by the treaties of 1916, but French economic interest could be guaranteed without interfering with the political sovereignty of the Armenians in Armenian territory. (pp. 18–19)

24. *Petition by 25,000 clergymen,* presented to President Wilson on March 3, 1919 and quoted in *The Lausanne Treaty, Turkey and Armenia,* 1923:

We, the undersigned, servants of Christ, representing all the denominations of the Protestant Church and the Holy Catholic Church in the United States of America, and heartily sympathizing with the aspirations of the Armenian people and speaking for them and for the Christian people of America, ask you respectfully to do your utmost to secure and insure the independence of Armenia including the six vilayets, Cilicia, and the littoral of Trebizond in Turkish Armenia, Russian Armenia and Persian Armenia to exert your great influence to the end that the Peace Conference may make requisite arrangements for helping Armenia to establish an independent Republic, and to obtain adequate reparation for the terrible losses the Armenian people have suffered during the war. (p. 189)

25. *Henry Morgenthau,* in *All in a Life Time,* 1922:

Mr. Morgenthau's several books have been of immeasurable value and excellent sources for material on the Armenian genocide. His present volume is more or less an autobiography from which he has omitted intentionally, it seems, his experiences in Constantinople during the Armenian massacres and deportations. The only reference to the Armenians pertains to the 'appointment of the memorable Harbord Commission to Armenia' (p. 336), and his recommendation to President Wilson for 'a triple mandate; one to cover Armenia, another Anatolia, and a third the Constantinople district, where the chief administrator would reside, with an administrator in each of the other territories." (p. 337)

His report to President Wilson was published in the *New York Times*, of November 9, 1919, and reprinted in *All in a Life Time*. Several pertinent paragraphs are herein reproduced for the benefit of our readers:

A brief survey of the history of Turkey in Europe will suffice to make clear the danger of accepting in this late day any promises of reform from that quarter. I have always thought that the final word on Turkey was spoken by an American friend of mine who had spent a large part of his life in the East, and who, on a visit to Berlin, was asked by Herrn von Gwinner, the President of the Deutsche Bank A.G., to spend an evening with him to discuss the future of the Sultan's empire. When my friend came to keep this appointment he began this way: "You have set aside the whole evening to discuss the Ottoman Empire. We do not need all that time. I can tell you the whole story in just four words: *Turkey is not reformable!*"

"You have summed up the whole situation perfectly," replied von Gwinner.

The character of the Turk, was the same in 1853 as it is now (1922); he was just as incapable politically then as he is today; his attitude toward the Christian populations whom the accident of history had placed in his power was identically the same as it is now. These populations were merely "filthy infidels," hated by Allah, having no rights to their own lives or property, who would be permitted to live only as slaves of the mighty Musulmans, and who could be tortured and murdered at will. All European statesmen knew in 1852 that the ultimate disappearance of the Ottoman Empire was inevitable; all understood that was only the support of certain European powers that permitted it to exist, even temporarily.

It was about this time that Czar Nicholas I applied to Turkey the name "sick man of the East," which has ever since been accepted as an accurate description of its political and social status. The point which I wish to make here is that that phrase is just as appropriate to-day as it was then. *The Turk had long since learned the great resources of Ottoman statesmanship—the adroit balancing*

*of one European power against the other as the one se-
curity of his own existence.* [Emphasis mine—Ed.] (pp.
425–427)

Mr. Morgenthau believes that "The British conscience has
changed since the days of the Crimean and Russo-Turkish
wars . . . Gladstone's idea of 'public right as the governing
idea of European politics' is more and more gaining the
upper hand. The ideals in foreign policy represented by
(Richard) Cobden and (John) Bright are the ideals that now
control British public opinion. . . . The England that will
deal with the Ottoman Empire in 1919 is the England of
Lloyd George, not the England of Palmerston and Disraeli.

> For the first time, therefore, [continues Mr. Morgenthau]
> the world approaches the problem of the Ottoman Empire,
> the greatest blight on modern civilization, with an abso-
> lutely free hand. The decision will inform us, more elo-
> quently than any other detail in the settlement, precisely
> what forces have won in this war. We shall learn from it
> whether we have really entered upon a new epoch;
> whether, as we hope, medieval history has ended and
> modern history has begun.
> If Constantinople is left to the Turk; if the Greeks, the
> Syrians, the Armenians, the Arabs and the Jews are not
> freed from the most revolting tyranny that history has
> ever known, we shall understand that the sacrifices of the
> last four years have been in vain, and that the much-dis-
> cussed new ideals in the government of the world are the
> merest cant. (pp. 432–433)

The idea of a triple mandate for (a) Constantinople, (b)
Turkish Anatolia, (c) Armenia, to be assumed by America
found favor among many European and American statesmen. Aside from the United States, Great Britain was the
only power that was capable of assuming the Ottoman mandate, but for "political and economic reasons" was unable to
do so, as frankly expressed by Lord Curzon and Lloyd
George. Mr. Morgenthau states in his article that in May,
1919 "William Buckler, Professor Philip M. Brown, and myself joined in a memorandum to President Wilson outlining

briefly a proposed system of government for the Ottoman dominions." The first paragraph of that memorandum elucidates the train of thought of its authors:

"The government of Asia Minor should be dealt with under three different mandates, (1) for Constantinople, and its zone, (2) for Turkish Anatolia, (3) for Armenia."

26. *Memorandum to President Wilson*, December 18, 1919, presented by prominent Americans, published in *England and France in Armenia*, by James W. Gerard, February 18, 1920:

The following is part of a memorandum which was telegraphed to the President on December 18, 1919:

'To The President, Washington, D. C.

Representative American opinion has already expressed itself with convincing emphasis in favor of the creation of an Armenian State that will unite Ararat with Cilicia and which alone can become an effective barrier against the Pan-Turanian ambition of the Turks of Anatolia. We believe the American people will gladly sanction America's extending necessary aid to Armenia during the formative period. We therefore respectfully ask that the Administration declare itself in favor of America's extending direct aid to Armenia; to that end, formulate a definite continuing policy, and, as a preliminary step in that direction, recognize at once the Armenian Republic. This recognition will enable the Armenian government to borrow the necessary funds to meet the most pressing needs of its starving people, and will also be a practical step toward the creation of a united Armenia.

Signed—James W. Gerard
Charles Evans Hughes
Alton B. Parker
Elihu Root
Frederic Courtland Penfield
Nicholas Murray Butler
Jacob Gould Schurman
John Grier Hibben
Philip N. Rhinelander
Bradley A. Fiske

27. *United States Senate*, Resolution #332, March 10, 1920, *Congressional Record*, March 10, 1920:

> *Whereas*, The affairs of the Armenian people, and particularly their relations to the Turks, have reached a critical state which can only be relieved by the proper arming of the Armenian people for the defense of their political liberties and ancient territorial rights: Now, therefore be it
>
> *Resolved*, That it is the sense of the Senate that the Government of the U.S. recognize the independence of Armenia under the Government of the Armenian Republic, having its seat at Erivan in Russian Armenia; and be it further
>
> *Resolved*, That it is the sense of the Senate that the Allied powers and the U.S. forthwith furnish to the Armenian Republic adequate arms, munitions, equipage, and military stores to enable the Armenian Republic to raise and maintain an army for the defense of the liberty and independence of Armenia, the protection of the Armenian people, and the *recovery and occupation of the territories from which the Armenians have been driven by the Turks;* [Emphasis mine—Ed.] and be it
>
> *Resolved*, further, That it be the sense of the Senate that the *proper and historic territories of Armenia be preserved in their integrity for the use and occupation of the Armenian people and for the support of their national life, and that all projects for the partition of Armenia be rejected.* [Emphasis mine—Ed.]

28. *Senator William H. King*, speech on the atrocities in Cilicia, *Congressional Record*, March 10, 1920, quoted in *The Near East*, April 1920.

During the consideration by the Senate of the Resolution recognizing the independence of Armenia, Senator William H. King made the following remarks:

> As long as it was believed that the U.S. would take some interest in the Near East in Turkey and in Armenian affairs there was a cessation of the atrocities which the Turks were committing against the Armenians, but now that the Ottoman Turks have reached the conclusion that the U.S. has withdrawn from world affairs, there has been

a recrudescence of the murders and massacres which have
for so many centuries characterized their treatment of the
Armenian people. Only recently, upon the withdrawal of
some French troops from one of the cities in Cilicia, more
than 16,000 Armenians were butchered. There is a determination upon the part of the Turks to destroy the Armenian race, in order that their lands and possessions may
become the property of the Turks. They know of the superior virtues of the Armenians, of their capacity to build
and govern, and of their own incapacity to organize a
government or build a civilized community. Fearing the
ultimate freedom of the Armenians and their permanency
in Western Asia and Asia Minor, the cruel barbarous Turks
seek their extermination. I propose to keep before the Senate and the public the awful conditions in Armenia and
the failure of the civilized nations to do their duty toward
a people who for centuries were an outpost protecting
Europe against Asiatic hordes and who in the World War
battled bravely with the allied nations for the cause of
freedom and the overthrow of the autocracy which Germany sought to impose upon the world.

29. *Bainbridge Colby,* Secretary of State, message to the
French Ambassador M. Jusserand, March 24, 1920, quoted
in *The Foreign Relations of the U.S.,* Volume III, 1920:

There can be no question as to the genuine interest of
the Government in the plans for Armenia, and the Government of the United States is convinced that the civilized world demands and expects the most liberal treatment
for that unfortunate country. Its boundaries should be
drawn in such a way as to recognize all the legitimate
claims of the Armenian people and particularly to give
them easy and unencumbered access to the sea. While unaware of the considerations governing the decision reached
by the supreme council, it is felt that the special rights
over Lazistan would hardly assure to Armenia that access
to the sea is indispensable to its existence.

30. *Senator William H. King,* speech before the Senate,
August 1, 1919.

Senator William H. King delivered a stirring address before the Senate of the United States on August 1, 1919. We

reproduce from the Congressional Record—Senate, page 3483–4 that speech in its entirety together with an article by Charles A. Selden, dated at Paris July 30, 1919 and published in the *New York Times:*

AFFAIRS IN ARMENIA

Mr. KING. Mr. President, the situation in Armenia is so serious that I have felt impelled to offer the resolution which has just been submitted and referred to the Committee on Foreign Relations. I sincerely hope the committee will immediately consider the resolution and report it in some form back to the Senate for approval.

The sufferings of Armenia have appealed to the civilized world for many years. Their history is written in blood and is full of tragedy and sorrow. For centuries the Armenian people have been under the tyrannous yoke of the Ottoman Empire. It seems incredible that a nation which has enjoyed diplomatic relations with civilized nations and which has been regarded as a nation with whom the great Christian peoples of the world could hold commercial and political relations would follow for centuries a policy of cruelty, bloodshed, and oppression with respect to peoples within its own territorial dominion and acknowledging its sovereignty and control. We have been compelled, however, to admit the fact that the Turkish Government deliberately sought the extermination of the Armenian race. This is not the time to enter into a discussion of the reasons which prompted the Ottoman Turks to butcher and destroy several million of brave, industrious, and progressive people who constituted such an important part of the strength of the Turkish Empire. During the recent war, while Turkey was fighting for her existence against the allied nations, she carried on her predetermined policy to destroy the Armenian people. The most savage cruelties were inflicted upon defenseless men, women, and children, and the edge of the sword was turned against these unfortunate people when it might have been used against the allied forces. I do not mean to convey the idea that Turkey did not fight with Germany and Austria and Bulgaria against the allied forces. Indeed, she gave strong support to the nations with which she was associated. It was known, of course, that the sympathies of the Armenian people were with the allied cause, and this doubtless increased the hatred of the Turks for the Armenians and intensified their purpose to destroy the entire race. It was the fervent hope of all civilized nations that with the end of the war freedom and liberty would come to Armenia; that the dark day of her sufferings and sorrows would end and the light of a bright and glorious period shine upon her devastated territory and the survivors of the horrors and persecutions of the past. I believe that each of the allied nations desired that the Armenian people should be restored to their ancient territory and should enjoy a government of their own choosing. As a matter of fact, the Armenians have erected a government of their own, democratic in form and in spirit. Suffering for so many centuries under the iron rule of an imperial and tyrannous government, they have sought the establishment of a Republic under which liberty and justice might be secured. These people, however, have been weakened by reason of the course pursued by Turkey, and as a result of the robberies and exploitation to which they have been subjected many of their cities and towns have been destroyed, extensive areas of Armenia have been laid waste, and property to the extent of millions have been destroyed. Tens of thousands of men have been murdered and hundreds of thousands of men, women, and children have been driven from their homes and have perished either at the hands of the sword or from exposure and starvation to which they have been subjected by their brutal oppressors.

In the circumstances it will perhaps be impossible for Armenia to maintain herself for a number of years to come without aid from friendly powers. She will require material aid and support in order to meet her obligations and to maintain herself as a nation in the struggle for national existence. I believe, however, that the Armenians are capable of self-government, and that their country possesses resources so rich and limitless as that within a reasonable time a government stable and strong will arise, and the support of friendly nations will not longer be required. For the present, however, the needs of Armenia are such as to call for aid from this and other nations. It would be a tragedy and an international crime if Armenia were to perish. The Allied nations have not completed their work by freeing Armenia from the Turks. A duty still exists to give succor and support to this unfortunate people.

The Associated Press dispatch of yesterday portrays the dangerous situation in which the Armenians are now placed. The Turks and Tartars are moving upon them from three sides, seeking the overthrow of their Government, the seizing of their property, and the extermination of all classes. Maj. Joseph C. Green, who is directing the American relief work in Tiflis, in the northern part of Armenia, has called the attention of the world to the serious condition there prevailing. The same dispatch states that Mr. Hoover, after learning of the precarious condition of the Armenians, submitted Maj. Green's message to the peace conference, 'which had already received similar reports from American and British observers.'

I call particular attention to Maj. Green's message, which bears date of July 23. He states:

"Had a long conference with the Armenian President today. The situation is worse. The Turkish Army, well prepared, and Tartars are advancing from three sides. If military protection is not afforded to Armenia immediately the disaster will be more terrible than the massacres in 1915, and the Armenian nation will be crushed, to the everlasting shame of the Allies.

Relief work is impossible in the present situation unless order is restored. Can not something be done to have the British forces in the Caucasus intervene to save Armenia?"

Under date of July 25 Maj. Green also telegraphs:

The Turks and Tartars are advancing in the districts of Karabagh and Alaghoz. They now occupy approximately the reopened territory of Russian Armenia. Khalil Bey, a Turkish colonel, is commanding the Azerbaijan Tartars.

Mr. Charles A. Selden, one of the very best journalists and one of the keenest observers in Europe, the correspondent of the New York Times, writes to his paper this article, which appeared in yesterday's issue of the Times:

The situation in Asia Minor, due to hostilities by Turkish troops, is admitted in Paris to be about the gravest menace now confronting the peace conference. Furthermore, it is attributed chiefly in French and American quarters to uncertainty among the Turks themselves as to what they may expect in the future, so far as a mandate government is concerned.

I shall not read the entire article, but shall ask that it

be inserted in the RECORD as a part of these informal observations. I desire, however, to call attention to the concluding part of Mr. Selden's statement:

The most effective thing that could happen to put an end to the present menace of disorder which is involving the Kurds and threatening Armenian extinction would be, according to opinion in Paris, a declaration from leaders of the American Congress that they intended when the time came to authorize the American Government to take the mandates for Constantinople and Armenia.

Such a declaration would quell the fighting Turkish troops much more quickly and effectively than the allied forces now in Asia Minor seem able to do. Actual acceptance of the mandate or formal action by Congress at this moment is not essential, but merely some sign of action in the future that would convince the Turks.

If America is not to take the mandate, certain knowledge of that fact would also be far better than the present uncertainty, for with the United States definitely eliminated from the situation the European powers could at least make an attempt to agree among themselves and settle the mandate on one of their own number, thereby removing the present vagueness which gives the Turks their excuse and chief opportunity for starting a new war.

Mr. President, I do not mean to convey the idea that I am advocating that the United States should accept the mandatory of Armenia, but Mr. Selden's article is a very strong argument in favor of that policy.

Of course, until the treaty of peace shall have been ratified, it would be improper to talk of the United States becoming a mandatory of any province or territory. It may be that after such ratification there will be great opposition to our Government assuming such obligation with respect to any of the lands or territory formerly belonging to the Governments with which our Nation has been at war. I believe, however, that the American people have such an abiding interest in Armenia and sympathize so deeply with her because of past and present misfortunes that if the United States should become a mandatory for any country or territory Armenia would most strongly appeal for such protecting care. The views, however, of Mr. Selden indicate that some positive step should be taken immediately by this Government and by the Allies for the purpose of protecting Armenia. It is clear from the article referred to that if our Government should announce its determination to see that justice is done to the Armenian people, it would have a deterring effect upon the Turks and their military forces now menacing the Armenian people. I believe that if the Paris conference should adopt a strong statement demanding the withdrawal of all Turkish military forces from Armenia it would have a most salutory effect upon those forces now moving into Armenian territory.

I believe that a declaration by the Senate of the United States, expressing the hope that steps will be taken to afford protection to the Armenian people, would stay the hand of the enemies of this unhappy people. It would be, as Maj. Green said, "an everlasting shame" if the allied nations should sit supinely by and permit the extermination of this brave and heroic people.

Mr. President, more than 1,000,000 Armenians perished at the hands of the Turks and the Germans associated with them during the war. There are approximately 2,000,000 Armenians still living. They reside in a vast territory extending from the Mediterranean Sea to the Black Sea. These people have no military resources. Much of the man power has been destroyed, and those remaining have been denuded of means for their defense. There are approximately 15,000 Armenians constituting the national military forces, but they are without arms or military supplies. If the Armenian people had guns and munitions and sufficient military supplies, perhaps they might be able to defend themselves against those now invading their land. But because of their impoverished condition it is manifestly impossible for them to resist military forces coming from three different directions and equipped with the modern implements of war.

The situation calls for immediate aid. This Nation and the allied nations will be guilty of a great delinquency if they fail at this juncture to protect Armenia from the peril now impending and which threatens her destruction.

The Vice President. "The resolution introduced by the Senator from Utah will be referred to the Committee on Foreign Relations, and, without objection, the article referred to will be printed in the RECORD."

The article is as follows:

Paris, July 30.

The situation in Asia Minor, due to hostilities by Turkish troops, is admitted in Paris to be about the gravest menace now confronting the peace conference. Furthermore, it is attributed chiefly in French and American quarters to uncertainty among the Turks themselves as to what they may expect in the future so far as a mandate government is concerned.

The activity of the Turkish troops under Mustapha Kemal Pasha, who calls himself 'Dictator of National Defense,' would not have been started if the Turks themselves had assurances that the United States was to govern Armenia and Constantinople. For a long time it was taken for granted in Asia Minor that such a mandate would be accepted by the United States, and in expectation of such powerful rule the Turks behaved. This certainty was based largely on what President Wilson said concerning Armenia in his Boston speech on his first return to the United States.

That speech was interpreted in Europe as showing conclusively that President Wilson himself was in favor of taking the mandate, and Europe, as well as Asia Minor, was well pleased. Since then there has been increasing uncertainty due to adverse criticism in the United States of the whole question of mandates and to the delay of Congress in indicating its future course in the matter.

That uncertainty concerning America is now supplemented by uncertainty as to what England is going to do. The leaders of the Turkish uprising are making much capital out of the insistence on the part of labor in England that British troops shall be withdrawn from Asia Minor as well as from Russia. The Turks are also fully aware of the present controversy between England and France over the limits of their respective zones in central Asia Minor as provided for in the agreement of 1916.

TURKS PROFIT BY EUROPE'S DIFFERENCES

The net result of all this is that the Turks see a repetition of their traditional opportunity to make capital for themselves while the European Powers fail to agree among themselves on Turkish policy.

The most effective thing that could happen to put an end to the present menace of disorder, which is involving the Kurds and threatening Armenian extinction, would be according to opinion in Paris, a declaration from leaders of the American Congress that they intended when the time came to authorize the American Government to take the mandates for Constantinople and Armenia.

Such a declaration would quell the fighting Turkish troops much more quickly and effectively than the allied forces now in Asia Minor seem able to do. Actual acceptance of the mandate or formal action by Congress at this moment is not essential, but merely some sign of action in the future that would convince the Turks.

If America is not to take the mandate, certain knowledge of that fact would also be far better than the present uncertainty, for with the United States definitely eliminated from the situation the European powers could at least make an attempt to agree among themselves and settle the mandate on one of their own number, thereby removing the present vagueness which gives the Turks their excuse and chief opportunity for starting a new war.

APPENDIX A

Chapter 6

Pertinent Articles of the Treaty of Sevres presented to the Turks on April 24, 1920, and signed at Sevres, France, on August 10.

THE COVENANT OF THE LEAGUE OF NATIONS

Treaty of Sevres

THE HIGH CONTRACTING PARTIES,

In order to promote international co-operation and to achieve international peace and security
   by the acceptance of obligations not to resort to war,
   by the prescription of open, just and honorable relations between nations,
   by the firm establishment of the understandings of international law as the actual rule of conduct among Governments, and
   by the maintenance of justice and scrupulous respect for all treaty obligations in the dealings of organised peoples with one another,
Agree to this Covenant of the League of Nations.

(Editor's Note: The Articles specifically pertaining to Armenians and other minorities are the following:)

SECTION VI.

ARMENIA

Article 88

Turkey, in accordance with the action already taken by the Allied Powers, recognises Armenia as a free and independent State.

Article 89

Turkey and Armenia as well as the other High Contracting Parties agree to submit to the arbitration of the President of the United States of America the question of the frontier to be fixed between Turkey and Armenia in the Vilayets of Erzerum, Trebizond, Van and Bitlis, and to accept his decision thereupon, as well as any stipulation he may prescribe as to access for Armenia to the sea, and as to the demilitarisation of any portion of Turkish territory adjacent to the said frontier.

Article 90

In the event of the determination of the frontier under Article 89 involving the transfer of the whole or any part of the territory of the said Vilayets to Armenia, Turkey hereby renounces as from the date of such decision all rights and title over the territory so transferred. The provision of the present Treaty applicable to territory detached from Turkey shall thereupon become applicable to the said territory.

The proportion and nature of the financial obligations of Turkey which Armenia will have to assume, or of the rights which will pass to her, on account of the transfer of the said territory will be determined in accordance with Articles 241 to 244, Part VIII (Financial Clauses) of the present Treaty.

Subsequent agreements will, if necessary, decide all questions which are not decided by the present Treaty and which may arise in consequence of the transfer of the said territory.

Article 91

In the event of any portion of the territory referred to in Article 89 being transferred to Armenia, a Boundary Commission, whose composition will be determined subsequently, will be constituted within three months from the delivery of the decision referred to in the said Article to trace on the spot the frontier between Armenia and Turkey as established by such decision.

Article 92

The frontiers between Armenia and Azerbaijan and Georgia respectively will be determined by direct agreement between the States concerned.

If in either case the States concerned have failed to determine the frontier by agreement at the date of the decision referred to in Article 89, the frontier line in question will be determined by the Principal Allied Powers, who will also provide for its being traced on the spot.

Article 93

Armenia accepts and agrees to embody in a treaty with the principal Allied Powers such provisions as may be deemed necessary by these Powers to protect the interests of inhabitants of that State who differ from the majority of the population in race, language, or religion.

Armenia further accepts and agrees to embody in a Treaty with the Principal Allied Powers such provisions as these Powers may deem necessary to protect freedom of transit and equitable treatment for the commerce of other nations.

PROTECTION OF MINORITIES.

Article 140.

Turkey undertakes that the stipulations contained in Articles 141, 145, and 147 shall be recognised as fundamental laws, and that no civil or military law or regulation, no Imperial *Iradeh* nor official action shall conflict or interfere with these stipulations, nor shall any law, regulation, Imperial *Iradeh* nor official action prevail over them.

Article 141.

Turkey undertakes to assure full and complete protection of life and liberty to all inhabitants of Turkey without distinction of birth, nationality, language, race or religion.

All inhabitants of Turkey shall be entitled to the free exercise, whether public or private, of any creed, religion or belief.

The penalties for any interference with the free exercise of the right referred to in the preceding paragraph shall be the same whatever may be the creed concerned.

Whereas, in view of the terrorist regime which has existed in Turkey since November 1, 1914, conversions to

Islam could not take place under normal conditions, no conversions since that date are recognised and all persons who were non-Moslems before November 1, 1914, will be considered as still remaining such, unless, after regaining their liberty, they voluntarily perform the necessary formalities for embracing the Islamic faith.

In order to repair so far as possible the wrongs inflicted on individuals in the course of the massacres perpetrated in Turkey during the war, the Turkish Government undertakes to afford all the assistance in its power or in that of the Turkish authorities in the search for and deliverance of all persons, of whatever race or religion, who have disappeared, been carried off, interned or placed in captivity since November 1, 1914.

The Turkish Government undertakes to facilitate the operations of mixed commissions appointed by the Council of the League of Nations to receive the complaints of the victims themselves, their families or their relations, to make the necessary enquiries, and to order the liberation of the persons in question.

The Turkish Government undertakes to ensure the execution of the decisions of these commissions, and to assure the security and the liberty of the persons thus restored to the full enjoyment of their rights.

Article 143.

Turkey undertakes to recognise such provisions as the Allied Powers may consider opportune with respect to the reciprocal and voluntary emigration of persons belonging to racial minorities.

Turkey renounces any right to avail herself of the provisions of Article 16 of the Convention between Greece and Bulgaria relating to reciprocal emigration, signed at Neuilly-sur-Seine on November 27, 1919. Within six months from the coming into force of the present Treaty Greece and Turkey will enter into a special arrangement relating to the reciprocal and voluntary emigration of the populations of Turkish and Greek race in the territories transferred to Greece and remaining Turkish respectively.

In case agreement cannot be reached as to such arrangements, Greece and Turkey will be entitled to apply to the Council of the League of Nations, which will fix the terms of such arrangement.

Article 144.

The Turkish Government recognises the injustice of the law of 1915 relating to Abandoned Properties (*Emval-i-Metroukeh*), and of the supplementary provisions thereof, and declares them to be null and void, in the past as in the future.

The Turkish Government solemnly undertakes to facilitate to the greatest possible extent the return to their homes and re-establishment in their businesses of the Turkish subjects of non-Turkish race who have been forcibly driven from their homes by fear of massacre or any other form of pressure since January 1, 1914. It recognises that any immovable or movable property of the said Turkish subjects or of the communities to which they belong, which can be recovered, must be restored to them as soon as possible, in whatever hands it may be found. Such property shall be restored free of all charges or servitudes with which it may have been burdened and without compensation of any kind to the present owners or occupiers, subject to any action which they may be able to bring against the persons from whom they derived the title.

The Turkish Government agrees that arbitral commissions shall be appointed by the Council of the League of Nations wherever found necessary. These commissions shall each be composed of one representative of the Turkish Government, one representative of the community which claims that it or one of its members has been injured, and a chairman appointed by the Council of the League of Nations. These arbitral commissions shall hear all claims covered by this Article and decide them by summary procedure.

The arbitral commissions will have power to order:

(1) The provision by the Turkish Government of labour for any work of reconstruction or restoration deemed necessary. This labour shall be recruited from the races inhabiting the territory where the arbitral commission considers the execution of the said works to be necessary;

(2) the removal of any person who, after enquiry, shall be recognised as having taken an active part in massacres or deportations or as having provoked them; the measures to be taken with regard to such person's possessions will be indicated by the commission;

(3) the disposal of property belonging to members of a

community who have died or disappeared since January 1, 1914, without leaving heirs; such property may be handed over to the community instead of to the State;

(4) the cancellation of all acts of sale or any acts, creating rights over immovable property concluded after January 1, 1914. The indemnification of the holders will be a charge upon the Turkish Government, but must not serve as a pretext for delaying the restitution. The arbitral commission will however have the power to impose equitable arrangements between the interested parties, if any sum has been paid by the present holder of such property.

The Turkish Government undertakes to facilitate in the fullest possible measure the work of the commissions and to ensure the execution of their decisions, which will be final. No decision of the Turkish judicial or administrative authorities shall prevail over such decisions.

Article 145.

All Turkish nationals shall be equal before the law and shall enjoy the same civil and political rights without distinction as to race, language or religion.

Difference of religion, creed or confession shall not prejudice any Turkish national in matters relating to the enjoyment of civil or political rights, as for instance admission to public employments, functions, and honours, or the exercise of professions and industries.

Within a period of two years from the coming into force of the present Treaty the Turkish Government will submit to the Allied Powers a scheme for the organisation of an electoral system based on the principle of proportional representation of racial minorities.

No restriction shall be imposed on the free use by any Turkish national of any language in private intercourse, in commerce, in religion, in the press or in publications of any kind, or at public meetings. Adequate facilities shall be given to Turkish nationals of nonTurkish speech for the use of their language, either orally or in writing, before the courts.

Article 146.

The Turkish Government undertakes to recognize the validity of diplomas granted by recognised foreign universities and schools, and to admit the holders thereof to the free exercise of the professions and industries for which such diplomas qualify.

This provision will apply equally to nationals of Allied Powers who are resident in Turkey.

Article 147.

Turkish nationals who belong to racial, religious or linguistic minorities shall enjoy the same treatment and security in law and in fact as other Turkish nationals. In particular they shall have an equal right to establish, manage and control at their own expense, and independently of and without interference by the Turkish authorities, any charitable, religious and social institutions, schools for primary, secondary and higher instruction and other educational establishments, with the right to use their own language and to exercise their own religion freely therein.

Article 148.

In towns and districts where there is a considerable proportion of Turkish nationals belonging to racial, linguistic or religious minorities, these minorities shall be assured an equitable share in the enjoyment and application of the sums which may be provided out of public funds under the State, municipal or other budgets for educational or charitable purposes.

The sums in question shall be paid to the qualified representatives of the communities concerned.

Article 149.

The Turkish Government undertakes to recognise and respect the ecclesiastical and scholastic autonomy of all racial minorities in Turkey. For this purpose, and subject to any provisions to the contrary in the present Treaty, the Turkish Government confirms and will uphold in their entirety the prerogatives and immunities of an ecclesiastical, scholastic or judicial nature granted by the Sultans to non-Moslem races in virtue of special orders or imperial decrees (firmans, hattis, berats, etc.) as well as by ministerial orders or orders of the Grand Vizier.

All laws, decrees, regulations and circulars issued by the Turkish Government and containing abrogations, restrictions or amendments of such prerogatives and immunities shall be considered to such extent null and void.

Any modification of the Turkish judicial system which may be introduced in accordance with the provisions of the provisions of the present Treaty shall be held to override this Article, in so far as such modification may affect individuals belonging to racial minorities.

Article 150.

In towns and districts where there is resident a considerable portion of Turkish nationals of the Christian or Jewish religions the Turkish Government undertakes that such Turkish nationals shall not be compelled to perform any act which constitutes a violation of their faith or religious observances, and shall not be placed under any disability by reason of their refusal to attend courts of law or to perform any legal business on their weekly day of rest. This provision, however, shall not exempt such Turkish nationals (Christians or Jews) from such obligations as shall be imposed upon all other Turkish nationals for the preservation of public order.

Article 151.

The Principal Allied Powers, in consultation with the Council of the League of Nations, will decide what measures are necessary to guarantee the execution of the provisions of this Pact. The Turkish Government hereby accepts all decisions which may be taken on this subject.

Article 226.

The Turkish Government recognises the right of the Allied Powers to bring before military tribunals persons accused of having committed acts in violation of the laws and customs of war. Such persons shall, if found guilty, be sentenced to punishments laid down by law. This provision will apply notwithstanding any proceedings or prosecution before a tribunal in Turkey or in the territory of her allies.

The Turkish Government shall hand over to the Allied Powers or to such one of them as shall so request all persons accused of having committed an act in violation of the laws and customs of war, who are specified either by name or by the rank, office or employment which they held under the Turkish authorities.

Article 227.

Persons guilty of criminal acts against the nationals of one of the Allied Powers shall be brought before the military tribunals of that Power.

Persons guilty of criminal acts against the nationals of more than one of the Allied Powers shall be brought before military tribunals composed of members of the military tribunals of the Powers concerned.

In every case the accused shall be entitled to name his own counsel.

Article 228.

The Turkish Government undertakes to furnish all documents and information of every kind, the production of which may be considered necessary to ensure the full knowledge of the incriminating acts, the prosecution of offenders and the just appreciation of responsibility.

Article 229.

The provisions of Articles 226 to 228 apply similarly to the Governments of the States to which territory belonging to the former Turkish Empire has been or may be assigned, in so far as concerns persons accused of having committed acts contrary to the laws and customs of war who are in the territory or at the disposal of such States.

If the persons in question have acquired the nationality of one of the said States, the Government of such State undertakes to take, at the request of the Power concerned and in agreement with it, or upon the joint request of all the Allied Powers, all the measures necessary to ensure the prosecution and punishment of such persons.

Article 230.

The Turkish Government undertakes to hand over to the Allied Powers the persons whose surrender may be required by the latter as being responsible for the massacres committed during the continuance of the state of war on territory which formed part of the Turkish Empire on August 1, 1914.

The Allied Powers reserve to themselves the right to designate the tribunal which shall try the persons so accused, and the Turkish Government undertakes to recognise such a tribunal.

In the event of the League of Nations having created in sufficient time a tribunal competent to deal with the said massacres, the Allied Powers reserve to themselves the right to bring the accused persons mentioned above before such a tribunal, and the Turkish Government undertakes equally to recognise such a tribunal.

The provisions of Article 228 apply to the cases dealt with in this Article.

Referring to Article 144 of the treaty, Andre N. Mandelstam makes the following, significant remarks, *in La Societe des Nations et les Puissances devant le Probleme Armenien:*

This article obliges the Ottoman government to make it possible for the non-Turkish dependents, driven away from their homes by force of violence, since January 1, 1914, to return to their homes as soon as their affairs are settled. It ordains the restoration to their owners of their movable or immovable goods, *which can be retrieved* [Emphasis by A.M.]. And the Treaty provides that all the demands of the mixed commissions of arbitration shall be recognized wherever the Council of the League of Nations shall deem necessary. . . The Commissions of Arbitration shall have power to decide: the furnishing of man-power by the Ottoman government for all the work of reconstruction or restoration; the annulment of all the sales or the establishment of rights over all the real properties having taken place after August 1, 1914, the holders to be indemnified by the State; the ascription (attribution) of all goods and properties having belonged to members of a community, deceased or disappeared since August 1, 1914, to that community instead of to the State, so that the State would not benefit from any of the property acquired by it by escheat following the massacres and deportations it had ordered. (p. 86)

These dispositions guarantee in a certain measure the recovery of personal properties and the restitution of real estate. Article 144 has, unfortunately, an important deficiency: it is silent about damages which the victims deprived of their goods and real estate certainly have the right to reclaim from unlawful holders; it is equally silent about what is more serious, indemnities to be paid by the principal massacrers themselves, who have left in misery a number of orphans and widows, not mentioning all the injury caused to the Armenian and Greek nations; in other ways, it (the article) deals only with restitutions and restorations within the Ottoman jurisdiction. (p. 86)

In a footnote M. Mandelstam strongly criticizes this lack of consideration on the part of the authors of the Sevres Treaty. It is worth reproducing here his comments in entirety:

The only course open to the Armenians and Greeks about the territories detached from Turkey, is, in our opinion, expressed in article 230. That article in part makes provisions for the trial of persons 'responsible for the massacres which were committed during the war, in all the territories which formed a part of the Ottoman Empire, as of August 1, 1914.' The Greeks and Armenians, subjects of Turkey or not, victims of massacres committed during the war, should be able to reclaim indemnities from the authors of the massacres, and should be recognized by the Allied Powers as parties in the proceedings before the designated tribunal, by virtue of article 230.

This view, though aleatory, does not, however, exonerate, in our opinion, the authors of the Treaty of Sevres from blame for not having clearly stipulated the right of indemnity for the victims of massacres. The system (the co-ordinated plan) of the Treaty of Sevres will not be justified by historic precedents. Certainly one can recall that in the course of history States from which certain parts have been taken away have paid no indemnity for the loss of life and effects suffered by their former subjects during periods of disturbances prior to the separation, nor (which is a stronger reason) the losses suffered by those who are of the same blood as the new nation but remained subjects of those states. But one of the results of the war has been the just consecration of a new law, the law of humanity. The dispositions of which, under the form of protectors of minorities have been fully incorporated in a series of treaties; the violation of these rules gives the unquestionable right to recourse against the state which has been adjudged guilty. Truly, one can object that this new law cannot be retroactive in every instance. But this objection, established for other states, does not apply to the special case of Turkey. As we have shown above, the intervention of mankind before passing into common law, has been applied for more than a century to the Ottoman Empire only.

In the course of its history Turkey has made many agreements with the Great Powers to respect the life, the honor, the freedom and the property of its Christian subjects. Therefore, in stipulating indemnities for the benefit of persons injured by the massacres and deportations, measures which have been unquestionably governmental and not due to a civil war, the Powers should not have given a retroactive force to dispositions over the minorities, but should have sanctioned the articles of many former treaties with the Porte by which the intervention of mankind is manifested.

Finally, the last agreement, whatever the legal basis which has empowered the Powers to insert in the Treaty of Sevres sanctions against the authors of the massacres of 1915, the demand for the liberation of the captives, the reconstruction of the properties and the restitution of the goods confiscated, one cannot see how these dispositions, considering the past, could not have been extended to the indemnification of widows and orphans deprived of their sustenance and to the compensation of persons deprived of their belongings. (pp. 86–87)

APPENDIX B

Chapter 6

*Comments on the Treaty of Lausanne and the
Turko-American Treaty*

1. *David Lloyd George*

(a) Speech in London, July 25, 1923, on the Treaty of Lausanne, reproduced in his book entitled *Is It Peace?*. The following is a small part of the speech made by Lloyd George:

The vanquished have returned to their spiritual home at Angora throwing their fezzes in the air. The victors have returned with tails well between their legs. . . . The Turk may be a bad ruler, but he is the prince of anglers. The cunning and the patience with which he lands the most refractory fish once he has hooked it is beyond compare. . . . Time never worries him, he can sit and wait. . . . Time and patience rewarded him. At last the tarpon are all lying beached on banks—Britain, France, Italy, and the United States—high and dry, landed and helpless, without a swish left in their tails, glistening and gasping in the summer sun.

(b) *Reflections on the Treaty:*

The Pact of Mudania was not Sevres, but it certainly was better than Lausanne. From Sevres to Mudania was a retreat. From Mudania to Lausanne is a rout.

What next? Lausanne is not a terminus, it is only a milestone. Where is the next? No one claims that this Treaty is peace with honour. It is not even peace. If one were dealing with a regenerated Turk, then there might be hope. But the burning of Smyrna, and the cold-blooded murders of tens of thousands of young Greeks in the interior, prove that the Turk is still unchanged. To quote again from the correspondent of The Times at Lausanne:—

All such evidence as can be obtained here confirms the belief that the new Turk is but the old, and that the coming

477

era of enlightenment and brotherly love in Turkey, for which it is the correct thing officially to hope, will be from the foreigners' point of view at best a humiliating, and at worst a bloody, chaos.'

2. *James W. Gerard,* former American Ambassador to Germany in an article entitled "The Senate and the Lausanne Treaty," quoted in *The New Armenia,* September-October 1923, writes in part:

The Treaty of Commerce and Amity that the United States, on August 6 (1923) concluded with Turkey at Lausanne, dishonors America. It leaves at the mercy of the Turks American lives; surrenders to them time-honored American rights; ignores the solemn pledges that American statesmen had repeatedly made to the Armenian people; and recognizes by implication calculated murder as a policy of government. It is a humiliating treaty. One searches in vain for any advantage which this treaty might hold for the United States. . . . By signing the Lausanne Treaty, we abdicated the high moral position which we had heretofore occupied in the Near East and fell into the category of petty concession hunters. By this act, we have cast serious reflection upon the motives of the men and women whom we send to the four corners of the earth as missionaries of American ideas and ideals; and we have discredited our professions of disinterestedness and altruism in our dealings with dependent nations.

If we accept, at the hands of the Turks, the counterfeit blood-money that the Lausanne Treaty offers, we shall be humiliated and discredited. Cynical European diplomats will smile at our professions of humanitarianism. In these circumstances, the church and the press of America, which interpret the conscience and the mind of our people, have a clear duty to perform. The honor of America, no less than every dictate of reason, demands that the Senate reject the Turkish Treaty.

3. *The New York Times.* In connection with the two treaties signed by the United States at Lausanne, a writer commenting in the *New York Times* in its editorial "Amity

and Commerce," quoted in *The New Armenia,* September-October, 1923, writes in part:

> The long and bloody record of Turkey proves but too well that the Turk is hopelessly incompetent to rule even himself and is a positive menace to others. Were the only results of his rule inefficiency, waste and corruption, he might claim consideration on the ground that these faults exist in other parts of the world. Alas! The record shows that these same venial faults, combined with a peculiar ethnological condition, rather than inherent cruelty, cause the pages to be stained with tales of murder, rape and bloodshed—tales that disgrace humanity.

4. *Edward Hale Bierstadt, in The Great Betrayal,* 1924

(a) The American position:

> The American delegation, though not negotiating a peace treaty nor submitting definite plans for adjustments to which the United States Government cannot become a signatory, has stated to the conference its full approval of the demand of Lord Curzon and other Allied statesmen for any practicable plan for a National Armenian Home and for an acceptance of such a plan. The American delegation has sought and obtained the views of those who represent the movement in the United States for a National Armenian Home and who may be considered as representative experts upon the subject and has laid these views before the conference today. In addition to this and in behalf of the Armenians and Americans interested we have given assurances that the case for a National Armenian Home would be put before the conference and have a hearing. We have contributed and will contribute to insistence that Turkey shall give consideration to any practicable concrete plan which may be put forward.

Here is what E. H. Bierstadt, as Executive Secretary of the Emergency Committee for Near East Refugees, says about the Lausanne Treaty, signed on July 24, 1923:

> The Treaty represented a complete revision of the Treaty of Sevres, and a profound modification of the tentative agreements reached at the first Lausanne conference. Tur-

key won the war at Lausanne. . . . The Allies capitulated for two reasons: first, because Turkey had an active army in the field, the size of which she vastly exaggerated for the Allies' benefit, and no one of the Powers was ready to fight; second, because the absolute conflict of aims represented by the rival oil interests made it impossible for the Allies to act together. It was a strange drama—Turkey, beaten to her knees in 1918, dictating the terms of peace to the great Powers of the world in 1923. Nothing but economic imperialism made it possible. Not one of the Allies, including the United States, had gone to the council table with clean hands, and knowing that, the Turkish delegates treated them with cynical disregard.

(b) Mr. Bierstadt sums up the Armenian situation after the Lausanne Treaty as follows:

"1. The Allies, both severally and jointly, pledged themselves to: (a) The relief of the Armenians from Turkish oppression; (b) the establishment of an autonomous Armenian state.

"2. France expressed through her spokesmen her willingness to accept a mandate over Armenia.

"3. The United States expressed through her spokesman her willingness to accept a mandate over Armenia.

"4. Thereupon Armenia turned to the United States.

"5. At the request of the United States the Allies postponed a final settlement with Turkey, pending the active cooperation of America.

"6. The United States did nothing for one and a half years.

"7. That delay directly resulted in:
    (a) The complete resurrection of Turkish power.
    (b) The massacre and expulsion of all Armenians in Turkey.
    (c) The overwhelming victory of Turkey at Lausanne."
(p. 183–184)

5. *The Democratic National Platform*, June 24, 1924:

"We condemn the Lausanne Treaty. It barters legitimate American rights and betrays Armenia for the Chester oil concession. We favor the protection of American rights in Turkey and the fulfillment of President Wilson's arbitral award respecting Armenia."

6. *Charles W. Eliot,* American educator and President of Harvard University, in *The Lausanne Treaty, Turkey and Armenia:*

How strange it is that nobody gives the real reason why we should have nothing to do with the Turks! The present Turks are the descendants and heirs of those Turks who for centuries have harassed and butchered the Christian population within their borders, and are themselves continuing the same practices to an even more revolting degree. (p. 17)

7. *110 Americans.* A memorandum signed by 110 Americans, among whom were such outstanding men as Newton D. Baker, Executive Secretary of War, Channing H. Cox, Governor of Massachusetts, Charles W. Eliot, President-Emeritus of Harvard University, James W. Gerard, Ex-Ambassador to Germany, Robert Underwood Johnson, Ex-Ambassador to Italy, Henry Morgenthau, Ex-Ambassador to Turkey, Oscar S. Straus, Ex-Ambassador to Turkey, Rabbi Stephen S. Wise and Governors of many states, presidents of numerous colleges and universities and other men of great renown, summed up the Lausanne Treaty as follows:

"It is morally an indefensible Treaty. It is an utterly humiliating and purposeless Treaty. . . . It ignores our solemn pledges to Armenia. . . . The Turks have broken thus early their promises of good behavior and their guarantees to our missionaries and to the remnants of the Christians in Turkey. . . . America stands to gain absolutely nothing by resuming relations with a Turkey in this state, and can lose nothing further by maintaining the status quo and awaiting developments. . . ."

8. *Dr. Fridtjof Nansen,* comments on the Lausanne Treaty, in *Armenia and the Near East,* 1928:

The nations of Europe and the statesmen of Europe are tired of the everlasting Armenian question. Of course. It has only brought them one defeat after another, the very mention of it recalling to their slumbering consciences a grim tale of broken and unfulfilled promises which they have never in practice done anything to keep. And after all, it was only a massacred, but gifted little nation, with no oil-fields or gold-mines.

Woe to the Armenians, that they were ever drawn into European politics! It would have been better for them if the name of Armenia had never been uttered by any European diplomatist.

But the Armenian people have never abandoned hope; they have gone on bravely working, and waiting. . . . waiting year after year.

They are waiting still.

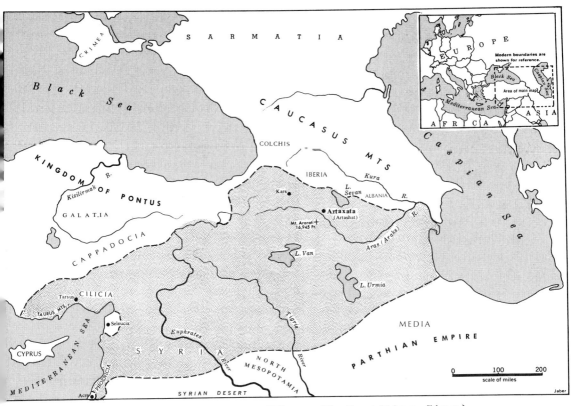

1. Armenia during the reign of Tigranes The Great (94 B.C.–54 B.C.)

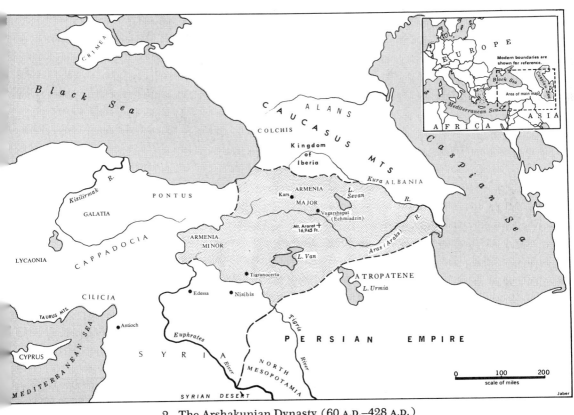

2. The Arshakunian Dynasty (60 A.D.–428 A.D.)

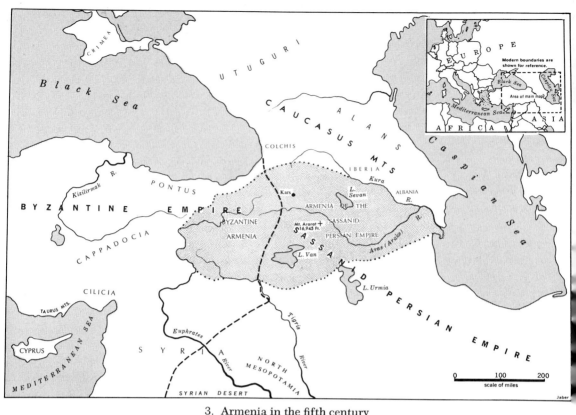

3. Armenia in the fifth century

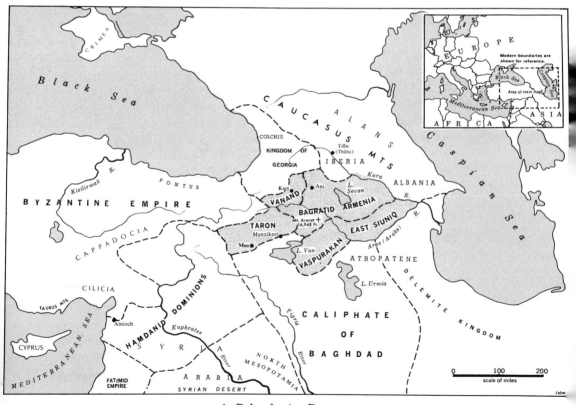

4. Pakradunian Dynasty

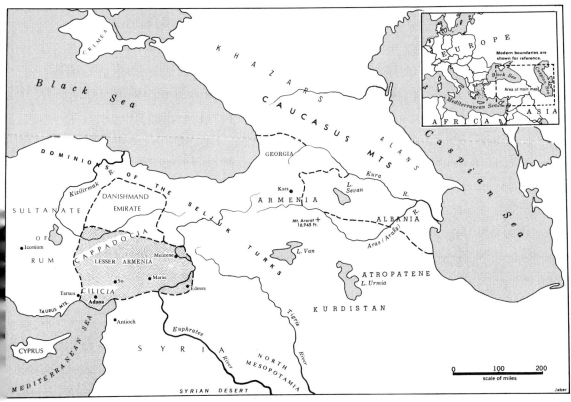

5. The Cilician Kingdom

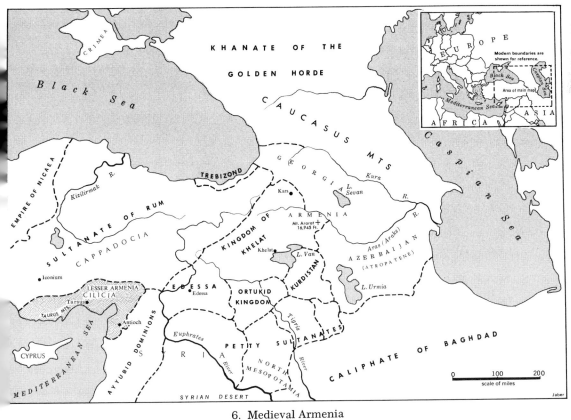

6. Medieval Armenia

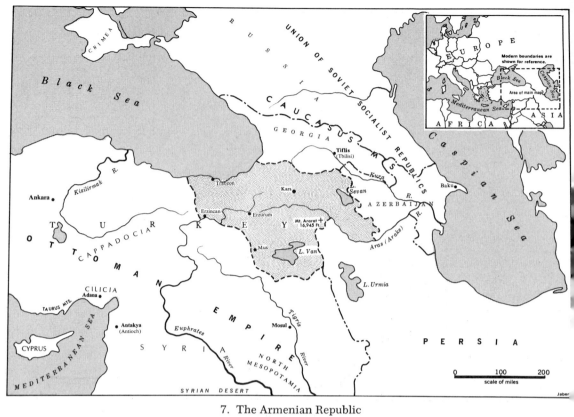

7. The Armenian Republic

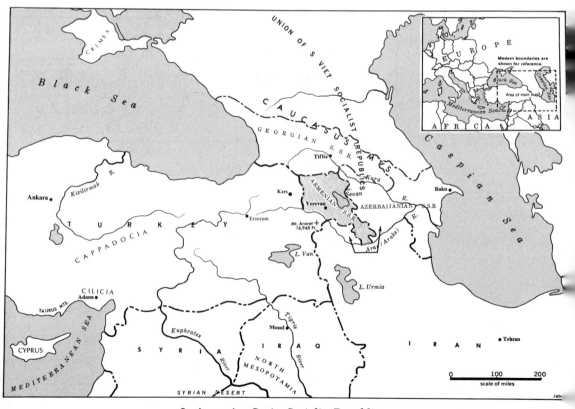

8. Armenian Soviet Socialist Republic

Index

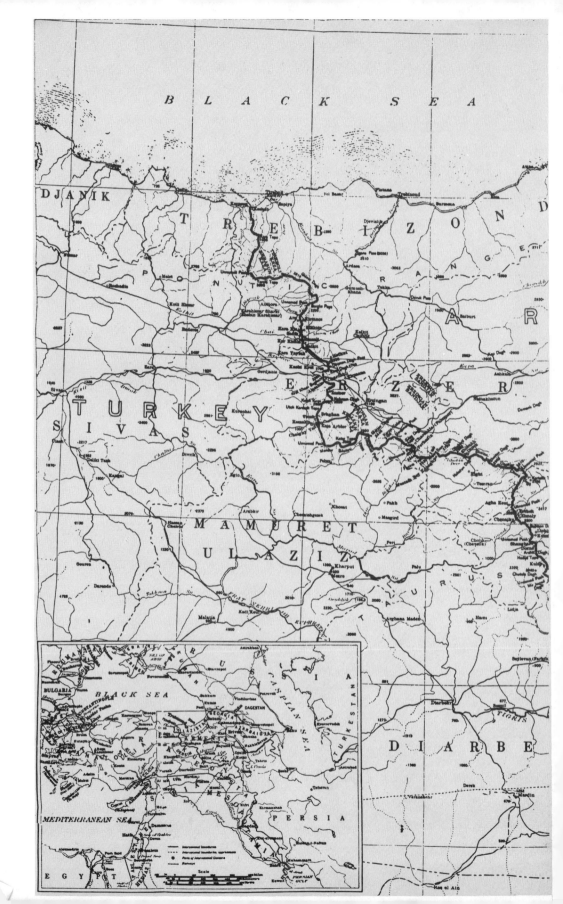